AF339307

ADVANCES IN ROBOT NAVIGATION

Edited by **Alejandra Barrera**

INTECHOPEN.COM

Advances in Robot Navigation

Edited by Alejandra Barrera

CBS, Edition **2016**

Published by InTech

Janeza Trdine 9, 51000 Rijeka, Croatia

All chapters are distributed under the Creative Commons Attribution 3.0 license, which allows users to download, copy and build upon published articles even for commercial purposes, as long as the author and publisher are properly credited, which ensures maximum dissemination and a wider impact of our publications. After this work has been published by InTech, authors have the right to republish it, in whole or part, in any publication of which they are the author, and to make other personal use of the work. Any republication, referencing or personal use of the work must explicitly identify the original source.

As for readers, this license allows users to download, copy and build upon published chapters even for commercial purposes, as long as the author and publisher are properly credited, which ensures maximum dissemination and a wider impact of our publications.

Notice

Statements and opinions expressed in the chapters are these of the individual contributors and not necessarily those of the editors or publisher. No responsibility is accepted for the accuracy of information contained in the published chapters. The publisher assumes no responsibility for any damage or injury to persons or property arising out of the use of any materials, instructions, methods or ideas contained in the book.
Copyright © 2011 InTech

Publishing Process Manager Natalia Reinić

Technical Editor Teodora Smiljanic

Cover Designer Jan Hyrat

Image Copyright VikaSuh, 2010. Used under license from Shutterstock.com

Additional hard copies can be obtained from orders@intechopen.com

Advances in Robot Navigation Edited by Alejandra Barrera

p. cm.

ISBN 978-953-307-346-0

INTECH

open science | open minds

Contents

Preface

Robot navigation includes different interrelated activities such as perception - obtaining and interpreting sensory information; exploration - the strategy that guides the robot to select the next direction to go; mapping - the construction of a spatial representation by using the sensory information perceived; localization - the strategy to estimate the robot position within the spatial map; path planning - the strategy to find a path towards a goal location being optimal or not; and path execution, where motor actions are determined and adapted to environmental changes.

The book integrates results from the research work of several authors all over the world, addressing the abovementioned activities and analyzing the critical implications of dealing with dynamic environments. Different solutions providing adaptive navigation are taken from nature inspiration and diverse applications are described in the context of an important field of study, social robotics.

The book includes 11 chapters organized within 4 parts as follows.

Robot Navigation Fundamentals

In order to contextualize the different approaches proposed by authors, this part provides an overview of core concepts involved in robot navigation. Specifically, Chapter 1 introduces the basics of a mobile robot physical structure, its dynamic and kinematic modeling, the mechanisms for mapping, localization, and trajectory planning and reviews the state of the art of navigation methods and control architectures which enables high degree of autonomy. Chapter 2 describes a navigational system providing vision-based localization and topological mapping of the environment. Chapter 3 depicts potential problems which might arise during robot motion planning, while trying to define the appropriate sequence of movements to achieve a goal within an uncertain environment.

Closing this part, Chapter 4 presents a robot navigation method combining an exploratory strategy that drives the robot to the most unexplored region of the environment, a SLAM algorithm to build a consistent map, and the Voronoi Fast Marching technique to plan the trajectory towards the goal.

Adaptive Navigation

Real scenarios involve uncertainty, thus robot navigation must deal with dynamic environments. The chapters included within this part are concerned with environmental uncertainty proposing novel approaches to this challenge. Particularly, Chapter 5 presents a multilayered approach to wheeled mobile robot navigation incorporating dynamic mapping, deliberative planning, path following, and two distinct layers of point-to-point reactive control. Chapter 6 describes a robot path planning strategy within an indoor environment employing the Distance Transform methodology and the Gilbert–Johnson–Keerthi distance algorithm to avoid colliding with dynamic obstacles. This hybrid method enables the robot to select the shortest path to the goal during navigation. Finally, Chapter 7 proposes an adaptive system for natural motion interaction between mobile robots and humans. The system finds the position and orientation of people by using a laser range finder based method, estimates human intentions in real time through a Case-Based Reasoning approach, allows the robot to navigate around a person by means of an adaptive potential field that adjusts according to the person intentions, and plans a safe and comfortable trajectory employing an adapted Rapidly-exploring Random Tree algorithm. The robot controlled by this system is endowed with the ability to see humans as dynamic obstacles having social zones that must be respected.

Robot Navigation Inspired by Nature

In this part, authors focused on nature of proposing interesting approaches to robot navigation. Specifically, Chapter 8 addresses brain interfaces - systems aiming to enable user control of a device based on brain activity-related signals. The author is concerned with brain-computer interfaces that use non-invasive technology, discussing their potential benefits to the field of robot navigation, especially in difficult scenarios in which the robot cannot successfully perform all functions without human assistance, such as in dangerous areas where sensors or algorithms may fail.

On the other hand, Chapter 9 investigates the use of animal low level intelligence to control robot navigation. Authors took inspiration from insect eyes with small nervous systems mimicking a mosaic eye to propose a bio-mimetic snake algorithm that divides the robot path into segments distributed among different vision sensors producing collision free navigation.

Social Robotics

One of the most attractive applications of robotics is, without doubt, the human-robot interaction by providing useful services. This final part includes practical cases of robots serving people in two important fields: guiding and rehabilitation.

In Chapter 10, authors present a social robot specifically designed and equipped for human-robot interaction, including all the basic components of sensorization and navigation within real indoor/outdoor environments, and a two-level decision making framework to determine the most appropriate localization strategy. The ultimate goal of this approach is a robot acting as a guide for visitors at the authors' university.

Finally, Chapter 11 describes the architecture design of an exoskeleton device for gait rehabilitation. It allows free leg motion while the patient walks on a treadmill completely or partially supported by a suspension system. During experimentation, the patient movement is natural and smooth while the limb moves along the target trajectory.

The successful research cases included in this book demonstrate the progress of devices, systems, models and architectures in supporting the navigational behavior of mobile robots while performing tasks within several contexts. With a doubt, the overview of the state of the art provided by this book may be a good starting point to acquire knowledge of intelligent mobile robotics.

Alejandra Barrera
Mexico's Autonomous Technological Institute (ITAM)
Mexico

Part 1

Robot Navigation Fundamentals

Conceptual Bases of Robot Navigation Modeling, Control and Applications

Silas F. R. Alves[1], João M. Rosário[1], Humberto Ferasoli Filho[2],
Liz K. A. Rincón[1] and Rosana A. T. Yamasaki[1]

[1]State University of Campinas
[2]University of São Paulo State
Brazil

1. Introduction

The advancements of the research on Mobile Robots with high degree of autonomy is possible, on one hand, due to its broad perspective of applications and, on other hand, due to the development and reduction of costs on computer, electronic and mechanic systems. Together with the research in Artificial Intelligence and Cognitive Science, this scenario currently enables the proposition of ambitious and complex robotic projects. Most of the applications were developed outside the structured environment of industry assembly lines and have complex goals, such as planets exploration, transportation of parts in factories, manufacturing, cleaning and monitoring of households, handling of radioactive materials in nuclear power plants, inspection of volcanoes, and many other activities.

This chapter presents and discusses the main topics involved on the design or adoption of a mobile robot system and focus on the control and navigation systems for autonomous mobile robots. Thus, this chapter is organized as follows:

- The *Section 2* introduces the main aspects of the Robot design, such as: the conceptualization of the mobile robot physical structure and its relation to the world; the state of art of navigation methods and systems; and the control architectures which enables high degree of autonomy.

- The *Section 3* presents the dynamic and control analysis for navigation robots with kinematic and dynamic model of the differential and omnidirectional robots.

- And finally, *Section 4* presents applications for a robotic platform of Automation, Simulation, Control and Supervision of Navegation Robots, with studies of dynamic and kinematic modeling, control algorithms, mechanisms for mapping and localization, trajectory planning and the platform simulator.

2. Robot design and application

The robot body and its sensors and actuators are heavily influenced by both the application and environment. Together, they determine the project and impose restrictions. The process of developing the robot body is very creative and defies the designer to skip steps of a natural evolutionary process and achieve the best solution. As such, the success of a robot project depends on the development team, on the clear vision of the environment and its restrictions, and on the existence purpose of the robot. Many are the aspects which determine the robot structures. The body, the embedded electronics and the software modules are the result of a creativity intensive process of a team composed by specialists from different fields. On the majority of industrial applications, a mobile robot can be reused several times before its disposal. However, there are applications where the achievement of the objectives coincides with the robot end of life. Such applications may be the exploration of planets or military missions such as bomb disposal.

The project of a robot body is initially submitted to a critical analysis of the environment and its existence purposes. The environment must be studied and treated according to its complexity and also to the previous knowledge about it. Thus, the environment provides information that establishes the drive system in face of the obstacles it will find. Whether it is an aerial, aquatic or terrestrial, it implies the study of the most efficient structure for the robot locomotion trough the environment. It is important to note that the robot body project may require the development of its aesthetics. This is particularly important to robots that will subsist with humans.

The most common drive systems for terrestrial mobile robots are composed by wheels, legs or continuous track. The aerial robots are robotic devices that can fly in different environment; generally this robots use propellers to move. The aquatic robots can move under or over water. Some examples for these applications are: the AirRobot UK® (Figure 1a), an aerial quad rotor robot (AirRobot, 2011); the Protector Robot, (Figure 1b), built by Republic of Singapore with BAE Systems, Lockheed Martin and Rafael Enterprises (Protector, 2010); and the *BigDog* robot (Figure 1c), created by Boston Dynamics (Raibert et al., 2011), a robot that walks, runs and climbs in different environment.

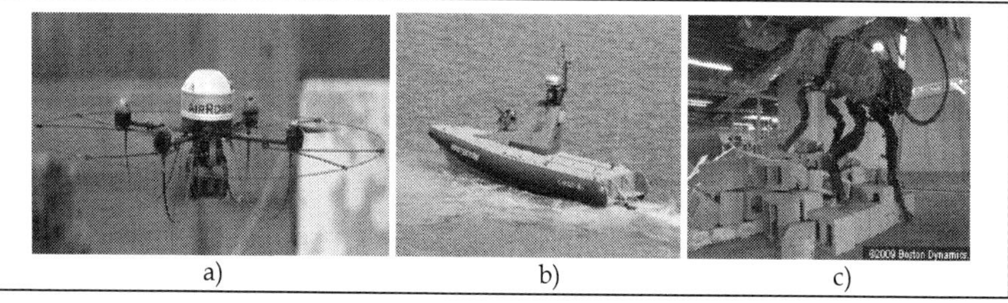

<table>
<tr><td align="center">a)</td><td align="center">b)</td><td align="center">c)</td></tr>
</table>

Fig. 1. Applications of Robot Navigation: a) Aerial Robot, b) Aquatic Robot, c)Terrestrial Robot

There are two development trends: one declares that the project of any autonomous system must begin with an accurate definition of its task (Harmon, 1987), and the other proclaims that a robot must be able to perform any task in different environments and situations (Noreils & Chatila, 1995). The current trend on industry is the specialization of robot systems, which is due by two factors: the production cost of general purpose robot is high, as it requires complex mechanical, electronic and computational systems; and a robot is generally created to execute a single task – or a task "class" – during its life cycle, as seem in Automated Guidance Vehicles (AVG). For complex tasks that require different sensors and actuators, the current trend is the creation of a robot group where each member is specialist on a given sub-task, and their combined action will complete the task.

2.1 Robot Navigation systems and methods

Navigation is the science or art of guiding of a mobile robot in the sense of how travel through the environment (McKerrow, 1991). The problems related to the navigation can be briefly defined in three questions: "Where am I", "Where am I going" and "How do I get there?" (Leonard & Durrant-White, 1991). The first two questions may be answered by an adequate sensorial system, while the third question needs an effective planning system. The navigation systems are directly related to the sensors available on the robot and the environment structure. The definition of a navigation system, just like any aspect of the robot we have seem so far, is influenced by the restrictions imposed by both the environment and the robot very purpose. The navigation may be obtained by three systems: a coordinates based system, a behavior based system and a hybrid system.

The coordinates based system, like the naval navigation, uses the knowledge of one's position inside a global coordinate system of the environment. It is based on models (or maps) of the environment to generate paths to guide the robot. Some techniques are Mapping (Latombe, 1991), Occupancy Grid Navigation (Elfes, 1987), and Potential Fields (Arkin et al., 1987). The behavior based system requires the robot to recognize environment features through its sensors and use the gathered information to search for its goals. For example, the robot must be able to recognize doors and corridors, and know the rules that will lead it to the desired location. In this case, the coordinate system is local (Graefe & Wershofen, 1991).

Information about the statistical features of the environment is important to both cited systems. The modeling of the environment refers to the representation of objects and the data structure used to store the information (the maps). Two approaches for map building are the geometric and phenomenological representation. Geometric representation has the advantage of having a clear and intuitive relation to the real world. However, the geometric representation has no satisfactory representation of uncertain geometries, as well as is not clear if knowing the world shape is really useful (Borenstein et al., 1995). The phenomenological representation is an attempt to overcome this problem. It uses a topological representation of the map with relative positioning which is based on local reference frames to avoid the accumulation of relative errors. Whenever the uncertainty grows too high, the robot sets a new reference frame; on the other hand, if the uncertainty decreases, the robot may merge frames. This policy keeps the uncertainty bound locally (Borenstein et al., 1995, as cited in Engelson & McDermott, 1992).

Mobile robots can navigate using relative or absolute position measures (Everett, 1995). Relative positioning uses odometry or inertial navigation. Odometry is a simple and inexpensive navigation system; however it suffers from cumulative errors. The inertial navigation (Barshan & Durrant-White, 1995) uses rotation and acceleration measures for extracting positioning information. Barshan and Durrant-White (1995) presented an inertial navigation system and discusses the challenges related to mobile robot movement based on non-absolute sensors. The most concerning issue is the accumulation of error found in relative sensors. The absolute positioning system can use different kinds of sensors which are divided in four groups of techniques: magnetic compass, active beacons, landmark recognition and model matching. Magnetic compasses are a common kind of sensor which uses Earth's natural electromagnetic field and does not require any change on the environment to be able to navigate through the world. Nevertheless, magnetic compasses readings are affected by power lines, metal structures, and even the robot movement, which introduces error to the system (Ojeda & Borenstein, 2000).

Active beacons are devices which emits a signal that is recognized by the robot. Since the active beacons are placed in known locations, the robot is able to estimate its position using triangulation or trilateration methods. In a similar fashion, the landmark system uses features of the environment to estimate its position. These landmarks may be naturally available on the environment, such as doors, corridors and trees; or they can be artificially developed and place on the environment, such as road signs. On one hand, natural landmarks do not require any modification in the world, but may not be easily recognized by the robot. On the other hand, artificial landmarks modifies the environment, but offer best contrast and are generally easier to be recognized. Nonetheless, the main problem with landmarks is detecting them accurately through sensorial data. Finally, the model matching technique uses features of the environment for map building or to recognize an environment within a previously known map. The main issues are related to finding the correspondence between a local map, discovered with the robot sensors, and a known global map (Borenstein et al., 1995).

Inside model matching techniques, we can point out the Simultaneous Localization and Mapping (SLAM). The SLAM addresses to the problem of acquiring the map of the environment where the robot is placed while simultaneously locating the robot in relation to this map. For this purpose, it involves both relative and absolute positioning techniques. Still, SLAM is a broad field and leaves many questions unanswered – mainly on SLAM in non-structured and dynamic environments (Siciliano & Khatib, 2008).

Other approach for mobile robot navigation is the biomimetic navigation. Some argue that the classic navigation methods developed on the last decades have not achieved the same performance flexibility of the navigation mechanisms of ants or bees. This has led researchers to study and implement navigation behaviors observed on biological agents, mainly insects. Franz and Mallot (Franz & Mallot, 2000) surveyed the recent literature on the phenomena of mobile robot navigation. The authors divide the techniques of biomimetic navigation into two groups: local navigation and path discovery. The local navigation deals with the basic problems of navigation, as the obstacle avoidance and track following, to move a robot from a start point (previously know or not) to a known destination inside the robot vision field. Most of recent researches objectives are to test the implementation of biological mechanisms, not to discover an optimal solution for a determined problem.

The navigation of mobile robots is a broad area which is currently the focus of many researchers. The navigation system tries to find an optimal path based on the data acquired by the robot sensors, which represents a local map that can be part, or not, of a global map (Feng & Krogh, 1990). To date, there is still no ideal navigation system and is difficulty to compare the results of researches, since there is a huge gap between the robots and the environment of each research (Borenstein et al., 1995). When developing the navigation system of a mobile robot, the designer must choose the best navigation methods for the robot application. As said by Blaasvaer et al. (1994): "each navigation context imposes different requirements about the navigation strategy in respect to precision, speed and reactivity".

2.2 Sensors

The mobile robots need information about the world so they can relate themselves to the environment, just like animals. For this purpose, they rely on sensor devices which transform the world stimuli into electrical signal. These signals are electrical data which represents state of about the world and must be interpreted by the robot to achieve its goals. There is wide range of sensors used to this end.

Sensors can be classified by some features as the application, type of information and signal. As for their usage, sensors can be treated as proprioceptive or exteroceptive. Proprioceptive sensors are related to the internal elements of the robot, so they monitor the state of its inner mechanisms and devices, including joints positions. In a different manner, exteroceptive sensors gather information from the environment where the robot is placed and generally are related to the robot navigation and application. From the viewpoint of the measuring method, sensors are classified into active and passive sensors. Active sensors apply an known interfering signal into the environment and verify the effect of this signal into the world. Contrastingly, passive sensors does not provoke any interfering signal to measure the world, as they are able to acquire "signals" naturally emitted by the world. Sensors can also be classified according to the electrical output signal, thus are divided into digital and analog sensors. In general, sensorial data is usually inaccurate, which raises the difficulty of using the information provided by them.

The sensor choice is determined by different aspects that may overlap themselves or are conflicting. The main aspects are: the robot goals, the accuracy of the robot and environment models, the uncertainty of sensor data, the overall device cost, the quantity of gathered information, the time available for data processing, the processing capabilities of the embedded computer (on-board), the cost of data transmission for external data processing (off-board), the sensors physical dimension in contrast to the required robot dimension, and the energy consumption.

In respect to the combined use of sensor data, there is not a clear division of data integration and fusion processes. Searching for this answer, Luo (Luo & Kay, 1989) presented the following definition: "The fusion process refers to the combination of different sensors readings into an uniform data structure, while the integration process refers to the usage of information from several sensor sources to obtain a specific application".

The arrangement of different sensors defines a sensor network. This network of multiple sensors when combined (through data fusion or integration) functions as a single, simple sensor, which provides information about the environment. An interesting taxonomy for multiple sensor networks is presented by Barshan and Durrant-White (1995) and complemented by Brooks and Iyengar (1997): *Complementary*: There is no dependency between the sensors, however they can be combined to provide information about a phenomena, *Competitive*: The sensors provides independent measures of the same phenomena, which reduces the inconsistency and uncertainties about of the information, *Cooperative*: different sensors which works together to measure a phenomena that a single sensor is not capable of measuring, *Independent*: independent sensors are those of which measures does not affect or complement other sensor data.

2.2.1 Robot Navigation sensors

When dealing with Robot Navigation, sensors are usually used for positioning and obstacle avoidance. In the sense of positioning, sensors can be classified as relative or absolute (Borenstein et al., 1995). Relative positioning sensors includes odometry and inertial navigation, which are methods that measures the robot position in relation to the robot initial point and its movements. Distinctively, absolute positioning sensors recognize structures on the environment which position is known, allowing the robot to estimate its own position.

Odometry uses encoders to measure the rotation of the wheels, which allows the robot to estimate its position and heading according to its model. It's the most available navigation system due to its simplicity, the natural availability of encoders, and low cost. Notwithstanding, this is often a poor method for localization. The rotation measuring may be jeopardized by the inaccuracy of the mechanical structure or by the dynamics of the interaction between the tire and the floor, such as wheel slippage. On the other hand, the position estimation takes into account all past estimations - it integrates the positioning. This means that the errors are also integrated and will grow over time, resulting in a high inaccurate system. Just like odometry, inertial navigation, which uses gyroscopes and accelerometers to measure rotation and acceleration rates, is highly inaccurate due to its integrative nature. Other drawback is the usual high costs of gyroscopes and accelerometers. The heading measure provided by compasses represents one of the most meaningful parameters for navigation. Magnetic compasses provides an absolute measure of heading and can function on virtually all of Earth surface, as the natural magnetic field of Earth is available on all of its surface. Nevertheless, magnetic compasses are influenced by metallic structures and power lines, becoming highly inaccurate near them.

Other group of sensors for navigation are the active beacons. These sensors provide absolute positioning for mobile robots through the information sent by three or more beacons. A beacon is a source of known signal, as structured light, sound or radio frequencies. The position is estimated by triangulation or trilateration. It is a common positioning system used by ships and airplanes due to its accuracy and high speed measuring. The Global Positioning System (GPS) is an example of active beacon navigation system.

The map based positioning consists in a method where robots use its sensors to create a local map of the environment. This local map is compared to a known global map stored on the robot memory. If the local map matches a part of the global map, then the robot will be able to estimate its position. The sensors used in this kind of system are called Time-of-Flight Range Sensors, which are active sensors that measures the distance of nearby objects. Some widely used sensors are sonars and LIDAR scanners (Kelly, 1995).

As sensor industry advances in high speed, this chapter does not cover all sensors available in the market. There are other sensors which may be used for navigation, as odor sensors (Russel, 1995, Deveza et al., 1994) for active beacon navigation, whereas the beacon emits an odor.

2.3 Control architectures for navigation

A mobile robot with a high degree of autonomy is a device which can move smoothly while avoiding static and mobile obstacles through the environment in the pursuit of its goal without the need for human intervention. Autonomy is desirable in tasks where human intervention is difficult (Anderson, 1990), and can be accessed through the robot efficiency and robustness to perform tasks in different and unknown environments (Alami et al., 1998), or the ability to survive in any environment (Bisset, 1997), responding to expected and unexpected events both in time and space, with the presence of independent agents or not (Ferguson, 1994).

To achieve autonomy, a mobile robot must use a control architecture. The architecture is closely linked to how the sensor data are handled to extract information from the world and how this information is used for planning and navigating in pursuit of the objectives, besides involving technological issues (Rich & Knight, 1994). It is defined by the principle of operation of control modules, which defines the functional performance of the architecture, the information and control structures (Rembold & Levi, 1987).

For mobile robots, the architectures are defined by the control system operating principle. They are constrained at one end by fully reactive systems (Kaelbling, 1986) and, in the other end, by fully deliberative systems (Fikes & Nilsson, 1971). Within the fully reactive and deliberative systems, lies the hybrid systems, which combines both architectures, with greater or lesser portion of one or another, in order to generate an architecture that can perform a task. It is important to note that both the purely reactive and deliberative systems are not found in practical applications of real mobile robots, since a purely deliberative systems may not respond fast enough to cope with the environment changes and a purely reactive system may not be able to reach a complex goal, as will be discussed hereafter.

2.3.1 Deliberative architectures

The deliberative architectures use a reasoning structure based on the description of the world. The information flow occurs in a serial format throughout its modules. The handling of a large amount of information, together with the information flow format, results in a slow architecture that may not respond fast enough for dynamic environments. However, as the performance of computer rises, this limitation decreases, leading to architectures with sophisticated planners responding in real time to environmental changes.

The CODGER (Communication Database with Geometric Reasoning) was developed by Steve Shafer et al. (1986) and implemented by the project NavLab (Thorpe et al., 1988). The Codger is a distributed control architecture involving modules that revolves a database. It distinguishes itself by integrating information about the world obtained from a vision system and from a laser scanning system to detect obstacles and to keep the vehicle on the track. Each module consists on a concurrent program. The Blackboard implements an AI (Artificial Intelligence) system that consists on the central Database and knows all other modules capabilities, and is responsible for the task planning and controlling the other modules. Conflicts can occur due to competition for accessing the database during the performance of tasks by the various sub-modules. Figure 2 shows the CODGER architecture.

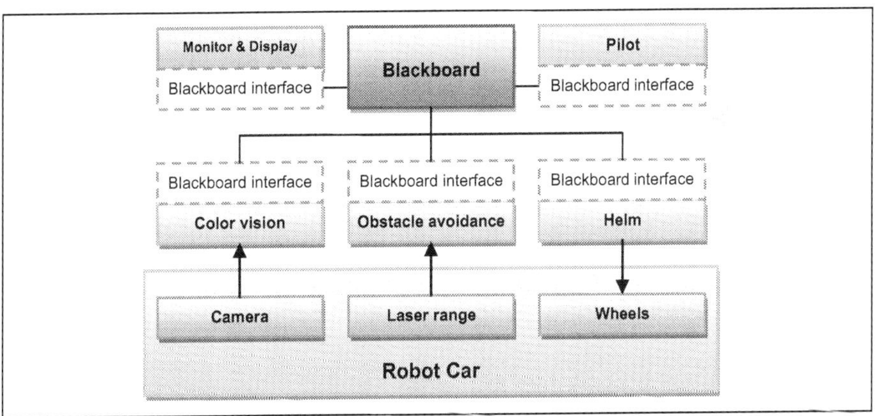

Fig. 2. CODGER Architecture on NavLab project (Thorpe et al., 1988)

The NASREM (NASA/NBS Standard Reference Model for Telerobot Control System Architecture) (Albus et al., 1987; Lumia, 1990) developed by the NASA/NBS consortium, presents systematic, hierarchical levels of processing creating multiple, overlaid control loops with different response time (time abstraction). The lower layers respond more quickly to stimuli of input sensors, while the higher layers answer more slowly. Each level consists of modules for task planning and execution, world modeling and sensory processing (functional abstraction). The data flow is horizontal in each layer, while the control flow through the layers is vertical. Figure 3. represents the NASREM architecture.

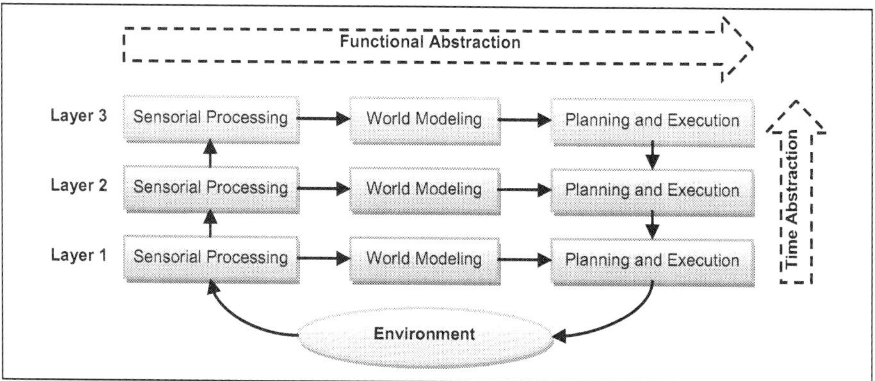

Fig. 3. NASREM architecture

2.3.2 Behavioral architectures

The behavioral architectures have as their reference the architecture developed by Brooks and thus follow that line of architecture (Gat, 1992; Kaelbling, 1986). The Subsumption Architecture (Brooks, 1986) was based on the constructive simplicity to achieve high speed of response to environmental changes. This architecture had totally different characteristics from those previously used for robot control. Unlike the AI planning techniques exploited by the scientific community of that time, which searched for task planners or problem solvers, Brooks (Brooks, 1986) introduced a layered control architecture which allowed the robot to operate with incremental levels of competence. These layers are basically asynchronous modules that exchange information by communication channels. Each module is an example of a finite state machine. The result is a flexible and robust robot control architecture, which is shown in Figure 4.

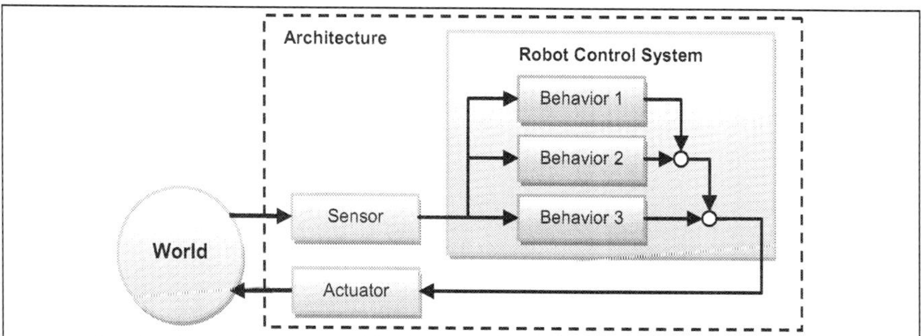

Fig. 4. Functional diagram of an behavioral architecture

Although the architecture is interesting from the point of view of several behaviors concurrently acting in pursuit of a goal (Brooks, 1991), it is unclear how the robot could perform a task with conflicting behaviors. For example, in a objects stacking task, the Avoiding Obstacles layer would repel the robot from the stack and therefore hinder the task execution, but on the other hand, if this layer is removed from the control architecture, then the robot would be vulnerable to moving or unexpected objects. This approach successfully deals with uncertainty and unpredictable environmental changes. Nonetheless, it is not clear how it works when the number of tasks increases, or when the diversity of the environment is increased, or even how it addresses the difficulty of determining the behavior arbitration (Tuijman et al., 1987; Simmons, 1994).

A robot driven only by environmental stimuli may never find its goal due to possible conflicts between behaviors or systemic responses that may not be compatible with the goal. Thus, the reaction should be programmable and controllable (Noreils & Chatila, 1995). Nonetheless, this architecture is interesting for applications that have restrictions on the dimensions and power consumption of the robot, or the impossibility of remote processing.

2.3.3 Hybrid architectures

As discussed previously, hybrid architectures combine features of both deliberative and reactive architectures. There are several ways to organize the reactive and deliberative subsystems in hybrid architectures, as saw in various architectures presented in recent years (Ferguson, 1994; Gat, 1992; Kaelbling, 1992). Still, there is a small community that research on the approach of control architectures in three hierarchical layers, as shown on Figure 5.

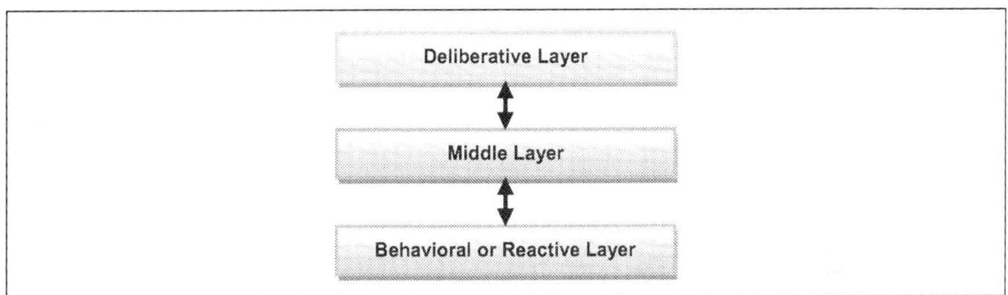

Fig. 5. Hybrid architecture in three layers

The lowest layer operates according to the behavioral approach of Brooks (Brooks, 1986) or are even purely reactive. The higher layer uses the planning systems and the world modeling of the deliberative approach. The intermediate layer is not well defined since it is a bridge between the two other layers (Zelek, 1996).

The RAPs (Reactive Action Packages) architecture (Firby, 1987) is designed in three layers combining modules for planning and reacting. The lowest layer corresponds to the skills or behaviors chosen to accomplish certain tasks. The middle layer performs the coordination of behaviors that are chosen according to the plan being executed. The highest layer accommodates the planning level based on the library of plans (RAP). The basic concept is centered on the RAP library, which determines the behaviors and sensorial routines needed to execute the plan. A reactive planner employ information from a scenario descriptor and the RAP library to activate the required behaviors. This planner also monitors these behaviors and changes them according to the plan. Figure 6 illustrates this architecture.

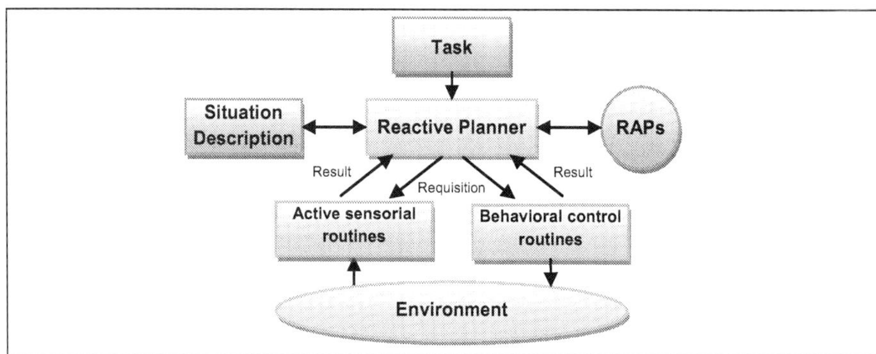

Fig. 6. RAPs architecture

The TCA (Task Control Architecture) architecture (Simmons, 1994) was implemented in the AMBLER robot, a robot with legs for uneven terrain (Krotkov, 1994). Simmons introduces deliberative components performing with layered reactive behavior for complex robots. In this control architecture, the deliberative components respond to normal situations while the reactive components respond to exceptional situations. Figure 7 shows the architecture. Summarizing, according to Simmons (1994): "The TCA architecture provides a comprehensive set of features to coordinate tasks of a robot while ensuring quality and ease of development".

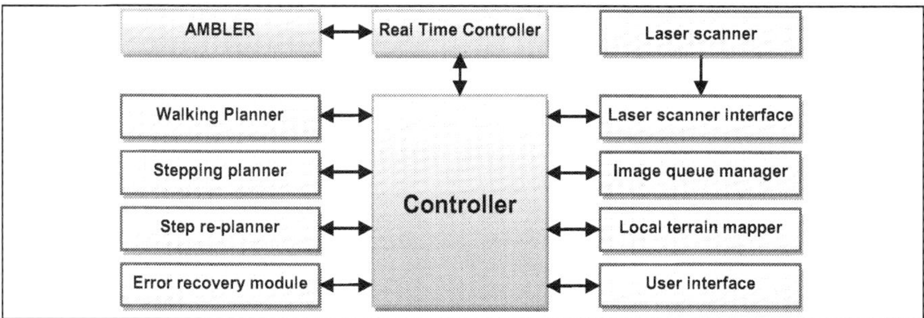

Fig. 7. TCA architecture

2.3.4 The choice of achitecture

The discussion on choosing an appropriate architecture is within the context of deliberative and behavioral approaches, since the same task can be accomplished by different control architectures. A comparative analysis of results obtained by two different architectures performing the same task must consider the restrictions imposed by the application (Ferasoli Filho, 1999). If the environment is known or when the process will be repeated from time to time, the architecture may include the use of maps, or get it on the first mission to use on the following missions. As such, the architecture can rely on deliberative approaches. On the other hand, if the environment is unknown on every mission, the use or creation of maps is not interesting – unless the map building is the mission goal. In this context, approaches based on behaviors may perform better than the deliberative approaches.

3. Dynamics and control

3.1 Kinematics model

The kinematics study is used for the design, simulation and control of robotic systems. This modeling is defined as the movement of bodies in a mechanism or robot system, without regard to the forces and torques that cause the movement (Waldron & Schmiedeler, 2008). The kinematics provides a mathematical analysis of robot motion without considering the forces that affect it. This analysis uses the relationship between the geometry of the robot, the control parameters and the system behavior in an environment. There are different representations of position and orientation to solve kinematics problems. One of the main objectives of the kinematics study is to find the robot velocity as a function of wheel speed, rotation angle, steering angles, steering speeds and geometric parameters of the robot configuration (Siegwart & Nourbakhsh, 2004). The study of kinematics is performed with the analysis of robot physical structure to generate a mathematical model which represents its behavior in the environment. The mobile robot can be distinguished by different platforms and an essential characteristic is the configuration and geometry of the structure body and wheels. The mobile robots can be divided according to their mobility. The maneuverability of a mobile robot is the combination of the mobility available, which is based on the sliding constraints and the features by the steering (Siegwart & Nourbakhsh, 2004). The robot stability can be expressed by the center of gravity, the number of contact points and the environment features. The kinematic analysis for navigation represents the robot location in the plane, with local reference frame $\{X_L, Y_L\}$ and global reference frame $\{X_G, Y_G\}$. The position of the robot is given by X_L and Y_L and orientation by the angle θ. The complete location of the robot in the global frame is defined by

$$\xi^T = \begin{bmatrix} x & y & \theta \end{bmatrix} \tag{1}$$

The kinematics for mobile robot requires a mathematical representation to describe the translation and rotation effects in order to map the robot's motion in tracking trajectories from the robot's local reference in relation to the global reference. The translation of the robot is defined as a P^G vector that is composed of two vectors which are represented by coordinates of local (P^L) and global ($Q_0{}^G$) reference system expressed as

$$P^G = Q_0^G + P^L, \quad Q_0^G = \begin{bmatrix} x_0 \\ y_0 \\ \theta \end{bmatrix} \quad P^L = \begin{bmatrix} x_1 \\ y_1 \\ 0 \end{bmatrix} \quad P^G = \begin{bmatrix} x_0 + x_1 \\ y_0 + y_1 \\ \theta + 0 \end{bmatrix} \tag{2}$$

The rotational motion of the robot can be expressed from global coordinates to local coordinates using the orthogonal rotation matrix (Eq.3)

$$R_G^L(\theta) = \begin{bmatrix} \cos(\theta) & \sin(\theta) & 0 \\ -\sin(\theta) & \cos(\theta) & 0 \\ 0 & 0 & 1 \end{bmatrix} \tag{3}$$

The mapping between the two frames is represented by:

$$\dot{\xi}_L = R_G^L(\theta)\dot{\xi}_G = R_G^L(\theta).\begin{bmatrix} \dot{x} \\ \dot{y} \\ \dot{\theta} \end{bmatrix} = \begin{bmatrix} \cos(\theta)\dot{x} + \sin(\theta)\dot{y} \\ -\sin(\theta)\dot{x} + \cos(\theta)\dot{y} \\ \dot{\theta} \end{bmatrix} \tag{4}$$

The kinematics is analyzed through two types of study: the forward kinematics and the inverse kinematics. The *forward kinematics* describes the position and orientation of the robot, this method uses the geometric parameters βi, the speed of each wheel αi, and the steering, expressed by

$$\dot{\xi} = \begin{bmatrix} \dot{x} \\ \dot{y} \\ \dot{\theta} \end{bmatrix} = f(\dot{\alpha}_1...\dot{\alpha}_n, \beta_1...\beta_m, \dot{\beta}_1...\dot{\beta}_m), \tag{5}$$

The *inverse kinematics* predicts the robot caracteristics as wheels velocities, angles and other geometrical parameters through the calculation of the final speed and its orientation angle:

$$\left[\dot{\alpha}_1...\dot{\alpha}_n, \beta_1...\beta_m, \dot{\beta}_1...\dot{\beta}_m\right] = f(\dot{x}, \dot{y}, \dot{\theta}) \tag{6}$$

In the kinematic analysis, the robot characteristics such as the type of wheels, the points of contact, the surface and effects of sliding or friction should be considered.

3.1.1 Kinematics for two-wheel differential robot

In the case of a two-wheeled differential robot, as presented in Figure 8, each wheel is controlled by an independent motor X_G and Y_G represents the global frame, while X_L and Y_L represents the local frame. The robot velocity is determined by the linear velocity $V_{robot}(t)$ and angular velocity $\omega_{robot}(t)$, which are functions of the linear and angular velocity of each wheel $\omega_i(t)$ and the distance L between the two wheels, $V_r(t)$, $\omega_r(t)$ are the linear and angular velocity of right wheel, $V_l(t)$, $\omega_l(t)$ are the linear and angular velocity of left wheel, θ is the orientation of the robot and the (r_l, r_r) are left and right wheels radius.

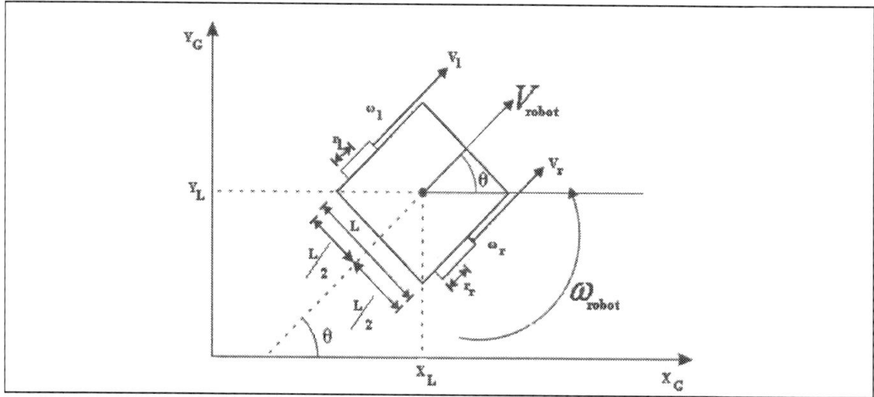

Fig. 8. Two-wheeled differential robot

The linear speed of each wheel is determined by the relationship between angular speed and radius of the wheel as

$$V_r(t) = \omega_r(t) r_r , \quad V_1(t) = \omega_1(t) r_1 \tag{7}$$

The robot velocities are composed of the center of mass's linear velocity and angular velocity generated by the difference between the two wheels.

$$V_1(t) = V_{robot}(t) - \left(\frac{L}{2}\right)\omega_{robot}(t) , \quad V_R(t) = V_{robot}(t) + \left(\frac{L}{2}\right)\omega_{robot}(t) \tag{8}$$

The robot velocities equations are expressed by

$$V_{robot} = \frac{V_r + V_1}{2} , \quad \omega_{robot} = \frac{V_r - V_1}{L} \tag{9}$$

The kinematics equations of the robot are expressed on the initial frame (Eq. 10a) and in local coordinates (Eq, 10b) by

$$
\begin{bmatrix} \dot{x}(t) \\ \dot{y}(t) \\ \dot{\theta}(t) \end{bmatrix} =
\begin{bmatrix} \cos(\theta) & 0 \\ \sin(\theta) & 0 \\ 0 & 1 \end{bmatrix}
\begin{bmatrix} v_{robot} \\ \omega_{robot} \end{bmatrix} , \quad
\begin{bmatrix} \dot{x}_L(t) \\ \dot{y}_L(t) \\ \dot{\theta}_L(t) \end{bmatrix} =
\begin{bmatrix} r/2 & r/2 \\ 0 & 0 \\ -r/L & r/L \end{bmatrix}
\begin{bmatrix} \omega_1(t) \\ \omega_r(t) \end{bmatrix} \tag{10}
$$

a)   b)

Therefore, with the matrix of the differential model shown in Eq. 10, it is possible to find the displacement of the robot. The speed in Y axis is always zero, demonstrating the holonomic constraint μ on the geometry of differential configuration. The holonomic constraint is explained by Eq.11, with $N(\theta)$ being the unit orthogonal vector to the plane of the wheels and p the robot velocity vector, it demonstrates the impossibility of movement on the Y axis, so the robot has to perform various displacements in X in order to achieve a lateral position.

$$\mu = 0 \rightarrow N(\theta).\dot{p} = \left[\sin(\theta) - \cos(\theta)\right]\begin{bmatrix} \dot{x} \\ \dot{y} \end{bmatrix} = \dot{x}\sin(\theta) - \dot{y}\cos(\theta) = 0 \tag{11}$$

Finally, with the direct kinematics it is possible to obtain the equations that allow any device to be programmed to recognize at every moment its own speed, position and orientation based on information from wheel speed and steering angle.

3.1.2 Kinematics for three-wheeled omnidirectional robot

The omnidirectional robot is a platform made up of three wheels in triangular configuration where the distance between these wheels is symmetric. Each wheel has an independent motor and can rotate around its own axis with respect to the point of contact with the surface. The Figure 9 shows the three-wheeled omnidirectional robot configuration.

As seen of Figure 9, X_G and Y_G are the fixed inertial axes and represent the global frame. X_L and Y_L are the fixed axis on the local frame in the robot coordinates; d_0 describes the current position of the local axis in relation to the global axis, d_i describes the location of the center of a wheel from the local axis. H_i are positive unit velocity vector of each wheel, θ describes the rotation axis of the robot X_{LR} and Y_{LR} compared to the global axis, α_i describes the rotation of the wheel in the local frame, β describes the angle between d_i and H_i. In order to obtain the kinematic model of the robot, the analysis of the speed of each wheel must be determined in terms of the local speed and its make the transformation to the global frame. The speed of each wheel has components in X and Y directions.

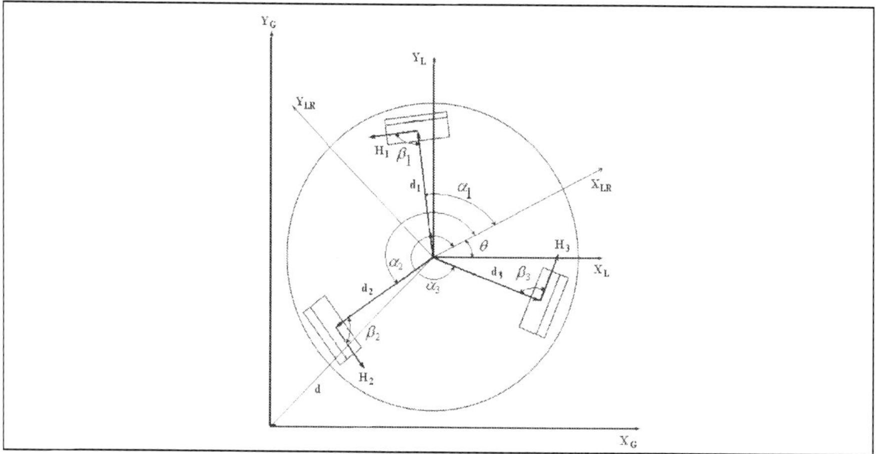

Fig. 9. Three-wheeled omnidirectional robot

The speed of each wheel is represented by the translation and rotation vectors in the robot frame. The position from the global frame $P_0{}^G$ is added to the position transformation and orientation of the wheel. The rotation $R_L{}^G (\theta)$ is calculated from local frame to global frame. The transformation matrix is obtained and provides the angular velocity of each wheel in relation to the global frame speeds represented in Eq.12, (Batlle & Barjau, 2009).

$$P_i^G = P_0^G + R_L^G(\theta)\,^L P_i\,, \quad \begin{bmatrix} \omega_1 \\ \omega_2 \\ \omega_3 \end{bmatrix} = \begin{bmatrix} v_1/r \\ v_2/r \\ v_3/r \end{bmatrix} = \frac{1}{r}\begin{bmatrix} -\sin(\theta+\alpha_1) & \cos(\theta+\alpha_1) & R \\ -\sin(\theta+\alpha_2) & \cos(\theta+\alpha_2) & R \\ -\sin(\theta+\alpha_3) & \cos(\theta+\alpha_3) & R \end{bmatrix}\begin{bmatrix} \dot{x}_G \\ \dot{y}_G \\ \dot{\theta} \end{bmatrix} \quad (12)$$

3.2 Dynamic model

The study of the movement dynamics analyzes the relationships between the forces of contact and the forces acting on the robot mechanisms, in addition to the study of the acceleration and resulting motion trajectories. This study is essential for the design, control and simulation of robots (Siciliano & Khatib, 2008). The kinematic model relates to the displacement, velocity, acceleration and time regardless of the cause of their movement, whereas the dynamic analysis relates to the generalized forces from the actuators, with the energy applied in the system (Dudek, 2000). There are different proposals for the dynamic model of robot navigation, but the general shape of the dynamic study is the analysis of the forces and torques produced inside and outside of the system. General equations of system motion, and the analysis of the system torques and energy allows developing the dynamic model of the robotic system. For this analysis, it is important to consider the physical and geometrical characteristics of the system such as masses, sizes, diameters, among others which are represented in the moments of inertia and static and dynamic torques of the system.

3.2.1 Dynamic model for robot joint

Each joint of a robot consists of a an actuator (DC motor, AC motor, step motor) associated with a speed reducer and transducers to measure position and velocity. These transducers can be absolute or incremental encoders at each joint. The motion control of robots is a complex issue, since the movement of the mechanical structure is accomplished through rotation and translation of their joints that are controlled simultaneously, which hinders the dynamic coupling. Moreover, the behavior of the structure is strongly nonlinear and dependent on operating conditions. These conditions must be taken into account in the chosen control strategy. The desired trajectory is defined by position, speed, acceleration and orientation of, therefore it is necessary to make coordinate transformations with set times and with great complexity of calculations. Normally the robot control on only considers the kinematic model, so joints are not coupled, and the control of each joint is independent. Each robotic joint commonly includes a DC motor, the gear, reducer, transmission, bearing and encoder. The dynamic model of DC motor is expressed by the electrical coupling and mechanical equation as

$$V(t) = L\dot{i}(t) + Ri(t) + e(t)$$
$$T(t) = K_m i(t) \tag{13}$$
$$T(t) = J\ddot{\theta}(t) + B\dot{\theta}(t) + T_r(t)$$

Where $i(t)$ is the current, R is the resistance, L is the inductance, $V(t)$ is the voltage applied to the armature circuit, $e(t)=k_e*\theta$ is the electromotive force, J and B are the moment of inertia and viscous friction coefficient, k_e and k_m are the electromotive torque coefficient and constant torque, T_r and T are the resistant torque due to system losses and mechanical torque. The joint model is shown in Figure 10.

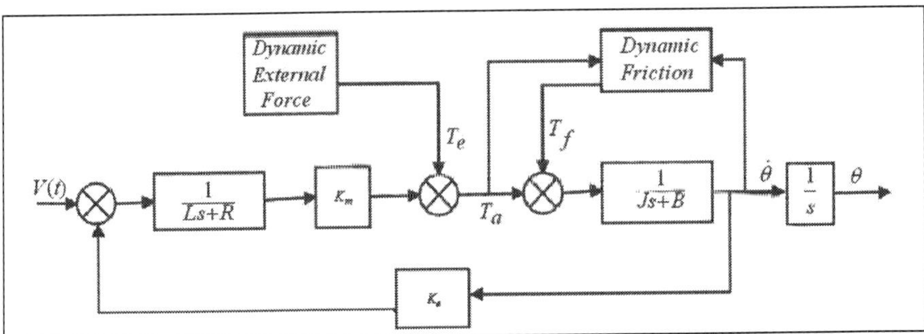

Fig. 10. Joint Model

The reduction model, with η as the rate of transmission, p as the teeth number of gear and r as the gear ratio, where the tangential velocity is the same between the gears. The system without slip can be expressed by

$$\eta = \frac{p_2}{p_1} \quad \text{and} \quad \theta_2 = \frac{r_1}{r_2}\theta_1 \; , \text{ then } v = \dot{\theta}_1 r_1 = \dot{\theta}_2 r_2 \text{ for } \frac{\dot{\theta}_1}{\dot{\theta}_2} = \frac{r_2}{r_1} = \eta \tag{14}$$

The model presented above will be increased by the dynamic effect of reducing the loads of coupled system through the motor model and load-reducer as

$$(T(s) - T_r(s))G_2(s) = \Omega_{motor}(s) \; , \quad (T_{load}(s) - T_{per}(s))G_3(s) = \Omega_{load}(s)$$

$$\Omega_{load}(s) = \frac{1}{\eta}\Omega_{motor}(s) \qquad T_{load}(s) = \eta T_{motor}(s) \tag{15}$$

3.2.2 Two-Wheeled differential dynamic model

The dynamic analysis is performed for the Two-Wheeled differential robot (Fierro & Lewis, 1997). The movement and orientation is due to each of the actuators, where the robot position in a inertial Cartesian frame (O, X, Y) is the vector q = {xc, yc, θ}, X_c and Y_c are the coordinates of center of mass of the robot. The robot dynamics can be analyzed from the Lagrange equation, expressed in terms as

$$\frac{d}{dt}\left(\frac{\partial T}{\partial \dot{q}}\right) - \frac{\partial T}{\partial q} = \tau + \mathbf{J}^T(\mathbf{q})\lambda \; , \quad T(\mathbf{q},\dot{\mathbf{q}}) = T\frac{1}{2}\dot{\mathbf{q}}^T M(q)\dot{\mathbf{q}} \tag{16}$$

The kinematic constraints are independent of time, and the matrix **D** represents the full range for a group of linearly independent vectors and the H(q) is the matrix associated with constraints of the system. The equation of motion is expressed with V1 and V2 as the linear velocities of the system in Eq.17.

$$\dot{\mathbf{q}} = \mathbf{D}(\mathbf{q})\mathbf{v}(t) = \begin{bmatrix} \dot{\mathbf{x}}_c \\ \dot{\mathbf{y}}_c \\ \dot{\theta} \end{bmatrix} = \begin{bmatrix} \cos(\theta) & -L\sin(\theta) \\ \sin(\theta) & L\cos(\theta) \\ 0 & 1 \end{bmatrix}\begin{bmatrix} v_1 \\ v_2 \end{bmatrix}, \; \mathbf{D}(\mathbf{q}) = \begin{bmatrix} \cos(\theta) & -L\cdot\sin(\theta) \\ \sin(\theta) & L\cdot\cos(\theta) \\ 0 & 1 \end{bmatrix}, \; \mathbf{v}(t) = \begin{bmatrix} \mathbf{v} \\ \omega \end{bmatrix} = \begin{bmatrix} v_1 \\ v_2 \end{bmatrix}, \tag{17}$$

The relationship between the parameters of inertia, information of the centripetal force and Coriolis effect, friction on surfaces, disturbances and unmodeled dynamics is expressed as

$$\mathbf{M}(\mathbf{q})\ddot{\mathbf{q}} + \mathbf{V}_m(\mathbf{q},\dot{\mathbf{q}})\dot{\mathbf{q}} + \mathbf{F}(\dot{\mathbf{q}}) + \mathbf{G}(\mathbf{q}) + \tau_d = \mathbf{B}(\mathbf{q})\tau - \mathbf{H}^T(\mathbf{q})\lambda \tag{18}$$

where M (q) is the inertia matrix, Vm (q, q) is the matrix of Coriolis effects, F (q) represents the friction of the surface, G (q) is the gravitational vector, Td represents the unknown disturbance including unmodelled dynamics. The dynamic analysis of the differential robot is a practical and basic model to develop the dynamic model of the omnidirectional robot. For the analysis of the dynamic model it is necessary to know the physical constraints of the system to get the array of restrictions, the matrix of inertia is expressed by the masses and dimensions of the robot with the geometrical characteristics of three-wheeled omnidirectional system.

3.3 Control structure

Control for robots navigation has been developed primarily with the trajectory tracking, with the aim to follow follow certain paths by adjusting the speed and acceleration parameters of the system, which are generally described by position and velocity profiles. Control systems are developed in open loop or closed loop. Some problems of control systems in open loop are the limitations to regulate the speed and acceleration in different paths, this control does not correct the system to disturbances or dynamic changes, resulting in paths that are not smooth (Siegwart & Nourbakhsh, 2004). Systems in closed loop control can regulate and compare its parameters with references to minimize errors. The feedback control is used to solve the navigation system when the robot has to follow a path described by velocity and position profiles as a function of time from an initial to a final position.

3.3.1 Control structure for robot joint

The controller is an important element of a complete control system. The goal of a controller in the control loop is to compare the output value with a desired value, determining a deviation and producing a control signal to reduce the error to regulate dynamic parameters. This error is generated by the comparison of the reference trajectory and the robot's current path, which is represented in terms of position and orientation (Figure 11).

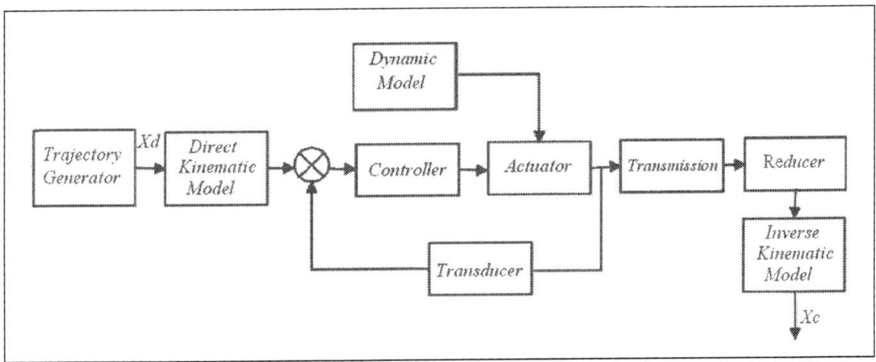

Fig. 11. Control Structure for Robot Joint

The control most used in robotic system is the PID Control that combines the Proportional (Kp), Integral (Ki) and Derivative (Kd) actions shown in the Eq. 19. This type of controller has good performance if the dynamic system is known and the controller parameter has been adjusted. The main limitation of a PID controller is the need to refine procedures of parameters adjustment, in addition it is very sensitive to the dynamic changes of the system.

$$G_c(s) = K_p + \frac{K_i}{s} + K_d s = \frac{K_d s^2 + K_p s + K_i}{s} \tag{19}$$

For setting parameters, different strategies in continuous time or discrete time can be applied as: Ziegler Nichols, Chien Hrones Reswick, and using control and stability analysis as Routh Hurwitz, Root Locus, Nyquist Criteria, Frequency response Analysis, and others.

4. Applications

Industry usually have a structured environment, which allows the integration of different mobile robots platforms. This chapter analyses the implementation of environments with robots in order to integrate multiple areas of knowledge. These environments applies the dynamic and kinematic model, control algorithms, trajectory planning, mechanisms for mapping and localization, and automation structures with the purpose of organizing the production chain, optimizing processes and reducing execution times.

4.1 Navigation robots platforms

The robots navigation platform uses one ASURO robot with hybrid control architecture AuRA (Mainardi, 2010), where the reactive layer uses motor-schemas based on topological maps for navigation. The environment perception is obtained through of signals from sensors. The ASURO robot has three types of sensors: contact, odometry and photosensors. Another robot of the platform is Robotino developed by FESTO. This robot has odometry, collision sensors and nine infrared distance sensors. Robotino is equipped with a Vision System, which consists of a camera to view images in real time. The modular structure allows the addition of new sensors and actuators. Both robots are shown in Figure 12. The odometry is performed with optical encoders. The phototransistors are used to detect the floor color while moving in a certain way. The robot navigates through line following and odometry.

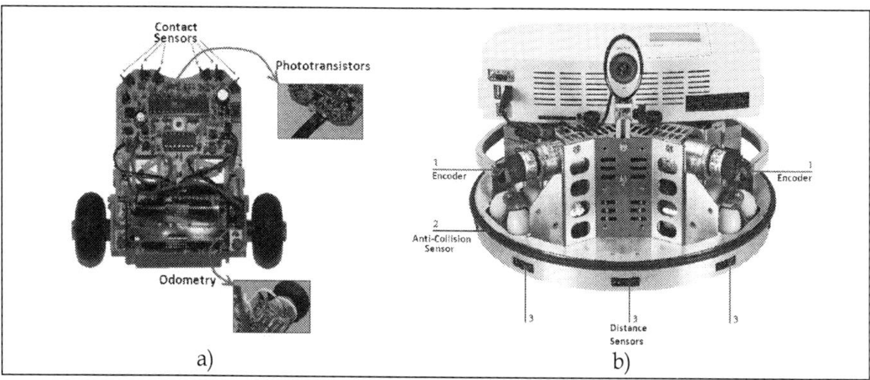

Fig. 12. Platform Robots (Mainardi, 2010): a)ASURO, b) Robotino

4.2 Mapping and location

The localization task uses an internal representation of the world as an map of environment to find the position through the environment perception around them. The topological maps divide the search space in nodes and paths (Figure 13). Mapping and location can guide the robot in different environments, these methods give information about of objects in the space.

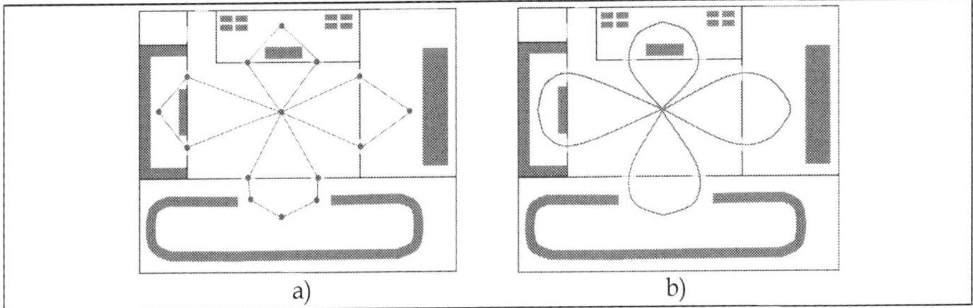

Fig. 13. a) Topological Map, b) Map with frame path (Mainardi,2010)

4.3 Path and trajectory planning

The path planning provides the points where the robot must pass. For this, the planning uses a search algorithm to analyze internal model of the world and find the best path, resulting in a sequence of coordinates to follow without colliding with known objects. For the purpose of determining the best path, the Dijkstra's algorithm is used to find the shortest path between all the nodes on the map. The discovered paths are then archived into a reminiscent table. Therefore, with the topological map of the environment shown in Figure 14, knowing the position and the goal, the path planning module access the reminiscent table to get the best path to the goal or, if necessary, it runs the Djikstra's algorithm to determine the best path. Finally, the path planning module applies two different techniques to generate the robot trajectories that compose the frame path. These techniques are the: Dubins path (geometric and algebraic calculations) and β-splines (polynomials parameterized).

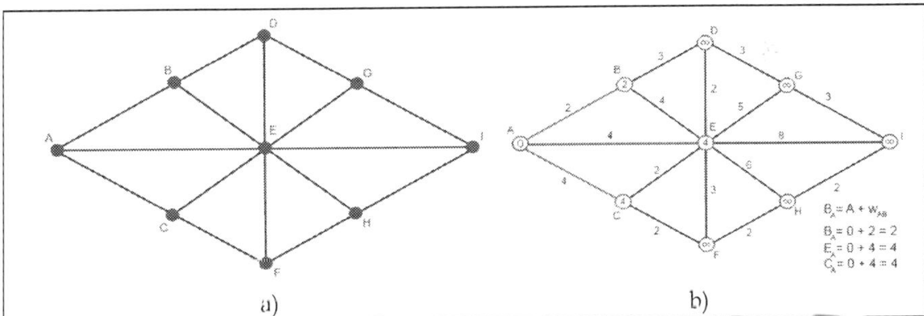

Fig. 14. a)Topological Map , b) Topological map with the weights

4.4 Trajectory execution

During the trajectory execution, the actuators are controlled based on the frame path and the environment perception. In this application, the execution of the trajectory will be conducted in a hybrid structure. The parameters are calculated in the path planning as the basis to adjust the robot parameter through perception of the environment. The stage of path execution is performed by motor-schemas, which are divided into three distinct components: perceptual schemas, motor-schemas and vector sum. The perceptual schemas are mechanisms of sensorial data processing. The motor-schemas are used to process behaviors, where each schema (behavior) is based on the perception of the environment provided by the perceptual schemas. These schemas apply a result vector indicating the direction that the robot should follow. The sum vector adds the vectors of all schemas, considering the weight of each schema to find the final resultant vector. In this case, the weights of each schema change according to the aim of the schema´s controller. The control signal changes due to the different objectives or due to the environment perception. The wheels speeds V_R and V_L are determined by Eq. 20, where vr_i and vl_i are speeds in each behavior, and p_i is weight behavior of the current state.

$$V_R = \sum_{i=1}^{n} vr_i * p_i \ , \ V_L = \sum_{i=1}^{n} vl_i * p_i \tag{20}$$

The robot behavior to follow a black line on the floor will be informed of the distance between the robot and the line, and calculates the required speeds for each wheel to correct the deviation , applying the Eq.21, where l_W is line width, V_M is maximum desired speed, K_R is reactive gain. The speed on both wheels must be less than or equal to the V_M.

$$V_R = V_M + K_R * \Delta S * V_M * \frac{2}{l_W} \ , \quad V_L = V_M - K_R * \Delta S * V_M * \frac{2}{l_W} \tag{21}$$

The odometric perception is responsible of the calculatation of the robot displacement. The execution of the paths made by motor schemas is represented by Figure 15.

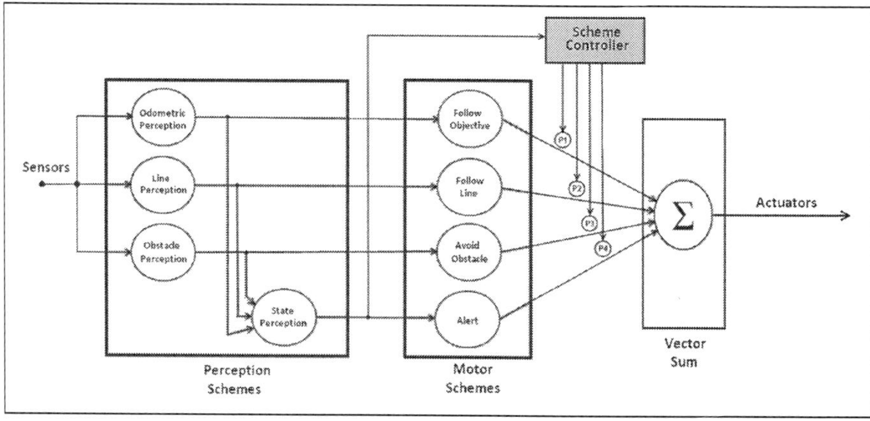

Fig. 15. Motor-schemas Structure (Mainardi,2010)

4.5 Trajectory and control simulator

The library DD&GP (Differential Drive and Global Positioning Blockset) of MATLAB®-Simulink is a simulation environment for dynamic modeling and control of mobile robotic systems, this library is developed from the GUI (Graphical User Interface) in MATLAB®, that allows the construction and simulation of mobile robot positioning within an environment. This Blockset consists of seven functional blocks. The integration of these blocks allows the simulation of mobile differential robot based on their technological and functional specifications. The kinematic, dynamic and control system can be simulated with the toolbox, where the simulator input is the trajectory generation. The velocities of deliberative behavior are easily found via the path planning, but the reactive velocities behavior is necessary to include two blocks in the simulator, one to determine the distance between robot and desired trajectory (CDRT) and another to determine the velocities (reactive speeds), this simulator is presented in Figure 16. Blocks DD & GP can be used for the simulation of two-wheeled diferential robot. However, to simulate the Robotino robot of three-wheeled omnidirectional, it is necessary to modify some of the blocks considering the differences in the dynamics and kinematics of robots for two and three wheels. In this case, a PID control block was added to control the motor speed of each wheel, and blocks were added according to the equations of kinematics model of three-wheeled omnidirectional robot (Figure 17).

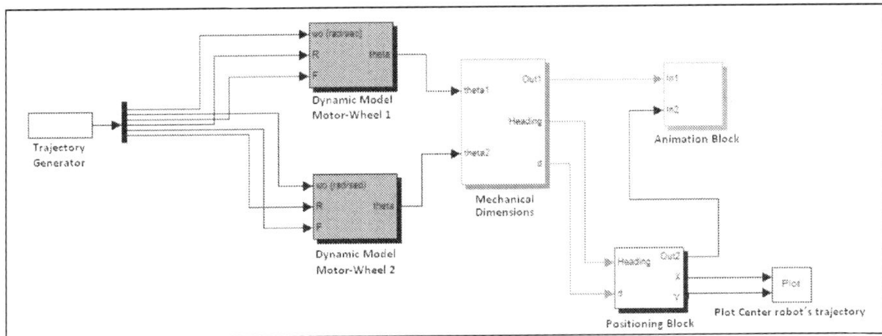

Fig. 16. Simulator with toolbox configuration in MATLAB® (Mainardi, 2010)

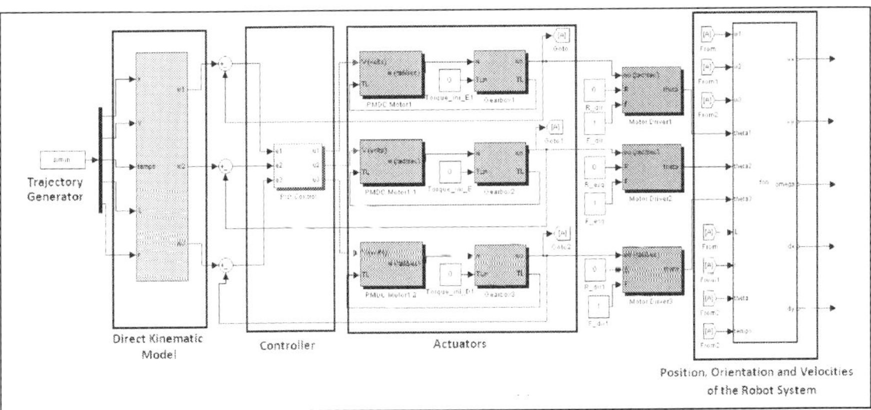

Fig. 17. Simulator for Three-Wheeled Omnidirectional

4.6 Results

First analysis simulated the path represented in Figure 13, with different number of control points to verify which control points respond better at proposed path. The simulations were realized with 17 points (Fig. 18a), 41 control points and 124 control points(Fig. 18b). To compare the results and set the values of desired weight p_d , reference weight p_r and reactive gain K_R, will use the square error in the simulation of paths, where the equation is the quadratic error shown in Eq. 22, where p_i is the current position and p_d is the desired position.

$$\Delta x \sqrt{\frac{\sum_{i=1}^{n}(p_i - pd_i)^2}{n*(n-1)}} \tag{22}$$

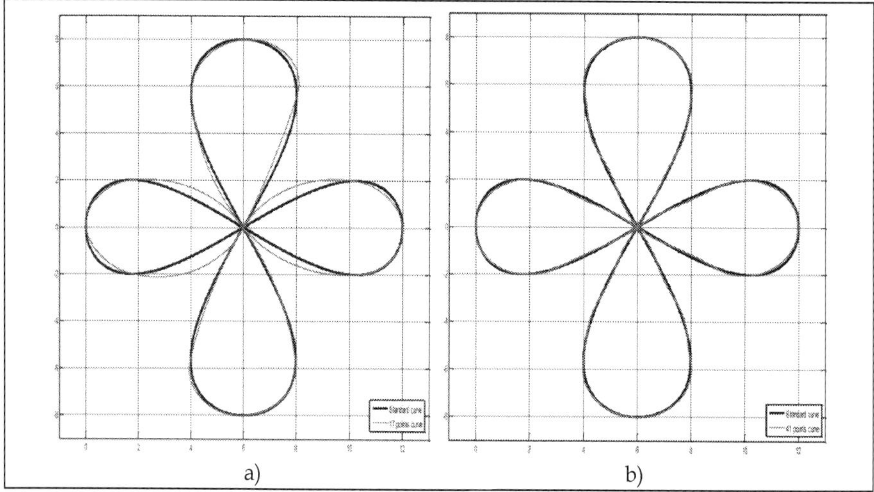

a)   b)

Fig. 18. a)First Path trajectory with 17 points, b) with 124 points (Maniardi, 2010)

Initially, the K_R values for each simulation were defined by simulation of trajectories using the quadratic error for different values of K_R. The optimal weights p_r and p_d were performed simulations varying the weights from 0 to 1 so that the sum of the weights should be equals 1, indicating that the overall speed should not exceed the desired speeds. The results of simulations of paths considering failures can be observed as : with the straight path, the best result was obtained with a purely reactive pair (0, 1), while on the curve path, the par purely deliberative (1, 0) had a better result. The pair (p_d, p_r)=(0.8, 0.2) had an excellent result on the straight and a good result in the curve, being the second best result in all simulations. For the analysis and selection of the best reactive gain K_R, the average was calculated with different simulations which resulted in the error graphs. The graph obtained is shown in Figure 19. The color lines represent different averages of the error in each gain K_R, where the lines is the result of the sum of simulations. The value K_R =10 was selected because the average error in this value is lower, with a better response in the control system.

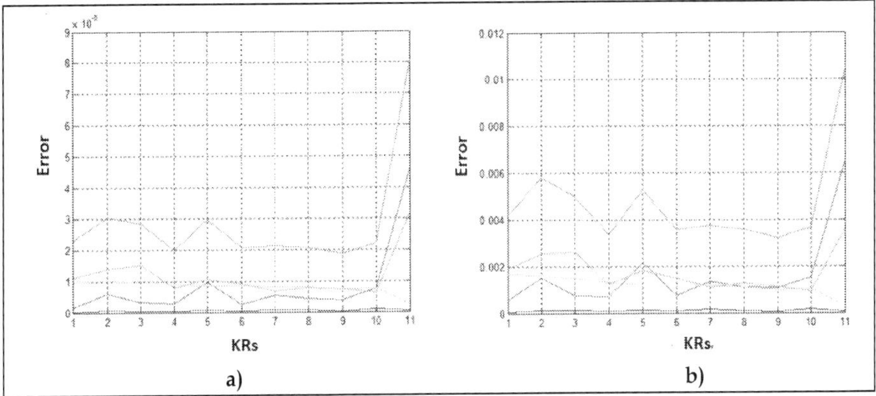

Fig. 19. Errors obtained in the simulations of the K_R's: a)Quadratic error, b) Maximum error

5. Conclusion

This chapter has presented the overall process of robot design, covering the conceptualization of the mobile robot, the modeling of its locomotion system, the navigation system and its sensors, and the control architectures. As well, this chapter provides an example of application. As discussed on this chapter, the development of an autonomous mobile robot is a transdisciplinary process, where people from different fields must interact to combine and insert their knowledge into the robot system, ultimately resulting on a robust, well modeled and controlled robot device.

6. Acknowledgment

The authors would like thanks the support of FAPESP (Fundação de Amparo à Pesquisa do Estado de São Paulo), under process 2010/02000-0.

7. References

Alami, R. ; Chatila, R.; Fleury, S.; Ghallab, M. & Ingrand, F. (1998). An Architecture for Autonomy. *International Journal of Robotics Research*, 1998.

Albus, J; McCain, H. & Lumia R. (1987). NASA/NBS Standart Reference Model for Telerobot Control System Architecture (NASREM). NBS Technical Note 1235, Robot Systems Division, National Bureau of Standart, 1987.

AirRobot UK. (2010). AirRobotUK, In: *AirRobot UK- links*, March 2011, Available from: < http://www.airrobot-uk.com/index.htm>

Anderson, T. & Donath, M. Animal Behavior as a Paradigm for Developing Robot Autonomy, Elsevier Science Publishers B.V. North-Holland, pp. 145-168, 1990.

Arkin, R. (1990). Integrating Behavioural, Perceptual and World Knowledge in Reactive Navigation. *Robotics and Autonomous Systems*, n6, pp.105-122, 1990.

Arkin, R.; Riseman, E. & Hanson, A. (1987). AuRA: An Architecture for Vision-based Robot Navigation, *Proceedings of the 1987 DARPA Image Understanding Workshop*, Los Angeles, CA, pp. 417-431.

Barshan, B. & Durrant-White, H. (1995) Inertial Systems for Mobile Robots. *IEEE Transactions on Robotics and Automation*, Vol. 11, No 3, pp. 328-351, June 1995.

Batlle, J.A & Barjau, A. (2009). Holonomy in mobile Robots. *Robotics and Autonomous Systems* Vol. 57, pp. 433-440, 2009.

Bisset, D. (1997). Real Autonomy. Technical Report UMCS-97-9-1, University of Kent, Manchester, UK, 1997.

Blaasvaer, H.; Pirjanian, P & Christensen, H. (1994) AMOR - An Autonomous Mobile Robot Navigation System. *IEEE International Conference on Systems, Man and Cybernetics*, San Antonio, Texas, pp. 2266-2277, october 1994.

Borenstein, J.; Everett, H. & Feng, L. (1995). Where am I? Sensors and Techniques for Mobile Robot Positioning. AK Peters, Ltd., Wellesley, MA), 1st ed., Ch. 2, pp. 28-35 and pp. 71-72, 1995.

Brooks, R. & Iyengar, S. (1997). Multi-sensor Fusion - Fundamentals and Applications with Software. Printice-Hall, New Jersey 1997.

Brooks, R. (1986). A Robust Layered Control System for a Mobile Robot. *IEEE Journal of Robotics and Automation*, Vol. RA-2, No 1, pp. 14-23, March 1986.

Brooks, R.A. (1991). Intelligence Without Representation. Intelligence Artificial Elsevier Publishers B.V, No 47, pages 139-159, 1991.

Deveza, R.; Russel, A. & Mackay-Sim, A. (1994). Odor Sensing for Robot Guidance. *The International Journal of Robotics Research*, Vol. 13, No 3, pp. 232-239, June 1994.

Dudek, G. & Jenkin, M. (2000). Mobile robot Hardware, In: Computational Principles of mobile robotics, (Ed.), 15-48, Cambridge University Press, ISBN 978-0-521-56021-4, New York,USA.

Elfes, A. (1987). Sonar-Based Real-World Mapping and Navigation. *IEEE Journal of Robotics and Automation*, Vol. RA-3, No 3, pages 249-265, June 1987.

Everett, H. (1995). Sensor for Mobile Robot - Theory and Application. A.K. Peters, Ltd, Wellesley, MA, 1995.

Feng, D. & Krogh, B. (1990). Satisficing Feedback Strategies for Local Navigation of Autonomous Mobile Robots. *IEEE Transactions on Systems, Man. and Cybernetics*, Vol. 20, No 6, pp. 476-488, November/December 1990.

Ferasoli Filho, H. (1999). Um Robô Móvel com Alto Grau de Autonomia Para Inspeção de Tubulação. Thesis, Escola Politécnica da Universidade de São Paulo, Brasil.

Ferguson, I. (1994). Models and Behaviours: a Way Forward for Robotics. *AISB Workshop Series*, Leeds, UK, April, 1994.

Fierro, R; Lewis, F.(1997). Control of a Nonholonomic Mobile Robot: Bac Backstepping Kinematics. *Journal of Robotic System*, Vol. 14, No. 3, pp. 149-163, 1997.

Fikes, R & Nilsson, N. (1971). STRIPS: A New Approach to the application of Theorem Proving to Problem Solving. *Artificial Intelligence*, 2, pp 189-208, 1971.

Firby, R. (1987). An investigation into reactive planning in complex domains. In *Sixth National Conference on Artificial Intelligence*, Seattle, WA, July 1987. AAAI.

Franz, M. & Mallot, H. (2000). Biomimetic robot navigation. *Robotics and autonomous Systems*, v. 30, n. 1-2, p. 133–154, 2000.

Gat, E. (1992) Integrating Planning and Reacting in a Heterogeneous Asynchronous Architecture for Controlling Real-World Mobile Robots. *Proceedings of the AAAI92.*

Graefe, V. & Wershofen, K. (1991). Robot Navigation and Environmental Modelling. *Environmental Modelling and Sensor Fusion*, Oxford, September 1991.

Harmon, S.Y. (1987). The Ground Surveillance Robot (GSR): An Autonomous Vehicle Designed to Transit Unknown Terrain. *IEEE Journal of Robotics and Automation*, Vol. RA-3, No.3, pp. 266-279, June 1987.

Kaelbling, L. (1992). An Adaptable Mobile Robot. *Proceedings of the 1st European Conference on Artificial Life.* 1992

Kaelbling, L. (1986). An Architecture for Intelligente Reactive Systems. Technical Note 400, Artficial Intelligence Center SRI International, Stanford University, October 1986.

Kelly, A. (1995) Concept Design of a Scanning Laser Rangerfinder for Autonomous Vehicles. Technical Report CMU-RI-TR-94-21, The Robotics Institute Carnegie Mellon University, Pittsburgh, January 1995.

Krotkov, E. (1994). Terrain Mapping for a Walking Planetary Rover. *IEEE Transaction on Robotics and Automation*, Vol. 10, No 6, pp. 728-739, December 1994.

Latombe, J. (1991). Robot Motion Planning, Kluwer,Boston 1991.

Leonard, J. & Durrant-White, H. (1991) Mobile Robot Localization by Tracking Geometric Beacons. *IEEE Transactions on Robotics and Automation*, Vol. 7, No 3, pp. 376-382, July 1991.

Lumia, R.; Fiala, J. & Wavering, A. (1990). The NASREM Robot Control System and Testbed. *International Journal of Robotics and Automation*, no.5, pp. 20-26, 1990.

Luo, R. & Kay, M. (1989). Multisensor Integration and Fusion in Intelligent Systems. *IEEE Transactions on Systems, Man. And Cybernetics*, Vol. 19, No 5, pages 900-931, September/October 1989.

Mainardi, A; Uribe, A. & Rosario, J. (2010). Trajectory Planning using a topological map for differential mobile robots, *Proceedings of Workshop in Robots Application*, ISSN 1981-8602, Bauru-Brazil, 2010.

Mckerrow, P.J. (1991). Introduction to Robotics. Addison-Wesley, New York, 1991.

Medeiros, A. A. (1998). A survey of control architectures for autonomous mobile robots. *Journal of the Brazilian Computer Society*, v. 4, 1998.

Murphy, R. (1998). Dempster-Shafer Theory for Sensor Fusion In Autonomous Mobile Robot. *IEEE Transaction on Robotics and Automation*, Vol. 14, No 2, pp. 197-206, April 1998.

Noreils, F. & Chatila, R.G. (1995). Plan Execution Monitoring and Control Arquiteture for Mobile Robots. *IEEE Transactions on Robotics and Automation*, Vol. 11, No 2, pp. 255-266, April 1995.

Ojeda, L. & Borenstein, J. (2000). Experimental results with the KVH C-100 fluxgate compass in mobile robots. Ann Arbor, v. 1001, p. 48109–2110.

Protector. (2010). Protector USV, In: *The Protector USV: Delivering anti-terror and force protection capabilities*, April 2010, Available from: < http://www.ws-wr.com/epk/BAE_Protector/>

Raibert, M., Blankespoor, K., Playter, R. (2011). BigDog, the Rough-Terrain Quadruped Robot, In: *Boston Dynamics, March 2011*, Available from: <http://www.bostondynamics.com/>

Rembold, U. & Levi, P. (1987) Sensors and Control for Autonomous Robots. *Encyclopedia of Intelligence Artificial.* pp. 79-95, John Wiley and Sons, 1987.

Rich, E. & Knight, K. (1994). Inteligência Artificial, Makron Books do Brasil, 1994, São Paulo.

Russell, R. (1995). Laying and Sensing Odor Markings as a Strategy for Assistent Mobile Robot Navigation Tasks. *IEEE Robotics & Automation Magazine*, pp. 3-9, September 1995.

Shafer, S.; Stentz, A. & Thorpe, C. (1986). An Architecture for Sensor Fusion in a Mobile Robot. *Proc. IEEE International Conference on Robotics and Automation, San Francisco, CA*, pp. 2002-2011, April 1986.

Siciliano, B.; Khatib, O. (ORGS.). Springer Handbook of Robotics. Heidelberg: Springer, 2008.

Siegwart, R. & Nourbakhsh, I. (2004). Mobile Robot Kinematics, In: Introduction to Autonomous Mobile Robots, MIT Press, 47-82., Massachussetts Institute of Technology, ISBN 0-262-19502, London, England.

Simmons, R. (1994). Structured Control for Autonomous Robots. *IEEE Transactions on Robotics and Automation*, Vol. 10, No 1, pp. 34-43, February 1994.

Thorpe, C; Hebert, M.; Kanade, T. & Shafer, S. (1988). Vision and Navigation for the Carnegie-Mellon Navlab. IEEE Transaction on Pattern Analysis and Machine Intelligence, Vol. 10, No. 3, pp. 401-412, May 1988.

Tuijnman, F.; Beemster, M.; Duinker, W.; Hertzberger, L.; Kuijpers, E. & Muller, H. (1987). A Model for Control Software and Sensor Algorithms for an Autonomous Mobile Robot. *Encyclopedia of Intelligence Artificial*, pp. 610-615, John Wiley and Sons, 1987.

Waldron & Schmiedeler. (ORGS.). Springer Handbook of Robotics. Heidelberg: Springer, 2008.

Zelek, J. (1996). SPOTT: A Real-Time, Distributed and Scalable Architecture for Autonomous Mobile Robot Control. Thesis, Centre for Intelligent Machines Departament of Eletrical Engineering McGill University, 1996.

Vision-only Motion Controller for Omni-directional Mobile Robot Navigation

Fairul Azni Jafar[1], Yuki Tateno[1], Toshitaka Tabata[1],
Kazutaka Yokota[1] and Yasunori Suzuki[2]
[1]Graduate School of Engineering, Utsunomiya University,
[2]Toyota Motor Corporation
Japan

1. Introduction

A major challenge to the widespread deployment of mobile robots is the ability to function autonomously, learning useful models of environmental features, recognizing environmental changes, and adapting the learned models in response to such changes.

Many research studies have been conducted on autonomous mobile robots that move by its own judgment. Generally, in many research studies of autonomous mobile robotics, it is necessary for a mobile robot to know environmental information from sensor(s) in order to navigate effectively. Those kinds of robots are expected for automation in order to give helps and reduce humans work load.

In previous research studies of autonomous mobile robots navigation, accurately control on the robot posture with a possibility of less error, was always required. For that, it is necessary to provide accurate and precise map information to the robot which makes the data become enormous and the application become tedious. However, it is believed that for a robot which does not require any special accuracy, it can still move to the destination like human, even without providing any details map information or precise posture control.

Therefore, in this research study, a robot navigation method based on a generated map and vision information without performing any precise position or orientation control has been proposed where the map is being simplified without any distance information being mentioned.

In this work we present a novel motion controller system for autonomous mobile robot navigation which makes use the environmental visual features capture through a single CCD camera mounted on the robot.

The main objective of this research work is to introduce a new learning visual perception navigation system for mobile robot where the robot is able to navigate successfully towards the target destination without obtaining accurate position or orientation estimation. The robot accomplishes navigation tasks based on information from images captured by the robot.

In the proposed approach, the robot identifies its own position and orientation based on the visual features in the images while moving to the desired position. The study focused on developing a navigation system where the robot will be able to recognize its orientation to the target destination through the localization process without any additional techniques or sensors required. It is believed that by having this kind of navigation system, it will minimize the cost on developing the robot and reduce burdens on the end-user.

For any robot which is developed for elementary missions such as giving a guide in an indoor environment or delivering objects, a simple navigation system will be good enough. The robot for these tasks does not require any precise position or orientation identification. Instead, qualitative information regarding the robot posture during the navigation task that is sufficient to trigger further actions is needed. As it is not necessary for the robot to know the exact and absolute position, a topological navigation will be the most appropriate solution.

This research work developed a visual perception navigation algorithm where the robot is able to recognize its own position and orientation through robust distinguishing operation using a single vision sensor. When talking about robot, precise and accurate techniques always caught our mind first. However, our research group proved that robots are able to work without precise and accurate techniques provided. Instead, robust and simple learning and recognizing methods will be good enough.

The remainder of this chapter is organized as follows. The next section will explain the topological navigation method employed in the research work. Section 3 gives an overview of the related work. In section 4, the omni-directional robot is introduced. Section 5 explains the environmental visual features used in the approach, section 6 describe the evaluation system of neural network, and section 7 details the motion control system. We conclude with an overview of experimental results (section 8) and a conclusion (section 9).

2. Topological navigation

The proposed navigation method presented here uses a topological representation of the environment, where the robot is to travel long distances, without demanding accurate control of the robot position along the path. Information related to the desired position or any positions that the robot has to get through is acquired from the map.

The proposed topological navigation approach does not require a 3D model of the environment. It presents the advantage of working directly in the sensor space. In this case, the environment is described by a topological graph. Each node corresponds to a description of a place in the environment obtained using sensor data, and a link between two nodes defines the possibility for the robot to move autonomously between two associated positions.

The works presented here require a recording run before the robot navigate in an environment, in order to capture representative images which are associated with the corresponding nodes (places).

An advantage of the proposed approach is that the robot does not have to 'remember' every position (image) along the path between two nodes. During the recording run, the robot will only capture images around the corresponding node. This exercise will help to reduce the data storage capacity.

At the end of the recording run, a topological map of the environment will be build by the robot. Data of visual features obtained from the images of each node are used as instructor data and a neural network (NN) data is produced for each node after trained by NN, before the actual navigation is conducted in the environment.

The topological navigation approach here allows the distance between nodes to be far from each other. The topological map in this approach may have only a few nodes as distance between each node can be quite far. Each node corresponds to a description of a place in the environment obtained using sensor data.

When the robot is moving to the target destination during autonomous run, it will first identify its own position. By knowing its own starting node, the robot will be able to plan the path to move to the target position and obtain the information about the next node from the map. Based on the information, the robot will start moving until it is able to localize that it has arrived at the next node. When the robot find that it is already at the next node, it will then obtain information for the next moving node from the map and start moving toward it. This action will be repeatedly carried out until the robot arrives at the desired destination. An overview of the navigation method is presented in Fig. 1.

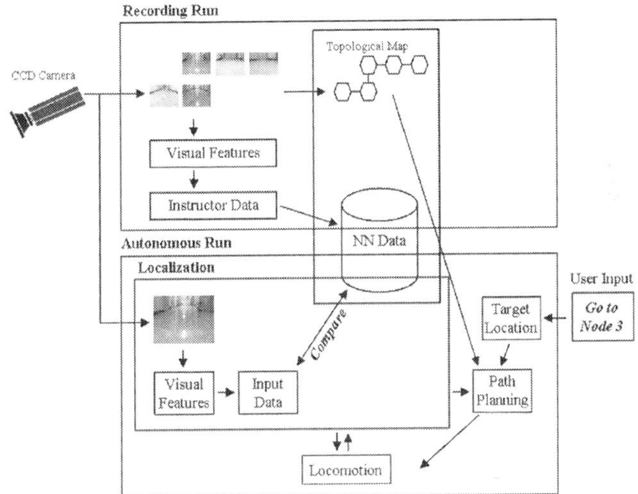

Fig. 1. Overview of the navigation process

In the localization process performed during navigating towards the target destination, the robot compares the extracted visual features from the image captured during the robot movement, with the stored visual features data of the target destination using NN. The NN output result will lead to the knowledge of whether the robot is already arriving near the respective node or not.

In this research study, a robust navigation method where the robot will take advantage of the localization process not only to identify its own position but also the orientation is proposed. By applying this method on the robot, it is believed that the robot is able to correct its own pose and navigate towards the target destination without loosing the direction while moving to the target destination.

2.1 Map information

The representations of large-scale spaces that are used by humans seem to have a topological flavour rather than a geometric one (Park & Kender, 1995). For example, when providing directions to someone in a building, directions are usually of the form "go straight to the hall, turn left at the first corner, use the staircase on your right," rather than in geometric form.

When using a topological map, the robot's environment is represented as an adjacency graph in which nodes represent places (that the robot needs to identify in the environment) and arcs stand for the connections between places. A link (show by the arc) on the topological map means that the robot can successfully travel between the two places (landmarks). A link can only be added to the map if the robot has made the corresponding journey. In some instances the links are established at the same time as the places are identified. Evidence has been provided that localization based on topological map, which recognizes certain spots in the environment, is sufficient to navigate a mobile robot through an environment.

The use of topological maps (graphs) has been exploited by many robotic systems to represent the environment. A compact topological map with fewer locations requires less memory and allow for faster localization and path planning. Topological representations avoid the potentially massive storage costs associated with metric representations. In order to reach the final goal, the navigation problem is decomposed into a succession of sub goals that can be identified by recognizable landmarks. An example of topological map is shown in Fig. 2.

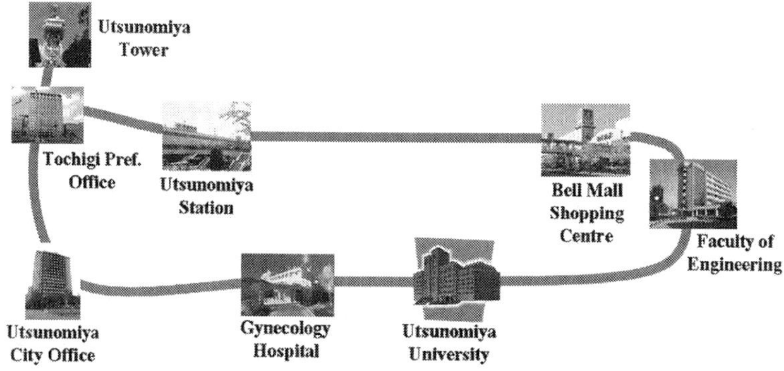

Fig. 2. A topological map of landmarks in the city of Utsunomiya, Japan

3. Related work

An intelligent robot navigation system requires not only a good localization system but also a dexterous technique to navigate in environment. The mobile robot has to be able to determine its own position and orientation while moving in an environment in order for the robot to follow the correct path towards the goal. Most current techniques are based on complex mathematical equations and models of the working environment, however following a predetermined path may not require a complicated solution.

Applications of additional sensors to control robot posture have been widely introduced (Morales et al., 2009). Conversely, in the approach introduced in this research work, there is no application of additional sensor to control the orientation of the robot. The only sensor that is used in the robot system is vision sensor. Many researchers presented methods of controlling robot pose by combining the problem with navigation towards the goal using only vision sensor, where visual servoing is most popular.

In a research work introduced by Vasallo et al. (Vasallo et al., 1998), the robot is able to correct its own orientation and position through a vanishing point calculated from the corridor guidelines where the robot is navigating. The method allows the robot to navigate along the centre of the corridor, where the progress along the path (links) is monitored using a set of reference images. These images are captured at selected positions along the path. The robot will be able to determine its own position through a comparison between the acquired image and the reference image set. They used SSD (sum of squared differences metric) method to perform the comparison. In these research works, they separated the task on detecting position and orientation. In addition, the methods require tedious techniques for both localization and navigation tasks in order to control the robot precisely from losing the actual direction.

Mariottini et al. (Mariottini et al., 2004) employed a visual servoing strategy for holonomic mobile robot based on epipolar geometry retrieved from current and desired image grabbed with the on-board omnidirectional camera to control the pose of the robot during navigation. Their servoing law is divided in two independent steps, dealing with the compensation, respectively, of rotation and translation occurring between the actual and the desired views. In the first step a set of bi-osculating conics, or bi-conics for short, is controlled in order to gain the same orientation between the two views. In the second step epipoles and corresponding feature points are employed to execute the translational step necessary to reach the target position.

There is a method introduced by Goedeme et al. (Geodome et al., 2005) which is comparable to the proposed approach. They developed an algorithm for sparse visual path following where visual homing operations are used. In this research work, they focus on letting the robot to re-execute a path that is defined as a sequence of connected images. An epipolar geometry estimation method is used to extract the position and orientation of the target during navigating towards the target point. The epipolar geometry calculation is done based on visual features found by wide baseline matching. Information obtained from the epipolar geometry calculation enables the robot to construct a local map containing the feature world positions, and to compute the initial homing vector. However, the method of using epipolar geometry requires difficult computation tasks.

In contrast to the approach introduced by Geodome the autonomous run operation in the proposed navigation method in this research work is straightforward and does not comprise any complicated tasks. In the work done by Geodome, the robot needs to perform an initialization phase in order to calculate the epipolar geometry between starting position and the target position. The robot will have to extract a trackable feature to be use as a reference during driving in the direction of the homing vector. In the tracking phase performed after the initialization phase, the feature positions of a new image are tracked, and thus the robot position in the general coordinate system is identified through the epipolar geometry measurements. The tasks perform by the robot in this approach are rather complicated. Dissimilar to this method, the robot in the proposed approach identifies its own starting position and immediately moves towards the target destination. All the identification works are done directly based on the environmental visual features explained in section 5. Moreover, the robot in the proposed approach does not have to measure the distance to move to the following place.

In spite of that, all the studies introduced in the literature have been a very successful achievement. However, they require complicated techniques to let the robot identify its own position and to control the robot from losing the actual direction during navigating towards the target destination. In the proposed approach here, a simple yet robust technique for both robot localization and navigation is developed with the main objective is to let the robot arrive safely at the proximity of the target destination. An emphasis is put on situations where robot does not require accurate localization or precise path planning but is expected to navigate successfully towards the destination. The approach also does not aim for accurate route tracing.

With this consideration, a robust navigation method for autonomous mobile robot where the robot will take advantage of the localization process not only to identify its own position but also the orientation is proposed. It is believed that both robot position and orientation can be identified through a single technique, and it is not necessary to have separate technique to control the robot orientation. A method with less technique required for identifying both position and orientation, will reduce the robot navigation time.

The proposed method is based on environmental visual features evaluated by neural network. By applying this method on the robot, it is believed that the robot is able to correct its own pose and navigate towards the target destination without losing the direction while moving to the target destination.

In a simple navigation method which does not require for any precise or accurate techniques as introduced in this research study, the robot programming will become less tedious. The method that is introduced in this research work will able to help minimizing cost in robot development.

An earlier contribution in the area of mobile robot navigation using image features and NN is the work of Pomerleau (Pomerleau, 1989)}. It was then followed by many other research works where they have successively let the robot navigate in the human working environments (Burrascano et al., 2002; Meng & Kak, 1993; Na & Oh, 2004; Rizzi et al., 2002).

One very similar research work with the proposed method is the one introduced by Rizzi et al. (Rizzi et al., 2002)}. The robot in this approach uses an omnidirectional image sensor to grab visual information from the environment and applies an artificial NN to learn the information along the path. The visual information, which composed of RGB color values, is preprocessed and compacted in monodimensional sequences called *Horizon Vectors* (HV), and the path is coded and learned as a sequence of HVs. The system in this approach guides the robot back along the path using the NN position estimation and orientation correction. The orientation identification is performed by a circular correlation on the HVs.

4. The omni-directional mobile robot

The autonomous mobile robot system in this research study is based on the Zen360 omni-directional mobile robot which was developed by RIKEN Research Centre (Asama et al., 1996). The driven mechanism part of the robot was developed by the previous members of the Robotics and Measurement Engineering Laboratory of Utsunomiya University. The robot consists of a computer and a CCD colour camera. Each image acquired by the system has a resolution of 320 x 240. The entire system is shown in Fig. 3.

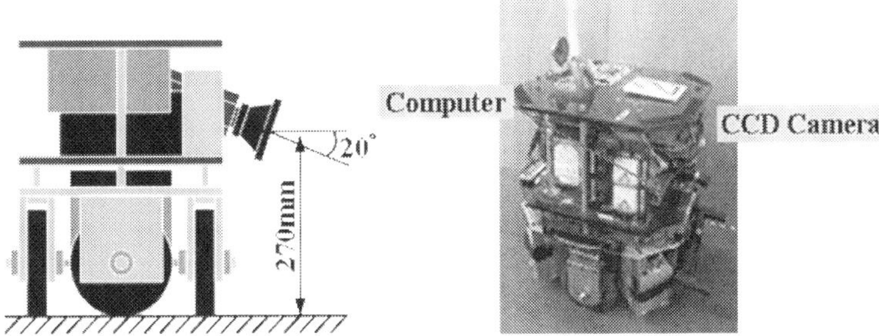

Fig. 3. The Omni-directional mobile robot

Model	Sony XC999
Heel Angle	106.30°
Tilt Angle	79.18°
Resolution	320 X 240 [pixel]

Table 1. Camera specification

The robot has 4 wheels where the wheel diameter is 360mm on the circumference of circle with the rotating shaft is pointing towards the centre. The robot mechanism possesses 2 translatory DOF and 1 rotating DOF, which in total of 3 DOF (Degree of Freedom).

During the actual locomotion, the opposing 2 wheels are rotating on the same translation direction derived through the activation of the 2 wheels bearing, therefore a stabilize translation motion towards x axis or y axis is feasible. Furthermore, a turning motion is also feasible due to the same direction driven of the 4 wheels.

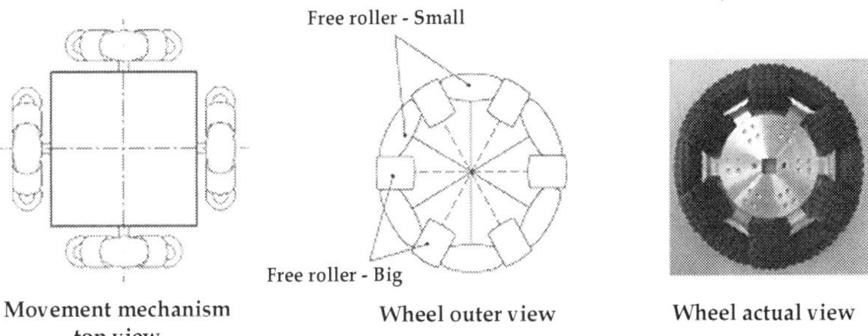

Fig. 4. Robot wheel with free rollers

Under ordinary circumstances, the arranged wheels become resistance to the travelling direction and the vertical direction. However, there are free rollers fixed on the wheel periphery of all the wheels as shown in Fig. 4, where it reduced the resistance on the wheel rotating direction and allowed for a smooth movement. Each wheel is built up from 6 big free rollers and 6 small free rollers. The two type of free rollers are arranged 30[deg] in angle alternately, and the free roller outer envelope form the outer shape of the wheel. With this condition, the robot is able to perform feasible omni-directional locomotion where it can move in all directions without affecting its posture.

5. Features extraction

Feature extraction is a process that begins with feature selection. The selected features will be the major factor that determines the complexity and success of the analysis and pattern classification process. Initially, the features are selected based on the application requirements and the developer's experience. After the features have been analyzed, with attention to the application, the developer may gain insight into the application's needs which will lead to another iteration of feature selection, extraction, and analysis. When selecting features, an important factor is the robustness of the features. A feature is robust if it will provide consistent results across the entire application domain.

5.1 Colour features

The concept of using colour histograms as a method of matching two images was pioneered by Swain and Ballard (Swain & Ballard, 1991). A number of research works also use colour histogram in their method for robot localization (Kawabe et al., 2006; Rizzi & Cassinis, 2001; Ulrich & Nourbakhsh, 2000). These research works previously verified that colour can be use as the features in mobile robot localization. However, unlike those studies, we examine all the colours in an image, and use their dispositions, rather than histograms, as features.

In examining the colour, CIE XYZ colour scheme is use as it can be indicated in x and y numerical value model. CIE XYZ considered the tristimulus values for red, green, and blue to be undesirable for creating a standardized colour model. They used a mathematical formula to convert the RGB data to a system that uses only positive integers as values.

In the proposed method, the CIE chromaticity diagram is separate into 8 colours with a non-colouring space at the centre. It is regarded that those colours which are located in the same partition as the identical colour. The separation of chromaticity diagram is shown in Fig. 5.

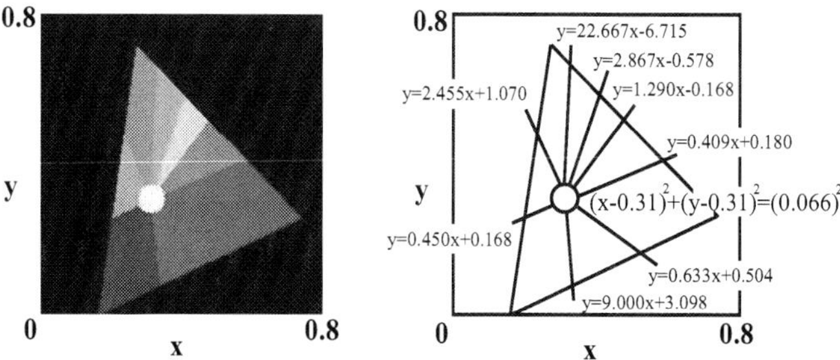

Fig. 5. Separating the chromaticity diagram into 8 colour partitions

Colours in an image are considered black when the lightness of the colour is low. It is necessary to take these circumstances into consideration when applying colour features. Therefore, luminosity L is applied to classify between black and the primary colour of each partition in the separated chromaticity diagram. L is presented as follow;

$$L = 0.299R + 0.597G + 0.114B \tag{1}$$

We also use the luminosity to classify the non-coloring space into white, grey and black color as we learned that the degree in lightness in the non-coloring space is changing gradually from white to black through grey color.

$L\geq50$ is classify as white and black for $L<35$ at the non-coloring space of $x=0.31$ and $y=0.31$. Grey color is considered when $50>L>35$. For other partitions, black color is considered when $L\leq10$. The value for L in this approach is determined empirically.

Formulating a simple way using the details of colour information, by roughly separating the colours into 11 classifications as explained above is considered.

Pixels whose colours fall into one colour domain are considered to have the same colour. Through this, the colour disposition in a captured image is evaluated based on area ratio in the entire image and coordinates of the centre of area (x and y coordinates) of each 10 colours in the entire image, which means total of 30 data of visual features can be acquire from colour features.

5.2 Shape features

A shape is made when the two ends of a line meet. Some shapes have *curved* lines while other shapes may have *straight* lines. For example, a wheel has a shape made from a curved line. One kind of shape is called *geometric*. Geometric shapes are simple shapes that can be drawn with straight lines and curves, for example a desk. The work in this research study is dealing with lines and points which are connected through the lines, in term of shape feature.

Edge detection methods are used as a first step in the line detection process. Edge detection is also used to find complex object boundaries by marking potential edge points corresponding to places in an image where rapid changes in brightness occur. After these edge points have been marked, they can be merged to form lines and object outlines.

In the proposed approach, the edge extraction is carried out based on a simple gradient operation using Robert operator. The original colour image is converted to gray level and then normalized so that the range of gray value is within [0,255]. From this, lines in an image can be extracted through the edge extraction process.

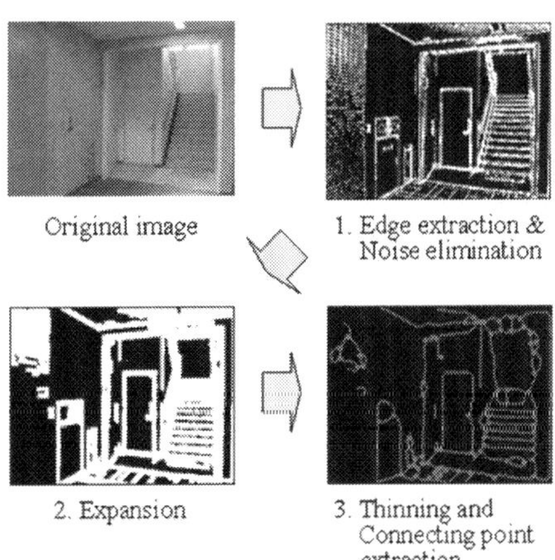

Fig. 6. Extracting lines and connecting points

When further image processing done on the extracted edges, points which are connected through the lines can be extracted and together with the extracted lines, they can be use as information to recognize a place. The processes on extracting the points include noise elimination, expansion and finish up with a thinning process. These processes can be seen in Fig. 6. From the extracted connecting points and lines, it is able to acquire 2 data of visual features, which consist;

- Ratio of the lines in the entire image
- Ratio of the connecting points in the entire image

5.3 Visual features data

An example of colour separation work and shape (lines and connecting points) extraction work which is done on an image is shown in Fig. 7.

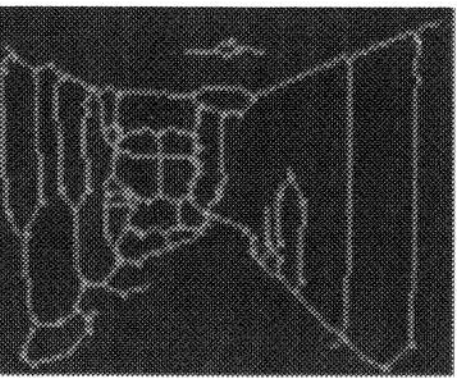

Original image   Color separation   Shape extraction

Fig. 7. Example of colour separation work and shape extraction work carried out on an image

Based on the extraction process which explained earlier, each captured image (either for the database data or for the position identification process) will produce a set of visual features data after going through the features extraction processes. The visual features data possess a total of 35 data where 33 data are from the colour features and another 2 data are from the shape features data. The data set can be seen in Table 2. C in Table 2 is colour area ratio, x and y are the coordinates of the colour area ratio, while S is representing the shape features.

C[0]	C[1]	C[2]	C[3]	C[4]	C[5]	C[6]	C[7]	C[8]	C[9]
$x[0]$	$x[1]$	$x[2]$	$x[3]$	$x[4]$	$x[5]$	$x[6]$	$x[7]$	$x[8]$	$x[9]$
$y[0]$	$y[1]$	$y[2]$	$y[3]$	$y[4]$	$y[5]$	$y[6]$	$y[7]$	$y[8]$	$y[9]$
S[1]	S[2]	S[3]	S[4]	S[5]	S[6]	S[7]	S[8]	S[9]	S[10]
S[11]									

Table 2. Architecture of the visual features data

6. Evaluation system

Neural networks (NN) are about *associative memory* or *content-addressable* memory. If content is given to the network, then an address or identification will be return back. Images of object could be storage in the network. When image of an object is shown to the network, it will return the name of the object, or some other identification, e.g. the shape of the object.

A NN is a massive system of parallel-distributed processing elements (neurons) connected in a graph topology. They consist of a network of processors that operate in parallel. This means they will operate very fast. To date, the most complex NN that operate in parallel consist of a few hundred neurons. But the technology is evolving fast. To recognize images, one needs about one processor per pixel. The processors, also called neurons, are very simple, so they can be kept small.

NN will learn to associate a given output with a given input by adapting its weight. The weight adaptation algorithm considered here is the steepest descent algorithm to minimize a nonlinear function. For NN, this is called *backpropagation* and was made popular in (Mcclelland et al., 1986; Rumelhart et al., 1986). One of the advantages of the backpropagation algorithm, when implemented in parallel, is that it only uses the communication channels already used for the operation of the network itself. The algorithm presented incorporates a minimal amount of tuning parameters so that it can be used in most practical problems. Backpropagation is really a simple algorithm, and it has been used in several forms well before it was invented.

NN is recommended for intelligent control as a part of well known structures with adaptive critic. Recently, much research has been done on applications of NNs for control of nonlinear dynamic processes. These works are supported by two of the most important capabilities of NNs; their ability to learn and their good performance for the approximation of nonlinear functions. At present, most of the works on system control using NNs are based on multilayer feedforward neural networks with backpropogation learning or more efficient variations of this algorithm.

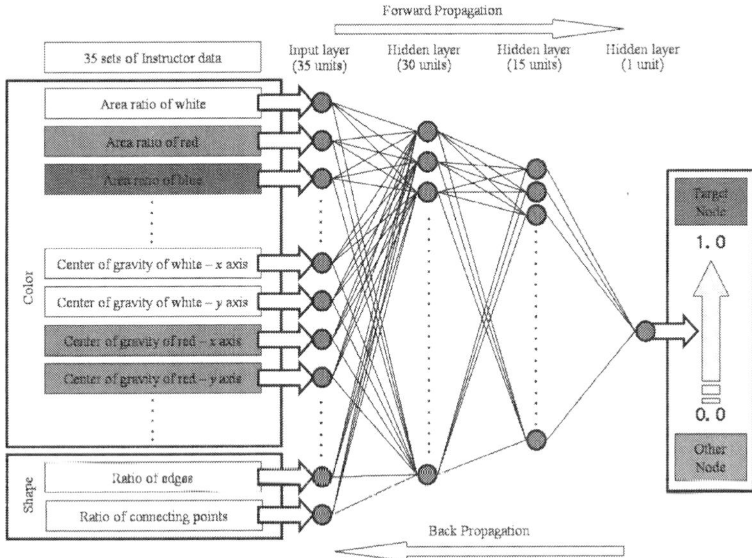

Fig. 8. Multilayer perceptron neural network

Essentially, NN deals with cognitive tasks such as learning, adaptation, generalization and optimization. NN improve the learning and adaptation capabilities related to variations in the environment where information is qualitative, inaccurate, uncertain or incomplete. The processing of imprecise or noisy data by the NN is more efficient than classical techniques because NN are highly tolerant to noises.

Furthermore, evaluation using NN will make recognition process robust and decreases the computational cost and time. NN offer a number of advantages, including requiring less formal statistical training and the availability of multiple training algorithms. With this consideration, NN has been choose in the proposed approach as the computational tool to evaluate the similarity between images captured during learning and localization phase.

In this work, a stratum type of multilayer perceptron NN as shown in Fig. 8 is used as the computation tool. The 4 layers NN is used where the number of input layer depends on the number of combination data between colour features and shape features, and the unit number of each middle layer is depends on the number of input data.

6.1 Instructor data

In order to let the robot in the proposed approach achieve a sufficiently cursory and stable recognition during the navigation, if the robot arrives in the proximity around the centre of the memorized node, the robot must be able to identify that it has reached the node. It is important to provide each node with a domain of area which can be identified by the robot.

For that, a set of the instructor data is need to be provided with consideration that the robot will be able to localize itself within a certain area around each place, rather than the exact centre of the place. The robot is assign to capture few images around the centre of the node during the recording run. From the captured images, visual features data are extracted.

Data taken at all nodes along the expected path is used as the instructor data for the NN. The back-propagation learning rules are then used to find the set of weight values that will cause the output from the NN to match the actual target values as closely as possible. Standard back-propagation uses steepest gradient descent technique to minimize the sum-of squared error over instructor data.

7. Motion control system design

To navigate along the topological map, we still have to define a suitable algorithm for the position and orientation recognition in order to let the robot move on the true expected path. This is mainly due to the inconsistency of the floor surface flatness level of where the robot is navigating, that might cause to large error in robot displacement and orientation after travelling for a certain distance.

In this work paper, we introduce a new method for mobile robot navigation, where the robot recognizes its own orientation on every step of movement through NN, using the same method for position recognition. In the proposed method, NN data for orientation recognition is prepared separately with NN data for the position recognition. By separating the NN into 2 functions, the width of the domain area for position recognition can be organized without giving influence to the orientation recognition. Furthermore, it is believed that through this, extensively efficient orientation recognition is achievable.

As mentioned earlier in is paper, in the proposed approach the robot need to conduct a recording run first to capture images for instructor data collection. The robot will be brought to the environment where it will have to navigate. At each selected node, the robot will allow to capture images to prepare instructor data and NN data for both position and orientation recognition. Topological map of the environment is prepared as soon as the recording run is completed.

Next, when the robot performs autonomous run in the environment, visual features extracted from the captured image is fed through the NN for position recognition first. This recognition operation will be based on the NN data prepared for the position recognition. If the result shows that the robot is not arriving near the target node yet, the orientation recognition process will be executed. The robot will apply the same visual features to each NN data of 5 different directions of the target node. This process is illustrated in Fig. 9. The robot will need to capture only 1 image at each movement which will help to improve the robot navigation time.

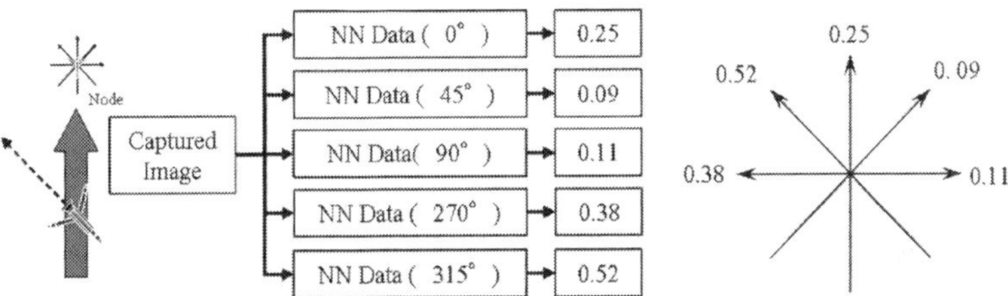

Fig. 9. NN evaluation against NN data of the 5 different directions

From the results produced by the 5 NN data, the robot will be able to determine its current progress direction by computing the median point of the results. An example of this evaluation method is demonstrated by Fig. 10. After the current progress direction is understood, the robot will calculate the difference in angle between target node and current progress direction, and correct its direction towards the target node. The same procedure is repeated until the robot able to recognize that it is within the domain of the target node and stop. This exercise will help keeping the robot on the true expected path. Through this, the robot will able to move on the path to the target destination. Fig. 11 presents an algorithm of the robot movement from TNm (target node of m order) to TNn including the orientation recognition process.

7.1 Positioning control

At every step of the robot movement, the robot will perform a self-localization task first in order to determine whether it has reached the target node or not. In order to perform the self-localization task, the robot can simply capture one image and feed the extracted visual features into the NN. Based on our empirical studies, we found out that the NN output is gradually increasing when the robot is approaching towards the target node.

The work in this research study does not put aim on letting the robot to perform a precise localization task. Therefore, when preparing the instructor data for NN of each node, a fact that the robot will be able to localize itself within a certain area around each node, rather than the exact centre of the node, need to be considered. This is necessary to ensure that the robot will not stop rather far from the centre of the node. Thus it will help the robot to avoid such problems like turning earlier than expected at a corner place which might cause a crash to the wall.

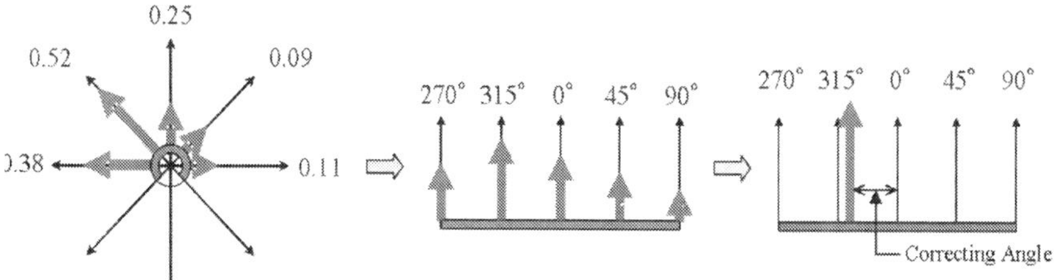

Fig. 10. Evaluation method for current progress direction

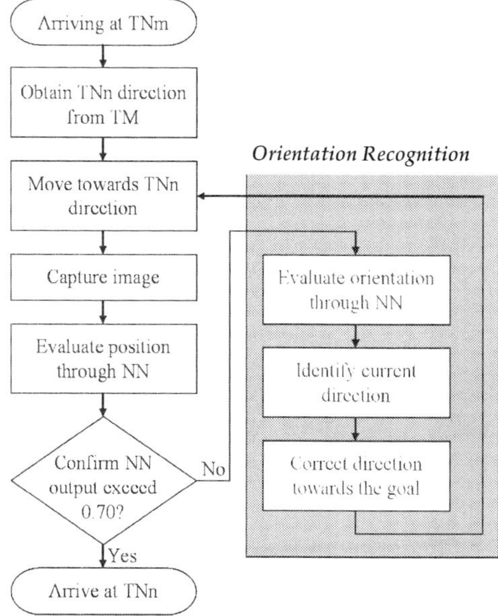

Fig. 11. Navigation algorithm consists of robot movement from a TNm to TNn

To be able to get a sufficiently robust localization output, the robot is arranged to capture 3 images around the centre of each corresponding nodes. 1 image is captured at the centre of the node and the other 2 images are about 5mm to the left and right from the centre, as shown in Fig. 12 (a). We believe that the domain area of the node which help the robot to robustly identify the node, will be constructed in this way.

It is important to evaluate the ability of the robot on recognizing its own position (localization) at around the specified nodes, before the robot is put to navigate in the real environment. Tests were conducted at 3 places (nodes) in a corridor environment to see how a domain of area for localization exists. The robot is moved manually every 5 cm between -80 and 80 cm on the X, Y, Zr and Zl axis of the place midpoint as shown in Fig. 12 (b). The robot is also rotated by 5 degree in an angle range between -60 and 60 degree as depicted in Fig. 12 (c). The result is presented in Fig. 13.

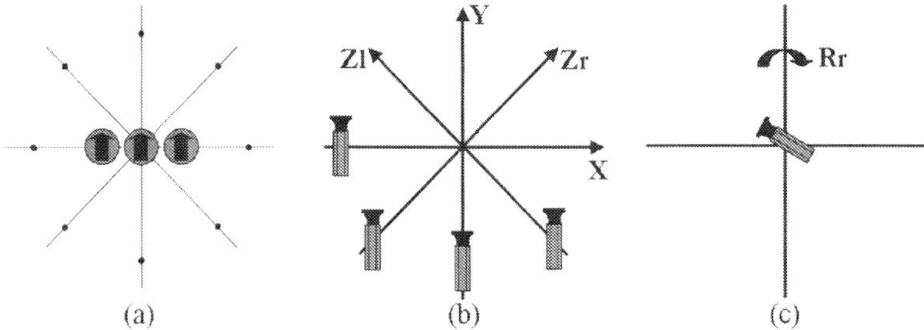

Fig. 12. (a) Positions where the image of instructor data is captured. (b)(c) Robot moves along each X, Y Zr, Zl and R axis of the place midpoint to evaluate the domain around the place

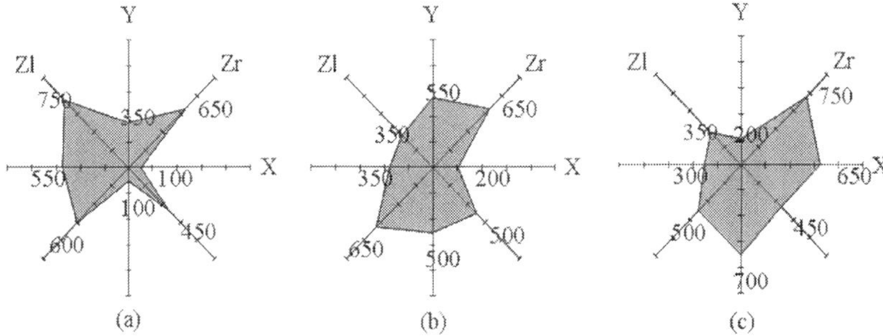

Fig. 13. Domain area acquired at the 3 places; (a) Place 1, (b) Place 2, (c) Place 3

7.2 Localization assessment

A manual localization experiment was performed in order to see the ability of the robot to recognize its own position and thus localize the selected nodes. The experiment took place at the 3rd floor corridor environment of the Mechanical Engineering Department building in our university (Fig. 14). In this experiment, the localization is carried out against all the 3 nodes.

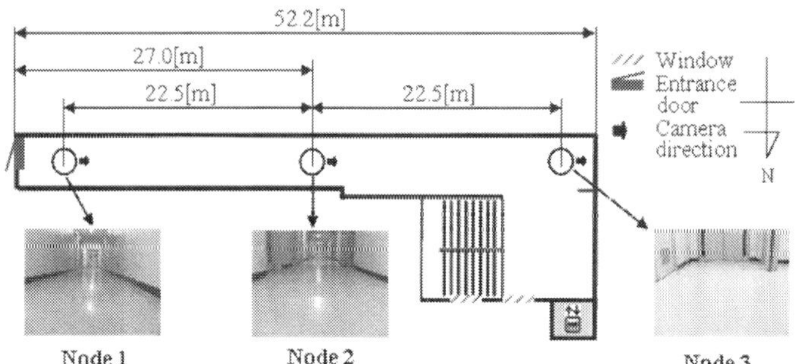

Fig. 14. Experiment layout of the corridor environment with the selected 3 nodes

After the instructor data is fed into NN for NN data preparation, the robot was brought back to the corridor and manually moved to capture image at every 15mm from a starting position which is about 150cm away from the Node 1 (see Fig. 14) until the last position which is about 150cm ahead of Node 3. All the captured images are tested against NN data of each 3 nodes.

The result of the localization experiment is shown in Fig. 15 (the graph with blue color). A localization is considered achieved when NN output is higher than 0.7 (red line in the result graph).

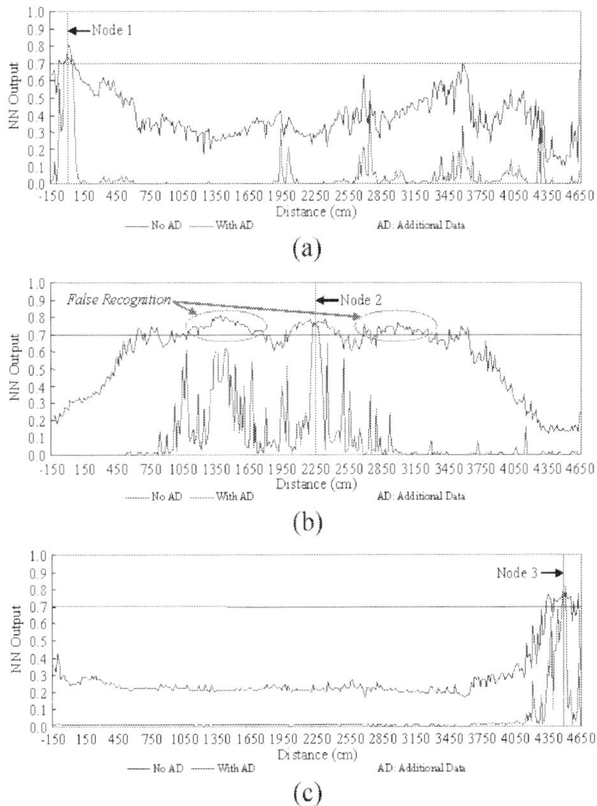

Fig. 15. Result of the test images localization test against NN data of each node; (a) Output from Node 1 NN, (b) Output from Node 2 NN, (c) Output from Node 3 NN

There are some errors occurred in the result against NN data of Node 2, where images around distance of 1200~1800cm mistakenly responded to the NN of Node 2 (Fig. 15 (b)). The same phenomenon can be seen at the distance of about 3000~3600cm from the starting point.

The set of instructor data described in previous section does not result in any particular width, depth, and shape of the domain area for position recognition. Even though we do not aim at the exact center of the node, it is desirable to have a way to somewhat control the size and shape of the domain area so that it is more compact and the robot will be able to converge and stop as much nearer as possible to the center of the node. In fact, the unnecessary mis-recognitions as occurred in the localization result against NN data of Node 2 (Fig. 15 (b)), should be prevented. The idea is to add few instructor data to the current method of preparation, which is believed will reduce the NN output just outside the desired area.

After some preliminary tests, result of the tests indicated that if 2 instructor data of images taken at distanced points of front and back from the center of the node, is added, and trained the NN to output 0.1 for them, the localization domain of the node will be less smaller (Fig. 16). However, distance of the additional data is different for each node to obtain the best domain area for localization. It should be at 90cm for Node 1, 100cm for Node 2 and 30 cm for Node 3. Localization results against NN data of the new method of instructor data is shown in purple graph of Fig. 15.

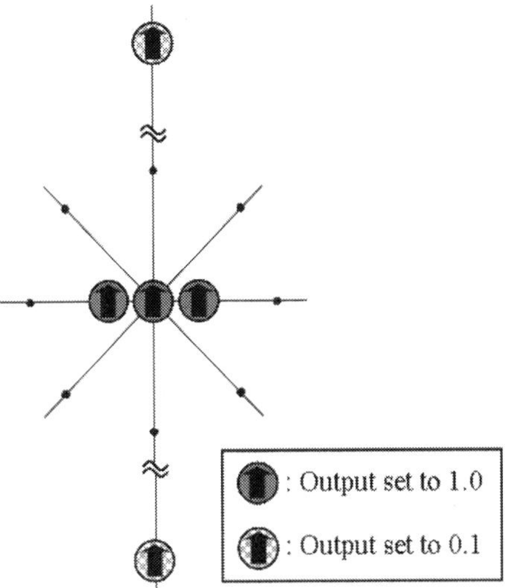

Fig. 16. New method of acquiring instructor data; additional data whose output is set to 0.1 assigned at distanced points of front and back from the centre of the node

As a conclusion to this result, the width, depth and shape of the domain area might be suffering by influences from the environment condition. A different method for preparing the instructor data (with unfixed distance of additional data which trained to output 0.1) might be necessary for different nodes even in the same environment. The shape and the width of the domain area are not identical on every places. They vary and depend much on the environment condition. For example when setting a place at a corner in the corridor, it is necessary to put a consideration on the width of the domain area in order to avoid a problem where the robot turns earlier and crashes into the wall. Furthermore, to let a robot navigate in a narrow environment, it may be necessary to provide a smaller domain area of each place.

7.3 Orientation control

When the robot is navigating through the environment, it is important for the robot to know its own moving direction in order to move on the true expected path. By knowing its own moving direction, the robot will be able to correct the direction towards the target destination.

In the approach which is proposed in this research study, visual features from the image captured at each step of the robot movement will be fed into the 5 NN data of different directions of the target destination (node). The visual features are the same features used for the position recognition. From the output results of the 5 NNs, the robot will be able to determine its current moving direction.

To prepare the instructor data and NN data for the orientation recognition, the robot is arranged to capture 5 images as shown in Fig. 17; 1 image at the centre and 1 image each to forward and backward from the centre along the x and y axis. For each node, the instructor data images are captured on 5 different directions during the recording run phase, as depicted in Fig. 18. A set of instructor data, which consist of visual features extracted from the images is prepared for each direction. The instructor data comprises 5 sets of features data of the direction whose output is set to 1, and 1 set of features data from each other directions whose output is set to 0. The instructor data are then going through a learning process in the NN to obtain NN data. 5 sets of NN data in total are prepared for each node in an environment.

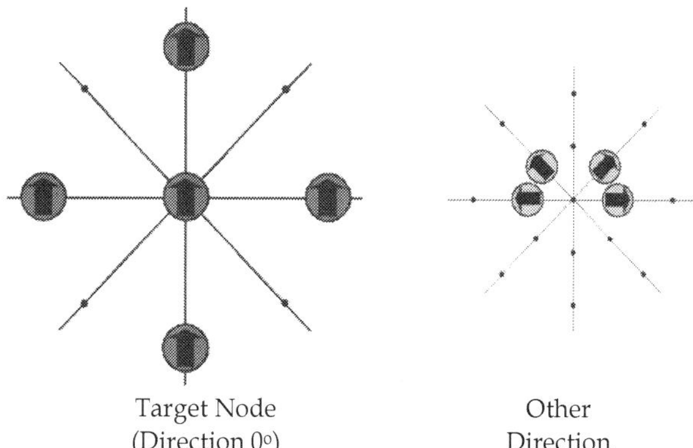

Fig. 17. Positions where images for instructor data are captured for orientation recognition

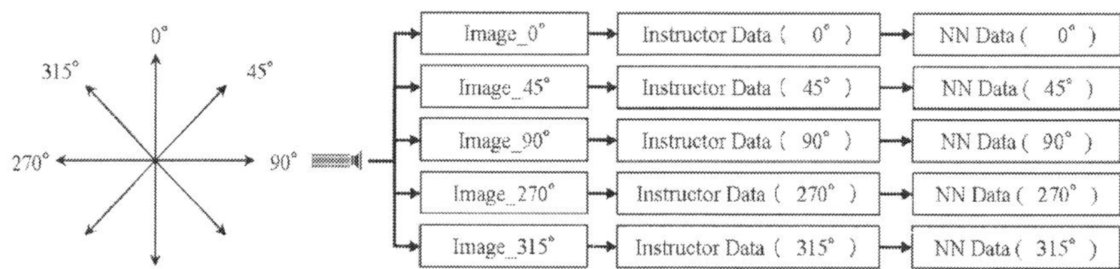

Fig. 18. Preparing the instructor data for orientation recognition of 5 different directions

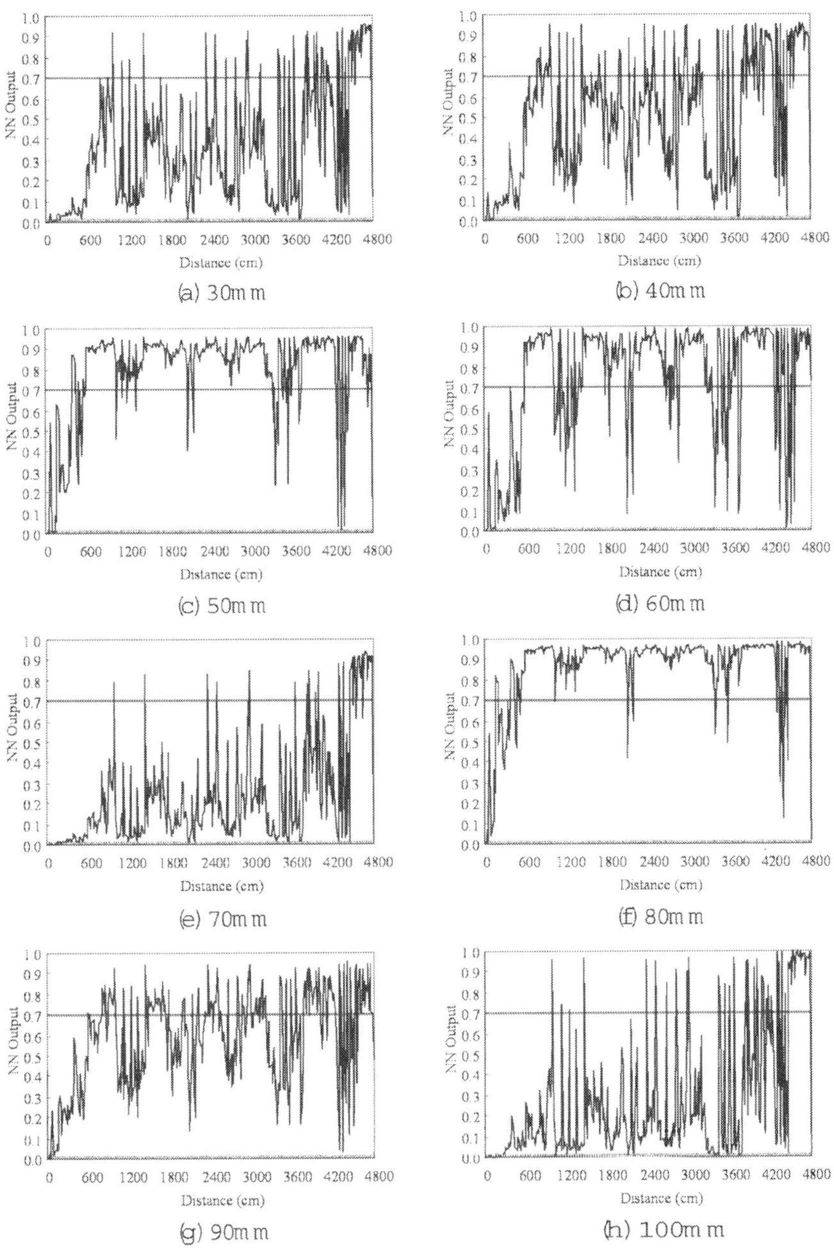

Fig. 19. Results of recognition capability against NN for orientation recognition in which distance for images captured at x axis is fixed

In order to recognize the finest distance for the 4 images on the x and y axis, a series of tests have been conducted at the Node 3 of the corridor environment (see Fig. 14). The test has been divided into two stages where in the first stage, 2 images of x axis are fixed to the distance of 30mm from the centre. As for the y axis, the 2 images are captured on every 10mm between distances of 30mm to 100mm, which means 8 sets of instructor data are prepared. After the instructor data is fed into NN for NN data preparation, a set of test images have been captured at every 15mm from a starting position which is about 4650cm far from the node. The output results of the test images which are tested against each NN data are shown in Fig. 19.

The results show that NN data which consists of instructor data images captured at 80mm from the centre of the node on the y axis produced the best recognition result. The test images output is mostly constant above 0.7 from a distance of about 4000cm, with few failure recognitions happened. With this condition, it is believed that mobile robot will be able to determine the current progress direction from as far as 40m from the centre of the node.

Next, in the second stage of the test, the 2 images on the y axis have been fixed to the distance of 80mm from the centre of the node. This is appropriate to the result of the first stage test. Images have been captured at 4 distances of 5mm, 10mm, 15mm and 30mm on x axis. 4 sets of instructor data and NN data are prepared. Using the same set of test images from the first stage test, a series of tests have been conducted against the 3 sets of NN data. The results which presented in Fig. 20 show that NN data with instructor data images captured at the distance of 30mm produced the finest result.

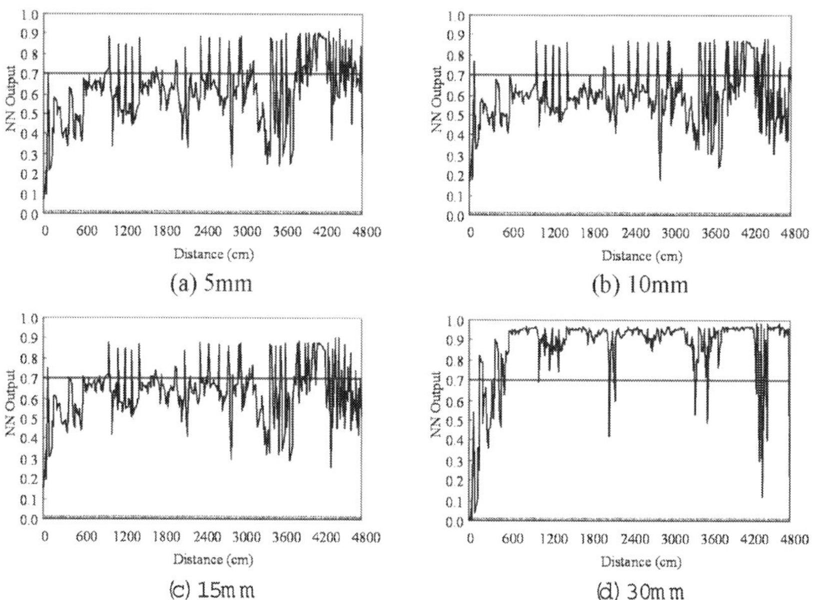

Fig. 20. Results of recognition capability against NN for orientation recognition in which distance for images captured at y axis is fixed

8. Navigation experiments

Navigation experiments have been scheduled in two different environments; the 3rd floor corridor environment and the 1st floor hall environment of the Mechanical Engineering Department building. The layout of the corridor environment can be seen in Fig. 14 and for the hall environment, the layout and representative images is presented in Fig. 21.

The corridor has been prepared with a total of 3 nodes separated from each other about 22.5m. The total length of the corridor is about 52.2m with 1.74m in width. Meanwhile, in the hall environment, 5 nodes have been arranged. Distance between each node is vary, where the longest distance is between node 2 and node 3 which is about 4 meter as shown in Fig. 21.

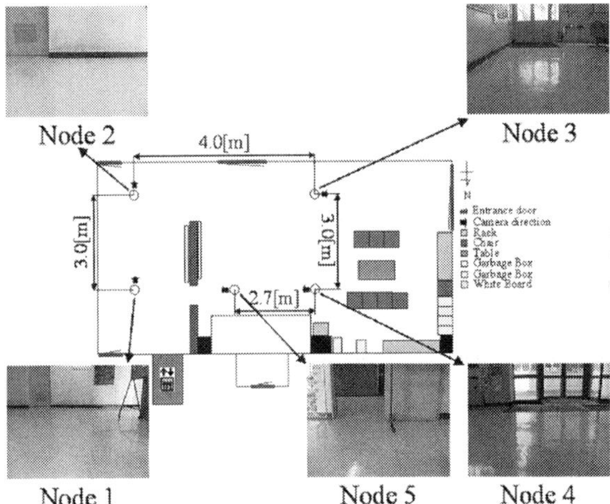

Fig. 21. Experiment layout of the hall environment with representative images of each node

8.1 Experimental setup

For the real-world experiments outlined in this research study, the ZEN360 autonomous mobile robot was used. It is equipped with a CCD colour video camera. The robot system is explained in section 4. Each image acquired by the system has a resolution of 320 x 240.

The robot is scheduled to navigate from Node 1 to Node 3, passing through Node 2 at the middle of the navigation in the corridor environment. Meanwhile, in the hall environment, the robot will have to navigate from Node 1 to Node 5 following the sequences of the node, and is expected to perform a turning task at most of the nodes.

The robot was first brought to the environments and a recording run has been executed. The robot is organized to capture images in order to supply environmental visual features for both position and orientation identification. The images were captured following the method explained in section 7.1 and 7.3, at around each specified nodes. Then, the robot generated a topological map and the visual features were used for training NNs.

After the recording run, the robot was brought once again to the environments to perform the autonomous run. Before start moving, the robot will identify its current position and based on the input of target destination, it will then plan the path to move on. Path planning involves determining how to get from one place (node) to another, usually in the shortest manner possible. The work in this research study does not deal with this problem explicitly, though the topological map produced can be used as input to any standard graph planning algorithm.

A number of autonomous runs were conducted to see the performance of the proposed navigation method. In the experiments conducted at the corridor, the robot navigates from Node 1 and while moving towards Node 2, the robot corrects its own orientation at each step of movement based on the result of a comparison between visual features of the captured image against the 5 directions NN data of Node 2. The same procedure is used for a movement towards Node 3 from Node 2. The robot is set to localize itself at each node along the path during the navigation. An identical process is employed by the robot when navigating in the hall environment, where it starts navigating from Node 1 to Node 2, and followed by Node 3 and 4 before finished at the Node 5.

8.2 Experiment results

The result of the navigation experiments are displayed in Fig. 22 and Fig. 23. The robot successfully moved on the expected path towards Node 3 in each run of the result in Fig. 22. Even though at some points, especially during the first run test, the robot moved slightly away from the expected path on the centre of the corridor (to the right and left), it still came back to the path. The results demonstrated the proposed method to be asymptotically dexterous as the robot displacement in x axis along the expected path during the navigation is small.

Simultaneously, the experiments conducted at the hall environment are producing successful results as well (Fig. 23). The robot was able to navigate along the expected path, identified Node 2, 3 and 4 and turned safely towards the next node. Incidentally, after navigating half of the journey between Node 2 and Node 3 in the second run, the robot movement fell out from the path (to the left). Nevertheless, it still accomplished to move back to the path just before recognizing Node 3. This proved that the robot is able to determine its own moving direction and correct it towards the target.

The localized positions were very much near to the centre of the nodes except for Node 4 where the robot identified the node a bit earlier. The environmental factor surrounding might give influence to the localization performance that caused the robot to localize the node slightly far before reaching near the node. As the node is assigned quite near to the door at the north side of the hall environment, and furthermore the door width is quite large, there are possibilities that sunlight from the outside might entering the door and affected the robot localization performance. In fact, the robot is facing directly towards the door when navigating from Node 3 to Node 4. Although the discussed factors may give influences to the robot localization performance, the robot is still able to turn to the right successfully and move towards the correct path and arrived at Node 5, safely and successfully.

As an overall conclusion, the navigation results proved that the proposed navigation components have successfully operating properly under experimental conditions, allowing the robot to navigate in the environments while successfully recognize its own position and the direction towards the target destination. The robot is able to control its own posture while navigating and moved along the expected path without losing the direction to the target destination.

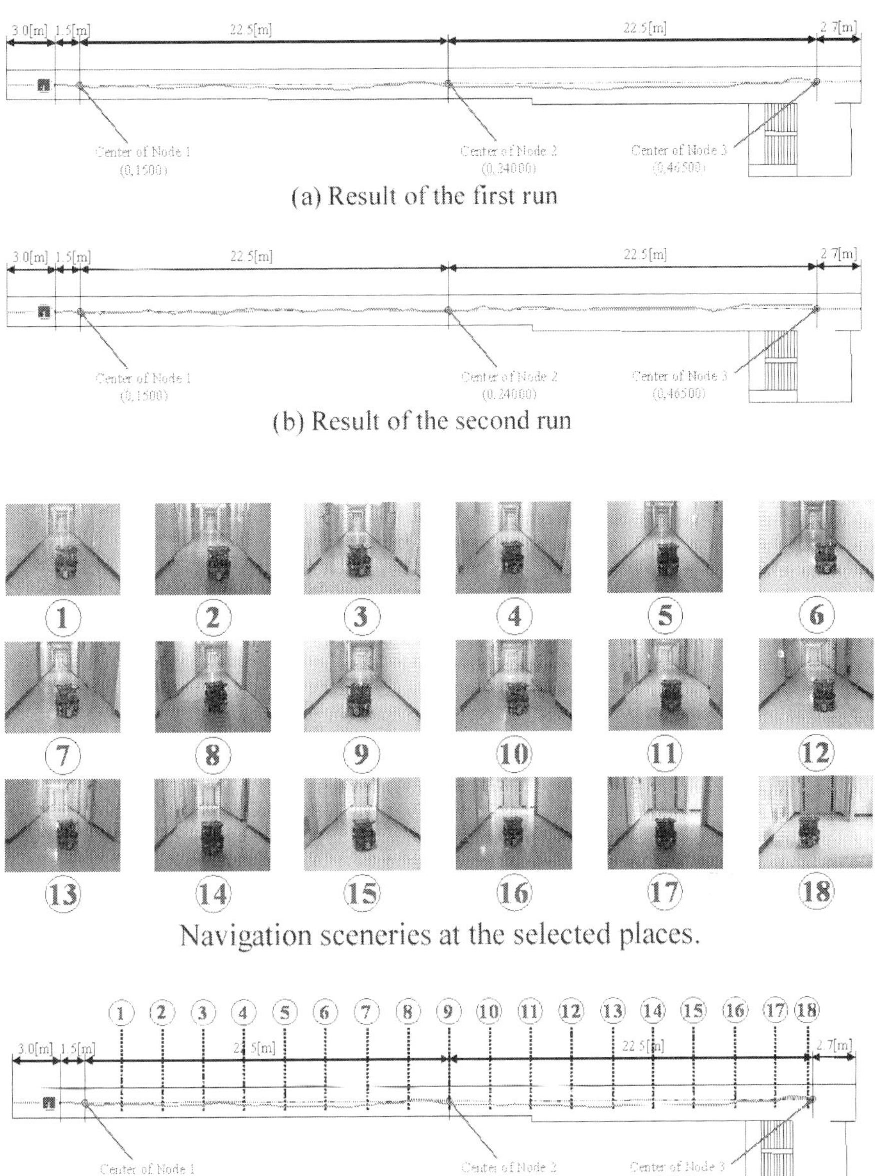

(a) Result of the first run

(b) Result of the second run

Navigation sceneries at the selected places.

Fig. 22. Results of the navigation experiment conducted at the corridor environment

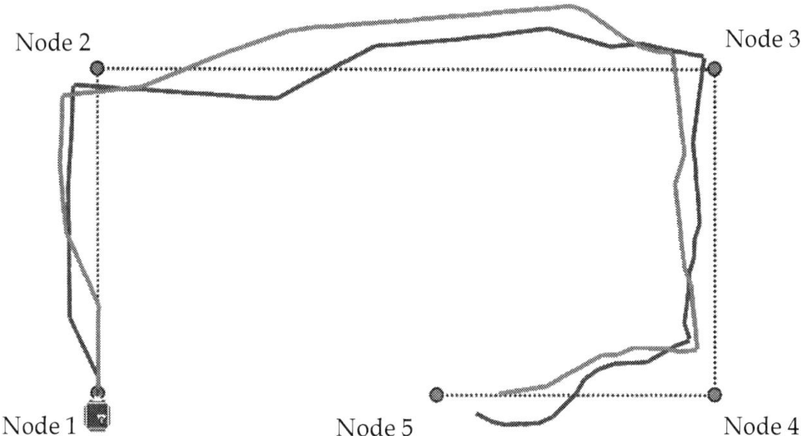

a) Experimental result; blue path – first run, red path – second run

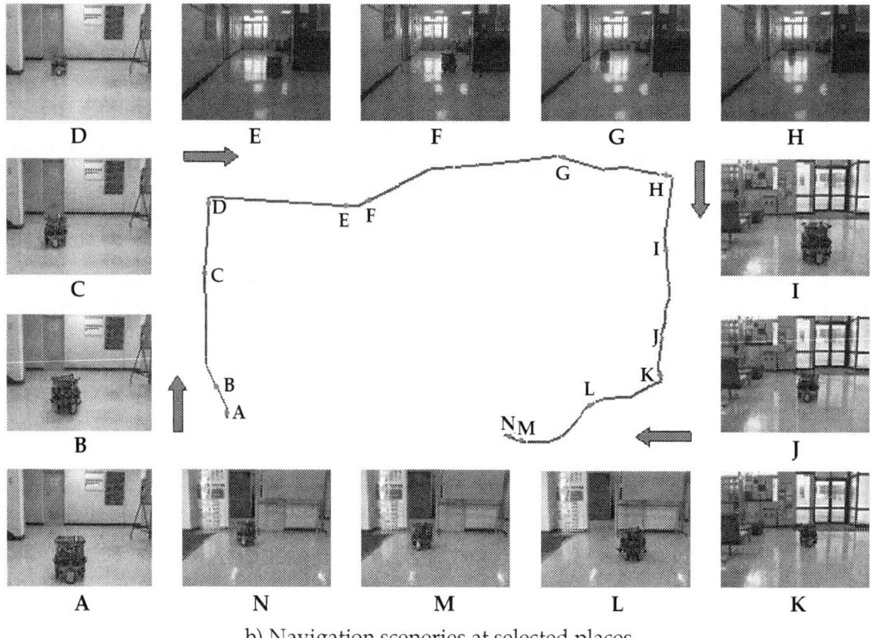

b) Navigation sceneries at selected places

Fig. 23. Result of the navigation experiment conducted at the hall environment

9. Conclusion

This chapter was concerned with the problem of vision-based mobile robot navigation. It built upon the topological environmental representation described in section 2.1. From the outset of this work, the goal was to build a system which could solve the navigation problem by applying a holistic combination of vision-based localization, a topological environmental representation and a navigation method. This approach was shown to be successful.

In the proposed control system, NN data is prepared separately for place and orientation recognition. By separating the NN data of place and orientation recognition, the navigation task was superbly achieved without any effect caused by the recognition domain area. This is mainly due to the fact that the width of the domain area for orientation recognition is practically wide under the method of preparing the instructor data as explained in section 7.3. At the same time, the width of domain area for position recognition is small in order to control the width and to prevent from robot stop slightly early before reaching certainly near around the target destination (node).

Furthermore, results from several navigation experiments lead the research work to identify a new way of preparing the instructor data for position recognition and hence improve the efficiency of localization process during navigation. With the new preparation method, it is believed that the domain area for localization of selected node can be control and the width could be smaller. This condition will help to prevent for early position recognition and help the robot to stop in somehow much more nearer to the centre of the node. Moreover, recognizing node at nearer point, it will help the robot to avoid other problems such as turning to early and crash to wall etc. at a node which is selected at a junction. In fact, the new instructor data acquiring method will help to reduce burdens on the end user during the recording run.

10. References

Asama, H.; Sato, M.; Kaetsu, H.; Ozaki, K.; Matsumoto, A. & Endo, I. (1996). Development of an Omni-directional Mobile Robot with 3 DoF Decoupling Drive Mechanism, *Journal of the Robotics Society of Japan (in Japanese)*, Vol.14, No.2, pp. 249-254, 1996.

Burrascano, P.; Fiori, S.; Frattale-Mascioli, F.M.; Martinelli, G.; Panella, M.; & Rizzi, A. (2002). Visual Path Following and Obstacle Avoidance by Artificial Neural Networks, *In "Enabling Technologies for the PRASSI Autonomous Robot" (S. Taraglio and V. Nanni, Ed.s), ENEA Research Institute*, pp. 30-39, 2002.

Geodome, T.; Tuytelaars, T.; Van Gool, L.; Vanacker, G.; & Nuttin, M. (2005). Omnidirectional Sparse Visual Path Following with Occlusion-robust Feature Tracking, *Proceedings of the 6th Workshop on Omnidirectional Vision, camera Networks and Nonclassical Cameras in conjunction with ICCV*, 2005.

Kawabe, T.; Arai, T.; Maeda, Y.; & Moriya, T. (2006). Map of Colour Histograms for Robot Navigation, *Intelligent Autonomous Systems 9*, pp. 165-172, 2006.

Mariottini, G.; Alunno, E.; Piazzi, J.; & Prattichizo, D. (2004). Epipole-based Visual Servoing with Central Catadioptric Camera, *Proceedings of the IEEE International Conference on Robotics and Automation*, pp. 497-503, 2005.

McClelland, J.L.; Rumelhart, D.E.; & the PDP Research Group (1986). Parallel Distributed Processing: Explorations in the Microstructure of Cognition, Volume 2, Psychological and Biological Models, *MIT Press, Cambridge, Massachusetts*, 1986.

Meng, M. & Kak, A.C. (1993). Mobile Robot Navigation Using Neural Networks and Nonmetrical Environment Models, *IEEE Control Systems Magazine*, Vol.13, No.5, pp. 30-39, 1993.

Morales, Y.; Carballo, A.; Takeuchi, E.; Aburadani , A.; & Tsubouchi, T. (2009). Autonomous Robot Navigation in Outdoor Pedestrian Walkways, *Journal of Field Robotics*, Vol.26, No.2, pp. 609-635, 2009.

Na, Y.K. & Oh, S.Y. (2004). Hybrid Control for Autonomous Mobile Robot Navigation Using Neural Network based Behavior Modules and Environment Classification, *Journal of Autonomous Robots*, Vol.15, No.2, pp. 193-206, 2004.

Park, I. & Kender, J.R. (1995). Topological Direction-giving and Visual Navigation in Large Environments, *Journal of Artificial Intelligence*, Vol.78, No.1-2, pp. 355-395, 1995.

Pomerleau, D.A. (1989). ALVINN: An Autonomous Land Vehicle in a Neural Network, *Technical Report CMU-CS-89-107*, 1989.

Rizzi, A. & Cassinis, R. (2001). A Robot Self-localization System Based on Omnidirectional Colour Images, *Journal of Robotics and Autonomous Systems*, Vol.34, No.1. pp. 23-38, 2001.

Rizzi, A.; Cassinis, R.; & Serana, N. (2002). Neural Networks for Autonomous Path-following with an Omnidirectional Image Sensor, *Journal of Neural Computing & Applications*, Vol.11, No.1. pp. 45-52, 2002.

Rumelhart, D.E.; McClelland, J.L.; & the PDP Research Group (1986). Parallel Distributed Processing: Explorations in the Microstructure of Cognition, Volume 1, Foundations, *MIT Press, Cambridge, Massachusetts*, 1986.

Swain, M. & Ballard, D. (1991). Colour Indexing, *International Journal of Computer Vision*, Vol.7, No.1, pp. 11-32, 1991.

Ulrich, I. & Nourbakhsh, I. (2000). Appearance-based Place Recognition for Topological Localization, *Proceedings of the IEEE International Conference on Robotics and Automation*, pp. 1023-1029, 2000.

Vassallo, R.F.; Schneebeli, H.J.; & Santos-Victor, J. (1998). Visual Navigation: Combining Visual Servoing and Appearance Based Methods, *Proceedings of the 6th International Symposium on Intelligent Robotic Systems*, pp. 137-146, 1998.

3

Application of Streaming Algorithms and DFA Learning for Approximating Solutions to Problems in Robot Navigation

Carlos Rodríguez Lucatero
Universidad Autónoma Metropolitana Unidad Cuajimalpa
México

1. Introduction

The main subject of this chapter is the robot navigation what implies motion planning problems. With the purpose of giving context to this chapter, I will start making a general overview of what is robot motion planning. For this reason, I will start giving some abstract of the general definitions and notions that can be frequently found in many robot motion planning books as for example (Latombe (1990)). After that I will talk about some robot motion problems that can be found in many research articles published in the last fifteen years and that have been the subject of some of my own research in the robot navigation field.

1.1 Robot motion planning and configuration space of a rigid body

The purpose of this section is to define the notion of configuration space when a robot is a rigid object without cinematic and dynamic limitations. One of the main goals of robotics is to create autonomous robots that receive as input high level descriptions of the tasks to be performed without further human intervention. For high level description we mean to specify the *what* task moreover than the *how* to do a task. A robot can be defined as a flexible mechanical device equiped with sensors and controled by a computer. Among some domains of application of these devices it can be mentioned the following:

- Manufacturing
- Garbage recolection
- Help to inabilited people
- Space exploration
- Submarine exploration
- Surgery

The robotics field started up big challenges in Computer Science and tends to be a source of inspiration of many new concepts in this field.

1.2 Robot motion planning

The development of technologies for autonomous robots is in strong relationship with the achievements in computational learning, automatic reasoning systems, perception and control research. Robotics give place to very interesting and important issues such as the *motion planning*. One of the concerns of *motion planning* is for example, what is the sequence of movements that have to be performed by a robot to achieve some given objects configuration. The less that can be hoped from an autonomous robot is that it has the hability to plan his own motions. At first sight it seems an easy job for a human because we normally do it all the time, but it is not so easy for the robots given that it has strong space and time computational constrains for performing it in an computational efficient way. The amount of mathematical as well as algorithmic that are needed for the implementation of a somehow general planner is overhelming. The first computer controlled robots appear in the 60's. However the biggest efforts have been lead during the 80's. Robotics and robot motion planning has been benefitted by the thoretical and practical knowledge produced by the research on Artificial Intelligence, Mathematics, Computer Science and Mechanical Engineering. As a consequence the computational complexity implications of the problems that arise in motion planning can be better grasped. This allow us to understand that robot motion planning is much more than to plan the movements of a robot avoiding to collide with obstacles.

The motion planning have to take into account geometrical as well as physical and temporal constrains of the robots. The motion planning under uncertainty need to interact with the environment and use the sensors information to take the best decision when the information about the world is partial. The concept of configuration space was coined by (Lozano-Perez (1986)) and is a mathematical tool for representing a robot as a point in an appropiate space. So, the geometry as well as the friction involved on a task can be mapped such configuration space. Many geometrical tool such as the geometrical topology and algebra are well adapted to such a representation. An alternative tool used frequently for motion planning is the *potential fields approach*. The figures 1 and 2 are an example of a motion planning simulation of a robot represented by a rectangular rod that moves in a 2D work space and with 3D configuration space $((x_i, y_i)$ position in the plane,(θ_i) orientation). This simulation uses a combination of configuration space planner and *potential method* planner.

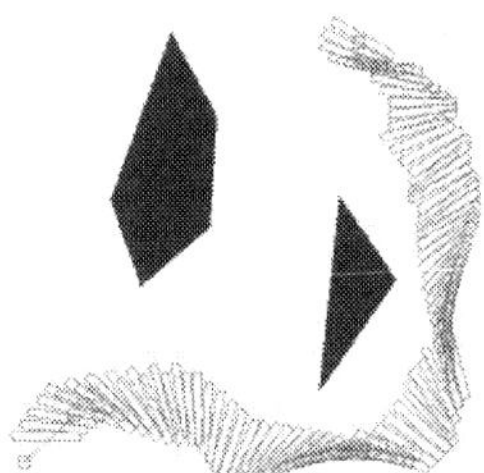

Fig. 1. Robot motion planning simulation

1.3 Path planning

A robot is a flexible mechanical device that can be a manipulator, an articulated hand, a wheled vehicle, a legged mechanical device, a flying platform or some combination of all the mentioned possibilities. It has a *work space* and then it is subject to the nature laws. It is autonomous in the sense that it has capability to plan automatically their movements. It is almost impossible to preview all the possible movements for performing a task. The more complex is the robot more critcal becomes the motion planning process. The motion planning

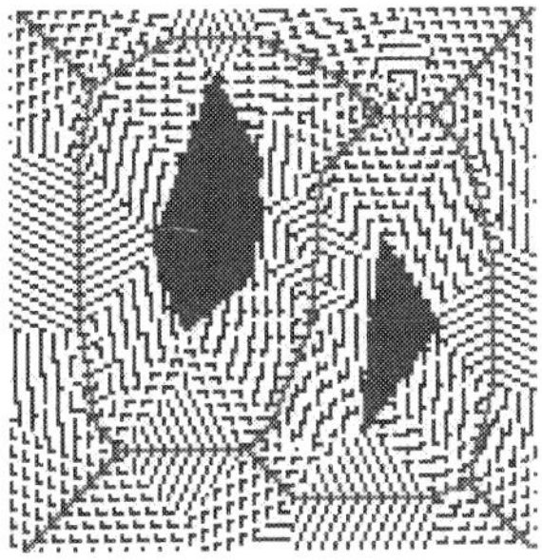

Fig. 2. Potential fields over a Voronoi diagram

is just one of the many aspects involved in the robot autonomy, the other could be for instance the real time control of the movement or the sensing aspects. It is clear that the motion planning is not a well defined problem. In fact it is a set of problems. These problems are variations of the robot motion planning problem whose computational complexity depend on the size of the dimension of the configration space where the robot is going to work, the presence of sensorial and/or control uncertainties and if the obstacles are fix or mobile. The robot motion navigation problems that I have treated in my own research are the following

- Robot motion planning under uncertainty
- Robot motion tracking
- Robot localization and map building

The methods and results obtained in my research are going to be explained in the following sections of this chapter.

2. Robot motion planning under uncertainty

As mentioned in the introduction section the robot motion planning become compuitionally more complex if the dimension of the configuration space grows. In the 80's many computationally efficient robot motion planning methods have been implemented for euclidean two dimensional workspace case, with plannar polygonal shaped obstacles and a robot having three degrees of freedom (Latombe et al. (1991)). The same methods worked quite well for the case of a 3D workspace with polyhedral obstacles and a manipulator robot with 6 articulations or degrees of freedom. In fact in this work (Latombe et al. (1991)) they proposed heuristically to reduce the manipulators degrees of freedom to 3 what gives a configuration space of dimension 3. By the same times it was proved in (Canny & Reif (1987); Schwartz & Sharir (1983)) that in the case of dealing with configuration spaces of dimension n or when obstacles in 2-dimensional work spaces move, the robot motion planning problem become computationally untractable ($NP - hard, NEXPTIME$, etc.). All those results were obtained under the hipothesis that the robot dont have to deal with sensorial uncertainties and that the robot actions were performed without deviations. The reality is not so nice and when those algorithms and methods were executed on real robots, many problems arised due to the uncertainties. The two most important sources of uncertainties were the sensors and the actuators of the robot. The mobile robots are equiped with proximity sensors and cameras for trying to perform their actions without colliding on the walls or furniture that are placed on the offices or laboratories where the plans were to be executed. The proximity sensors are ultrasonic sensors that present sonar reflection problems and give unaccurate information about the presence or absence of obstacles. In figure 3 it is shown a simulation example, running over a simulator that we have implemented some years ago, of a mobile robot using a model of the sonar sensors. The planner used a *quadtree* for the division of the free space. It can be noticed in figure 3 that the information given by the sonar sensors is somehow noisy.

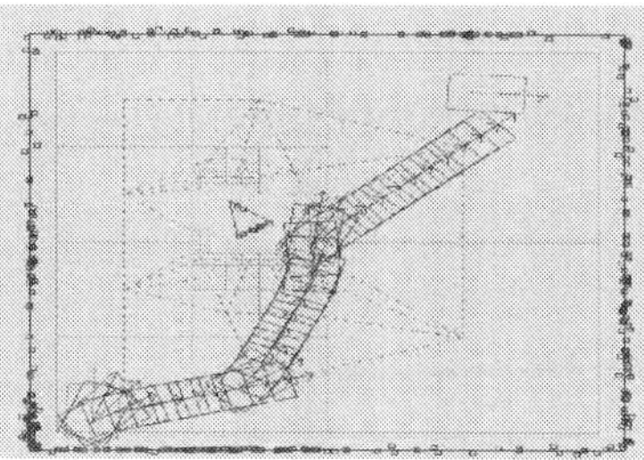

Fig. 3. Planner with sonar sensor simulation

The visual sensors present calibration problems and the treatment of 3D visual information some times can become very hard to deal with. If we take into account these uncertainties the motion planning problem become computationally complex even for the case of 2D robotic workspaces and configurations of low dimension (2D or 3D)(Papadimitriou (1985);Papadimitriou & Tsitsiklis (1987)). The motion planning problems that appear due to the sensorial uncertainies attracted many researches that proposed to make some abstractions of the sensors and use bayesian models to deal with it (Kirman et al. (1991); Dean & Wellman (1991); Marion et al. (1994)). In (Rodríguez-Lucatero (1997)) we study the three classic problems, evaluation, existence and optimization for the *reactive motion strategies* in the frame of a robot moving with uncertainty using various sensors, based on traversing colored graphs with a probabilistic transition model. We first show how to construct such graphs for geometrical scenes and various sensors. We then mention some complexity results obtained on evaluation, optimization and approximation to the optimal in the general case strategies, and at the end we give some hints about the approximability to the optimum for the case of reactive strategies. A planning problem can classically be seen as an optimum-path problem in a graph representing a geometrical environment, and can be solved in polynomial time as a function of the size of the graph. If we try to execute a plan π, given a starting point s and a terminating point t on a physical device such as a mobile robot, then the probability of success is extremely low simply because the mechanical device moves with uncertainty. If the environment is only partially known, then the probability of success is even lower. The robot needs to apply certain strategies to readjust itself using its sensors: in this paper, we define such strategies and a notion of *robustness* in order to compare various strategies. Concerning the research that we have done in (Rodríguez-Lucatero (1997)), the motion planning under uncertainty problem that interested us was the one that appears when there are deviations in execution of the commands given to the robot. These deviations produced robot postion uncertainties and the need to retrieve his real position by the use of landmarks in the robotic scene. For the sake of clarity in the exposition of the main ideas about motion planning under uncertainty, we will define formally some of the problems mentioned. Following the seminal work of Schwartz and Sharir (Schwartz & Sharir (1991)), we look at the problem of *planning with uncertainty*, and study its computational complexity for graph-theoretical models, using the complexity classes BPP and IP. Given a graph with uncertainty, one looks at the complexity of a path problem in terms of the existence of a strategy of expectation greater than S (a threshold value). Such problems have been considered in (Valiant (1979);Papadimitriou (1985)) with slightly different probabilistic models, and the problem is *#P-complete* in Valiant's model, and *PSPACE-complete* in Papadimitriou's model.

2.1 Valiant's and Papadimitriou's model

Let $G = < V, E >$ be an oriented graph of domain V with $E \subseteq V^2$ the set of edges, and let $s, t \in V$ be given. Let $p(e)$ be the probability that the edge e exists: $p : E \rightarrow [0, 1]$, and let S be a numerical value, used as a threshold. The problem is to decide if the expectation to reach s from t is greater than S.
In (Valiant (1979)) it is shown that this problem is #P-complete, i.e. can't be solved in polynomial time, unless some unlikely complexity conjectures were true.
This problem with uncertainty is $PSPACE$, although not $PSPACE-$complete. In (Papadimitriou (1985)) a different probabilistic model is considered where the probability of edge-existence is more complex. Let $p : E.V \rightarrow [0, 1]$. $p(e, v)$ is the probability that e exists, when we are on v.
The problem DGR or *Dynamic Graph Reliability* is the decision problem where given G, s, t, S, p, we look for the existence of a strategy whose probability of success is greater than S.
DGR is $PSPACE$-complete, and is the prototype of problems that can be approached as *games against nature*.
In (Rodríguez-Lucatero (1997)), I considered a global model of uncertainty, and defined the notion of a *robust strategy*. We then give simple examples of robust and non-robust strategies, by evaluating the probability of success. This task can be quite complex on a large scene with unknown obstacles, and hence we wanted to study strategies that are easy to be evaluated and try to keep its level of performance by using sensors.
Under this colored graph model I defined the *existence of one coloration and one Markovian strategy* denoted as EPU and obtained some complexity results.

2.2 The colored graph model

In our model, the free space is represented with a labeled hypergraph in which the vertices are associated with both the robot's state and the expected sensor's measures in this state, and the label edges indicates the recommended action for reaching a vertex from one another.

2.2.1 The coloration method

In (Kirman et al. (1991)) a model of sensors is used to relate the theoretical model with the physical model. It is used for the description of specific strategies, which would reduce the uncertainty in a planning system. Our approach is interested in the comparison of different strategies, that include the ones described in (Kirman et al. (1991)).
Rather than using strictly quantitative measures from the sensors, we model with colors some qualitative features in the environement. It can be the detection of a more or less close wall from US sensors, the localisation of a landmark with vision .
So we defined for a graph $G = (V, E)$:

- **COLOR**, a finite set of colors,

- $clr : V \to$ **COLOR**, the coloration of the vertices.

In the case clr is bijective, we talk about *public uncertainty* : after each move, though it is uncertain, we know the exact position of the robot. Otherwise, we talk about *private uncertainty*. This distinction is essential, because the complexity of the studied problems depends on it.

When we want to represent a *real* scene using our model, we first proceed in a simple cell decomposition of the free space. For simplicity, we are choosing right now to use a grid as accessibility graph (generally 4 or 8- connected). Then we mark those cells with the measure (i.e. the color) expected by the sensors, eventually using *sensor data fusion* as described later.

2.2.1.1 Ultrasonic sensors

As the few ultrasonic sensors of our robot are not very reliable, we first choose an extremly simple model (1 in figure 4) with three different colors; the only thing we expect to detect is a local information : we can observe either **NOTHING**, a **WALL** or a **CORNER**. Being more confident, we then introduce an orientation criterion which bring us to a model (2 in figure 4) with nine colors;

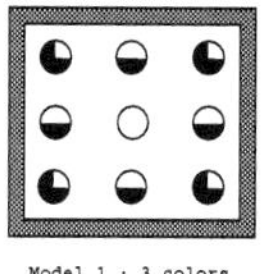

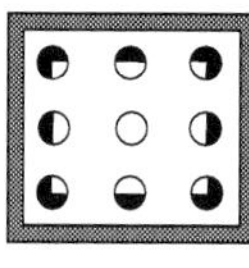

Fig. 4. Some simple models of US sensors

Many variations can be obtained by integrating some quantitative measures in qualitative concepts, like the colors previously described with a notion of *close* or *far*. For special types of graphs and related problems, many models have been introduced, one of them was presented in (Dean & Wellman (1991)),

Using the second model of coloration, we can obtain a scene such as figure 5. We first drew a grid on which we have suppressed the vertices occupied by obstacles. We then drew the color of the expected US measure on each vertex.

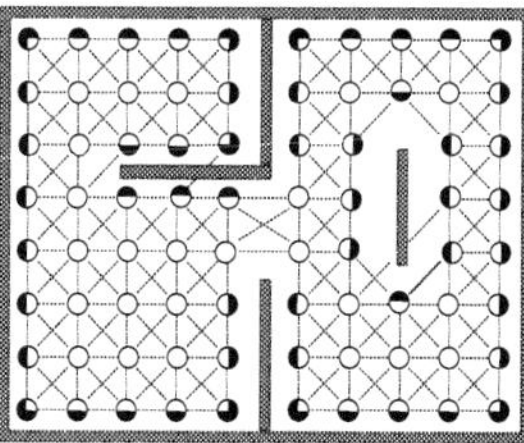

Fig. 5. A scene with two rooms and a door, using model 2 of US sensors

2.2.2 Moving with uncertainty

When executing an action, the new robot state can be different from the expected one. For this reason we use a hypergraph: each edge determines in fact a set of possible arriving vertices, with certain probabilities. *The uncertainty is then coded by a distribution probability over the labeled edges.*

In (Diaz-Frias (1991)) we can find a more formal definition of this model, in which two kinds of plans are considered: fixed plans and dynamical plans or strategies. In the rest of the section, we review the notion of *robust strategy* and we discuss the probability of robustness.
On a graph $G = (V, E)$, we define :

- $LABEL$, a finite set of basic command on G;
  on a 4-connected graph, for instance, we can have :
  $\textbf{LABEL} = \{STOP, EAST, NORTH, WEST, SOUTH\}$,

- $lbl : V \times \textbf{LABEL} \to V \vee \{FAIL\}$;

we then define the uncertainty on the moves by :

- $\delta : V \times \textbf{LABEL} \times V \to [0, 1]$; $\delta(v_i, l, v_j)$ is the probability beeing in $v_i \in V$, executing the command $l \in LABEL$, to arrive in $v_j \in V$. We assume δ is really a probability function, i.e. :

$$\forall v_i \in V, \forall l \in LABEL, \sum_{v_j \in V} \delta(v_i, l, v_j) = 1$$

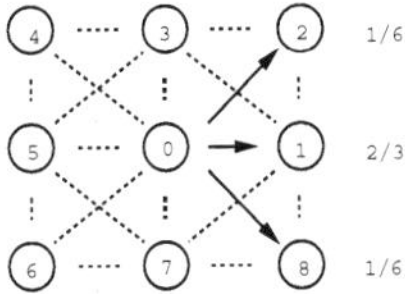

Fig. 6. An instance of the δ function : $\delta(0, EAST, 1) = \frac{2}{3}, \delta(0, EAST, 2) = \delta(0, EAST, 8) = \frac{1}{6}$ on an 8-connected grid.

2.2.3 Strategies

2.2.3.1 General case :

In the general case the strategies use his whole history for taking a decision. For more information see (Marion et al. (1994)) . We define the history, which is a record of all the actions and measures : $h \in H \subset (\textbf{COLOR} \times LABEL)^*$. The history is first initialized with $clr(s)$; and then, during a realization, at the step t, the color of the current vertex is the last element of the history.

Definition 1. *A strategy with history, or* **H-strategy**, *is a function* $\sigma_H : H \to LABEL$.

2.2.3.2 Strategies without memory :

We then define two basic cases of strategies which are of interest because of their properties in the case of public uncertainty, and also because they are easy to evaluate.

Definition 2. *A Markov-strategy, or* **M-strategy**, *is a function* σ_M :

$$\sigma_M : \textbf{COLOR} \to \textbf{LABEL}$$

A Markov-strategy is a *time-independent* strategy. It depends only on the color of the current vertex. In the case of public uncertainty, it is a function of the current vertex.

Definition 3. *A* **T-strategy** *is a function σ_T :*

$$\sigma_T : \mathbf{COLOR} \times \mathbf{N} \to \mathbf{LABEL}$$

A T-strategy is a *time-dependent* strategy; It depends only of the color of the current vertex, and the number of steps. **remark :** A notion of **plan** is often defined. It is a particular kind of

T-strategy which depend only of the time : $\sigma_P : \mathbf{N} \to \mathbf{LABEL}$

For more details about other types of strategies more embeded that use a bounded memory see (Marion et al. (1994)).

2.2.3.3 Strategies using history :

If the two different strategies described above are efficient in some cases (as we will see in a further section, see section 4.2), other strategies using history can be more efficient. That is why we define a new kind of strategy named **D-strategy**.

For a graph $G = (V, E)$, a model of uncertainty δ, and a strategy σ, let's define at step k :

- $s_k \in V$ the position and h_k the history ; s_{k+1} is a function of $G, \delta, \sigma, h_k, s_k$, and $h_{k+1} = h_k \cup (col(s_{k+1}), \sigma(h_k))$.

- $\forall v \in V, f_{h_k}(v) = Pr(s_k = v \mid h_k)$, the probability of being in v at the step t, **knowing** the history.

At the step $k + 1$, $f_{h_{k+1}}(v)$ is defined by :

$$[\xi_{h_{k+1}}(v) = \begin{cases} \sum_{u \in V} f_{h_k}(u)\delta(u, \sigma(h_k), v) & \text{if } col(v) = col(s_{k+1}) \\ 0 & \text{otherwise} \end{cases}] \; [f_{h_{k+1}}(v) = \frac{\xi_{h_{k+1}}(v)}{\sum_{u \in V} \xi_{h_{k+1}}(u)}]$$

Let be $\Phi : H \to [0, 1]^{|V|}$, the function which associate for all h, $\Phi(h) = f_h$ the distribution over the vertices. We note $\mathcal{F} = \Phi(H)$.

Definition 4. *A* **D-strategy** *is a function :* $\sigma : \mathcal{F} \times \mathbf{N} \to \mathbf{LABEL}$

A D-strategy only depends on the time and the distribution over the vertices.

2.2.4 Criteria of evaluation of a strategy

2.2.4.1 Reliability :

We are first interested in reaching t from s with the maximal possible probability, but in a limited time k :

$$\mathbf{R}(\sigma, k) = Prob(s \xrightarrow{\sigma} t \mid \; |h| \le k)$$

We note, at the limit:

$$\mathbf{R}(\sigma) = \mathbf{R}(\sigma, \infty) = \lim_{k \to \infty} \mathbf{R}(\sigma, k)$$

This criterion is essentially uses for M-strategy, for which we have means to compute this value (see section 3.1).

Definition 5. *A strategy σ_{opt} is* **R-k**-*optimal iff :*

$$\forall \sigma : \mathbf{R}(\sigma, k) \le \mathbf{R}(\sigma_{opt}, k)$$

Definition 6. *A strategy σ_{opt} is* **R-optimal** *iff :*

$$\forall \sigma : \mathbf{R}(\sigma) \le \mathbf{R}(\sigma_{opt})$$

2.3 Definition of the problems

Given $G = (V, E)$, an uncertainty function δ, a coloration function clr, a command function lbl, two points $s, t \in G$ (resp. source and target), and a criterion C, let us consider the following problem :

- **PU**, the decision problem
  Output : 1, if there exists a strategy which satisfies the criterion, else 0.

- **PU**$_{opt}$, the optimization problem
  Output : the optimal strategy for the criterion.

And for a given strategy σ :

- **PU**$_\sigma$, the evaluation problem
  Output : the value $C(\sigma)$.

3. M-strategies vs. T-strategies

3.1 The public uncertainty case

In that case T-strategy and M-strategy are interesting :

Theorem 1. *A T-strategy **R**-optimal for a given k does exist and can be constructed in time polynomial in k and the size of the input graph with uncertain moves.*

Theorem 2. *For every graph with uncertain moves and a source/target pair of vertices there exists an **R**-optimal M-strategy.*

Note that the first theorem consider finite time criterion, and the second one infinite time criterion. (The demonstration of these theorems and the methods to construct those optimal strategies can be found in (Burago et al. (1993)).

Using these criteria we can compare different types of strategies under an unified frame. In (Marion et al. (1994)) we can find un exemple of graph where for a given number of steps a T-strategy works better than an M-strategy. In this same paper we showed that we can construct more involved strategies that can be more performants but harder to evaluate, so we proposed the simulation as a tool for estimating the performances of this kind of strategies.

3.2 Example: Peg-in-hole

We assume that we have a robot manipulator with a tactil sensor in the end effector. This sensor allows us to move compliantly over a planar surface. We suppose too that we have a workspace limited by a rectangular frame, so we can detect with the fingers of the end effector if we are touching the frame or an obstacle, by interpretation of the efforts in the fingers of the end effector. The robotic scene is as follows:

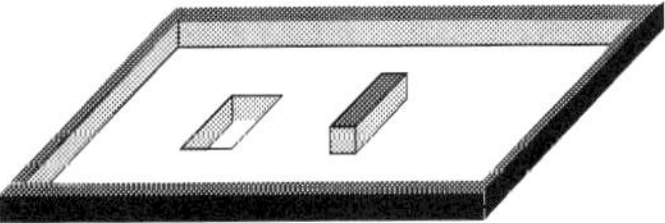

Fig. 7. A scene for the Peg-in-hole

If we use a sensorial model of the tactil sensor in a similar way as we used for the ultrasonic sensors we can obtain a colored graph representation like the next figure:

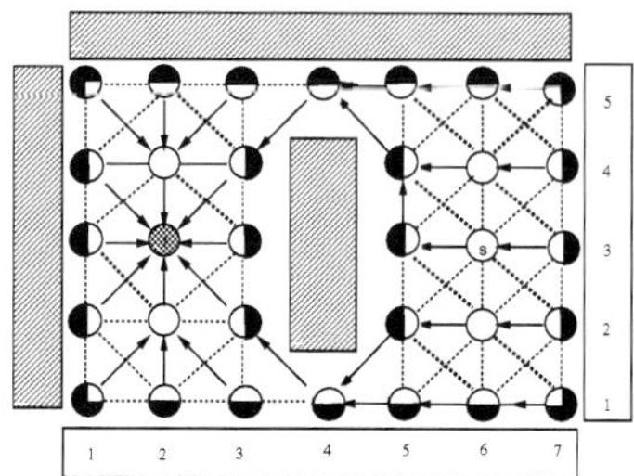

Fig. 8. Associated colored graph the arrows represents the M-strategy actions

If we evaluate this M-stretegy for a number of steps $k = 7$ we obtain: $R(\sigma_M, 20) = 0.16627$ as we can see this strategy is not performant even allowing a big number of steps. We can remark too that the coloration is not bijective so we can't distinguish between the limiting right frame and the right face of the rectangular obstacle. So we can propose a T-strategy (a little variation of the M-strategy) that for this color if $k \geq 5$ we execute the action E instead of making N The reliability for this new strategy is $R(\sigma_T, 20) = 0.8173582$ that makes a very big difference. In the case of finite polynomial time, there may not be an optimal M-strategy as shown on figure 9. In this example, the uncertainty is public. The command are RIGHT, LEFT and STRAIGHT, on the directed edges. The goal is to reach t from s in less than 6 steps. The moves are certain except for some edges :

- $\delta(s, RIGHT, 4) = \delta(s, RIGHT, 1) = \delta(s, LEFT, 4) = \delta(s, LEFT, 1) = \frac{1}{2}$,

- $\delta(8, LEFT, t) = \delta(8, LEFT, trap) = \frac{1}{2}$,

An *optimal* strategy first choose RIGHT to arrive at 4 in one step; but in case it fails, it will arrive there in four steps. An *optimal* M-strategy σ_M will **always** choose on vertex 4 :

- either LEFT, taking the risk not to arrive before the time is gone (6 steps maximum),

- either RIGHT, taking the risk to fall in the trap.

The optimal T-strategy σ_T will choose on vertex 4 :

- LEFT a (the safe way) if it arrive there in only one step,

- otherwise RIGHT (a more risky path).

Thus the probability of success of those two strategies are : $[\mathbf{R}(\sigma_M, 6) = \frac{1}{2} \leq \mathbf{R}(\sigma_T, 6) = \frac{3}{4}]$

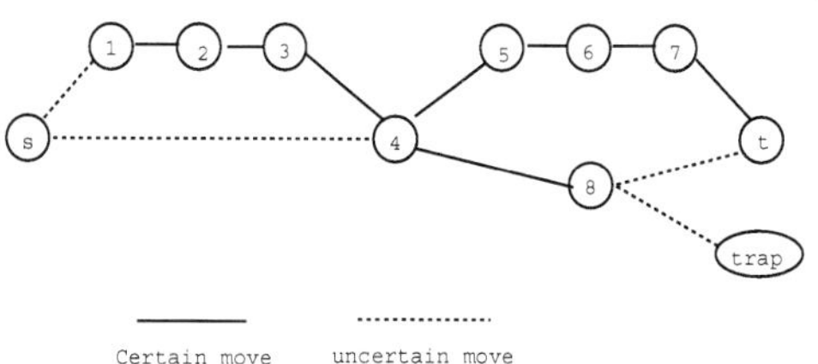

Fig. 9. σ_T is optimal though σ_M is not.

3.3 The private uncertainty case

In the case of total uncertainty (i.e. all the vertices have the same color),

Theorem 3. *It is $NP-hard$ to decide if there exists a strategy which succeeds with probability 1.*

Another result that we consider interesting concerns the approximability of this problem in the case of total uncertainty, that we can state as:

Theorem 4. *It is $NP-hard$ to decide if there exists an approximate solution.*

4. Complexity of the evalution problem

4.1 Evaluation in the general case

The computation of $R(\sigma, k)$ for some strategy σ may be very hard. This can be shown by a reduction of $3SAT$ to the evaluation problem. We represent F as a table. Let be:

$$F = \bigwedge_{1 \le i \le m} \bigvee_{1 \le j \le 3} z_{i,j}$$

a formula where $z_{i,j}$ are literals of the set

$$\{x_1, \ldots, x_n, \overline{x_1}, \ldots, \overline{x_n}\})$$

. His tabular representation is

$$
\begin{array}{l}
z_{1,1}\ z_{2,1}\ \cdots\ z_{m,1} \\
z_{1,2}\ z_{2,2}\ \cdots\ z_{m,2} \\
z_{1,3}\ z_{2,3}\ \cdots\ z_{m,3}
\end{array}
$$

where the height is 3 and the length is m (the i-th column corresponds to the i-th clause in the formula). We say that two literals z_1 et z_2 are opposed iff $z_1 \Leftrightarrow \overline{z_2}$. We assume that there is not contradictory literals in a column. One path in F is an horizontal path P in the table build taking one literal by column (clause), we mean that P is a list of literals as $(z_{1,j_1}, z_{2,j_2}, \ldots, z_{m,j_m})$, $1 \le j_i \le 3, 1 \le i \le m$. We interpret this paths as truth value assignments. In the case that a path have no pair of contradictory literals we say that is a model of the logic formula. The paths without contradictions are named as *opened* otherwise *closed*.
In this way we can construct a graph as:

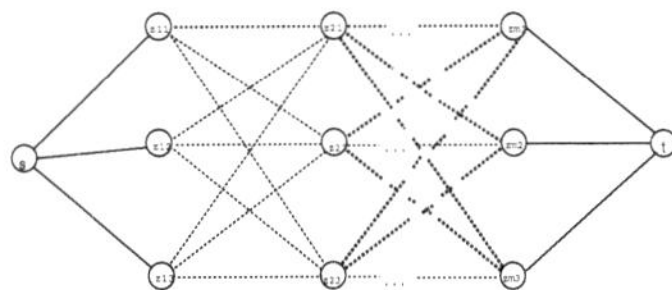

Fig. 10. Example multilayer graph for the reduction of 3SAT to PU

The triplets of vertex in the vertical sense represents the columns of the table. The dashed lines are probabilistic transitions of the strategy σ, that is, when the strategy takes a dashed line he arrives to one of the vertex in the next layer with a probability of $1/3$ it doesn't matter what edge has been taken.
In the case of continue lines, they are safe lines, that is if the strategy takes it, she follows it certainly. The strategy selects the edge seeing the walked path (i.e. a prefix of a path in F). If at this moment the path is an *opened* one the strategy takes a dashed line (i.e. makes a random mouvement), otherwise it takes a safe line going through the *trap*. If the strategy arrives to the

last layer by an *opened* path, then it transits to the goal by a safe line. We conclude that if F satisfaied then $R(\sigma, k) > 0$.

Before this result, the evaluation problem is a hard one in the general case. Even that we can try to work with strategies that are easy to evaluate as the M-strategies and T-strategies.

4.2 Evaluation of M-strategy & T-strategy

Theorem 5. *Computing* $\mathbf{R}(\sigma, k)$ *if* σ *is a M-strategy, or a T-strategy which stops in polynomial time* k, *can be done in polynomial time (idem* $\mathbf{E}(\sigma, k)$).

proof : It follows from Markov chain theory : Let us note μ_k the distribution over the vertices at step k. $\mu_0(s) = 1$.
A M-strategy σ_M can be seen as a transition matrix $\mathbf{M} = [m_{ij}]$. If the decision of the M-strategy in i is $l(i)$: from i, move to j.

$$m_{ik} = \begin{cases} 1 & \text{if } k = j, \\ 0 & \text{otherwise} \end{cases}$$

We compute $\mathbf{P} = [p_{ij}]$ with : $p_{ij} = \delta(i, l(i), j)$ Then, $\forall i \in \mathbf{N} : \mu_{i+1} = \mathbf{P}\mu_i$ and $\mathbf{R}(\sigma_M, k) = \mu_k$.

We can do the same thing with a T-strategy σ_T, except that in this case, the decision depends also of the time : $l(i, t)$. Then we define $\mathbf{P}(t)$ in the same way, and :
$\forall i \in \mathbf{N} : \mu_{i+1} = \mathbf{P}(i)\mu_i$ and $\mathbf{R}(\sigma_T, k) = \mu_k$. $\square$

Theorem 6. *The problems of evaluating a M-strategy for a infinite time criterion can be solved in polynomial time.*

proof : An other result from Markov chain theory : we just compute the stationary distribution over the vertices π (ie. solve $P\pi = \pi$). $\square$

4.3 Definition of EPU and complexity

One other approach for trying to deal with this problem is to explore the posibility of working with strategies that are easy to evaluate (M-strategies) and use some fixed amount of colours for keeping his performance. In this section we deal with this problem and give some complexity results about that.

Definition 7. *Problem* **KNAPSACK**: *to find a subset of a set where each element is affected by two values, one given by a size function s and the other given by a weight function v. The addition of all the sizes in this sub-set must be lesser than a given value and the addition of the weights bigger than another given value.*
INPUT: $U = \{u_1, \ldots, u_n\}$ *a function* $s : u \in U \to Z^+$ *a function* $v : u \in U \to Z^+$ *two integers* B *et* K
OUTPUT: *1 if* $\exists U' \subset U$, *such that* $\sum_{u' \in U'} s(u') \leq B$ *and* $\sum_{u' \in U'} v(u') \geq K$, *and 0 otherwise.*

Definition 8. **EPU**: *problem of the existence of one coloration and one M-strategy given a fixed number of colors and a threshold.*
INPUT: $G(V, E), s, t \in V, k, q \in Q, T, \mu$
OUTPUT: *1 if* $\exists clr : v \in V \to \{1, \ldots, k\} : \exists \sigma_M$ *such that* $R(\sigma_M, T) \geq q$, *and 0 otherwise.*

Theorem 7. **EPU** *is NP-complet*

proof :   We show it by a reduction of **KNAPSACK** to **EPU**. It belongs to **NP** because if we want to obtain a **M**-strategy with T steps, given k colours and a threshold, we colour the graph randomly an associate an action to each color. Based on this, we calculate a Markov matrix an we evaluate the strategy in polynomial time. In this way we prouve that $EPU \in NP$.

The goal is to find a polynomial transformation of **KNAPSACK** to **EPU**. For this end we build 2 graphs having $n + 2$ vertices as we show in the figure 11.

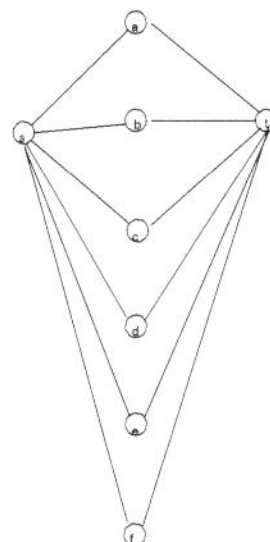

Fig. 11. Example of the graph for knapsack to EPU

We associate each graph to each restriction of **KNAPSACK**.

As it can be verified in the figure 11 we defined a graph that has one layer that contains n vertices that we name selection points.

This layer associates each selection vertex to an element of the **KNAPSACK** set U. We have two additional vertices s for the starting point and t for the goal. We draw n edges between s and each element of the selection layer, and we assign a uniform probability $1/n$ to each one.

Similarly we define an edge going from each element of the selection layer to the goal vertex t. Then we fix the number of steps $T = 2$, one for going from s to the selection layer an the other one for going from the selection layer to the goal vertex t

We fix the nomber of available colors k to 2 because we want to interpret the selection of elements in U as an assignement of colors and associate to each color one action. Next we define a probabilistic deviation model in function of the associated weights of elements for the second restriction of **KNAPSACK** as follows:

$$\forall 1 \leq i \leq B \ (u(i),t) \ \in E\mu_1(u,\sigma_M(clr(u(i))),t) = \begin{cases} p_1 = \frac{u(i)}{V} \\ 1 - p_1 \quad \text{trap} \end{cases}$$

As we can see we introduced a parameter **V** that represents the total weight of the set U. This give us probability values between 0 and 1.

In the same way we define for the first restriction of **KNAPSACK** a probabilistic deviation model in function of the sizes associated to each element of the U as follows:

$$\forall 1 \leq i \leq B \ (u(i),t) \ \in E\mu_2(u,\sigma_M(clr(u(i))),t) = \begin{cases} p_2 = \frac{s(i)}{S} \ \text{trap} \\ 1 - p_2 \end{cases}$$

As we can see we introduced a parameter **S** that represents the total size of the set U. This give us probability values between 0 and 1.

We have 2 label actions : one for **move to t** and the other for **stop**. Next we relate the color **selected** and the action **move to t** and the color not selected with the action **stop**.

For finishing the transformation we relate the thresholds q_1 et q_2 for each graph with the parameters of the **KNAPSACK** as follows:

$$q_1 = \frac{K}{n \times V}$$

and

$$q_2 = 1 - \frac{B}{n \times S}$$

Remark : In the definition of the distribution μ_1 we talked about a probability to get traped equal to $1 - p$, and a probability p to have succes in the mouvement. So we cant arrive to the goal since a vertex coloured with **non selected**. The same is valid for μ_2 too.

Before that we have for the first graph:

$$R_1(\sigma_M, T) = \sum_{\pi \in PATHS} \mathbf{Prob}(\pi \text{ réalisation } de\ \sigma_M) =$$

$$\sum_{i=0}^{T} \sum_{j=1}^{n} \mu_1(i, \sigma_M, j)$$

and for the second one:

$$R_2(\sigma_M, T) = \sum_{\pi \in PATHS} \mathbf{Prob}(\pi \text{ réalisation } de\ \sigma_M) = \sum_{i=0}^{T} \sum_{j=1}^{n} \mu_2(i, \sigma_M, j)$$

So we can proclaim that it exists a subset for the **KNAPSACK** iff it exists a colouring clr and an associated strategy σ_M that fullfils the performance q_1 for the first graph an simultaneously q_2 for the second one. That is that we have shown that **KNAPSACK** $\Rightarrow EPU$.

For showing the reduction in the oposite sense we say that if we have one colouring and an $M-$strategy associated that fullfils the performace q_1 and q_2 en each graph then it exist a subset $U' \subset U$ for **KNAPSACK**. For this we only need to label vertex of the selection layer with one element of the U and take the vertices that have a **selected** color. This gives a subset that works for **KNAPSACK**. In this way we prouved that **KNAPSACK** $\Leftarrow EPU$ and we can proclaim that:

$$\mathbf{KNAPSACK} \Leftrightarrow EPU$$

$\square$

This result show that EPU is a hard one but what is intresting is that $KNAPSACK$ is one of the rare problems that are **NP-complet** and at the same time arbitrarly approximable. That is that $KNAPSACK$ has a fully polynomial approximation schema (**FPTAS**). So if we can make a special kind of transformation from EPU to $KNAPSACK$ called $L - reduction$ (for details see (Papadimitriou & Yannakakis (1991)) and (Papadimitriou & Steiglitz (1982))), we can find good approximations to the optimal for the EPU optimazing problem.

5. Robot motion tracking, DFA learning, sketching and streaming

Another robot navigation problem that has attracted my attention in the last six years has been the robot tracking problem. In this problem we are going to deal with another kind of uncertainty. The uncertainty on the setting of two robots that, one that plays de rôle of *observer* and the other that of *target*. This problem has to do with other kind of uncertainty that appears in robot navigation problems. The uncertainty on the knowledge of the other reactions in a given situation. This situation arise when there are two or more robots or agents in general that have to perform their tasks in the same time and to share the working space. Many everyday life situations can be seen as an interaction among agents, as can be to play football , to drive a car in Mexico city streets, or to play chess with your wife. The robot tracking is not the exception. In the examples given above as well as in the robot tracking case, the agents observe the actions taken by the other agents, and try to predict the behaviour of them and react in the best possible way. The fundamental difference between the examples that we have given and the robot tracking problem is that the agents in the last case are robots and as consequence they are limited in computational power. Because of that we proposed in (Lucatero et al. (2004)) to pose the robot tracking problem as a repeated game. The main motivation of this proposal was that in many recent articles on the robot tracking problem (La Valle & Latombe (1997) La Valle & Motwani (1997)) and (Murrieta-Cid & Tovar (2002)) they make the assumption that the strategy of the target robot is to evade the *observer robot* and based on that they propose geometrical and probabilistic solutions of the tracking problem which consists on trying to maximize, by the *observer*, the minimal distance of escape of the *target*. We feel that this solution is limited at least in two aspects. First the target don't interact with the *observer* so there is no evidence that the strategy of the *target* will be to try to escape if it doesn't knows what are the actions taken by the observer. The second aspect is that even if it take place some sort of interaction between the *target* and the *observer*, the *target* is not necessarily following an evasion strategy so this may produce a failure on the tracking task. Because of that we proposed a DFA learning algorithm followed by each robot and obtained some performance improvements with respect to the results obtained by the methods used in (Murrieta-Cid & Tovar (2002)). In the last few years many research efforts have been done in the design and construction of efficient algorithms for reconstructing unknown robotic environments (Angluin & Zhu (1996);Rivest & Schapire (1993);Blum & Schieber (1991);Lumelsky & Stepanov (1987)) and apply learning algorithms for this end (Angluin & Zhu (1996);Rivest & Schapire (1993)). One computational complexity obstacle for obtaining efficient learning algorithms is related with the fact of being a passive or an active learner. In the first case it has been shown that it is impossible to obtain an efficient algorithm in the worst case (Kearns & Valiant (1989);Pitt & Warmuth (1993)). In the second case if we permit the learner to make some questions (i.e. to be an active learner) we can obtain efficient learning algorithms (Angluin (1981)) . This work done on the DFA learning area has given place to many excellent articles on learning models of intelligent agents as those elaborated by David Carmel and Shaul Markovitch (Carmel & Markovitch (1996);Carmel & Markovitch (1998)) and in the field of Multi-agent Systems those written about Markov games as a framework for multi-agent reinforcement learning by M.L. Littman (Littman (1994)). In (Lucatero et al. (2004)) we proposed to model the robot motion tracking problem as a repeated game. So, given that the agents involved have limited rationality, it can be assumed that they are following a behaviour controled by an automata. Because of that we can adapt the learning automata algorithm proposed in (Carmel & Markovitch (1996)) to the case of the robot motion tracking problem. In (Lucatero et al. (2004)) we assume that each robot is aware of the other robot actions, and that the strategies or preferences of decision of each agent are private. It is assumed too that each robot keeps a model of the behavior of the other robot. The strategy of each robot is adaptive in the sense that a robot modifies his model about the other robot such that the first should look for the best response strategy w.r.t. its utility function. Given that the search of optimal strategies in the strategy space is very complex when the agents have bounded rationality it has been proven in (Rubinstein (1986)) that this task can be simplified if we assume that each agent follow a Deterministic Finite Automate (DFA) behaviour. In (Papadimitriou & Tsitsiklis (1987)) it has been proven that given a DFA opponent model, there exist a best response DFA that can be calculated in polynomial time. In the field of computational learning theory it has been proven by E.M. Gold (Gold (1978)) that the problem of learning minimum state DFA equivalent to an unknown target is NP-hard. Nevertheless D. Angluin has proposed in (Angluin (1981)) a supervised learning algorithm called ID which learns a target DFA given a live-complete sample and a knowledgeable teacher to answer membership queries posed by the learner. Later Rajesh Parekh, Codrin Nichitiu and Vasant Honavar proposed in (Parekh & Honavar (1998)) a polynomial time incremental algorithm for learning DFA. That algorithm seems to us well adapted for the tracking problem because the robots have to learn incrementally the other robot strategy by taking as source of examples the visibility information and the history of the actions performed by each agent. So, in (Lucatero et al. (2004)) we implemented a DFA learning that learned an aproximate DFA followed by the othe agent. For testing the performance of that algorithm it was necesary the creation of an automata for playing the role of target robot strategy, with a predefined behavior, and to watch the learning performance on the observer robot of the target robot mouvements. The proposed target robot behavior was a wall-follower. The purpose of this automata is to give an example that will help us to test the algorithm, because in fact the algorithm can learn other target automatas fixing the adequate constraints. The target automata strategy was simply to move freely to the North while the way was free, and at the detection of a wall to follow it in a clockwise sense. Besides the simplicity of the automata we need a discretization on the possible actions for being able to build the automata. For that reason we have to define some constraints. The first was the discretization of the directions to 8 possibilities (N, NW, W, SW, S, SE, E, NE). The second constraint is on the discretization of the possible situations that will become inputs to the automata of both robots. It must be clearly defined for each behavior what will be the input alphabet to which will react both robots. This can be done without modifying the algorithm The size of the input alphabet afect directly the learning algorithm performance, because it evaluates for each case all possible course of action. So, the table used for learning grows proportionaly to the number of elements of the input alphabet. It is worth mentioning that in the simulation we used, to compare with our method, an algorithm inspired on the geomety based methods proposed in (La Valle & Latombe (1997); La Valle & Motwani (1997)) and (Murrieta-Cid & Tovar (2002)). In this investigation, we have shown that the one-observer-robot/one-target-robot tracking problem can be solved satisfactorily using DFA learning algorithms inspired in the formulation of the robot motion tracking as a two-player repeated game and enable us to analyse it in a more general setting than the evader/pursuer case. The prediction of the target movements can be done for more general target behaviours than the evasion one, endowing the agents with learning DFA's abilities. So, roughly speaking we have shown that learning an approximate or non minimal DFA in this setting was factible in polynomial time. The question that arises is, *how near is the obtained DFA to the minimal one ?*. This problem can reduces to the problem of automata equivalece. For giving an answer to this question we have used the sketching and streaming algorihms. This will be developped in the following subsection.

5.1 DFA equivalence testing via sketch and stream algorithms

Many advances have been recently taking place in the approximation of several classical combinatorial problems on strings in the context of *Property Testing* (Magniez & de Rougemont (2004)) inspired on the notion of *Self-Testing* (Blum & Kannan S. (1995); Blum et al. (1993); Rubinfeld & Sudan (1993)). What has been shown in (Magniez & de Rougemont (2004)) is that, based on a statistical embedding of words, and constructing a tolerant tester for the equality of two words, it is possible to obtain an approximate normalized distance algorithm whose complexity don't depend on the size of the string. In the same paper (Magniez & de Rougemont (2004)) the embedding is extended to languages and get a geometrical approximate description of regular languages consisting in a finite union of polytopes. As an application of that its is obtained a new tester for regular languages whose complexity does not depend on the automaton. Based on the geometrical description just mentioned it is obtained an deterministic polynomial equivalent-tester for regular languages for a fixed threshold distance. Computing *edit distance* between two words is an important subproblem of many applications like text-processing, genomics and web searching. Another field in Computer Science that where important advances recently have been taking place is that of embeddings of sequences (Graham (2003)). The sequences are fundamental objects in computer science because they can represent vectors, strings, sets and permutations. For beeing able to measure their similarity a distance among sequences is needed. Sometimes the sequences to be compared are very large so it is convenient to map or embed them in a different space where the distance in that space is an approximation of the distance in the original space. Many embeddings are computable under the streaming model where the data is too large to store in memory, and has to be processed as and when it arrives piece by piece. One fundamental notion introduced in the approximation of combinatorial objects context is the *edit-distance*. This concept can be defined as follows:

Definition 9. *The* **edit distance** *between two words is the minimal number of character substitutions to transform one word into the other. Then two words of size n are ϵ-far if they are at distance greater than ϵn.*

Another very important concept is the *property testing*. The *property testing* notion introduced in the context of program testing is one of the foundations of our research. If **K** is a class of finite structures and P is a property over **K**, we wish to find a **Tester**, in other words, given a structure U of **K**:

- It can be that U satisfy P.

- It can be that U is ϵ-far from P, that means, that the minimal distance between U and U' that satisfy P is greater than .

- The randomized algorithm runs in $O(\epsilon)$ time independently of n, where n represent, the size of the structure U.

Formally an ϵ-tester can be defined as follows.

Definition 10. *An ϵ-tester for a class $K_0 \subseteq K$ is randomized algorithm which takes a structure U_n of size n as input and decides if $U_n \in K_0$ or if the probability that U_n is ϵ-far from K_0 is large. A class K_0 is testable if for every sufficiently small ϵ there exists an ϵ-tester for K_0 whose time complexity is in $O(f(\epsilon))$, i.e. independent of n*

For instance, if **K** is the class of graphs and P is a property of being colorable, it is wanted to decide if a graph U of size n is 3-colorable or ϵ-far of being 3-colorable, i.e. the Hamming distance between U and U' is greater than $\epsilon \cdot n^2$. If **K** is the class of binary strings and P is a regular property (defined by an automata), it is wished to decide if a word U of size n is accepted by the automata or it is ϵ-far from being accepted, i.e., the *Edition distance* between U and U' is greater than $\epsilon \cdot n$. In both cases, it exists a **tester**, that is, an algorithm in that case take constant time, that depends only on and that decide the proximity of these properties. In the same way it can be obtained a **corrector** that in the case that U does not satisfy P and that U is not ϵ-far, finds a structure U' that satisfy P. The existence of **testers** allow us to approximate efficiently a big number of combinatorial problems for some privileged distances. As an example, we can estimate the distance of two words of size n by means of the *Edition distance* with shift, we mean, when it is authorized the shift of a sub-word of arbitrary size in one step. To obtain the distance it is enough to randomly sample the sub-words between two words, to observe the statistics of the random sub-words and to compare with the L_1 norm. In a general setting, it is possible to define distances between automata and to quickly test if two automata are near knowing that the exact problem is NEXPTIME hard. By other side, an important concept that is very important in the context of sequence embeddings is the notion of *sketch*. A *sketch* algorithm for *edit distance* consit of two compression procedures, that produce a finger print or *sketch* from each input string, and a reconstrucction procedure that uses the sketches for approximating the *edit distance* between the to strings. A sketch model of computation can be described informally as a model where given an object x a shorter *sketch* x can be made so that compairing to *sketches* allow a function of the original objects to be approximated. Normally the function to be approximated is the distance. This allow efficient solutions of the next problems:

- Fast computation of short *sketches* in a variety of computing models, wich allow sequences to be comapred in constant time and spaces non depending on the size of the original sequences.

- Approximate nearest neighbor and clustering problems faster than the exact solutions.

- Algorithms to find approximate occurrences of pattern sequences in long text sequences in linear time.

- Efficient communication schemes to approximate the distance between, and exchange, sequences in close to the optimal amount of communication.

Definition 11. *A distance sketch function $sk(a,r)$ with parameters ϵ, δ has the property that for a distance $d(\cdot, \cdot)$, a specified deterministic function f outputs a random variable $f(sk(a,r), sk(b,r))$ so that*

$$(1 - \epsilon)d(f(sk(a,r), sk(b,r)))$$
$$\leq f(sk(a,r), sk(b,r))$$
$$\leq (1 + \epsilon)d(f(sk(a,r), sk(b,r)))$$

for any pairs of points a and b with probability $1 - \delta$ taken over small choices of a small seed r chosen uniformly at random

The sketching model assumes complete access to a part of the input. An alternate model is the streaming model, in which the computation has limited access to the whole data. In that model the data arrive as a stream but the space for storage for keeping the information is limited.

6. Applications to robot navigation problems

As I mentioned in section 5 one automata model based aproach for solving the robot motion tracking has been proposed in (Lucatero & Espinosa (2005)). The problem consited in building a model in each robot of the navigation behaviour of the other robot under the assumption that both robots, target and observer, were following an automata behaviour. Once the approximate behaviour automata has been obtained the question that arises is, *how can be measured the compliance of this automata with automata followed by the target robot ?*. Stated otherwise *How can be tested that the automata of the target robot is equivalent to the one obtained by the observer robot ?* Is exactly in that context that the property testing algorithms can be applied for testing the equivalence automata in a computationally efficient way. It is well known that the problem of determining equivalence between automatas is hard computationally as was mentioned in section 5. The map learning can be as well formulated as an automata with stochastic output inferring problem (Dean et al. (1985)). It can be usefull to compare the real automata describing the map of the environment and the information inferred by the sensorial information. This can be reduced to the equivalence automata problem, and for this reason, an approximate property testing algorithm can be applied. In (Goldreich et al. (1996)) can be found non obvious relations between property testing and learnability. As can be noted testing mimimics the standar frameworks of learning theory. In both cases one given access to an unknown *target* function. However there are important differences between testing and learning. In the case of a learning algorithm the goal is to find an approximation of a function $f \in K_0$, whereas in the case of testing the goal is to test that $f \in K_0$. Apparently it is harder to learn a property than to test it. (Goldreich et al. (1996)) it shown that there are some functions class which are harder to test than to learn provided that $NP \not\subset BPP$. In (Goldreich et al. (1996)) when they speak about the complexity of random testing algorithms they are talking about query complexity (number test over the input) as well as time complexity (number of steps) and hey show there that both types of complexities depend polynomially only on ϵ not on n for some properties on graphs as colorability, clique, cut and bisection. Their definition of property testing is inspired on the PAC-learning model (Valiant (1984)), so there it is considered de case of testers that take randomly chosen instances with arbitrarly distribution instead of querying. Taking into account the progress on property testing mentioned , the results that will be defined further can be applied to the problem of testing how well the automata inferred by the *observer robot* in the robot motion tracking problem solved in (Lucatero & Espinosa (2005)), fits the behaviour automata followed by the *target robot*. The same results can be applied to measure how much the automata obtained by explorations fits the automata that describes the space explored by the robot. Roughly speaking, the equivalence ϵ-tester for regular languages obtained in (Fisher et al. (2004)), makes a statistical embedding of regular languages to a vectorial statistical space which is an approximate geometrical description of regular languages as a finite union of polytopes. That embedding enables to approximate the *edit distance* of the original space by the ϵ-tester under a *sketch* calculation model. The automata is only required in a preprocessing step, so the ϵ-tester does not depend on the number of states of the automata. Before stating the results some specific notions must be defined

Definition 12. Block statistics. *Let w and w' two word in Σ each one of length n such that k dived n. Let $\epsilon = \frac{1}{k}$. The statitistics of block letters of w denoted as $b - stat(w)$ is a vector of dimension $|\Sigma|^k$ such that its u coordinate for $u \in \Sigma^k$ (Σ^k is called the block alphabet and its elements are the block letters) satisfies $b - stat(w)[u] \stackrel{def}{=} Pr_{j=1,...,n/k} [w[j]_b = u]$ Then $b - sta(w)$ is called the block statistics of w*

A convenient way to define block statistics is to use the underlying distribution of word over Σ of size k that is on block letter on Σ^k. Then a uniform distribution on block letters $w[1]_b, w[2]_b, \dots, w[\frac{n}{k}]_b$ of is the block distribution of w. Let X be a random vector of size $|\Sigma|^k$ where all the coordinates are 0 except its u-coordinate which is 1, where u is the index of the random word of size k that was chosen according to the block distribution of w. Then the expectation of X satisfies $E(X) = b - stat(w)$. The *edit distance* with moves between two word $w, w' \in \Sigma$ denoted as $dist(w, w')$ is the mininimal number of elementary operations on w to obtain w'. A class $K_0 \in K$ is testable if for every $\epsilon > 0$, there exists an ϵ-tester whose time complexity depends only on ϵ.

Definition 13. *Let $\epsilon \geq 0$. Let $K_1, K_2 \subseteq K$ two classes. K_1 is ϵ-contained in K_2 if every but finitely many structures of K_1 are ϵ-close to K_2. K_1 is ϵ-equivalent to K_2 if K_1 is ϵ-contained in K_2 and K_2 is ϵ-contained in K_1*

The following results that we are going to apply in the robotics field, are stated without demonstration but they can be consulted in (Fisher et al. (2004)).

Lemma 1. .-

$$dist(w, w') \leq \left(\frac{1}{2} |b - stat(w) - bstat(w')| + \epsilon \right) \times n$$

So we can embed a word w into its block statistics $b - stat(w) \in \Re^{|\Sigma|^{1/\epsilon}}$

Theorem 8. *For every real $\epsilon > 0$ and regular language L over a finite alphabet Σ there exists an ϵ-tester for L whose query complexity is $O(\frac{\lg |\Sigma|}{\epsilon^4})$ and time complexity $2^{|\Sigma|^{O(1/\epsilon)}}$*

Theorem 9. *There exists a deterministic algorithm T such that given two autimata A and B over a finite alphabet Σ with at most m states and a real $\epsilon > 0$, $T(A, B, \epsilon)$*

1. *accepts if A and B recognize the same language*

2. *rejects if A and B recognize languages that are not ϵ-equivalent. Moreover the time complexity of T is in $m^{|\Sigma|^{O(1/\epsilon)}}$*

Now based on 9 our main result can be stated as a theorem.

Theorem 10. *The level of approximability of the inferred behaviour automata of a **target robot** by an **observer robot** with respect to the real automata followed by the **target robot** in the motion tracking problem can be tested efficiently.*

Theorem 11. *The level of approximability of the sensorialy inferred automata of the **environment** by an **explorator robot** with respect to the real environment automata can be tested efficiently.*

7. Application of streaming algorithms on robot navigation problems

The starting premise of the sketching model is that we have complete access to one part of the input data. That is not the case when a robot is trying to build a map of the environemet based on the information gathered by their sensors. An alternative calculation model is the streaming model. Under this model the data arrives as a stream or predetermined sequence and the information can be stored in a limited amount of memory. Additionally we cannot backtrack over the information stream, but instead, each item must be processed in turn. Thus a stream is a sequence of n data items $z = (s_1, s_2, \ldots, s_n)$ that arrive sequentially and in that order. Sometimes, the nomber n of items is known in advance and some other times the last item s_{n+1} is used as an ending mark of the data stream. Data streams are fundamental to many other data processing applications as can be the atmospheric forecasting measurement, telecommunication network elements operation recording, stock market information updates, or emerging sensor networks as highway traffic conditions. Frequently the data streams are generated by geografically distributed information sources. Despite the increasing capacity of storage devices, it is not a good idea to store the data streams because even a simple processing operation, as can be to sort the incoming data, becomes very expensive in time terms. Then, the data streams are normally processed *on the fly* as they are produced. The stream model can be subdivided in various categories depending on the arrival order of the attributes and if they are aggregated or not. We assume that each element in the stream will be a pair $\langle i, j \rangle$ that indicates for a sequence a we have $a[i] = j$.

Definition 14. *A streaming algorithm accepts a data stream z and outpus a random variable $str(z, r)$ to approximate a function g so that*

$$(1 - \epsilon)g(z) \leq str(z,r) \leq (1 - \epsilon)g(z)$$

with probability $1 - \delta$ over all choices of the random seed r, for parameters ϵ and δ

The streaming models can be adapted for some distances functions. Let suppose tha z consists of two interleaved sequences, a and b, and that $g(z) = d(a,b)$. Then the streaming algorithm to solve this proble approximates the distance between a and b. It is possible that the algorithm can can work in the sketching model as well as in the streaming model. Very frequently a streaming algorithm can be initially conceived as a sketching one, if it is supposed that the sketch is the contents of the storage memory for the streaming algorithm. However, a sketch algorithm is not necesarilly a streaming algorithm, and a streaming algorithm is not always a sketching algorithm. So, the goal of the use of this kind of algorithms, is to test equality between two object, approximately and in an efficient way.

Another advantage of using *fingerprints* is that they are integers that can be represented in $O(\log n)$ bits. In the commonly used RAM calculation model it is assumed that this kind of quantities can be worked with in $O(1)$ time. This quantities can be used for building has tables allowing fast access to them without the use of special complex data structures or sorting preprocessing. Approximation of L_p distances can be considered that fit well with sketching model as well as with the streaming model. Initially it can be suppossed that the vectors are formed of positive integers bounded by a constant, but it can be extended the results to the case of rational entries. An important property possesed by the sketches of vectors is the *composability*, that can be defined as follows:

Definition 15. *A sketch function is said to be composable if for any pair of sketches $sk(a,r)$ and $sk(b,r)$ we have that $sk(a + b, r) = sk(a,r) + sk(b,r)$*

One theoretical justification that enables us to embed an Euclidean vector space in a much smaller space with a small loss in accuracy is the Johnson-Lindenstrauss lema that can be stated as follows:

Lemma 2. *.- Let a, b be vectors of length n. Let v be a set of k different random vectors of length n. Each component $v_{i,j}$ is picked independently from de Gaussian distribution $N(0,1)$, then each vector v_i is normalised under the L_2 norm so that the magnitude of v_i is 1. Define the sketch of a to be a vector $sk(a,r)$ of length k so that $sk(a,r)_i = \sum_{j=1}^{n} v_{i,j}a_j = v_i \cdot a$. Given parameters δ and ϵ, we have with probability $1 - \delta$*

$$\frac{(1 - \epsilon)\|a - b\|_2^2}{n} \leq \frac{\|sk(a,r) - sk(b,r)\|_2^2}{k}$$
$$\leq \frac{(1 + \epsilon)\|a - b\|_2^2}{n}$$

where k is $O(1/\epsilon^2 \log 1/\delta)$

This lemma means that we can make a sketch of dimension smaller that $O(1/\epsilon^2 \log 1/\delta)$, from the convolution of each vector with a set of randomly created vectors drawn from the Normal distribution. So, this lemma enable us to map m vectors into a reduced dimension space. The sketching procedure cannot be assimilated directly to a streaming procedure, but it has been shown recently how to extend the sketching approach to the streaming environement for L_1 and L_2 distances. Concerning streaming algorithms, some of the first have been published in (?) for calculating the frequency moments. In this case, we have an unordered and unaggregated stream of n integers in the range of $1, \ldots, M$, such that $z = (s_1, s_2, \ldots, s_n)$ for integers s_j. So, in (?) the authors focus on calculating the frequency moments F_k of the stream. Let it be, from the stream, $m_i = |\{j|s_j = i\}|$, the number of the occurrences of the integer i in the stream. So the frequency moments on the stream can be calculated as $F_k = \sum_{i+1}^{M}(m_i)^k$. Then F_0 is the number of different elements in the sequence, F_1 is the length of the sequence n, and F_2 is the repeat rate of the sequence. So, F_2 can be related with the distance L_2. Let us suppose that we build a vector v of length M with entries chosen at random, we process the stream $s_1, s_2, \ldots, s_n$ entry by entry, and initialise a variable $Z = 0$. So, after whole stream has been processed we have $Z = \sum_{i=1}^{M} v_i m_i$. Then F_2 can be estimated as

$$
\begin{aligned}
Z^2 &= \sum_{i=1}^{M} v_i^2 m_i^2 \\
&+ \sum_{i=1}^{M} \sum_{j \neq i} v_i m_i v_j m_j \\
&= \sum_{i=1}^{M} m_i^2 \\
&+ \sum_{i=1}^{M} \sum_{j \neq i} m_i m_j v_i v_j
\end{aligned}
$$

So, if the entries of the vector v are pairwise independent, then the expectation of the cross-terms $v_i v_j$ is zero and $\sum_{i=1}^{M} m_i^2 = F_2$. If this calculation is repeated $O(1/\epsilon^2)$ times, with a different random v each time, and the average is taken, then the calculation can be guaranteed to be an $(1 \pm \epsilon)$ approximation with a constant probability, and if additionallly, by finding the median of $O(1/\delta)$ averages, this constant probability can be amplified to $1 - \delta$. It has been observed in (Feigenbaum et al. (1999)) that the calculation for F_2 can be adapted to find the L_2 distance between two interleaved, unaggregated streams a and b. Let us suppose that the stream arrives as triples $s_j = (a_i, i, +1)$ if the element is from a and $s_j = (b_i, i, -1)$ if the item is from stream b. The goal is to find the square of the L_2 distance between a and b, $\sum_i (a_i - b_i)^2$. We initialise $Z = 0$. When a triple $(a_i, i, +1)$ arrives we add $a_i v_i$ to Z and when a triple $(b_i, i, -1)$ arrives we subtract $a_i v_i$ from Z. After the whole stream has been processed $Z = \sum(a_i v_i - b_i vi) = \sum_i(a_i - b_i)vi$. Again the expectation of the cross-terms is zero and, then the expectation of Z^2 is L_2 difference of a and b. THe procedure for L_2 has the nice property of being able to cope with case of unaggregated streams containing multiple triples of the form $(a_i, i, +1)$ with the same i due to the linearity of the addition. This streaming algorithm translates to the sketch model: given a vector a the values of Z can be computed. The sketch of a is then these values of Z formed into a vector $z(a)$. Then $z(a)_i = \sum_j(a_j - b_j)v_{i,j}$. This sketch vector has $O(1/\epsilon^2 \log 1/\delta)$ entries, requiring $O(\log Mn)$ bits each one. Two such sketches can be combined, due to the composability property of the sketches, for obtaining the sketch of the difference of the vectors $z(a - b) = (z(a) - z(b))$. The space of the streamin algorithm, and then the size of the sketch is a vector of length $O(1/\epsilon^2 \log 1/\delta)$ with entries of size $O(\log Mn)$. A natural question can be if it is possible to translate sketching algorithms to streaming ones for distances different from L_2 or L_1 and objects other than vectors of integers. In (Graham (2003)) it shown that it is possible the this translation for the Hamming distance. This can be found in the next theorem of (Graham (2003)).

Theorem 12. *The sketch for the Symmetric Difference (Hamming distance) between sets can be computed in the unordered, aggregated streaming model. Pairs of sketches can be used to make $1 \pm \epsilon$ approximmations of the Hamming distance between their sequences, which succeed with probability $1 - \delta$. The sketch is a vector of dimension $O(1/\epsilon^2 \log 1/\delta)$ and each entry is an integer in the range $[-n \ldots n]$.*

Given that, under some circumstances, streaming algorithms can be translated to sketch algorithms, then the theorem 10 can be applied for the robot motion tracking problem, under the streaming model as well.

In general, the mobile robotics framework is more complex because we should process data flows provided by the captors under a dynamic situation, where the robot is moving, taking into account two kind of uncertainty:

- The sensors have low precision

- The robot movements are subject to deviations as any mechanical object.

The data flow provided by the captors produce similar problems to those that can be found on the databases. The robot should make the fusion of the information sources to determine his motion strategy. Some sources, called bags, allow the robot to self locate geometrically or in his state graph. While the robot executes his strategy, it is subject to movement uncertainties and then should find robust strategies for such uncertainty source. The goal is to achieve the robustness integrating the data flow of the captors to the strategies. We consider the classical form of simple Markovian strategies. In the simplest version, a Markov chain, MDP, is a graph where all the states are distinguishable and the edges are labeled by actions $L_1, L_2, \ldots, L_p$. If the states are known only by his coloration in k colors $C_1, C_2, \ldots, C_k$. Two states having the same coloration are undistinguishable and in this case we are talking about POMDP (Partially Observed Markov Decision Process). A simple strategy σ is a function that associates an action simplex to a color among the possible actions. It is a probabilistic algorithm that allows to move inside the state graph with some probabilities. With the help of the strategies we look for reaching a given node of the graph from the starting node (the initial state) or to satisfy temporal properties, expressed in LTL formalism. For instance, the property C_1 Until C_2 that express the fact that we can reach a node with label C_2 preceded only by the node C_1. Given a property θ and a strategy σ, let $Prob_\sigma(\theta)$ be the probability that θ is true over the probability space associated to σ. Given a POMDP M two strategies σ and π can be compared by means of ther probabilities, that is, $Prob_\sigma(\theta) > Prob_\pi(\theta)$. If $Prob_\sigma(\theta) > b$, it is frequent to test such a property while b is not very small with the aid of the path sampling according to the distribution of the POMDP. In the case that $b < Prob_\sigma(\theta) < b - \epsilon$ it can be searched a corrector for σ, it means, a procedure that lightly modify σ in such a way that $Prob_\sigma(\theta) > b$. It can be modified too the graph associated and in that case, we look for comparing two POMDPs. Let be M_1 and M_2 two POMDPs, we want to compare this POMDPs provided with strategies σ and π in the same way as are compared two automata in the sense that they are approximately equivalent (refer to the section concerning distance between DTDs). How can we decide if they are approximately equivalent for a property class? Such a procedure is the base of the strategy learning. It starts with a low performance strategy that is modified in each step for improvement. The tester, corrector and learning algorithms notions find a natural application in this context. One of the specificities of mobile robotics is to conceive robust strategies for the movements of a robot. As every mechanical object, the robot deviates of any previewed trajectory and then it must recalculate his location. At the execution of an action L_i commanded by the robot, the realization will follow L_i with probability p, an action L_{i-1} with probability $(1 - p)/2$ and an action L_{i+1} with probability $(1 - p)/2$. This new probabilistic space induce robustness qualities for each strategy, in other words, the $Prob_\sigma(\theta)$ depends on the structure of the POMDP and on the error model. Then the same questions posed before can be formulated: how to evaluate the quality of the strategies, how to test properties of strategies, how to fix the strategies such that we can learn robust strategies. We can consider that the robots are playing a game against nature that is similar to a Bayesian game. The criteria of robust strategy are similar to those of the direct approach. Another problem that arise in robot motion is the relocalization of a robot in a map. As we mentioned in the initial part of the section 6, one method that has been used frequently in robot exploration for reducing the uncertainty in the position of robot was the use of landmarks and triangulation. The search of a landmark in an unknown environment can be similar to searching a pattern in a sequence of characters or a string. In the present work we applied sketching and streaming algorithms for obtaining distance approximations between objects as vectors in a dimensional reduced, and in some sense, deformated space. If we want to apply sketching or streaming for serching patterns as landmarks in a scene we have to deal with distance between permutations.

8. Conclusion and future work

The property testing algorithms under the sketch and streaming calculation model for measuring the level of approximation of inferred automata with respect to the true automata in the case of robot motion tracking problem as well as the map construction problem in robot navigation context. The use of sketch algorithms allow us to approximate the distance between objects by the manipulation of sketches that are significantly smaller than the original objects. Another problem that arise in robot motion is the relocalization of a robot in a map. As we mentioned in the section 2, one method that has been frequently used in robot exploration for reducing the uncertainty in the position of robot was the use of landmarks and triangulation. The search of a landmark in an unknown environment can be similar to searching a pattern in a large sequence of characters or a big string. For doing this task in an approximated and efficient way, sketch and streaming algorithms can be usefull.

9. References

A. Blum, P. R. & Schieber, B. (1991). Navigating in unfamiliar geometric terrain, *ACM STOC 91*, pp. 494–504.

Angluin, D. (1981). A note on the number of queries needed to identify regular languages.

Blum, M., Luby M. & Rubinfeld R. (1993). Self-testing/correcting with application to numerical problems.

Blum, M. & Kannan S. (1995). Designing programs that check their work.

Burago, D., de Rougemont, M. & Slissenko, A. (1993). Planning of uncertain motion, *Technical report*, Université de Poitiers.

Canny, J. & Reif, J. (1987). New lower-bound techniques for robot motion planning problems, *Proc. 28st. FOCS*, pp. 49–60.

Carmel, D. & Markovitch, S. (1996). Learning models of intelligent agents, *Technical Report CIS9606*, Department of Computer Science, Technion University.

Carmel, D. & Markovitch, S. (1998). How to explore your oponentŠs strategy (almost) optimally, *Proceedings ICMAS98 Paris France*.

C.Rodríguez Lucatero, A. Albornoz. & R.Lozano (2004). A game theory approach to the robot tracking problem.

Dana Angluin, Westbrook J. & Zhu, W. (1996). Robot navigation with range queries, *ACM STOC 96*, pp. 469–478.

Dean T., Angluin D., Basye K., Engelson S., Kaelbling L., Kokkevis E. & Maron O. (1985). Inferring finite automata with stochastic output functions and an application to map learning.

Dean, T. & Wellman, M. (1991). *Planning and Control*, Morgan Kaufmann Publishers.

Diaz-Frias, J. (1991). About planning with uncertainty, *8e. Congres Reconnaisance des Formes et Intelligence Artificielle*, pp. 455–464.

Magniez F. & de Rougemont, M. (2004). Property testing of regular tree languages, *ICALP 2004*.

Feigenbaum J., Kannan S., Strauss M.& Viswanathan M. (1999). An approximmate l_1 difference algorithm for massive data streams., *Proceedings of the 40th Annual Symposium on Foundations of Computer Science*, pp. 501–511.

Fisher E., Magniez F. & de Rougemont, M. (2004). Property and equivalence testing on strings, *ECCC 2004*.

Gold, E. (1978). Complexity of automaton identification from given data.

Goldreich, O., S.Goldwasser & D.Ron.Property (1996). Testing and its connection to learning and approximation, *IEEE Symposium on Foundations of Computer Science*.

Graham, C. (2003). Sequence distance embeddings, *Phd thesis in cs university of warmick*, University of Warmick.

Kirman, J., Bayse, K. & Dean, T. (1991). Sensor abstractions for control of navigation, *Proc. IEEE Robotics & Automation*, pp. 2812–2817.

Latombe, J. (1990). *Robot motion planning*, Kluwer.

Latombe, J., Lazanas, A. & Shekhar, S. (1991). Robot motion planning with uncertainty in control and sensing, *Artificial Intelligence* 52: 1–47.

Valiant, L.G. (1984). A theory of the learnable, *CACM*, pp. 1134–1142.

Littman, M. (1994). Markov games as a framework for multiagent reinforcement learning, *Proceedings of the eleventh International Conference on Machine Learning*, pp. 157–163.

Lozano-Perez, T. (1986). A simple motion planning algorithm for general robot manipulators.

Lucatero, C. R. & Espinosa, R. L. (2005). Application of automata learning algorithms to robot motion tracking.

Lumelsky, V. & Stepanov, A. (1987). Path planning strategies for a point mobile automaton moving amidst unknown obstacles of arbitrary shape.

Marion, J., Rodriguez, C. & de Rougemont, M. (1994). The evaluation of strategies in motion planning with uncertainty, *Proc. IEEE Robotics & Automation*.

M.Kearns & Valiant, L. (1989). Cryptographic limitation on learning boolean formulae and finite automata, *Proc. 21th ACM Symposium on Theory of Computing*, pp. 433–444.

Papadimitriou, C. (1985). Games against nature, *Journal of Computer and System Sciences* (31): 288–301.

Papadimitriou, C. & Steiglitz, K. (1982). *Combinatorial Optimization: Algorithms and Complexity*, Prentice-Hall Inc.

Papadimitriou, C. & Tsitsiklis, J. (1987). The complexity of markov decision processes, *Mathematics of operations research* (3): 441–450.

Papadimitriou, C. & Yannakakis, M. (1991). Optimization, approximation and complexity classes, *Journal of Computer and System Sciences* (43): 425–440.

Pitt, L. & Warmuth, M. (1993). The minimal consistent dfa problem cannot be approximated within any polynomial.

R. Murrieta-Cid, H. G.-B. & Tovar, B. (2002). A reactive motion planner to maintain visibility of unpredictable targets, *Proceedings of the IEEE International Conference on Robotics and Automation*.

Rajesh Parekh, C. N. & Honavar, V. (1998). A polynomial time incremental algorithm for learning dfa, *Proceedings of the Fourth International Colloquium on Grammatical Inference (ICGI'98), Ames, IA. Lecture Notes in Computer Science vol. 1433*, pp. 37–49.

Rivest, R. L. & Schapire, R. E. (1993). Inference of finite automata using homing sequences.

Rodríguez-Lucatero, C. (1997). Evaluation, existence and optimization of reactive strategies in motion with uncertainty.

Rubinfeld, R. & Sudan, M. (1993). Robust characterizations of polynomials with applications to program testing.

Rubinstein, A. (1986). Finite automata play the repeated prisionerŠs dilemma.

Schwartz, J. & Sharir, M. (1983). On the piano movers problem ii general techniques for computing topological properties of real algebraic manifolds, *Advances in Applied Mathematics Academic Press* .

Schwartz, J. & Sharir, M. (1991). Algorithmic motion planning in robotics., *Handbook of theoretical Computer Science* A: 391–425.

La Valle S.M., David Lin, L. J. G. J. L. & Motwani, R. (1997). Finding an unpredictable target in a workspace with obstacles, *Proceedings of the IEEE International Conference on Robotics and Automation*, pp. 731–736.

S.M. La Valle, H.H. González Baños, C. B. & Latombe, J. (1997). Motion strategies for maintaining visibility of a moving target, *Proceedings of the IEEE International Conference on Robotics and Automation*, pp. 731–736.

Valiant, L. (1979). The complexity of enumeration and reliability problems, *SIAM* 8(3).

4

SLAM and Exploration using Differential Evolution and Fast Marching

Santiago Garrido, Luis Moreno and Dolores Blanco
Robotics Lab, Carlos III University of Madrid
Spain

1. Introduction

The exploration and construction of maps in unknown environments is a challenge for robotics. The proposed method is facing this problem by combining effective techniques for planning, SLAM, and a new exploration approach based on the Voronoi Fast Marching method.

The final goal of the exploration task is to build a map of the environment that previously the robot did not know. The exploration is not only to determine where the robot should move, but also to plan the movement, and the process of simultaneous localization and mapping.

This work proposes the Voronoi Fast Marching method that uses a Fast Marching technique on the Logarithm of the Extended Voronoi Transform of the environment's image provided by sensors, to determine a motion plan. The Logarithm of the Extended Voronoi Transform imitates the repulsive electric potential from walls and obstacles, and the Fast Marching Method propagates a wave over that potential map. The trajectory is calculated by the gradient method.

The robot is directed towards the most unexplored and free zones of the environment so as to be able to explore all the workspace.

Finally, to build the environment map while the robot is carrying out the exploration task, a SLAM (Simultaneous Localization and Modeling) algorithm is implemented, the Evolutive Localization Filter (ELF) based on a differential evolution technique.

The combination of these methods provide a new autonomous exploration strategy to construct consistent maps of 2D indoor environments.

2. Autonomous exploration

Autonomous exploration and mapping are fundamental problems to solve as an autonomous robot carries out tasks in real unknown environments. Sensor based exploration, motion planning, localization and simultaneous mapping are processes that must be coordinated to achieve autonomous execution of tasks in unknown environments.

Sensor based planning makes use of the sensor acquired information of the environment in its latest configuration and generates an adequate path towards the desired following position. Sensor-based discovery path planning is the guidance of an agent - a robot - without a complete a priori map, by discovering and negotiating the environment so as to reach a goal location while avoiding all encountered obstacles. Sensor-based discovery (i.e., dynamic) path planning is problematic because the path needs to be continually recomputed as new information is discovered.

In order to build a map of an unknown environment autonomously, this work presents first a exploration and path planning method based on the Logarithm of the Extended Voronoi Transform and the Fast Marching Method. This Path Planner is called Voronoi Fast Marching (8). The Extended Voronoi Transform of an image gives a grey scale that is darker near the obstacles and walls and lighter when far from them. The Logarithm of the Extended Voronoi Transform imitates the repulsive electric potential in 2D from walls and obstacles. This potential impels the robot far from obstacles. The Fast Marching Method has been applied to Path Planning (34), and their trajectories are of minimal distance, but they are not very safe because the path is too close to obstacles and what is more important, the path is not smooth enough. In order to improve the safety of the trajectories calculated by the Fast Marching Method, avoiding unrealistic trajectories produced when the areas are narrower than the robot, objects and walls are enlarged in a security distance that assures that the robot does not collide and does not accept passages narrower than the robot's size.

The last step is calculating the trajectory in the image generated by the Logarithm of the Extended Voronoi Transform using the Fast Marching Method. Then, the path obtained verifies the smoothness and safety considerations required for mobile robot path planning.

The advantages of this method are the ease of implementation, the speed of the method and the quality of the trajectories. This method is used at a local scale operating with sensor information (sensor based planning).

To build the environment map while the robot is carrying out the exploration task, a SLAM (Simultaneous Localization and Modelling) is implemented. The algorithm is based on the stochastic search for solutions in the state space to the global localization problem by means of a differential evolution algorithm. This non linear evolutive filter, called Evolutive Localization Filter (ELF) (23), searches stochastically along the state space for the best robot pose estimate. The set of pose solutions (the population) focuses on the most likely areas according to the perception and up to date motion information. The population evolves using the log-likelihood of each candidate pose according to the observation and the motion errors derived from the comparison between observed and predicted data obtained from the probabilistic perception and motion model.

In the remainder of the chapter, the section 3 presents the state of the art referred to exploration and motion planning problems. Section 4 presents our Voronoi Fast Marching (VFM) Motion Planner. The SLAM algorithm is described briefly in Section 5. Then, section 6 describes the specific Exploration method proposed. Next, section 7 demonstrates the performance of the exploration strategy as it explores different environments, according to the two possible ways of working for the exploration task. And, finally the conclusions are summarized in section 8.

3. Previous and related works

3.1 Representations of the world

Roughly speaking there are two main forms for representing the spatial relations in an environment: metric maps and topological maps. Metric maps are characterized by a representation where the position of the obstacles are indicated by coordinates in a global frame of reference. Some of them represent the environment with grids of points, defining regions that can be occupied or not by obstacles or goals (22) (1). Topological maps represent the environment with graphs that connect landmarks or places with special features (19) (12). In our approach we choose the grid-based map to represent the environment. The clear advantage is that with grids we already have a discrete environment representation and ready to be used in conjunction with the Extended Voronoi Transform function and Fast Marching Method for path planning. The pioneer method for environment representation in a grid-based model was the certainty grid method developed at Carnegie Mellon University by Moravec (22). He represents the environment as a 3D or 2D array of cells. Each cell stores the probability of the related region being occupied. The uncertainty related to the position of objects is described in the grid as a spatial distribution of these probabilities within the occupancy grid. The larger the spatial uncertainty, the greater the number of cells occupied by the observed object. The update of these cells is performed during the navigation of the robot or through the exploration process by using an update rule function. Many researchers have proposed their own grid-based methods. The main difference among them is the function used to update the cell. Some of them are, for example: Fuzzy (24), Bayesian (9), Heuristic Probability (2), Gaussian (3), etc. In the Histogramic In-Motion Mapping (HIMM), each cell, has a certainty value, which is updated whenever it is being observed by the robots sensors. The update is performed by increasing the certainty value by 3 (in the case of detection of an object) or by decreasing it by 1 (when no object is detected), where the certainty value is an integer between 0 and 15.

3.2 Approaches to exploration

This section relates some interesting techniques used for exploratory mapping. They mix different localization methods, data structures, search strategies and map representations. Kuipers and Byun (13) proposed an approach to explore an environment and to represent it in a structure based on layers called Spatial Semantic Hierarchy (SSH) (12). The algorithm defines distinctive places and paths, which are linked to form an environmental topological description. After this, a geometrical description is extracted. The traditional approaches focus on geometric description before the topological one. The distinctive places are defined by their properties and the distinctive paths are defined by the twofold robot control strategy: follow-the-mid-line or follow-the-left-wall. The algorithm uses a lookup table to keep information about the place visited and the direction taken. This allows a search in the environment for unvisited places. Lee (16) developed an approach based on Kuipers work (13) on a real robot. This approach is successfully tested in indoor office-like spaces. This environment is relatively static during the mapping process. Lee's approach assumes that walls are parallel or perpendicular to each other. Furthermore, the system operates in a very simple environment comprised of cardboard barriers. Mataric (19) proposed a map learning method based on a subsumption architecture. Her approach models the world as a graph, where the nodes correspond to landmarks and the edges indicate topological adjacencies. The landmarks are detected from the robot movement. The basic exploration process is wall-following combined with obstacle avoidance. Oriolo et al. (25) developed a grid-based environment mapping process that uses fuzzy logic to update the grid cells. The mapping process runs on-line (24), and the local maps are built from the data obtained by the sensors and integrated into the environment map as the robot travels along the path defined by the A^* algorithm to the goal. The algorithm has two phases. The first one is the perception phase. The robot acquires data from the sensors and updates its environment map. The second phase is the planning phase. The planning module re-plans a new safe path to the goal from the new explored area. Thrun and Bucken (37) (38) developed an exploration system which integrates both evidence grids and topological maps. The integration of the two approaches has the advantage of disambiguating different positions through the grid-based representation and performing fast planning through the topological representation. The exploration process is performed through the identification and generation of the shortest paths between unoccupied regions and the robot. This approach works well in dynamic environments, although, the walls have to be flat and cannot form angles that differ more than 15° from the perpendicular. Feder et al. (4) proposed a probabilistic approach to treat the concurrent mapping and localization using a sonar. This approach is an example of a feature-based approach. It uses the extended Kalman filter to estimate the localization of the robot. The essence of this approach is to take actions that maximize the total knowledge about the system in the presence of measurement and navigational uncertainties. This approach was tested successfully in wheeled land robot and autonomous underwater vehicles (AUVs). Yamauchi (39) (40) developed the Frontier-Based Exploration to build maps based on grids. This method uses a concept of frontier, which consists of boundaries that separate the explored free space from the unexplored space. When a frontier is explored, the algorithm detects the nearest unexplored frontier and attempts to navigate towards it by planning an obstacle free path. The planner uses a depth-first search on the grid to reach that frontier. This process continues until all the frontiers are explored. Zelek (42) proposed a hybrid method that combines a local planner based on a harmonic function calculation in a restricted window with a global planning module that performs a search in a graph representation of the environment created from a CAD map. The harmonic function module is employed to generate the best path given the local conditions of the environment. The goal is projected by the global planner in the local windows to direct the robot. Recently, Prestes el al. (28) have investigated the performance of an algorithm for exploration based on partial updates of a harmonic potential in an occupancy grid. They consider that while the robot moves, it carries along an activation window whose size is of the order of the sensors range.

Prestes and coworkers (29) propose an architecture for an autonomous mobile agent that explores while mapping a two-dimensional environment. The map is a discretized model for the localization of obstacles, on top of which a harmonic potential field is computed. The potential field serves as a fundamental link between the modelled (discrete) space and the real (continuous) space where the agent operates.

3.3 Approaches to motion planning

The motion planning method proposed in this chapter can be included in the sensor-based global planner paradigm. It is a potential method but it does not have the typical problems of these methods enumerated by Koren- Borenstein (11): 1) Trap situations due to local minima (cyclic behavior). 2) No passage between closely spaced obstacles. 3) Oscillations in the presence of obstacles. 4) Oscillations in narrow passages. The proposed method is conceptually close to the navigation functions of Rimon-Koditscheck (33), because the potential field has only one local minimum located at the single goal point. This potential and the paths are smooth (the same as the repulsive potential function) and there are no degenerate critical points in the field. These properties are similar to the characteristics of the electromagnetic waves propagation in Geometrical Optics (for monochromatic waves with the approximation that length wave is much smaller than obstacles and without considering reflections nor diffractions).

The Fast Marching Method has been used previously in Path Planning by Sethian (36) (35), but using only an attractive potential. This method has some problems. The most important one that typically arises in mobile robotics is that optimal motion plans may bring robots too close to obstacles (including people), which is not safe. This problem has been dealt with by Latombe (14), and the resulting navigation function is called *NF2*. The Voronoi Method also tries to follow a maximum clearance map (7). Melchior, Poty and Oustaloup (21; 27), present a fractional potential to diminish the obstacle danger level and improve the smoothness of the trajectories, Philippsen (26) introduces an interpolated Navigation Function, but with trajectories too close to obstacles and without smooth properties and Petres

(30), introduces efficient path-planning algorithms for Underwater Vehicles taking advantage of the underwaters currents.

LaValle (15), treats on the feedback motion planning concept. To move in the physical world the actions must be planned depending on the information gathered during execution.

Lindemann and Lavalle (17) (18) present a method in which the vector field globally solves the navigation problem and provides robustness to disturbances in sensing and control. In addition to being globally convergent, the vector field's integral curves (system trajectories) are guaranteed to avoid obstacles and are C^∞ smooth, except in the changes of cells. They construct a vector field with these properties by using existing geometric algorithms to partition the space into simple cells; they then define local vector fields for each cell, and smoothly interpolate between them to obtain a global vector field that can be used as a feedback control for the robot.

Yang and Lavalle (41) presented a randomized framework motion strategies, by defining a global navigation function over a collection of spherical balls in the configuration space. Their key idea is to fill the collision free subset of the configuration space with overlapping spherical balls, and define collision free potential functions on each ball. A similar idea has been developed for collision detection in (31) and (32).

The proposed method constructs a vectorial field as in the work by Lindemann, but the field is done in the global map instead of having local cells maps with the problem of having trajectories that are not C^∞ in the union between cells. The method has also similitudes with the Yang and Lavalle method. They proposed a series of balls with a Lyapunov potential associated to each of them. These potentials are connected in such a way that it is possible to find the trajectory using in each ball the gradient method. The method that we propose, has a unique global Lyapunov potential associated with the vectorial field that permits build the C^∞ trajectory in a single pass with the gradient method.

To achieve a smooth and safe path,it is necessary to have smooth attractive and repulsive potentials, connected in such a way that the resulting potential and the trajectories have no local minima and curvature continuity to facilitate path tracking design. The main improvement of the proposed method are these good properties of smoothness and safety of the trajectory. Moreover, the associated vector field allows the introduction of nonholonomic constraints.

It is important to note that in the proposed method the important ingredients are the attractive and the repulsive potentials, the way of connecting them describing the attractive potential using the wave equation (or in a simplified way, the eikonal equation). This equation can be solved in other ways: Mauch (20) uses a Marching with Correctness Criterion with a computational complexity that can reduced to $\mathcal{O}(N)$. Covello (5) presents a method that can be used on nodes that are located on highly distorted grids or on nodes that are randomly located.

4. The VFM Motion Planner

Which properties and characteristics are desirable for a Motion Planner of a mobile robot? The first one is that the planner always drives the robot in a smooth and safe way to the goal point. In Nature there are phenomena with the same way of working: electromagnetic waves. If in the goal point, there is an antenna that emits an electromagnetic wave, then the robot could drive itself to the destination following the waves to the source. The concept of the electromagnetic wave is especially interesting because the potential and its associated vector field have all the good properties desired for the trajectory, such as smoothness (it is C^∞) and the absence of local minima. This attractive potential still has some problems. The most important one that typically arises in mobile robotics is that optimal motion plans may bring robots too close to obstacles, which is not safe. This problem has been dealt with by Latombe (14), and the resulting navigation function is called *NF2*. The Voronoi Method also tries to follow a maximum clearance map (6). To generate a safe path, it is necessary to add a component that repels the robot away from obstacles. In addition, this repulsive potential and its associated vector field should have good properties such as those of the electrical field. If we consider that the robot has an electrical charge of the same sign as the obstacles, then the robot would be pushed away from obstacles. The properties of this electric field are very good because it is smooth and there are no singular points in the interest space (C_{free}).

The third part of the problem consists in how to mix the two fields together. This union between an attractive and a repulsive field has been the biggest problem for the potential fields in path planning since the works of Khatib (10). In the VFM Method, this problem has been solved in the same way that Nature does so: the electromagnetic waves, such as light, have a propagation velocity that depends on the media. For example, flint glass has a refraction index of 1.6, while in the air it is approximately one. This refraction index of a medium is the quotient between the velocity of light in the vacuum and the velocity in the medium under consideration. That is the slowness index of the front wave propagation in a medium. A light ray follows a straight line if the medium has a constant refraction index (the medium is homogeneous) but refracts when there is a transition of medium (sudden change of refraction index value). In the case of a gradient change in refraction index in a given medium, the light ray follows a curved line. This phenomenon can be seen in nature in hot road mirages. In this phenomenon, the air closer to the road surface is warmer than the higher level layers. The warmer air has lower density and lower refraction index. For this reason, light rays coming from the sun are curved near the road surface and cause what is called the hot road mirage, as illustrated in fig. 1. This is the idea that inspires the way in which the attractive and the repulsive fields are merged in our work.

For this reason, in the *VFM* method, the repulsive potential is used as refraction index of the wave emitted from the goal point. In this way, a unique field is obtained and its associated vector field is attractive to the goal point and repulsive from the obstacles. This method inherits the properties of the electromagnetic field. Intuitively, the *VFM* Method gives the propagation of a front wave in an inhomogeneous media.

In Geometrical Optics, Fermat's *least time principle* for light propagation in a medium with space varying refractive index $\eta(\mathbf{x})$ is equivalent to the eikonal equation and can be written as $||\nabla\Phi(\mathbf{x})|| = \eta(\mathbf{x})$ where the eikonal $\Phi(\mathbf{x})$ is a scalar function whose isolevel contours are normal to the light rays. This equation is also known as the Fundamental Equation of the Geometrical Optics.

The eikonal (from the Greek "eikon", which means "image") is the phase function in a situation for which the phase and amplitude are slowly varying functions of position. Constant values of the eikonal represent surfaces of constant phase, or wavefronts. The normals to these surfaces are rays (the paths of energy flux). Thus the eikonal equation provides a method for "ray tracing" in a medium of slowly varying refractive index (or the equivalent for other kinds of waves).

The theory and the numerical techniques known as Fast Marching Methods are derived from an exposition to describe the movement of interfaces, based on a resolution of the equations on partial differential equations as a boundary condition problem. The Fast Marching Method has been used previously in Path Planning by Sethian(35; 36), but using only an attractive potential.

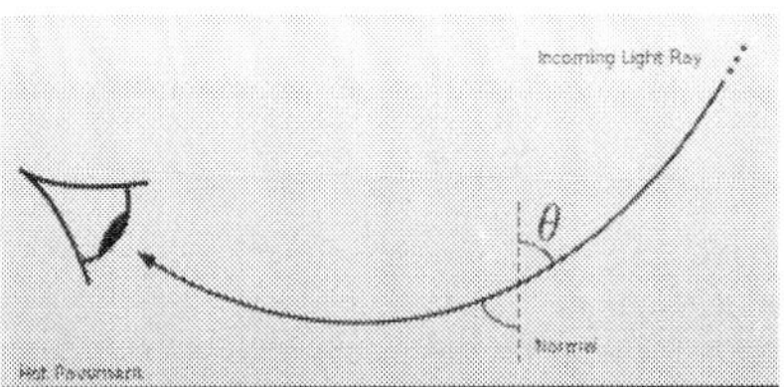

Fig. 1. Light rays bending due to changing refraction index in air with higher temperature near road surface.

The use of the Fast Marching method over a slowness (refraction or inverse of velocity) potential improves the quality of the calculated trajectory considerably. On one hand, the trajectories tend to go close to the Voronoi skeleton because of the optimal conditions of this area for robot motion (6).

An attractive potential used to plan a trajectory bring robots too close to obstacles as shown in fig. 2. For this reason, in the proposed method, the repulsive potential (fig. 3) is used as refraction index of the wave emitted from the goal point. This way a unique field is obtained and its associated vector field is attracted to the goal point and repulsed from the obstacles, as shown in fig. 4. This method inherits the properties of the electromagnetic field, i.e. it is C^∞, if the refraction index is C^∞. Intuitively, the VFM Method gives the propagation of a front wave in an inhomogeneous media.

The solution of the eikonal equation used in the VFM method is given by the solution of the wave equation:

$$\phi = \phi_0 e^{ik_0(\eta x - c_0 t)}$$

As this solution is an exponential, if the potential $\eta(x)$ is C^∞ then the potential ϕ is also C^∞ and therefore the trajectories calculated by the gradient method over this potential would be of the same class.

This smoothness property can be observed in fig. 5, where the trajectory is clearly good, safe and smooth. One advantage of the method is that it not only generates the optimum path, but also the velocity of the robot at each point of the path. The velocity reaches its highest values in the light areas and minimum values in the greyer zones. The VFM Method simultaneously provides the path and maximum allowable velocity for a mobile robot between the current location and the goal.

4.1 Properties

The proposed VFM algorithm has the following key properties:

- *Fast response.* The planner needs to be fast enough to be used reactively and plan new trajectories. To obtain this fast response, a fast planning algorithm and fast and simple treatment of the sensor information is necessary. This requires a low complexity order algorithm for a real time response to unexpected situations. The proposed algorithm has a fast response time to allow its implementation in real time, even in environments with moving obstacles using a normal PC computer.

  The proposed method is highly efficient from a computational point of view because the method operates directly over a 2D image map (without extracting adjacency maps), and due to the fact that Fast Marching complexity is $O(m \times n)$ and the Extended Voronoi Transform is also of complexity $O(m \times n)$, where $m \times n$ is the number of cells in the environment map. In table 1, orientative results of the cost average in time appear

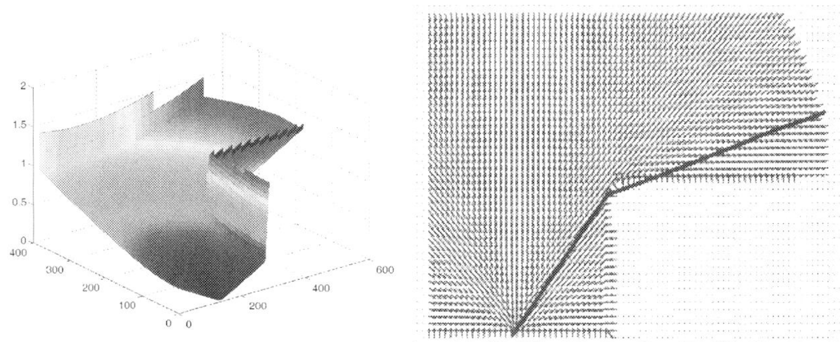

Fig. 2. Attractive potential, its associated vector field and a typical trajectory.

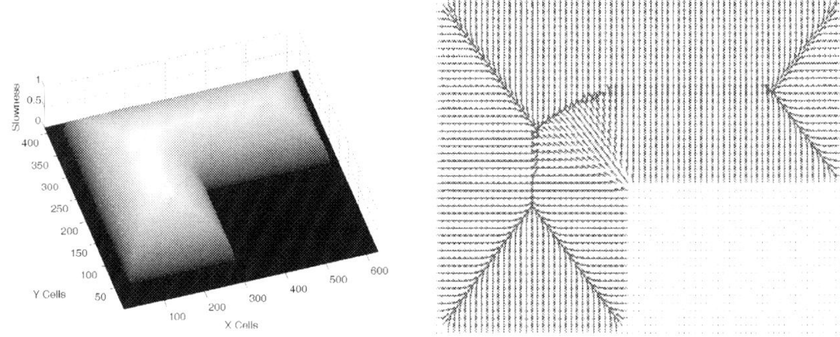

Fig. 3. The Fast Marching Method applied to a L-shaped environment gives: the slowness (velocity inverse) or repulsive potential and its associated vector field.

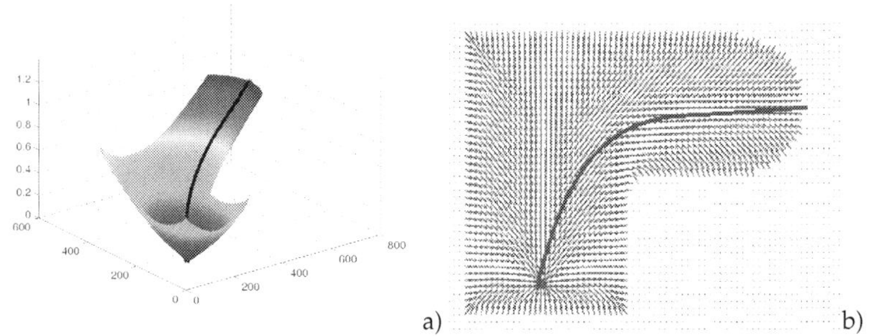

Fig. 4. a) Union of the two potentials: the second one having the first one as refractive index. b) Associated vector field and typical trajectories obtained with this method.

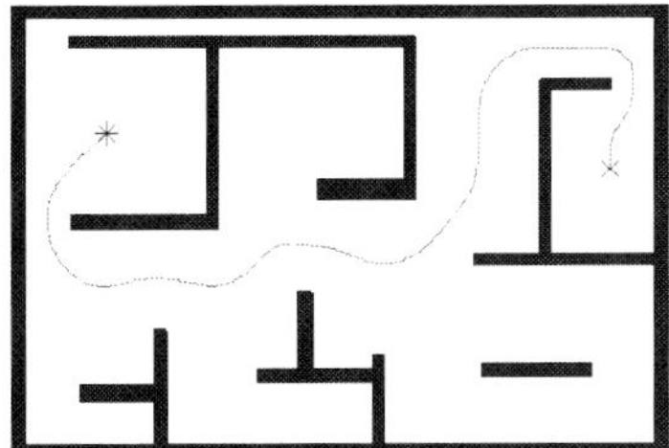

Fig. 5. Trajectories calculated applying the proposed algorithm with Fast Marching over the Logarithm Extended Voronoi Transform.

(measured in seconds), and each step of the algorithm for different trajectory lengths to calculate (the computational cost depends on the number of points of the image).

Alg. Step/Trajectory length	Long	Medium	Short
Obst. Enlarging	0.008	0.008	0.008
Ext. Voronoi Transf.	0.039	0.039	0.039
FM Exploration	0.172	0.078	0.031
Path Extraction	0.125	0.065	0.035
Total time	0.344	0.190	0.113

Table 1. Computational cost (seconds) for the room environment (966x120 pixels)

- *Smooth trajectories.* The planner must be able to provide a smooth motion plan which can be executed by the robot motion controller. In other words, the plan does not need to be refined, avoiding the need for a local refinement of the trajectory. The solution of the eikonal equation used in the proposed method is given by the solution of the wave equation:

$$\phi = \phi_0 e^{ik_0(\eta x - c_0 t)}$$

As this solution is an exponential, if the potential $\eta(x)$ is C^∞ then the potential ϕ is also C^∞ and therefore the trajectories calculated by the gradient method over this potential would be of the same class.

This smoothness property can be observed in fig. 5, where the trajectory is clearly good, safe and smooth. One advantage of the method is that it not only generates the optimum path, but also the velocity of the robot at each point of the path. The velocity reaches its highest values in the light areas and minimum values in the greyer zones. The VFM Method simultaneously provides the path and maximum allowable velocity for a mobile robot between the current location and the goal.

- *Reliable trajectories.* The proposed planner provides a safe (reasonably far from detected obstacles) and reliable trajectory (free from local traps). This is due to the refraction index, which causes higher velocities far from obstacles.

- *Completeness.* As the method consists of the propagation of a wave, if there is a path from the the initial position to the objective, the method is capable of finding it.

5. Differential evolution approach to the SLAM

Localization and map building are key components in robot navigation and are required to successfully execute the path generated by the VFM planner in the exploration method proposed in this work. Both problems are closely linked, and learning maps are required to solve both problems simultaneously; this is the SLAM problem. Uncertainty in sensor measures and uncertainty in robot pose estimates make the use of a SLAM method necessary to create a consistent map of the explored environment.

The SLAM algorithm used in this work is described in (23). It is based on the stochastic search of solutions in the state space to the localization problem by means of a differential evolution algorithm. A non linear evolutive filter, called Evolutive Localization Filter (ELF), searches stochastically along the state space for the best robot pose estimate. The proposed SLAM algorithm operates in two steps: in the first step the ELF filter is used at a local level to re-localize the robot based on the robot odometry, the laser scan at a given position and a local map where only a low number of the last scans have been integrated. In a second step, the aligned laser measures, together with the corrected robot poses, are used to detect when the robot is revisiting a previously crossed area. Once a cycle is detected, the Evolutive Localization Filter is used again to reestimate the robot position and orientation in order to integrate the sensor measures in the global map of the environment.

This approach uses a differential evolution method to perturb the possible pose estimates contained in a given set until the optimum is obtained. By properly choosing the cost function, a maximum a posteriori estimate is obtained. This method is applied at a local level to re-localize the robot and at a global level to solve the data association problem. The method proposed integrates sensor information in the map only when cycles are detected and the residual errors are eliminated, avoiding a high number of modifications in the map or the existence of multiple maps, thus decreasing the computational cost compared to other solutions.

6. Implementation of the explorer

In order to solve the problem of the exploration of an unknown environment, our algorithm can work in two different ways. First, the exploration process can be directed giving to the algorithm one or several successive goal points in the environment which the robot must drive to during the exploration process. Second, that is the second form to work of our algorithm, the exploration can be carried out without having any previously fixed objective point. In such case, the algorithm must automatically determine towards where the robot must drive in order to complete the exploration process.

6.1 Case I

In the first one, the initial information is the localization of the final goal. In this way, the robot has a general direction of movement towards the goal. In each movement of the robot, information about the environment is used to build a binary image distinguishing occupied space represented by value 0 (obstacles and walls) from free space, with value 1. The Extended Voronoi Transform of the known map at that moment gives a grey scale that is darker near the obstacles and walls and lighter far from them. The Voronoi Fast Marching Method gives the trajectory from the pose of the robot to the goal point using the known information. In this first way of working, the SLAM algorithm described in (23) is used to avoid localization errors being translated into the map built during the exploration process.

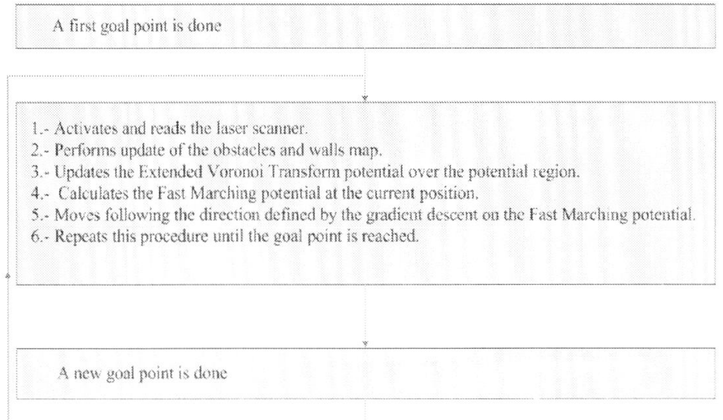

Fig. 6. Flowchart of case 1.

In this first case, the robot has a final goal: the exploration process the robot performs in the algorithm described in the flowchart of fig. 6.

6.2 Case II

In the second way of working of the algorithm, the goal location is unknown and robot behavior is truly exploratory. We propose an approach based on the incremental calculation of a map for path planning.

We define a neighborhood window, which travels with the robot, roughly the size of its laser sensor range. This window indicates the new grid cells that are recruited for update, i.e., if a cell was in the neighborhood window at a given time, it becomes part of the explored space by participating in the EVT and Fast Marching Method calculation for all times. The set of activated cells that compose the explored space is called the neighborhood region. Cells that were never inside the neighborhood window indicate unexplored regions. Their potential values are set to zero and define the knowledge frontier of the state space, the real space in our case. The detection of the nearest unexplored frontier comes naturally from the Extended Voronoi Transform calculation. It can also be understood from the physical analogy with electrical potentials that obstacles repel while frontiers attract.

Consider that the robot starts from a given position in an initially unknown environment. In this second method, there is no direction of the place where the robot must go.

A initial matrix with zeros in the obstacles and value 1 in the free zones is considered. This first matrix is built using the information provided by sensors and represents a binary image of the environment detected by sensors. The first step consists of calculating the EVT of the obstacles in this image. A value that represent the distance to the nearest obstacle is associated to each cell of the matrix. A matrix W of grays with values between 0 (obstacles) and 1 is obtained. This W matrix gives us the EVT of the obstacles found up until that moment.

A second matrix is built darkening the zones that the robot has already visited. Then, the EVT of this image is calculated and the result is the VT matrix.

Finally, matrix WV is the sum of the matrices VT and W, with weights 0.5 and 1 respectively.

$$WV = 0.5 * VT + W$$

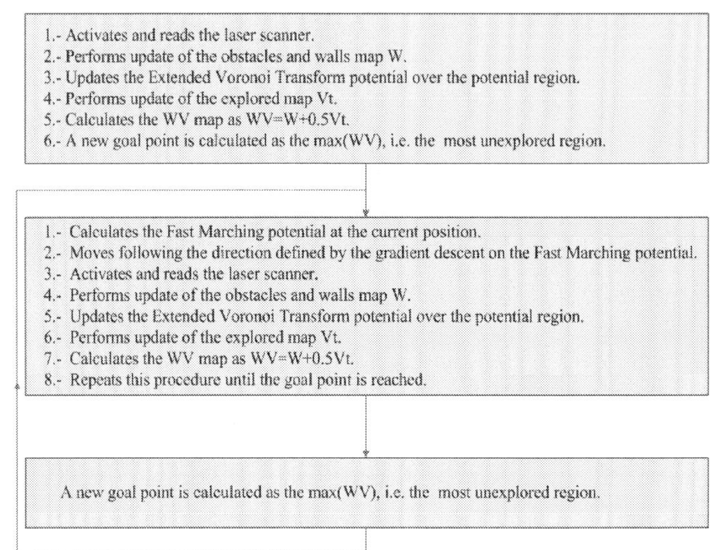

Fig. 7. Flowchart of algorithm 2.

In this way, it is possible to darken the zones already visited by the robot and impel it to go to the unexplored zones. The whitest point of matrix WV is calculated as $max(WV)$, that is, the most unexplored region that is in a free space. This is the point chosen as the new goal point. Applying the Fast Marching method on WV, the trajectory towards that goal is calculated. The robot moves following this trajectory. In the following steps, the trajectory to follow is computed, calculating first W and VT at every moment, and therefore WV, but without changing the objective point. Once the robot has been arrived at the objective, (that is to say, that path calculated is very small), a new objective is selected as $max(WV)$.

Therefore, the robot moves maximizing knowledge gain. In this case or in any other situation where there is no gradient to guide the robot, it simply follows the forward direction. The exploration process the robot performs in the second method described is summarized in the flowchart of fig. 7.

The algorithms laid out in fig. 6 (flowchart of case 1) can be inefficient in very large environments. To increase speed it is possible to pick a goal point, put a neighborhood window the size of the sensor range, run into the goal point, then look at the maximal initial boundary, and recast and terminate when one reaches the boundary of the computed region. Similar improvements can be made to algorithm 2.

7. Results

The proposed method, has been tested using the manipulator robot Manfred, see website: roboticslab.uc3m.es. It has a coordinated control of all degree of freedom in the system (the mobile base has 2 DOF and the manipulator has 6 DOF) to achieve smooth movement. This mobile manipulator use a sensorial system based on vision and 3-D laser telemetry to perceive and model 3-D environments. The mobile manipulator will include all the capabilities needed to navigate, localize and avoid obstacles safely through out the environment.

To illustrate the performance of the exploration method based on the VFM motion planner proposed, a test in a typical office indoor environment as shown in fig. 8, has been carried out. The dimensions of the environment are 116x14 meters (the cell resolution is 12 cm), that is the image has 966x120 pixels.

The VFM motion planning method provides smooth trajectories that can be used at low control levels without any additional smooth interpolation process. Some of the steps of the planning process between two defined points are shown in fig. 9. In this figure, the trajectory computed by the VFM planner is represented (the red line represents the crossed path, and the blue one represents the calculated trajectory from the present position to the destination point). This figure shows also the map built in each step using the SLAM algorithm.

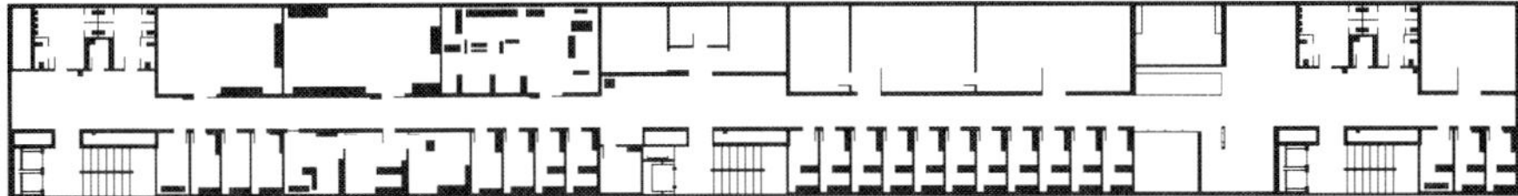

Fig. 8. Environment map of the Robotics Lab.

The results of two different tests are presented to illustrate both cases of exploration that this work contemplates in the same environment. In this case the size of image is 628x412 pixels.

Figs. 10 and 11 represent the first case for implementing the exploration method (directed exploration) on the Environment map shown in fig. 5. A final goal is provided for the robot, which is located with respect to a global reference system; the starting point of the robot movement is also known with respect to that reference system. The algorithm allows calculating the trajectory towards that final goal with the updated information of the surroundings that the sensors obtain in each step of the movement. When the robot reaches the defined goal, a new destination in an unexplored zone is defined, as can be seen in the third image of the figure.

The results of one of the tests done for the second case of exploration described are shown in figs. 12 and 13. Any final goal is defined. The algorithm leads the robot towards the zones that are free of obstacles and unexplored simultaneously (undirected exploration).

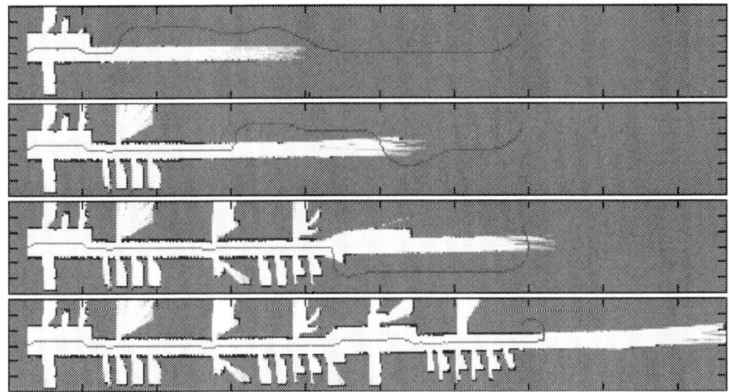

Fig. 9. Consecutive steps of the process using the first case of the exploration algorithm. The red line represents the crossed path and the blue one represents the calculated trajectory from the present position to the destination point.

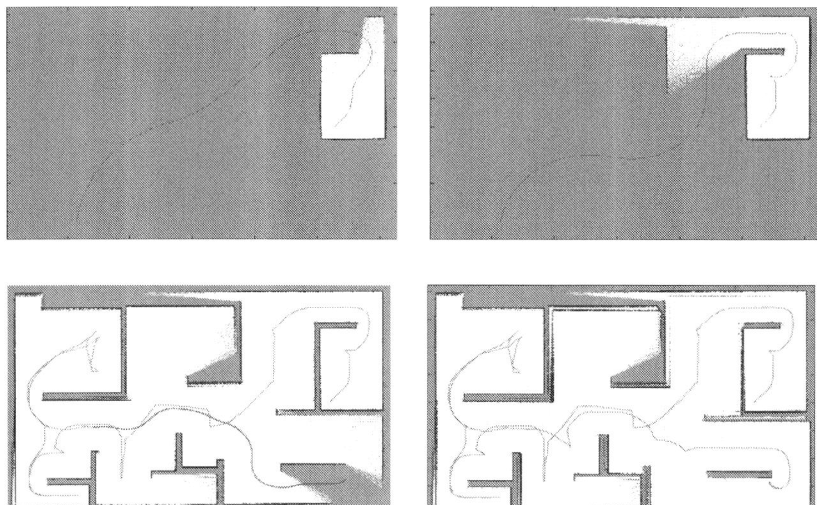

Fig. 10. Simulation results with method 1, with final objective. Trajectory calculated. The red line represents the crossed path and the blue one represents the calculated trajectory from the present position to the destination point.

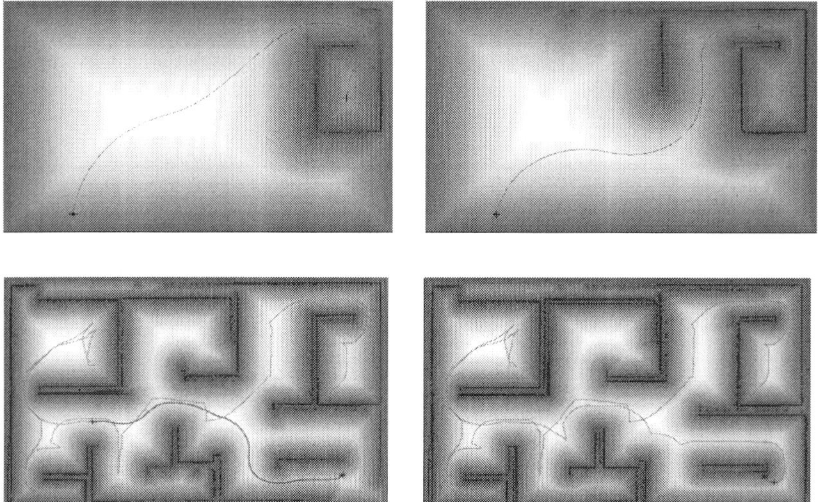

Fig. 11. Simulation results with method 1. Map built. The red line represents the crossed path and the blue one represents the calculated trajectory from the present position to the destination point.

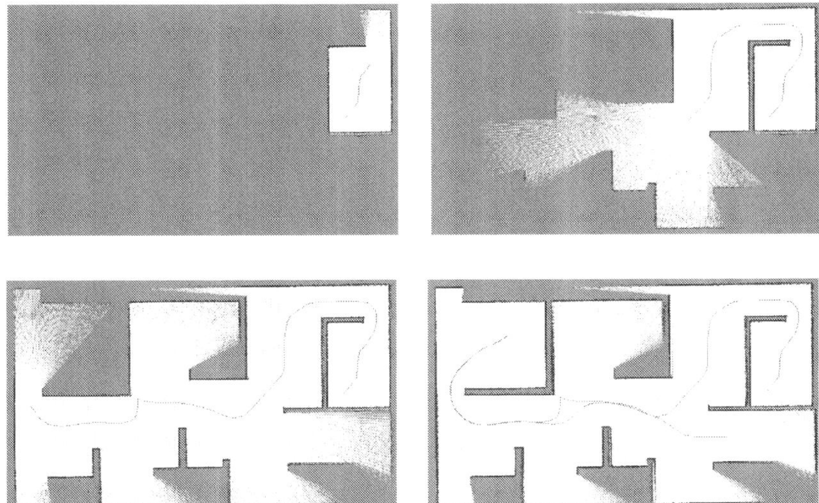

Fig. 12. Simulation results with method 2, without final objective. Trajectory calculated.

Fig. 13. Simulation results with method 2. Map built.

8. Conclusion

This work presents a new autonomous exploration strategy. The essential mechanisms used included the VFM method (8) applied to plan the trajectory towards the goal, a new exploratory strategy that drives the robot to the most unexplored region and the SLAM algorithm (23) to build a consistent map of the environment. The proposed autonomous exploration algorithm is a combination of the three tools which is able to completely construct consistent maps of unknown indoor environments in an autonomous way.

The results obtained show that the Logarithm of Extended Voronoi Transform can be used to improve the results obtained with the Fast Marching method to implement a sensor based motion planner, providing smooth and safe trajectories.

The algorithm complexity is $O(m \times n)$, where $m \times n$ is the number of cells in the environment map, which lets us use the algorithm on line. Furthermore, the algorithm can be used directly with raw sensor data to implement a sensor based local path planning exploratory module.

9. References

[1] J. Borenstein and Y. Koren, "Histogramic in-motion mapping for mobile robot obstacle avoidance.", *IEEE Journal of Robotics*, vol. 7, no. 4, pp. 535–539, 1991.

[2] A. Elfes, "Sonar-based real world mapping and navigation.", *IEEE Journal of Robotics and Automation*, vol. 3, no. 3, pp. 249–265, 1987.

[3] A. Elfes, "Using occupancy grids for mobile robot perception and navigation.", *Computer Magazine*, pp. 46–57, 1989.

[4] H. Feder, J. Leonard and C. Smith, "Adaptive mobile robot navigation and mapping.", *International Journal of Robotics Research*, vol. 7, no. 18, pp. 650–668, 1999.

[5] P. Covello and G. Rodrigue, "A generalized front marching algorithm for the solution of the eikonal equation.", *J. Comput. Appl. Math.*, vol. 156, no. 2, pp. 371–388, 2003.

[6] S. Garrido, L.Moreno, and D.Blanco, "Voronoi diagram and fast marching applied to path planning." in *2006 IEEE International conference on Robotics and Automation. ICRA 2006.*, pp. 3049–3054.

[7] S. Garrido, L. Moreno, M. Abderrahim, and F. Martin, "Path planning for mobile robot navigation using voronoi diagram and fast marching." in *Proc of IROS'06. Beijing. China.*, 2006, pp. 2376–2381.

[8] S. Garrido, L. Moreno, and D. Blanco, *Sensor-based global planning for mobile robot navigation.*, Robotica 25 (2007), 189–199.

[9] A. Howard and L. Kitchen, "Generating sonar maps in highly specular environments." in *Proceedings of the Fourth International Conference on Control, Automation, Robotics and Vision*, 1996.

[10] M. Khatib and R. Chatila, "An extended potential field approach for mobile robot sensor-based motions." in *Proceedings of the IEEE Int. Conf. on Intelligent Autonomus Systems*, 1995.

[11] Y. Koren and J. Borenstein, "Potential field methods and their inherent limitations for mobile robot navigation" in *Proceedings of the IEEE Int. Conf. on Robotics and Automation*, pp. 1398–1404, 2004.

[12] B. Kuipers and T. Levitt, "Navigation and mapping in large-scale space.", *AI Magazine*, vol. 9, pp. 25–43, 1988.

[13] B. Kuipers and Y. Byun, "A robot exploration and mapping strategy based on a semantic hierarchy of spatial representations.", *Robotics and Autonomous Systems*, vol. 8, pp. 47–63, 1991.

[14] J.-C. Latombe, *Robot motion planning.* Dordrecht, Netherlands: Kluwer Academic Publishers, 1991.

[15] S. M. LaValle, 2006. *Planning Algorithms*, Cambridge University Press, Cambridge, U.K.

[16] W. Lee, "Spatial semantic hierarchy for a physical robot.", Ph.D. dissertation, Department of Computer Sciences, The University of Texas, 1996.

[17] S. R. Lindemann and S. M. LaValle," Simple and efficient algorithms for computing smooth, collision-free feedback laws", *International Journal of Robotics Research*, 2007.

[18] S. R. Lindemann and S. M. LaValle, "Smooth feedback for car-like vehicles in polygonal environments." in *Proceedings IEEE International Conference on Robotics and Automation*, 2007.

[19] M. Mataric, "Integration of representation into goal-driven behavior-based robots.", *IEEE Transaction on Robotics and Automation*, vol. 3, pp. 304–312, 1992.

[20] S. Mauch, "Efficient algorithms for solving static hamilton-jacobi equations.", Ph.D. dissertation, California Inst. of Technology, 2003.

[21] P. Melchior, B. Orsoni, O. Laviale, A. Poty, and A. Oustaloup, "Consideration of obstacle danger level in path planning using A* and Fast Marching optimisation: comparative study.", *Journal of Signal Processing*, vol. 83, no. 11, pp. 2387–2396, 2003.

[22] H. Moravec and A. Elfes, "High resolution maps from wide angle sonar." in *Proceedings of the IEEE International Conference on Robotics and Automation*, March, 1985, pp. 116–121.

[23] L.Moreno, S.Garrido and F.Martin. "E-SLAM solution to the grid-based Localization and Mapping problem", in *2007 IEEE International Symposium on Intelligent Signal Processing (WISP'2007)*. Alcala Henares. Spain. pp.897-903, 2007.

[24] G. Oriolo, M. Vendittelli and G. Ulivi,"On-line map-building and navigation for autonomous mobile robots." in *Proceedings of the IEEE International Conference on Robotics and Automation*, 1995, pp. 2900–2906.

[25] G. Oriolo, G. Ulivi and M. Vendittelli, "Fuzzy maps: A new tool for mobile robot perception and planning.", *Journal of Robotic Systems*, vol. 3, no. 14, pp. 179–197, 1997.

[26] R. Philippsen and R. Siegwart, "An interpolated dynamic navigation function." in *2005 IEEE Int. Conf. on Robotics and Automation*, 2005.

[27] A. Poty, P. Melchior and A. Oustaloup, "Dynamic path planning by fractional potential." in *Second IEEE International Conference on Computational Cybernetics*, 2004.

[28] E. P. Silva., P. Engel, M. Trevisan, and M. Idiart, "Exploration method using harmonic functions.", *Journal of Robotics and Autonomous Systems*, vol. 40, no. 1, pp. 25–42, 2002.

[29] E. P. Silva, P. Engel, M. Trevisan, and M. Idiart, "Autonomous learning architecture for environmental mapping.", *Journal of Intelligent and Robotic Systems*, vol. 39, pp. 243–263, 2004.

[30] C. Petres, Y. Pailhas, P. Patron, Y. Petillot, J. Evans and D. Lane, "Path planning for autonomous underwater vehicles.", *IEEE Trans. on Robotics*, vol. 23, no. 2, pp. 331–341, 2007.

[31] S. Quinlan and O. Khatib. "Elastic bands: Connecting path planning and control. " in *IEEE Int. Conf Robot and Autom.*, pp 802-807, 1993.

[32] S. Quinlan and O. Khatib, "Efficient distance computation between nonconvex objects." in *IEEE Int. Conf Robot and Autom.*, pp. 3324-3329, 1994.

[33] E. Rimon and D.E. Koditschek, "Exact robot navigation using artificial potential functions.", *IEEE Transactions on Robotics and Automation*, vol. 8, no. 5, pp.501–518, 1992.

[34] J. A. Sethian, "A fast marching level set method for monotonically advancing fronts.", *Proc. Nat. Acad Sci. U.S.A.*, vol. 93, no. 4, pp. 1591–1595, 1996.

[35] J. A. Sethian, "Theory, algorithms, and aplications of level set methods for propagating interfaces.", *Acta numerica*, pp. 309–395, Cambridge Univ. Press, 1996.

[36] J. Sethian, *Level set methods.* Cambridge University Press, 1996.

[37] S. Thrun and A. Bücken, "Integrating grid-based and topological maps for mobile robot." in *Proceedings of the 13th National Conference on Artificial Intelligence (AAAI-96)*, 1996, pp. 944–950.

[38] S. Thrun and A. Bücken, "Learning maps or indoor mobile robot navigation." CMU-CS-96-121, Carnegie Mellon University, Pittsburgh, PA, Tech. Rep., 1996.

[39] B. Yamauchi, "A frontier-based exploration for autonomous exploration." in *IEEE International Symposium on Computational Intelligence in Robotics and Automation, Monterey, CA*, 1997, pp. 146–151.

[40] B. Yamauchi, A. Schultz, W. Adams and K. Graves, "Integrating map learning, localization and planning in a mobile robot." in *Proceedings of the IEEE International Symposium on Computational Intelligence in Robotics and Automation, Gaithersburg, MD*, 1998, pp. 331–336.

[41] L. Yang and S. M. LaValle, "A framework for planning feedback motion strategies based on a random neighborhood graph" in Proceedings IEEE International Conference on Robotics and Automation, pages 544–549, 2000.

[42] J. Zelek, "A framework for mobile robot concurrent path planning and execution in incomplete and uncertain environments." in *Proceedings of the AIPS-98 Workshop on Integrating Planning, Scheduling and Execution in Dynamic and Uncertain Environments, Pittsburgh, PA*, 1988.

Part 2

Adaptive Navigation

5

Adaptive Navigation Control for Swarms of Autonomous Mobile Robots

Yasuhiro Nishimura[1], Geunho Lee[1], Nak Young Chong[1],
Sang Hoon Ji[2] and Young-Jo Cho[3]
[1]Japan Advanced Institute of Science and Technology,
[2]Korea Institute of Industrial Technology,
[3]Electronics and Telecommunications Research Institute
[1]Japan
[2,3]Korea

1. Introduction

Deploying a large number of resource-constrained mobile robots performing a common group task may offer many advantages in efficiency, costs per system, and fault-tolerance (Sahin, 2005). Therefore, robot swarms are expected to perform missions in a wide variety of applications such as environment and habitat monitoring, exploration, odor localization, medical service, and search-and-rescue. In order to perform the above-mentioned tasks successfully, one of the most important concerns is how to enable swarms of simple robots to autonomously navigate toward a specified destination in the presence of obstacles and dead-end passageways as seen in Fig. 1. From the standpoint of the decentralized coordination, the motions of individual robots need to be controlled to support coordinated collective behavior.

We address the coordinated navigation of a swarm of mobile robots through a cluttered environment without hitting obstacles and being trapped in dead-end passageways. Our study is motivated by the observation that schools of fish exhibit emergent group behavior. For instance, when schools of fish are faced with obstacles, they can split themselves into a plurality of smaller groups to avoid collision and then merge into a single group after passing around the obstacles (Wilson, 1976). It is also worth noting that a group of fish facing a dead end can get out of the area.

Based on the observation of schooling behavior in fish, this work aims to present a novel adaptive group behavior, enabling large-scale robot swarms with limited sensing capabilities to navigate toward a goal that is visible only to a limited number of robots. In particular, the coordinated navigation is achieved without using any leader, identifiers, common coordinate system, and explicit communication. Under such a minimal robot model, the adaptive navigation scheme exploits the geometric local interaction which allows three neighboring robots to form an equilateral triangle. Specifically, the proposed algorithm allows robot swarms to 1) navigate while maintaining equilateral triangular lattices, 2) split themselves into multiple groups while maintaining a uniform distance of each other, 3) merge into a single group while maintaining a uniform distance of each other, and 4) escape from any dead-end passageways. During the adaptive navigation process, all robots execute the same algorithm and act independently and asynchronously of each other. Given any arbitrary initial positions, a large-scale swarm of robots is required to navigate toward a goal position in an environment while locally interacting with other robots. The basic necessities for the proposed solution are argued as follows. First, the robots can self-control their travel direction according to environmental conditions, leading to enhancing autonomy of their behavior. Secondly, by being split into multiple groups or re-united into a single swarm, the robots can self-adjust its size and shape depending on the conditions. By the capabilities above, robots have the emergent capability to maximize adaptability to operate in uncertain environments. Thirdly, the coordinated navigation of multiple robots in an equilateral triangle formation reduces a potential traffic jam and stragglers.

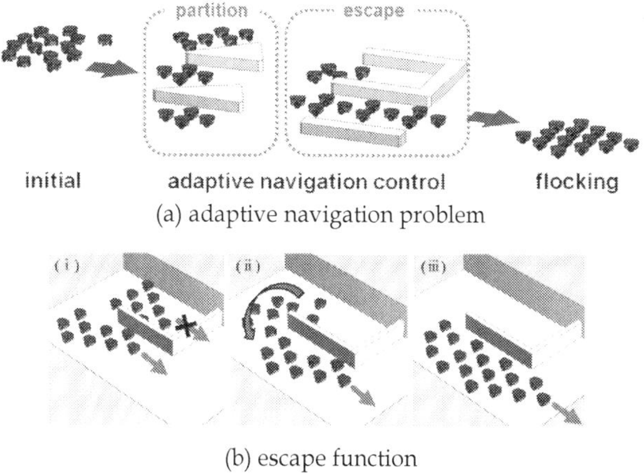

(a) adaptive navigation problem

(b) escape function

Fig. 1. Concept of adaptive navigation by autonomous mobile robot swarms

Consequently, the proposed adaptive navigation provides a cost-effective way to allow for an increase in efficiency and autonomy of group navigation in a highly cluttered environment. What is important from a practical standpoint is that the swarm flocking is considered as a good *ad hoc* networking model whose connectivity must be maintained while moving. In particular, maintaining the uniform distance enables the model to optimize efficient energy consumption in routing protocols (Fowler, 2001)(Lyengar *et al.*, 2005). This networking model can potentially be used in application examples such as exploration and search-and-rescue. This navigation can be further applied to swarms of unmanned vehicles and sensors performing autonomous operations such as capturing and transporting toxic and hazardous substances. We describe our algorithm in detail, and perform extensive simulations to demonstrate that a swarm of robots can navigate toward a specified destination while adapting to unknown environmental conditions in a scalable manner.

The rest of this paper is organized as follows. Section 2 introduces a brief description of research related to swarming and flocking and sheds light on our motivation. Section 3 presents the robot model and the formal definitions of the adaptive navigation problem. Section 4 describes the fundamental motion control of each robot locally interacting with their neighboring robots, leading to forming an equilateral triangle lattice. Section 5 gives the solution scheme of the adaptive navigation. Section 6 demonstrates the validity and applicability of the proposed scheme through extensive simulations. Section 7 draws conclusions.

2. Background

Wireless network-enabled mobile robotic sensors have been increasingly popular over the recent years (Yicka *et al.*, 2008). Such robotic sensors dispersing themselves into an area can be used for search-and-rescue and exploration applications by filling the area of interest and/or establishing an *ad hoc* network. To achieve a desired level of self-deployment of robotic sensors, many prior studies have attempted to use decentralized approaches in self-configuration (Lee & Chong, 2009)(Shucker *et al.*, 2008)(Spears *et al.*, 2004), pattern generation (Lee & Chong, 2009-b)(Ikemoto *et al.*, 2005), and navigation (Gu & Hu, 2010)(Lee & Chong, 2008)(Olfati-Saber, 2006). In particular, we have witnessed a great interest in distributed navigation control that enables a large number of robots to navigate from an initial position toward a desired destination without human intervention.

Recently, many navigation control studies have been reported in the field of swarm robotics, where the decentralized navigation controls are mainly based on interactions between individual robots mostly inspired by evidence from biological systems (*e.g.*, fish schools or bird flocks) or natural phenomena (*e.g.*, liquid diffusion). The navigation control can be further divided into biological emergence (Folino & Spezzano, 2002)(Reynolds, 1987), behavior-based (Lee & Chong, 2008)(Ogren & Leonard, 2005)(Balch & Hybinette, 2000), and virtual physics-based (Esposito & Dunbar, 2006)(Zarzhitsky *et al.*, 2005)(Spears *et al.*, 2006) approaches. Specifically, the behavior-based and virtual physics-based approaches are related to the use of such physical phenomena as gravitational forces (Zarzhitsky *et al.*, 2005)(Spears *et al.*, 2006) and potential fields (Esposito & Dunbar, 2006). Those works mostly use some sort of force balance between inter-individual interactions exerting an attractive or repulsive force on each other. This is mainly because the force-based interaction rules are considered simple yet effective, and provide an intuitive understanding on individual behavior. However, the computation of relative velocities or accelerations between robots is needed to obtain the magnitude of the interacting force.

Regarding the aspect of calculating the movement position of each robot, accuracy and computational efficiency issues have been attracted. In practice, many works on robot swarms use sensor-rich information and explicit means of communication. Note that if any means of communication would be employed, robots need to identify with each other or use a global coordinate or positioning system (Correll *et al.*, 2000)(Lam & Liu, 2006)(Nembrini *et al.*, 2002). In this paper, we attempt to achieve adaptive navigation without taking advantage of rich computational capabilities and communication. This will allow us to develop robot systems in simple, robust, and non-costly ways. A subset of this work was reported in (Lee & Chong, 2008) which provided mobile robot swarms with basic navigation and adaptation capabilities. The main objective of this paper is to present a completely new and general adaptive navigation coordination scheme assuming a more complicated arena with dead-end passageways. Specifically, we highlight the simplicity and intuition of the self-escape capability without incorporating a combination of sophisticated algorithms.

3. Problem statement

3.1 Robot model and notations

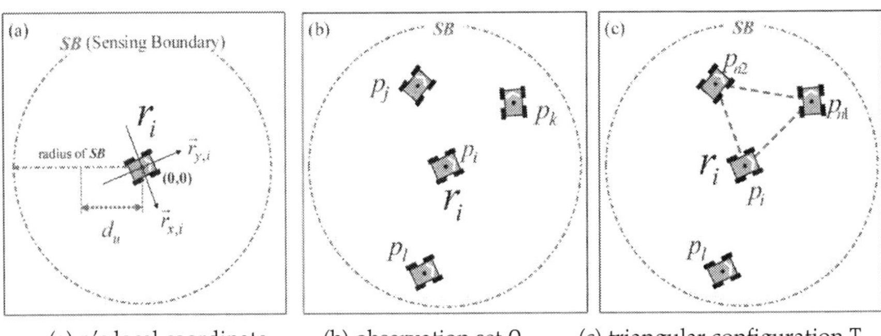

| (a) r_i's local coordinate | (b) observation set O_i | (c) triangular configuration T_i |

Fig. 2. Illustration of definition and notation

In this work, we consider a swarm of mobile robots denoted by $r_1, \cdots, r_n$. It is assumed that an initial distribution of all robots is arbitrary and their positions are distinct. Each robot autonomously moves on a two-dimensional plane. Robots have no leader and no identifiers. They do not share any common coordinate system. Due to a limited observation range, each robot can detect the positions of other robots only within its line-of-sight. In addition, robots are not allowed to communicate explicitly with each other.

Next, as illustrated in Fig. 2-(a), let's consider a robot r_i with local coordinate system $\vec{r}_{x,i}$ and $\vec{r}_{y,i}$. The robot's heading direction $\vec{r}_{y,i}$ is defined as the vertical axis of r_i's coordinate system. It is straightforward to determine the horizontal axis $\vec{r}_{x,i}$ by rotating $\vec{r}_{y,i}$ 90 degrees clockwise. The position of r_i is denoted by p_i. Note that p_i is $(0, 0)$ with respect to r_i's local coordinate system. The line segment $\overline{p_i p_j}$ is defined as a straight line between p_i and p_j occupied by another robot r_j. The distance between p_i and p_j is defined as $\text{dist}(p_i, p_j)$. In particular, the desired inter-robot distance between r_i and r_j is denoted by d_u. Moreover, $\text{ang}(\vec{m}_i, \vec{n}_i)$ denote the angle between two arbitrary vectors $\vec{m}_i$ and $\vec{n}_i$.

As shown in Fig. 2-(b), r_i detects the positions p_j, p_k and p_l of other robots located within its sensing boundary SB, yielding a set of the positions $O_i (=\{p_j, p_k, p_l\})$ with respect to its local coordinate system. When r_i selects two robots r_{n1} and r_{n2} within its SB, we call r_{n1} and r_{n2} the neighbors of r_i, and their position set $\{p_{n1}, p_{n2}\}$ is denoted by N_i as illustrated in Fig. 2-(c). Given p_i and N_i, a set of three distinct positions $\{p_i, p_{n1}, p_{n2}\}$ with respect to r_i is called the triangular configuration T_i, namely $\{p_i, p_{n1}, p_{n2}\}$. We further define the equilateral triangular configuration, denote by E_i, as the configuration that all distances between any two of p_i, p_{n1} and p_{n2} of T_i are equal to d_u.

3.2 Problem definition

It is known that the local geometric shape of schools of tuna represents a diamond shape (Stocker, 1999), whereby tuna exhibit their adaptive behavior while maintaining the local shape. Similarly, the local interaction in this work is to generate E_i from T_i. Formally, the *local interaction* is to have r_i maintain d_u with N_i at each time toward forming E_i. Now, we can address the coordination problem of *adaptive navigation* of robot swarms based on the local interaction as follows:

Given $r_1, \cdots, r_n$ located at arbitrarily distinct positions, how to enable the robots to autonomously travel through unknown territories using only local information in order to reach a destination?

It is assumed that the unknown environment to be navigated by a swarm of robots includes obstacles and dead-end passageways. Next, we advocate that adaptive flocking can be achieved by solving the following four constituent sub-problems.

- **Problem-1**(*Maintenance*): Given robots located at arbitrarily distinct positions, how to enable them to navigate with $\mathbb{E}_i$.

- **Problem-2**(*Partition*): Given that an obstacle is detected, how to enable a swarm to split into multiple smaller swarms to avoid the obstacle.

- **Problem-3**(*Unification*): Given that multiple swarms exist in close proximity, how to enable them to merge into a single swarm.

- **Problem-4**(*Escape*): Given some robots trapped in a dead-end passageway, how to enable them to escape from the area.

4. Geometric local interaction scheme

This section explains the local interaction among three neighboring robots. As presented in ALGORITHM-1, the algorithm consists of a function $\varphi_{interaction}$ whose arguments are p_i and N_i at each activation.

$$\text{constant } d_u := \text{uniform distance}$$
$$\textbf{FUNCTION } \varphi_{interaction}(\{p_{n1}, p_{n2}\}, p_i)$$
$$1 \quad (p_{ct,x}, p_{ct,y}) := centroid(p_{n1}, p_{n2}, p_i)$$
$$2 \quad \phi := \text{angle between } \overline{p_{n1}p_{n2}} \text{ and } r_i\text{'s local horizontal axis}$$
$$3 \quad p_{ti,x} := p_{ct,x} + d_u \cos(\phi + \pi/2)/\sqrt{3}$$
$$4 \quad p_{ti,y} := p_{ct,y} + d_u \sin(\phi + \pi/2)/\sqrt{3}$$
$$5 \quad p_{ti} := (p_{ti,x}, p_{ti,y})$$

Algorithm 1. Local Interaction (code executed by the robot r_i at point p_i)

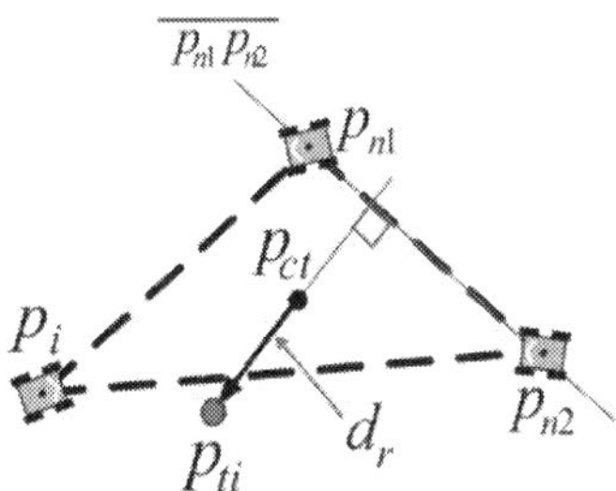

Fig. 3. Illustration of the local interaction algorithm

4.1 Local interaction algorithm

Let's consider a robot r_i and its two neighbors r_{n1} and r_{n2} located within r_i's SB. As shown in Fig. 3, three robots are configured into $\mathbb{T}_i$ whose vertices are p_i, p_{n1} and p_{n2}, respectively.

First, r_i finds the centroid of the triangle $\triangle p_i p_{n1} p_{n2}$, denoted by p_{ct}, with respect to its local coordinate system, and measures the angle ϕ between the line $\overline{p_{n1} p_{n2}}$ connecting the neighbors and $\vec{r}_{x,i}$ (r_i's horizontal axis). Using p_{ct} and ϕ, r_i calculates the next movement point p_{ti}. Each robot computes p_{ti} by its current observation of neighboring robots. Intuitively, under ALGORITHM-1, r_i may maintain d_u with its two neighbors at each time. In other words, each robot attempts to form an isosceles triangle for N_i at each time, and by repeatedly running ALGORITHM-1, three robots configure themselves into Ξ_i (Lee & Chong, 2009).

4.2 Motion control

As illustrated in Fig. 4-(b), let's consider the circumscribed circle of an equilateral triangle whose center is p_{ct} of $\triangle p_i p_{n1} p_{n2}$ and radius d_r is $d_u/\sqrt{3}$. Under the local interaction, the positions of each robot are determined by controlling the distance d_i from p_{ct} and the internal angle α_i (see Fig. 4-(a)). First, the distance is controlled by the following equation

$$\dot{d}_i(t) = -a(d_i(t) - d_r), \tag{1}$$

Where a is a positive constant. Indeed, the solution of (1) is $d_i(t) = |d_i(0)|e^{-at} + d_r$ that converges exponentially to d_r as t approaches infinity. Secondly, the internal angle is controlled by the following equation

$$\dot{\alpha}_i(t) = k\big(\beta_i(t) - \gamma_i(t) - 2\alpha_i(t)\big), \tag{2}$$

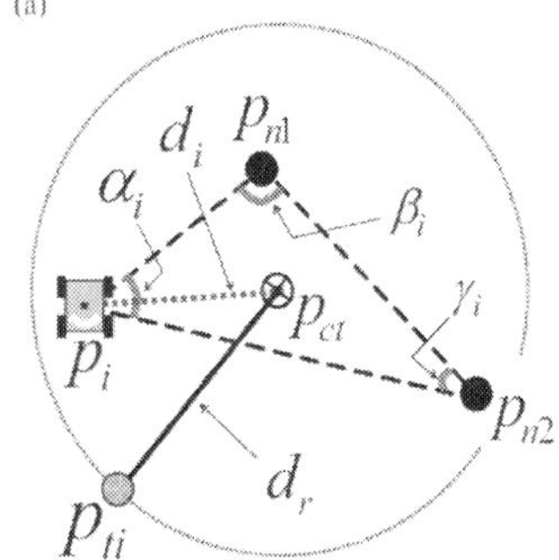

(a) control parameters range d_i and bearing α_i (b) desired equilateral triangle $\mathbb{E}_i$

Fig. 4. Two control parameter of local interaction

where k is a positive number. Because the total internal angle of a triangle is 180°, (2) can be rewritten as

$$\dot{\alpha}_i(t) = k'\big(60° - \alpha_i(t)\big), \tag{3}$$

where k' is 3k. Likewise, the solution of (3) is $\alpha_i(t) = |\alpha_i(0)|e^{-k't} + 60°$ that converges exponentially to 60° as t approaches infinity.

Note that (1) and (3) imply that the trajectory of r_i converges to d_r and 60°, an equilibrium state as termed $[d_r \quad 60°]^T$ shown in Fig. 4-(b). This also implies that three robots eventually form Ξ_i. In order to prove the convergence of the local interaction, we apply Lyapunov's stability theory (Slotine & Li, 1991). Lyapunov's stability theorem states that if there exists a scalar function $v(\mathbf{x})$ of the state $\mathbf{x}$ with continuous first order derivatives such that $v(\mathbf{x})$ is positive definite, $v'(\mathbf{x})$ is negative definite, and $v(\mathbf{x}) \to \infty$ as $\|\mathbf{x}\| \to \infty$, then the equilibrium at the origin is asymptotically stable. Now, the desired configuration can be regarded as one that minimizes the energy level of a Lyapunov function.

Consider the following scalar function of the state $\mathbf{x} = [d_i(t) \quad \alpha_i(t)]^T$ with continuous first order derivatives:

$$f_{l,i} = \frac{1}{2}(d_i - d_r)^2 + \frac{1}{2}(60° - \alpha_i)^2. \tag{4}$$

This scalar function is always positive definite except $d_i \neq d_r$ and $\alpha_i \neq 60$. The derivative of the scalar function is given by

$$\dot{f}_{l,i} = -(d_i - d_r)^2 - (60° - \alpha_i)^2, \tag{5}$$

which is obtained by differentiating $f_{l,i}$ to substitute for $\dot{d}_i$ and $\dot{\alpha}_i$. It is evident that (5) is negative definite and the scalar function $f_{l,i}$ is radially unbounded since it tends to infinity as $\|\mathbf{x}\| \to \infty$. Therefore, the equilibrium state is asymptotically stable, implying that r_i reaches a vertex of Ξ_i. Further details on the convergence proof are given in (Lee & Chong, 2009).

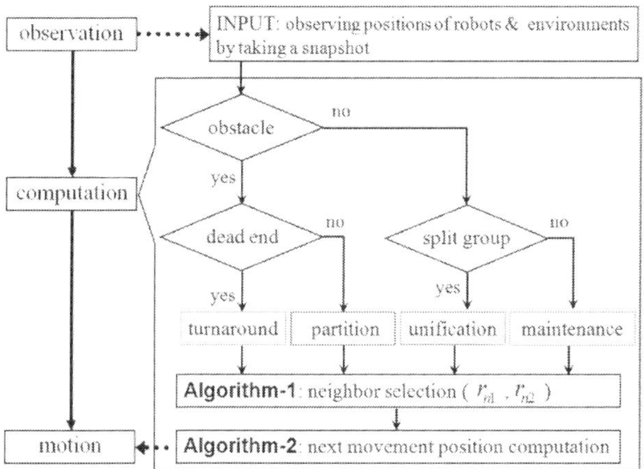

Fig. 5. Adaptive navigation algorithm flowchart

5. Adaptive navigation algorithm

As illustrated in Fig. 5, the input to the adaptive navigation algorithm at each time is O_i and the arena border detected with respect to r_i's local coordinate system, and the output is r_i's next movement position. When r_i observes the arena within its SB, depending on whether or not it can move forward, it either executes the partition function to avoid the obstacle or the escape function to break a stalemate. When r_i faces no arena border but observes other swarms, it executes the unification function. Otherwise, it basically performs the maintenance function to navigate toward a goal.

Function $\varphi_{rrsel}(O_i, p_i)$

1 $p_{n1} := \min\limits_{p \in O_i - \{p_i\}} [dist(p_i, p)]$

2 $p_{n2} := \min\limits_{p \in O_i - \{p_i, p_{n1}\}} [dist(p_{n1}, p) + dist(p, p_i)]$

3 Output: $\{p_{n1}, p_{n2}\}$ $(= N_i)$

Algorithm 2. Neighbor Selection -1 (code executed by the robot r_i at point p_i)

The four functions above should determine two positions p_{n1} and p_{n2} occupied by two neighbors r_{n1} and r_{n2}. These positions are the input arguments of ALGORITHM-1. Before explaining the four functions as individual solutions of each sub-problem, we introduce the neighbor selection algorithm commonly used in the four functions, enabling r_i to select its neighbor robots. To form $\mathbb{T}_i$, the first neighbor r_{n1} is selected as the one located the shortest distance away from r_i as shown in Fig. 6-(a). When there exist two or more candidates r_{n1_m} and r_{n1_n} for r_{n1}, r_i arranges their positions $p_{n1_m}=(x_{n1_m}, y_{n1_m})$ and $p_{n1_n}=(x_{n1_n}, y_{n1_n})$ with respect to r_i's local coordinate system. Then, r_i uniquely determines its r_{s1} by sorting their positions in the following increasing order with respect to its local coordinate system: if $(p_{n1_m} < p_{n1_n}) \Leftrightarrow [(y_{n1_m} < y_{n1_n}) \vee \{(y_{n1_m} = y_{n1_n}) \wedge (x_{n1_m} < x_{n1_n})\}]$ where the logic symbols $\vee$ and $\wedge$ indicate the logical conjunction and the logical disjunction, respectively. As presented in Fig. 6-(b), the second neighbor r_{n2} is selected such that the length of $\mathbb{T}_i$'s perimeter is minimized as follows: $\min[dist(p_{n1}, p_{n2}) + dist(p_{n2}, p_i)]$. In particular, when both r_i and the neighbors are all aligned, if there are three or more robots in O_i, r_{n2} is re-selected such that r_i is not located on the same line. Under ALGORITHM-2, r_i is able to select its neighbors and then form $\mathbb{T}_i$. Notice that the currently selected neighbors do not coincide with ones at the next time due to the assumption of anonymity. Using the current O_i by r_i, $\mathbb{T}_i$ is newly formed at each time.

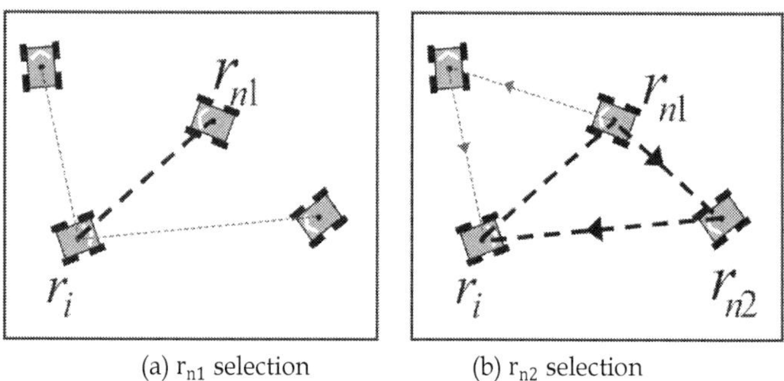

(a) r_{n1} selection   (b) r_{n2} selection

Fig. 6. Illustration of the neighbour selection algorithm

5.1 Maintenance function

The first problem is how to maintain Ξ_i with neighboring robots while navigating. As shown in Fig. 7-(a), r_i adjusts its traveling direction $\vec{T}_i$ with respect to its local coordinate system and computes O_i at the time t. By rotating $\vec{T}_i$ 90 degrees clockwise and counterclockwise, respectively, two vectors $\vec{T}_{i,c}$ and $\vec{T}_{i,a}$ are defined. Within r_i's SB, an area of traveling direction $A(\vec{T}_i)$ is defined as the area between $\vec{T}_{i,c}$ and $\vec{T}_{i,a}$ as illustrated in Fig. 7-(b). Under ALGORITHM-2, r_i checks whether there exists a neighbor in $A(\vec{T}_i)$. If any robots exist within $A(\vec{T}_i)$, r_i selects the first neighbor r_{n1} and defines its position p_{n1}. Otherwise, r_i spots a virtual point p_v located some distance d_v away from p_i along $A(\vec{T}_i)$, which gives p_{n1}. After determining p_{n1}, r_{n2} is selected and its position p_{n2} is defined.

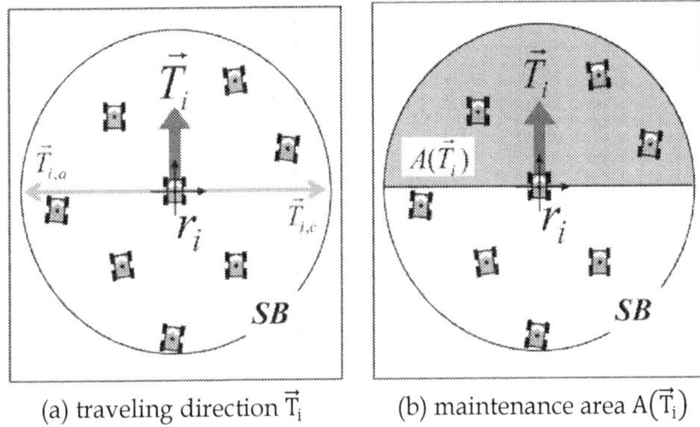

(a) traveling direction $\vec{T}_i$ (b) maintenance area $A(\vec{T}_i)$

Fig. 7. Illustration of the maintenance function

5.2 Partition function

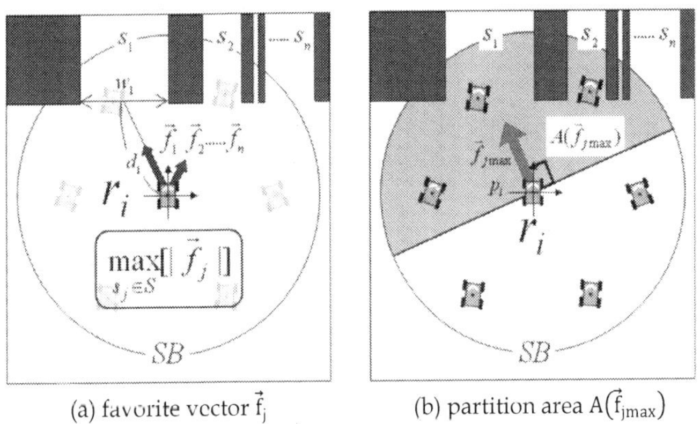

(a) favorite vector $\vec{f}_j$ (b) partition area $A(\vec{f}_{jmax})$

Fig. 8. Illustration of the partition function

When r_i detects an obstacle that blocks its way to the destination, it is required to modify the direction toward the destination avoiding the obstacle. In this work, r_i determines its direction by using the relative degree of attraction of individual passageways s_j, termed the favorite vector $\vec{f}_j$, whose magnitude is given:

$$\left| \vec{f}_j \right| = \left| \frac{w_j}{d_j^2} \right| \tag{6}$$

where w_j and d_j denote the width of s_j and the distance between the center of w_j and p_i, respectively. Note that if r_i can not exactly measure w_j beyond its SB, w_j may be shortened. Now, s_j can be represented by a set of favorite vectors $\{\vec{f}_j | 1 \leq j \leq m\}$, and then r_i selects the maximum magnitude of $\vec{f}_j$, denoted as $\left| \vec{f}_j \right|_{max}$. Similar to defining $A(\vec{T}_i)$ above, r_i defines a maximum favorite area $A(\vec{f}_{jmax})$ based on the direction of $\left| \vec{f}_j \right|_{max}$ within its SB. If neighbors are found in $A(\vec{f}_{jmax})$, r_i selects r_{n1} to define p_{n1}. Otherwise, r_i spots a virtual point p_v located at d_v in the direction of $\left| \vec{f}_j \right|_{max}$ to define p_{n1}. Finally, r_{n2} and its r_{n2} are determined under ALGORITHM-2.

5.3 Unification function

In order to enable multiple swarms in close proximity to merge into a single swarm, r_i adjusts $\vec{T}_i$ with respect to its local coordinate system and defines the position set of robots D_u located within the range of d_u. r_i computes $ang(\vec{T}_i, \overrightarrow{p_i p_u})$, where $\overrightarrow{p_i p_u}$ is the vector starting from p_i to a neighboring point p_u in D_u, and defines a neighbor point p_{ref} that gives the minimum $ang(\vec{T}_i, \overrightarrow{p_i p_u})$ between $\vec{T}_i$ and $\overrightarrow{p_i p_u}$. If there exists p_{ul}, r_i finds another neighbor point p_{um} using the same method starting from $\overrightarrow{p_i p_{ul}}$. Unless p_{ul} exists, r_i defines p_{ref} as p_{rn}. Similarly, r_i can decide a specific neighbor point p_{ln} while rotating 60 degrees counterclockwise from $\overrightarrow{p_i p_{ref}}$. The two points, denoted as p_{rn} and p_{ln}, are located at the farthest point in the right-hand or left-hand direction of $\overrightarrow{p_i p_u}$, respectively. Next, a unification area $A(U_i)$ is defined as the common area between $A(\vec{T}_i)$ in SB and the rest of the area in SB, where no element of D_u exists. Then, r_i defines a set of robots in $A(U_i)$ and selects the first neighbor r_{n1}. In particular, the second neighbor position p_{n2} is defined such that the total distance from p_{n1} to p_i can be minimized only through either p_{rn} or p_{ln}.

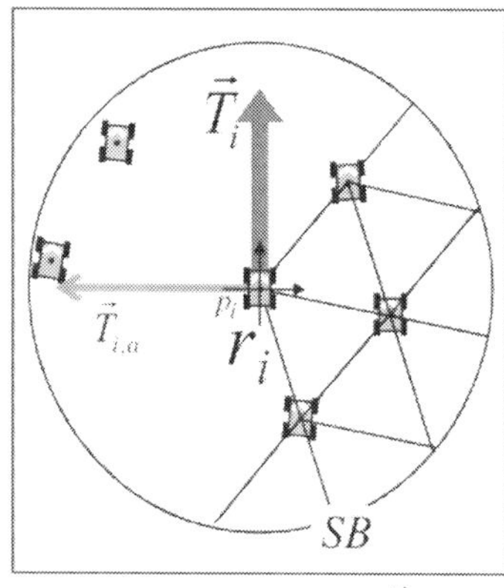

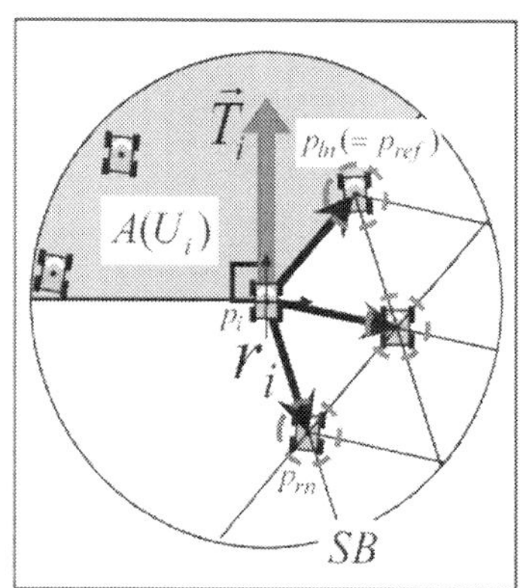

(a) traveling direction $\vec{T}_i$ (b) unification area $A(U_i)$

Fig. 9. Illustration of the unification function

5.4 Escape control

When r_i detects an arena border within its SB as shown in Fig. 10-(a), it checks whether T_i is equal to Ξ_i. Neighboring robots should always be kept d_u distance from r_i. Moreover, r_i's current position p_i and its next movement position p_{ti} remain unchanged for several time steps, r_i will find itself trapped in a dead-end passageway. r_i then attempts to find new neighbors within the area $A(E_i)$ to break the stalemate. Similar to the unification function, r_i adjusts $\vec{T_i}$ with respect to its local coordinate system and defines the position set of robots D_e located within SB. As shown in Fig. 10-(b), r_i computes $ang(\vec{T_i}, \overrightarrow{p_i p_e})$, where $\overrightarrow{p_i p_u}$ is the vector starting from p_i to a neighboring point p_e in D_e, and defines a neighbor point r_{ref} that gives the minimum $ang(\vec{T_i}, \overrightarrow{p_i p_e})$ between $\vec{T_i}$ and $\overrightarrow{p_i p_u}$. While rotating 60 degrees clockwise and counterclockwise from $\overrightarrow{p_i p_{ref}}$, respectively, r_i can decide the specific neighbor points p_{ln} and p_{rn}. Employing p_{ln} and p_{rn}, the escape area $A(E_i)$ is defined. Then, r_i adjusts a set of robots in $A(E_i)$ and selects the first neighbor r_{n1}. In particular, the second neighbor position p_{n2} is determined under ALGORITHM-2.

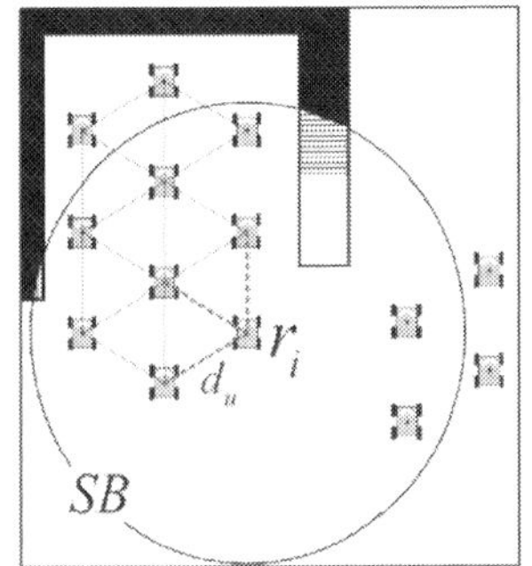

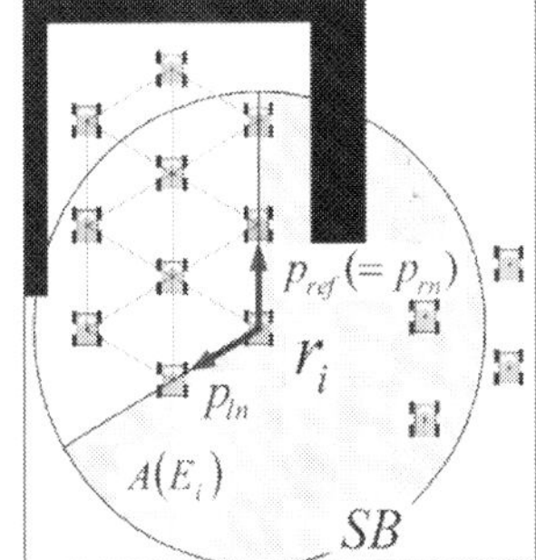

(a) encountered dead-end passageway   (b) merging with another adjacent swarm

Fig. 10. Illustration of the escape function

6. Simulation results and discussion

This section describes simulation results that tested the validity of our proposed adaptive navigation scheme. We consider that a swarm of robots attempts to navigate toward a stationary goal while exploring and adapting to unknown environmental conditions. In such an application scenario, the goal is assumed to be either a light or odor source that can only be detected by a limited number of robots. As mentioned in Section 3, the coordinated navigation is achieved without using any leader, identifiers, global coordinate system, and explicit communication. We set the range of SB to 2.5 times longer than d_u.

The first simulation demonstrates how a swarm of robots adaptively navigates in an environment populated with obstacles and dead-end passageway. In Fig. 11, the swarm navigates toward the goal located on the right hand side. On the way to the goal, some of the robots detect a triangular obstacle that forces the swarm split into two groups from 7 sec (Fig. 11-(c)). The rest of the robots that could not identify the obstacle just follow their neighbors moving ahead. After being split into two groups at 14 sec (Fig. 11-(d)), each group maintains their local geometric configuration while navigating. At 18 sec (Fig. 11-(e)), some robots happen to enter a dead-end passageway. After they find themselves trapped, they attempt to escape from the passageway by just merging themselves into a neighboring group from 22 sec to 32 sec (from Figs. 11-(f)) to (k)). After 32 sec (Fig. 11-(k)), simulation result shows that two groups merge again completely. At 38 sec (Fig. 11-(l)), the robots successfully pass through the obstacles.

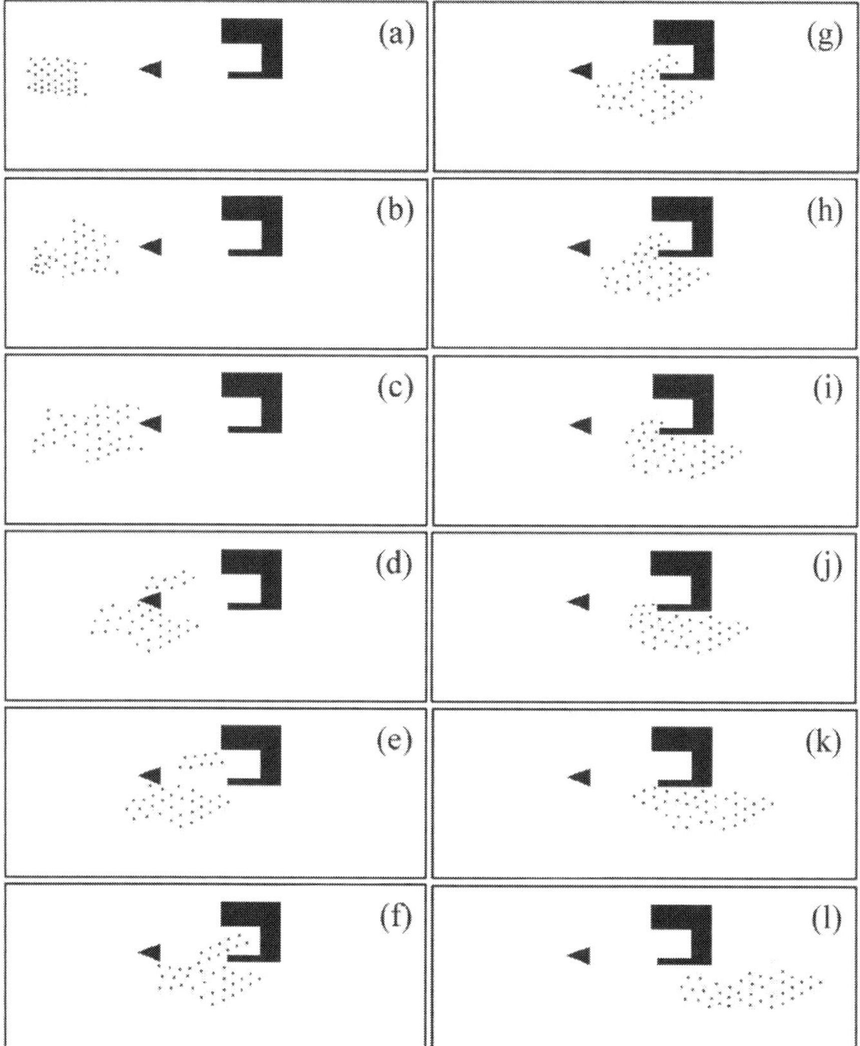

Fig. 11. Simulation results of adaptive flocking toward a stationary goal ((a)0 sec,(b)4 sec, (c)7 sec,(d)14 sec,(e)18 sec,(f)22 sec,(g)23 sec,(h)24 sec,(i)28 sec,(j)29 sec,(k)32 sec,(l)38sec)

Fig. 12 shows the trajectories of individual robots in Fig. 11. We could confirm that the swarm was split into two groups due to the triangular obstacle located at coordinates $(0,0)$. If we take a close look at Figs. 11-(f) through (j) (from 22 sec to 29 sec), the trapped ones escaped from the dead-end passageway located at coordinates $(x, 200)$. More important, after passing through the obstacles, all robots position themselves from each other at the desired interval d_u.

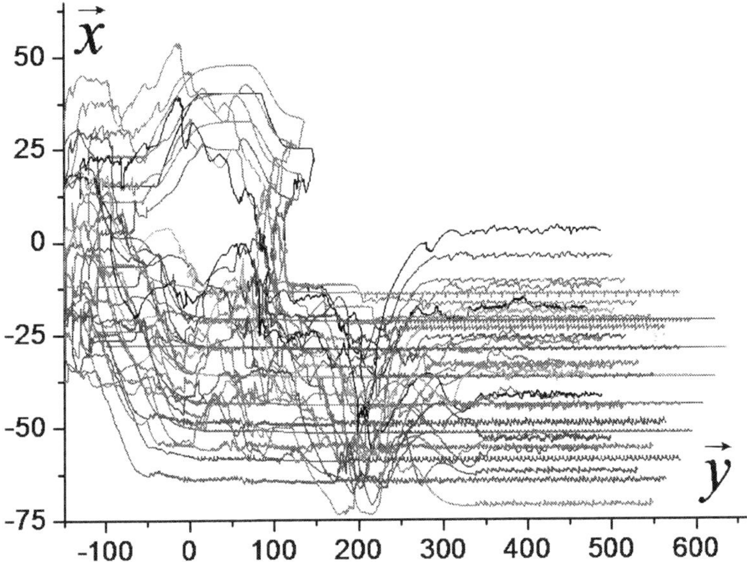

Fig. 12. Robot trajectory results for the simulation in Fig.11

Next, the proposed adaptive navigation is evaluated in a more complicated environmental condition as presented in Fig. 13. On the way to the goal, some of the robots detect a rectangular obstacle that forces the swarm split into two groups in Fig. 13-(b). After passing through the obstacle in Fig. 13-(d), the lower group encounters another obstacle in Fig. 13-(e), and split again into two smaller groups in Fig. 13-(g). Although several robots are trapped in a dead-end passageway, their local motions can enable them to escape from the dead-end passageway in Fig. 13-(i). This self-escape capability is expected to be usefully exploited for autonomous search and exploration tasks in disaster areas where robots have to remain connected to their *ad hoc* network. Finally, for a comparison of the adaptive navigation characteristics, three kinds of simulations are performed as shown in Figs. 14 through 16. All the simulation conditions are kept the same such as *du*, the number of robots, and initial distribution. Fig. 14 shows the behavior of mobile robot swarms without the partition and escape functions. Here, a considerable number of robots are trapped in the dead-end passageway and other robots pass through an opening between the obstacle and the passageway by chance. As compared with Fig. 14, Fig. 15 shows more robots pass through the obstacles using the partition function. However, a certain number of robots remain trapped in the dead-end passageway because they have no self-escape function. Fig.

16 shows that all robots successfully pass through the obstacles using the proposed adaptive navigation scheme. It is evident that the partition and escape functions will provide swarms of robots with a simple yet efficient navigation method. In particular, self-escape is one of the most essential capabilities to complete tasks in obstacle-cluttered environments that require a sufficient number of simple robots.

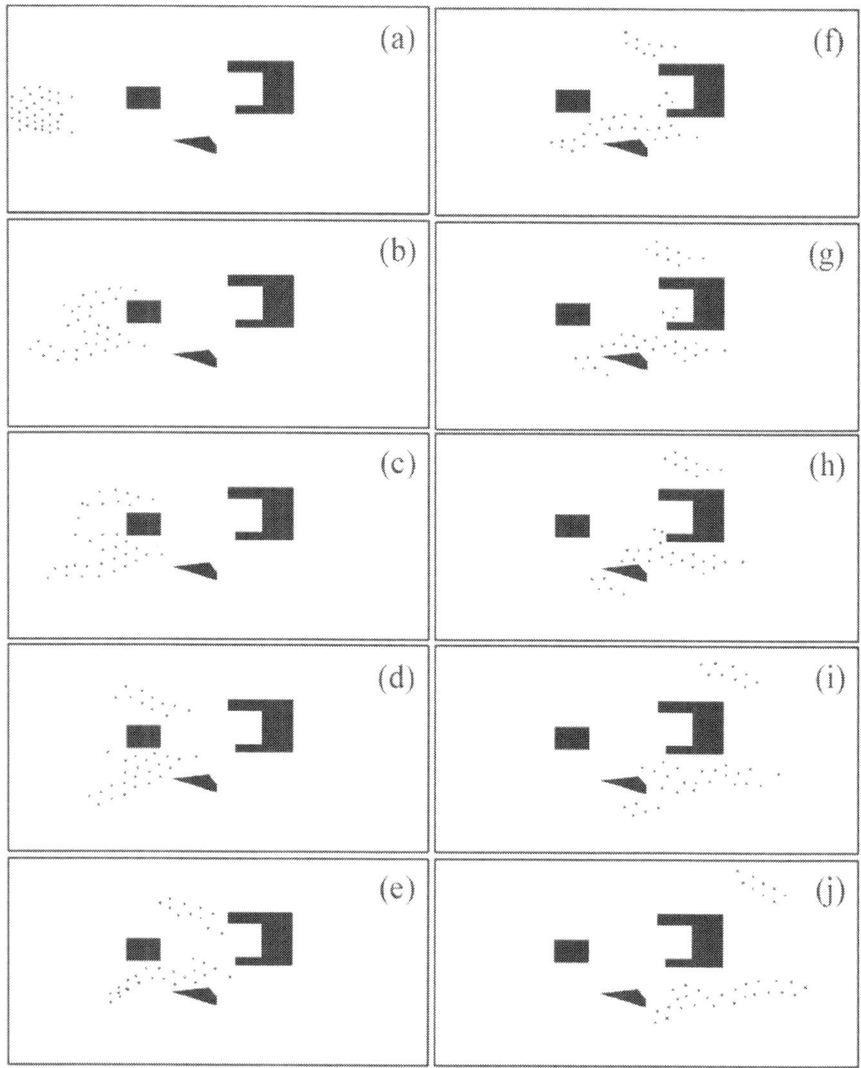

Fig. 13. Simulation results of adaptive flocking toward a stationary goal ((a)0 sec,(b)8 sec, (c)10 sec,(d)14 sec,(e)18 sec,(f)22 sec,(g)25 sec,(h)27 sec,(i)31 sec,(j)36)

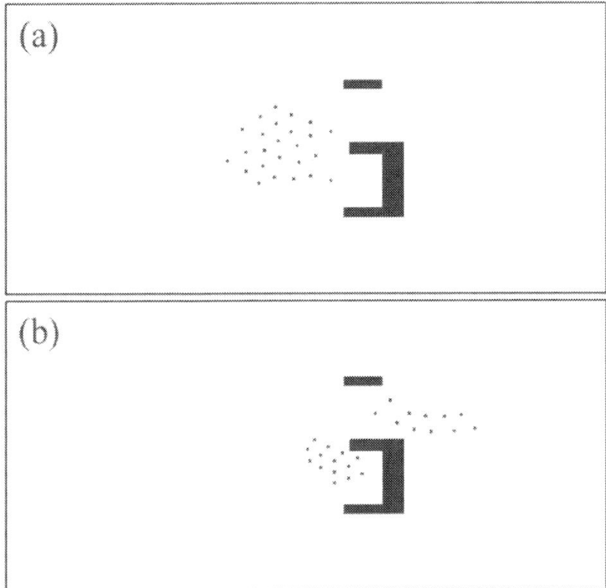

Fig. 14. Simulation results for flocking without partition and escape functions

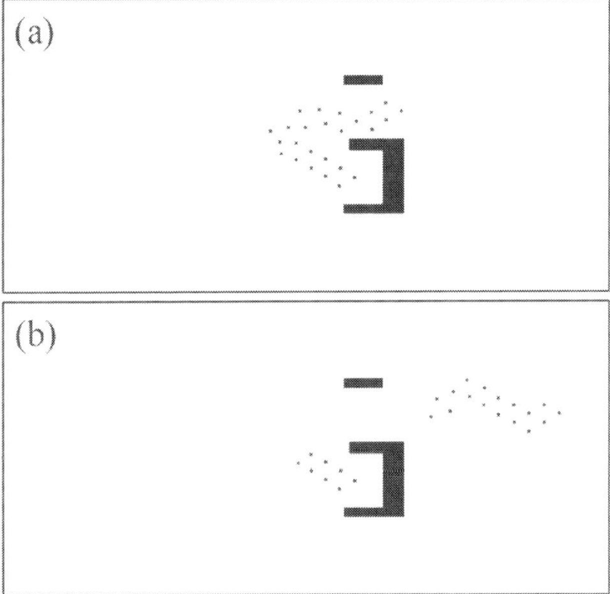

Fig. 15. Simulation results for flocking with only partition function

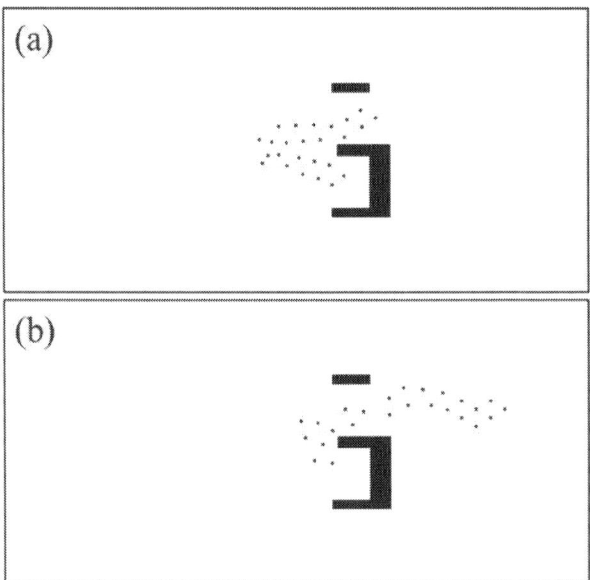

Fig. 16. Simulation results for flocking with the partition and escape functions

7. Conclusions

This paper was devoted to developing a new and general coordinated adaptive navigation scheme for large-scale mobile robot swarms adapting to geographically constrained environments. Our distributed solution approach was built on the following assumptions: anonymity, disagreement on common coordinate systems, no pre-selected leader, and no direct communication. The proposed adaptive navigation was largely composed of four functions, commonly relying on dynamic neighbor selection and local interaction. When each robot found itself what situation it was in, individual appropriate ranges for neighbor selection were defined within its limited sensing boundary and the robots properly selected their neighbors in the limited range. Through local interactions with the neighbors, each robot could maintain a uniform distance to its neighbors, and adapt their direction of heading and geometric shape. More specifically, under the proposed adaptive navigation, a group of robots could be trapped in a dead-end passage, but they merge with an adjacent group to emergently escape from the dead-end passage. Furthermore, we verified the effectiveness of the proposed strategy using our in-house simulator. The simulation results clearly demonstrated that the proposed algorithm is a simple yet robust approach to autonomous navigation of robot swarms in highly-cluttered environments. Since our algorithm is local and completely scalable to any size, it is easily implementable on a wide variety of resource-constrained mobile robots and platforms. Our adaptive navigation control for mobile robot swarms is expected to be used in many applications ranging from examination and assessment of hazardous environments to domestic applications.

8. References

Balch, T. & Hybinette, M. (2000). Social potentials for scalable multi-robot formations, *Proc. IEEE Int. Conf. Robotics and Automation*, pp. 73-80, IEEE

Correll, N., Bachrach, J., Vickery, D., & Rus, D. (2009). Ad-hoc wireless network coverage with networked robots that cannot localize, *Proc. IEEE Int. Conf. Robotics and Automation*, pp. 3878 - 3885, IEEE

Esposito, J. M. & Dunbar, T. W. (2006). Maintaining wireless connectivity constraints for swarms in the presence of obstacles, *Proc. IEEE Int. Conf. Robotics and Automation*, pp. 946-951, IEEE

Folino, G. & Spezzano, G. (2002). An adaptive flocking algorithm for spatial clustering, In: *Parallel Problem Solving from Nature* (LNCS), Yao, X., Burke, E., Lozano, J. A., Smith, J., Merelo-Guervos, J. J., Bullinaria, J. A., Rowe, J., Tino, P., Kaban, A., & Schwefel, H.-P. (Ed.), Vol. 2439, 924-933, Springer Berlin, ISBN: 978-3-540-23092-2

Fowler, T. (2001). Mesh networks for broadband access, IEE Review, Vol. 47, No. 1, 17-22

Gu, D. & Hu, H. (2010). Distributed minmax filter for tracking and flocking, *Proc. IEEE/RSJ Int. Conf. Intelligent Robots and Systems*, pp. 3562-3567, IEEE

Ikemoto, Y., Hasegawa, Y., Fukuda, T., & Matsuda, K. (2005). Graduated spatial pattern formation of robot group, *Information Science*, Vol. 171, No. 4, 431-445

Lam, M. & Liu, Y. (2006). ISOGIRD: an efficient algorithm for coverage enhancement in mobile sensor networks, *Proc. IEEE/RSJ Int. Conf. Intelligent Robots and Systems*, pp. 1458-1463, IEEE

Lee, G. & Chong, N. Y. (2009). A geometric approach to deploying robot swarms, *Annals of Mathematics and Artificial Intelligence*, Vol. 52, No. 2 – 4, 257-280

Lee, G. & Chong, N. Y. (2009-b). Decentralized formation control for small-scale robot teams with anonymity, *Mechatronics*, Vol. 19, No. 1, 85-105

Lee, G. & Chong, N. Y. (2008). Adaptive flocking of robot swarms: algorithms and properties, *IEICE Trans. Communications*, Vol. E91 – B, No. 9, 2848-2855

Lyengar, R., Kar, K., & Banerjee, S. (2005). Low-coordination topologies for redundancy in sensor networks, *Proc. 3rd Acm Int. Sym. Mobile Ad Hoc Networking and Computing*, pp. 332-342, ACM

Nembrini, J., Winfield, A., & Melhuish, C. (2002). Minimalist coherent swarming of wireless networked autonomous mobile robots, *Proc. 7th Int. Conf. Simulation of Adaptive Behavior*, pp. 373-382, IEEE

Olfati-Saber, R. (2006). Flocking for mult-agnet dynamic systems: algorithms and theory, *IEEE Trans. Automatic Control*, Vol. 51, No. 3, 401-420

Ogren, P. & Leonard, N. E. (2005). A convergent dynamic window approach to obstacle avoidance, *IEEE Trans. Robotics and Automation*, Vol. 21, No. 2, 188-195

Stocker, C. W. (1987). Flocks, herds, and schools: a distributed behavioral model, *Computer Graphics*, Vol. 21, No. 4, 25-34

Sahin, E. (2005). Swarm robotics: from sources of inspiration to domains of application, In: *Swarm Robotics* (LNCS), Sahin, E & Spears, W. M., (Ed.), Vol. 3342, 10-20, Springer Berlin, ISBN: 978-3-540-24296-3

Shucker, B., Murphey, T. D., & Bennett, J. K. (2008). Convergence-preserving switching for topology-dependent decentralized systems, *IEEE Trans. Robotics*, Vol. 24, No. 6, 1405-1415

Slotine, J. E. & Li,W. (1991). Applied nonlinear control, Prentice-Hall, ISBN: 0-13-040890-5

Spears, D., Kerr, W., & Spears, W. M. (2006). Physics-based robot swarms for coverage problems, *Int. Jour.Intelligent Control and Systems*, Vol. 11, No. 3, 124-140

Spears, W. M., Spears, D., Hamann, J., & Heil, R. (2004). Distributed, physics-based control of swarms of vehicles, *Autonomous Robots*, Vol. 17, No. 2 – 3, 137-162

Stocker, S. (1999). Models for tuna school formation, *Mathematical Biosciences*, Vol. 156, No. 1–2, 167-190

Wilson, E. O. (1976). Sociobiology: the new synthesis, Harvard University Press, ISBN: 0-674-00089-7

Yicka, J., Mukherjeea, B., & Ghosal, D. (2008). Wireless sensor network survey, *Computer Networks*, Vol. 52, No. 12, 2292-2330

Zarzhitsky, D., Spears, D., & Spears, W. M. (2005). Distributed robotics approach to chemical plume tracing, *Proc. IEEE/RSJ Int. Conf. Intelligent Robots and Systems*, pp. 4034-4039, IEEE

6

Hybrid Approach for Global Path Selection & Dynamic Obstacle Avoidance for Mobile Robot Navigation

D. Tamilselvi, S. Mercy Shalinie, M. Hariharasudan and G. Kiruba
Department of Computer Science and Engineering,
Thiagarajar College of Engineering, Madurai, TamilNadu, South India,
India

1. Introduction

In Robotics, path planning has been an area gaining a major thrust and is being intensively researched nowadays. This planning depends on the environmental conditions they have to operate on. Unlike industrial robots, service robots have to operate in unpredictable and unstructured environments. Such robots are constantly faced with new situations for which there are no pre programmed motions. Thus, these robots have to plan their own motions. Path planning for service robots are much more difficult due to several reasons. First, the planning has to be sensor-based, implying incomplete and inaccurate world models. Second, the real time constraints, provides only limited resources for planning. Third, due to incomplete models of the environment, planning could involve secondary objectives, with the goal to reduce the uncertainty about the environment. Navigation for mobile robots is closely related to sensor-based path planning in 2D, and can be considered as a mature area of research.

Mobile robots navigation in dynamic environments represents still a challenge for real world applications. The robot should be able to reach its goal position, navigating safely amongst, people or vehicles in motion, facing the implicit uncertainty of the surrounding world. Because of the need for highly responsive algorithms, prior research on dynamic planning has focused on re-using information from previous queries across a series of planning iterations. The dynamic path-planning problem consists in finding a suitable plan for each new configuration of the environment by re computing a collision free path using the new information available at each time step.

The problem of collision detection or contact determination between two or more objects is fundamental to computer animation, physical based modeling, molecular modeling, computer simulated environments (e.g. virtual environments) and robot motion planning. In robotics, an essential component of robot motion planning and collision avoidance is a geometric reasoning system which can detect potential contacts and determine the exact collision points between the robot and the obstacles in the workspace.

2. Mobile robot indoor environment

Indoor Environment Navigation is the kind of navigation restricted to indoor arenas. Here the environment is generally well structured and map of the part from the robot to the target is known. Mapping plays a vital role for Mobile Robot Navigation. Mapping the Mobile Robot environment representation is the active research in AI Field for the last two decades for machine intelligence device real time applications in various fields. Creating the spatial model with fine grid cells for physical indoor environment considering the geometric properties is the additional feature compared with the topological mapping. Grid mapping supports the conceptual motion planning for mobile robot navigation and extend the simulation into real time environments.

The robot and obstacle geometry is described in a 2D or 3D *workspace*, while the motion is represented as a path in (possibly higher-dimensional) configuration space. A configuration describes the pose of the robot, and the configuration space C is the set of all possible configurations. If the robot is a single point (zero-sized) translating in a 2-dimensional plane (the workspace), C is a plane, and a configuration can be represented using two parameters (x, y). The indoor physical environment is represented as two dimensional arrays of cells. Each cell of the map contains two kinds of configuration space depending upon the status of obstacles known as free space and obstacle space.

The term 'path planning' usually refers to the creation of an overall motion plan from a start to a goal location. Most path planners create a path plan in C-space and then use obstacle avoidance to modify this plan as needed. The idea of using C-space for motion planning was first introduced by Lozano-Perez and Wesley [1979]. The idea for motion planning in C-space is to 'grow' C-space obstacles from physical obstacles while shrinking the mobile robot down to a single point. In the cell decomposition approach to motion planning, the free C-space in the robot environment is decomposed into disjoint cells which have interiors where planning is simple. The planning process then consists of locating the cells in which the start and goal configurations are and then finding a path between these cells using adjacency relationships between the cells.

There are two types of cell decomposition, exact and approximate. In exact cell decomposition, the union of all the cells corresponds exactly to the free C-space. Therefore, if a path exists this approach will find it. However, all cells must be computed analytically, which quickly becomes difficult and time consuming for robots with many DOF. Schwartz and Sharir [1983] use exact cell decomposition to study the 'piano mover's' problem. Approximate cell decomposition avoids the difficulty of analytically computing cells by decomposing the free C-space into many simple cells (often squares or cubes). In addition to easing the decomposition process, computing the adjacency relationships is simplified due to the sameness of all cells. Lozano-Perez used approximate cell decomposition in developing a resolution complete planner for arbitrary, n-DOF manipulators [1987].

3. DT Algorithm for global path planning

The DT algorithm was devised by Rosenfield and Pfaltz as a tool to study the shape of objects in 2D images by propagating distance in tessellated space from the boundaries of shapes into their centers. Various properties of shape can be extracted from the resultant transform and it can be shown that the skeletons of local maxima can be used to grow back the original shapes without information loss. Jarvis discovered that, by turning the algorithm 'inside out' to propagate distance from goals in the free space that includes the shapes interpreted as obstacles and by repeating a raster order and inverse raster order scan used in the algorithm until no further change takes place, a space filling transform with direct path planning application is resulted. Multiple starting points, multiple goals and multidimensional space versions are easily devised. When the DT completes filling the free space with distance markers, the goal is achieved from any starting point through a steepest descent trajectory.

Using distance transforms for planning paths for mobile robot applications was first reported by R.A. Jarvis and J.C. Byrne. This approach considered the task of path planning to find paths from the goal location back to the start location. The path planner propagates a distance wave front through all free space grid cells in the environment from the goal cell. The distance wave front flows around obstacles and eventually through all free space in the environment. For any starting point within the environment representing the initial position of the mobile robot, the shortest path to the goal is traced by walking down hill via the steepest descent path. If there is no downhill path, and the start cell is on a plateau then it can be concluded that no path exists from the start cell to the goal cell i.e. the goal is unreachable. Global path planner finds the optimized path in the occupancy grid based environment.

DT (Distance Transform) method proved to be one of the best global path selection and effective way of path planning in the static known environment. DT methodology is versatile and can be used for path planning alone or integration of path planning with obstacle avoidance. To predict the dynamic obstacles in the environment, avoid collision with the mobile robot, GJK (Gilbert–Johnson–Keerthi) distance algorithm supports for collision avoidance of obstacles in the dynamic environment combined with DT Algorithm.

4. Collision Detection and Avoidance in mobile robots – an algorithmic approach

Collision Detection and Avoidance plays a vital role in mobile robot applications. Algorithms are used to achieve this. This Collision Detection and Avoidance is also employed in various other applications like simulated computer games, unmanned vehicle guidance in military based applications, etc. In these applications the Collision detection strategy is achieved by checking whether the objects overlap in space or if their boundaries intersect each other during their movement.

The obstacle avoidance problem for robotics can be divided into three major areas. These are mapping the world, determining distances between manipulators and other objects in the world, and deciding how to move a given manipulator such that it best avoids contact with other objects in the world. Unless distances are determined directly from the physical world using range-finding hardware, they are calculated from the world model that is stored during the world mapping process. These calculations are largely based on the types of objects that are used to model the world. One of the most popular ways of modelling the world is to use polyhedral [Canny, 1988] [Gilbert, Johnson, and Keerthi, 1988] [Lin and Canny, 1991] [Mirtich, 1997]. Models built using polyhedral are capable of providing nearly exact models of the world. Unlike many other distance algorithms, it does not require the geometry data to be stored in any specific format, but instead relies solely on a support mapping function and using the result in its next iteration. Algorithm stability, speed and small storage makes GJK suitable for real time collision detection.(eg., Physics Engine for Video Games – sony play stations).

GJK supports mappings for reading the geometry of an object. A support mapping fully describes the geometry of a convex object and can be viewed as an implicit representation of the object. The class of objects recursively constructed are

- Convex primitives

- Polytopes (line segments, triangles, boxes and other convex polyhedra)
- Quadrics (spheres, cones and cylinders)
- Images of convex objects under affine transformation
- Minkowski sums of two convex objects
- Convex hulls of a collection of convex objects
- Convex Polyhedra and Collision Detection

Convex polyhedra have been studied extensively in the context of the minimum distance problem. The reason is that the minimum distance problem in this case can be cast as a linear programming problem, allowing us to use well-known results from convex optimization. The algorithms for convex polyhedra fall into two main categories: simplex-based and feature-based. The simplex-based algorithms treat the polyhedron as the convex hull of a point set and perform operations on simplexes defined by subsets of these points. Feature-based algorithms, on the other hand, treat the polyhedron as a set of features, where the different features are the vertices, edges and faces of the polyhedron.

4.1 GJK (gilebert-Johnson-Keerthi) algorithm – simplex based

One of the most well-known simplex-based algorithms is the Gilbert- Johnson-Keerthi (GJK) algorithm. Conceptually, the GJK algorithm works with the Minkowski difference of the two convex polyhedra. The Minkowski difference is also a convex polyhedron and the minimum distance problem is reduced to find the point in that polyhedron that is closest to the origin; if the polyhedron includes the origin, then the two polyhedra intersect. However, forming the Minkowski difference explicitly would be a costly approach. Instead GJK work iteratively with small subsets, simplexes, of the Minkowski difference that quickly converge to a subset that contains the point closest to the origin. For problems involving continuous motion, the temporal coherence between two time instants can be exploited by initializing the algorithm with the final simplex from the previous distance computation.

Unlike many other distance algorithms, it does not require the geometry data to be stored in any specific format, but instead relies solely on a support mapping function and using the result in its next iteration. Relying on the support mapping function to read the geometry of the objects gives this algorithm great advantage, because every enhancement on the support mapping function leads to enhancement of the GJK algorithm.

5. Proposed methodology

Fig.1. shows the hybrid method proposed for the Global Path Selection and Dynamic Obstacle Avoidance. Path planning was based on the distance criteria for the simulation, and sensor values mapping for the FIRE BIRD V mobile robot, that was used for the real time study.

Distance Transform (DT) was generated through free space from the goal location using a cost function [17]. Path transform for the point c is calculated with the formula.1

$$\text{Cost function} = \min\left[\text{length}(p) + \sum_{c_i \in P} \alpha \, \text{obstacle}(c_i)\right] \tag{1}$$

Where P is the set of all possible paths from the point c to the goal, and $p \in P$ i.e. a single path to the goal. The function *length(p)* returns the Euclidean distance between the source and the goal through the path p. The function *obstacle(c)* is a cost function generated using the values of the obstacle transform. It represents the degree of discomfort the nearest obstacle exerts on a point c. The weight α is a constant ≥ 0 which determines how strongly the path transform will avoid obstacles. Local cost functions return the instantaneous cost for traversing a particular patch. Global Cost functions provide the estimated cost to reach a goal from a particular location.

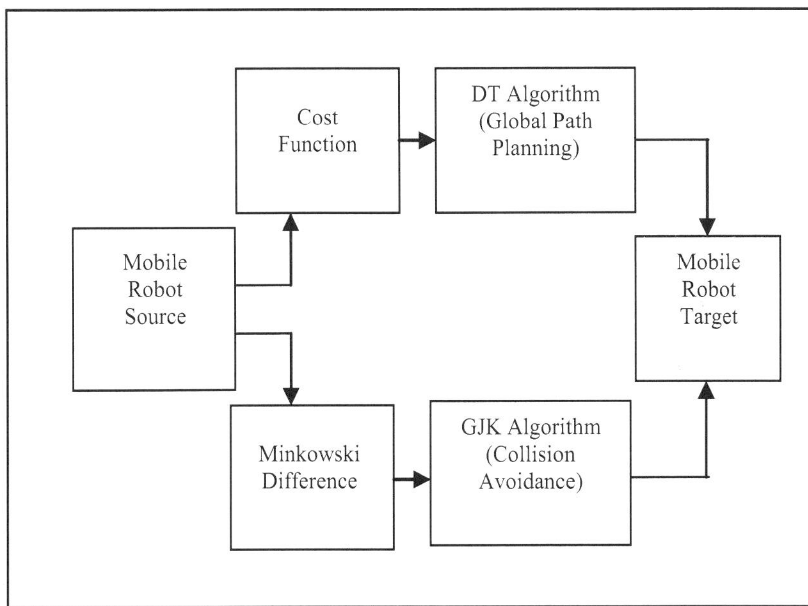

Fig. 1. Hybrid Method for Global Path Selection & Dynamic Obstacle Avoidance

GJK algorithm, involves the computationally intensive step of computing the supporting function of the set of vertices, is a set-theoretic approach in essence. Since in applications the distance between two objects needs to be updated from time to time, every possible enhancement of distance computation procedure can speed up the repetitive process as the time goes on[18].GJK key concept is instead of computing the minimum distance between A and B, the minimum distance between A-B and the origin is computed. This algorithm uses the fact that the shortest distance between two convex polygons is the shortest distance between their Minkowski Difference and the origin. If the Minkowski Difference encompasses the origin then the two objects intersect. Computing the collision translation of two convex bodies can be reduced to computing collision translations of pairs of planar sections and minimizing a bivariate convex function.

So this approach employs the concept of DT algorithm which returns the least Euclidean distant path p to the goal, then triggers the GJK algorithm to anticipate the possibility of a local collision through that path, for all the possible moves of the obstacle in the next instant. Accordingly the model employs the path which provides a least distant point which returns a 0 possibility of collision with the obstacle.

5.1 Flow chart representation for the proposed methodology

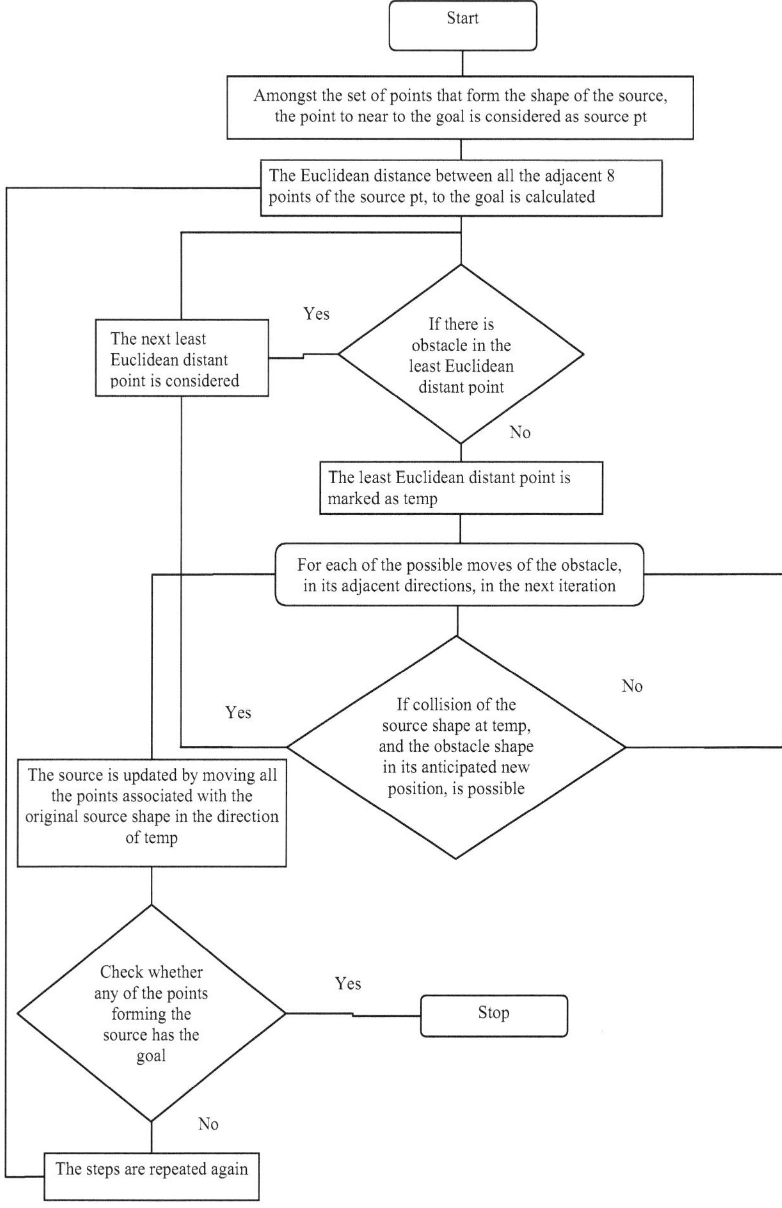

Fig. 2. Flowchart for the Proposed Method

The assumptions made in the simulation and real time environment are, the source and obstacle moves with the same speed of, one grid point per iteration. One dynamic obstacle is taken into consideration. Mobile Robot shape is assumed as triangle and square. The goal is fixed with green. Robot scans the 8 adjacent directions in the grid environment, to find the next adjacent position that promises the minimum Euclidean distance to the goal. From the calculated new position, it checks for all possible next iteration-movements of the obstacle in all its 8 adjacent directions and checks if collision would occur using GJK algorithm.

If not, the mobile robot moves to the calculated new position. If the mobile robot predicts the collision possibility, it repeats the above steps. GJK supports for the dynamic obstacle avoidance by calculating the Minkowski difference between the mobile robot and obstacle for every step movement in the grid environment. The simplex formula calculates the next step co ordinate values, and the zero value predicts the collision occurrences. Repeating the calculation of each Minkowski difference supports for prediction of collision and avoidance in the dynamic environment. The following example briefs about the calculation of distance values for dynamic obstacle prediction and avoidance.

Eg. Calulation for Minkowski difference for the Triangle Obstacle to predict and avoid the collision was given below.

Lets consider the source to be of a triangle shape at the coordinates (1,2), (0,3), (2,3) and the obstacle which is here taken as a quadrilateral, initially occupying the coordinates (3,2), (4,1), (3,4), (5,3). The goal is set at the point (8,3). Now the DT algorithm returns the coordinates (2,2), (3,3) and (1,3) as the new set of points for the source, returning a minimum Euclidean distance to the goal. Now the GJK algorithm detects that if the obstacle moves to the position (2,2), (3,1), (4,3), (2,4) then the new set of minkowski points would be

$$(0,0), (-1,1), (-2.-1), (0,-2), (1,1), (0,-2), (-1,0), (1,-1), (-1,1), (-2,-2), (-3,0), (-1,-1)$$

The shape that encloses these points would also enclose the origin. So a collision is possible with the obstacle if the source moves to that point. So it takes the next least Euclidean distant point and proceeds on till it finds a new position for the source which is devoid of any collision. If there is a possibility of collision in all the possible positions, then the source remains fixed to its current position for the next iteration also.

6. Simulation results

Grid environment (size 10x10) was created with the triangle shaped mobile robot and convex shaped obstacle. The dynamic obstacle movements were shown in Fig.3. Top rightmost green colour indicates the goal position. Mobile robot predicts movement using GJK and reaches the goal with DT.

The time taken for the mobile robot to reach the target was 0.32 seconds for Fig.3, which shows GJK predicts the obstacle by considering only the neighboring coordinates values and moves in the proposed environment. DT calculates the goal position in prior and checks for the optimal distance value to reach the goal.

Fig.4 shows the square shaped mobile robot with the same convex obstacle. Due to the dynamic nature of obstacle, mobile robot moving near the obstacle is not possible often. In this case, the time taken for the mobile robot to reach the goal is 0.29 seconds.

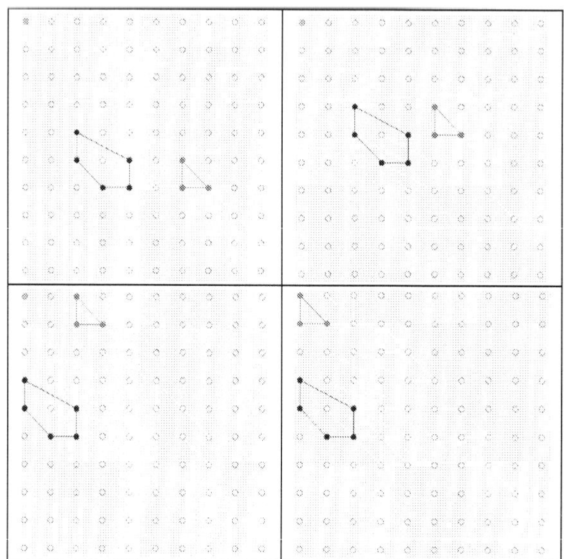

Fig. 3. Dynamic Obstacle Avoidance – Simulation Results

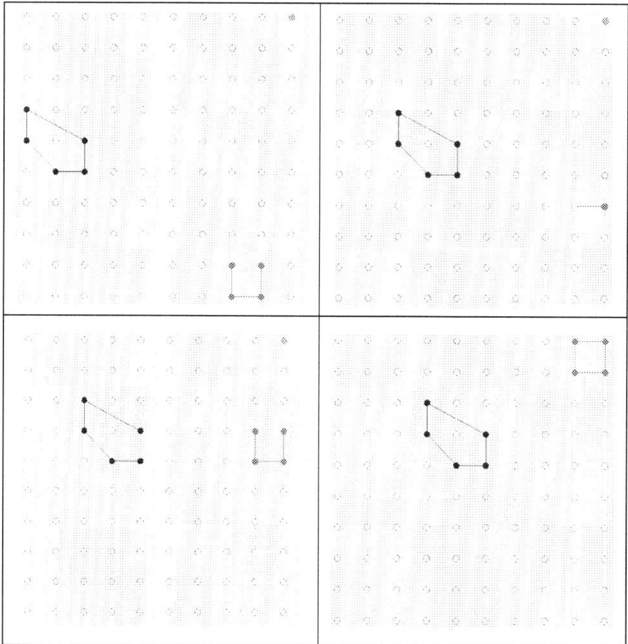

Fig. 4. Dynamic Obstacle Avoidance – Simulation Results

7. Real time results

The GJK was implemented in real time with Fire Bird V mobile robot. FIRE BIRD V robot has two DC geared motors for the locomotion. The robot has a top speed of 24cm/second. These motors are arranged in differential drive configuration. I.E. motors can move independently of each other. Front castor wheel provides support at the front side of the robot. Using this configuration, the robot can turn with zero turning radius by rotating one wheel in clockwise direction and other in counterclockwise direction. Position encoder discs are mounted on both the motor's axle to give a position feedback to the microcontroller.Fig.5 shows the Fire Bird V mobile robot with the IR Sensors to detect obstacles in all sides.

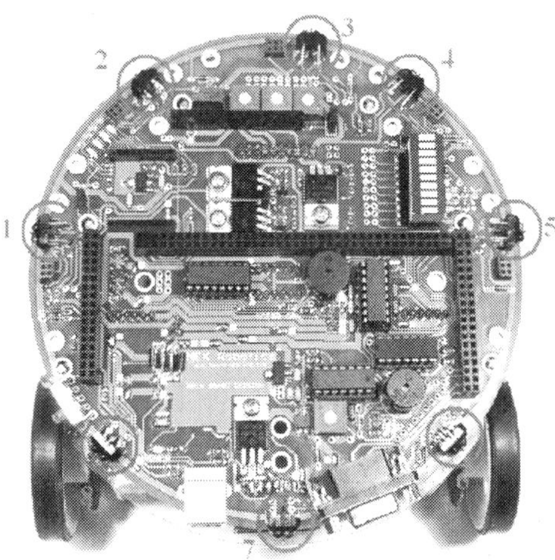

Fig. 5. Eight IR Sensors in Fire Bird V Mobile Robot

Instead of coordinates, mapping was created in real time with sensors. As GJK finds the distance between the objects using Minkowski Difference, we use the IR Range and IR Proximity Sensors in conjunction to detect the distance from the approaching object. The threshold values of each sensor are calculated already such that a collision does not occur. So if the threshold value is reached, it is an indication that a collision is about to happen in the near future. Sensor values are used for real time obstacle avoidance.

The distance mapping was created with sensor mapping values. Sharp IR range sensors consists of 2 parts - narrow IR beam for illumination and CCD array, which uses triangulation to measure the distance from any obstacle. A small linear CCD array is used for angle measurement. The IR beam generates light. The light hits the obstacle and reflects back to the linear CCD array. Depending on the distance from the obstacle, angle of the reflected light varies. This angle is measured using the CCD array to estimate distance from the obstacle. When away from obstacles, the sensor values are smaller. An obstacle can be a wall, any moving object. Near an obstacle or vice-versa, the sensor values increases. Table 1 shows the mapping of IR sensor values observed from the Fire Bird V Mobile Robot for obstacle prediction and avoidance.

Obstacle Position	IR1	IR2	IR3	IR4	IR5	IR6	IR7	IR8
No obstacle along any side	233	235	242	242	245	252	252	253
Obstacle at front	233	233	229	241	244	251	252	253
Obstacle at front and left	228	232	229	240	244	249	250	252
Obstacle at front and right	231	232	229	241	242	249	250	251
Obstacle at left only	229	235	240	241	245	251	252	253
Obstacle at right only	232	232	236	240	239	249	251	250
Obstacle at front, left and right	225	233	231	240	239	249	251	250
Obstacle at back	232	232	236	242	245	250	246	252

Table 1. Sensor Mapping Values for the Indoor Real Time Environment (80 cm x 75 cm)

The difference is distance values are mapped with IR sensor values and it predicts the behavior of mobile robot to avoid collision with obstacle. Rectangle and convex shapes obstacles were included in the dynamic environment. GJK predicts obstacle movement in the environment and plans the mobile robot for path selection. DT supports for the mobile robot to reach the target position. The sensor prediction for various obstacle position in real time and avoidance was described below.

- Obstacle at Front
  Initially when the robot is kept in open space with no obstacles in range, all the IR sensor values are high. It is then instructed to move forward, whereby it might sense obstacles at the front using sensor IR3. The threshold value for IR3 is 229 i.e. by GJK algorithm, the shortest possible distance that the robot can traverse forward is until IR3 value reaches 229. After this value has been reached, the robot has to take a turn to left or right to avoid the obstacle.

- Obstacle at two sides
  Consider the robot meets a corner i.e. obstacles at front and left (or) at front and right. Let's take the first case: obstacle at front and left. In this case, sensor values of IR3 and IR1 reduces on approaching the obstacle. These values are checked whether they meet the combinational threshold. If so, the robot is made to turn towards the free side, here it is the right side. The same is followed for the latter case where sensors IR3 and IR5 are taken into account. Here the robot makes a turn towards the left on meeting the threshold.
  The threshold values are as below:
  IR1: 228   IR3: 229
  IR5: 242   IR3: 229

- Obstacle at back
  This special case is taken into consideration only in a dynamic environment because in a static environment, any objects at the back do not account as obstacles. Here IR6, IR7, and IR8 help in detecting the obstacles. For activating these sensors, master-slave (microcontrollers) communication needs to be established. When an obstacle is sensed at the back, the robot needs to move forward with a greater velocity to avoid collision. The threshold value for IR7: 246.

White line sensors with the Fire Bird V mobile robot finds the target, localize itself and stop the navigation. White line sensors are used for detecting white line on the ground surface.

White line sensor consists of a highly directional phototransistor for line sensing and red LED for illumination.

Fig. 6 & Fig.7 shows Fire Bird V mobile robot path selection results with convex shape obstacles in the proposed real time environment.

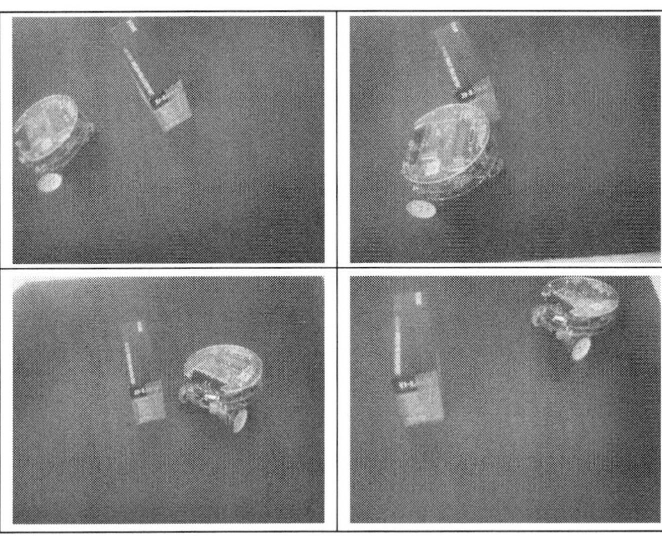

Fig. 6. Fire Bird V Mobile Robot Real Time Navigation Results

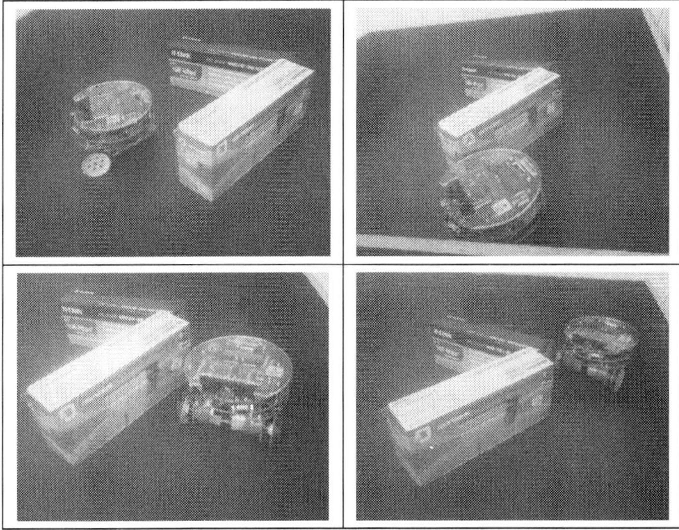

Fig. 7. Fire Bird V Mobile Robot Real Time Navigation Results

8. Conclusion

Proposed method builds the test bed with Fire Bird V Mobile Robot for future development of an intelligent wheelchair for elderly people assistance in the indoor environment. Real time results proves, DT computes the shortest path selection for the elderly people and movement of people/any object was predicted in prior by DT and collision avoidance with objects was effectively handled by GJK Algorithm. The proposed framework in real time with Fire Bird V Mobile Robot control program is easily scalable and portable for any indoor environment with various shapes of obstacles it encounters during navigation. Proposed method was tested successfully with various shapes of dynamic obstacles.

GJK Algorithm for computing the distance between objects shows the improved performance in simulation and real time results. The algorithm fits well especially for the collision detection of objects modelled with various types of geometric primitives such as convex obstacles. Unlike many other distance algorithms, it does not require the geometry data to be stored in any specific format, but instead relies solely on a support mapping function and using the result in its next iteration. Relying on the support mapping function to read the geometry of the objects gives this algorithm great advantage. The algorithm's stability, speed, and small storage footprint make it popular for real time collision detection.

9. Acknowledgement

This work is part of Research grant sponsored by Computer Society of India , Project titled" Intelligent Algorithmic Approach for Mobile Robot Navigation in an Indoor Environment" , File No. 1-14/2010-03 dated 29.03.2010.

10. References

[1] F. Belkhouche, B. Belkhouche, Kinematics-Based Characterization of the Collision Course. *International Journal of Robotics and Automation*, Vol. 23, No. 2, pp 1-10, 2008

[2] J.P. Laumond S. Sekhavat F. Lamiraux, Guidelines in Nonholonomic Motion Planning for Mobile Robots, *Lectures Notes in Control and Information Sciences Springer*, pp 343-347, ISBN 3-540-76219-1, 1998.

[3] Marcelo Becker, Carolina Meirelles Dantas, Weber Perdigão Macedo, Obstalce Avoidance Procedure for Mobile Robots, *ABCM Symposium on Mechatronics*, Vol.2,pp.250-257, 2006

[4] Andrew Price, Artificially Intelligent Autonomous Aircraft Navigation System Using a DT on an FPGA. *NIOS II, Embedded Processor Design Contest*, Star Award Paper, pp 1-14, 2006

[5] Christor Ericson, The GJK Algorithm,"The GJK Algorithm" *31st International Conference on Computer Graphics and Interactive Techniques*, pp1-12, 2004

[6] Davor Jovanoski. The Gilbert Johnson Keerthi Algorithm, Department of Computer Science, Bachelor Seminar, University of Salzburg, Feburary 2008

[7] K. J. Kyriakopoulos ,G. N. Saridis, Distance estimation and collision prediction for on-line robotic motion planning, NASA Center of Intelligent Robotic Systems for Space Exploration (CIRSSE), Electrical, Computer and Systems Engineering, Dept., February 2003

[8] A.Zelinsky, Using Path Transforms to Guide the Search for Find path in 2D, *International Journal of Robotics Research*,Vol.13, No.4, pp 315-325, 1994

[9] Sardjono Trihatmo, R.A. Jarvis, Short-Safe Compromise Path for Mobile Robot Navigation in a dynamic environment, *International Journal of Intelligent Systems*, Vol.20, pp 523-539, 2005

[10] O.Hachour, Path planning of Autonomous Mobile robot, *International Journal of Systems Applications, Engineering & Development* , Issue 4, Volume 2, pp178 – 190, 2008

[11] Morten Strandberg, Robot Path Planning: An Object-Oriented Approach, Automatic Control, Department of Signals, Sensors and Systems, Royal Institute of Technology (KTH),Ph.D thesis, 2004

[12] Enrique J. Bernabeu, Josep Tornero, Masayoshi Tomizuka, Collision Prediction and Avoidance Amidst Moving Objects for Trajectory Planning Applications, *Proceedings of the 2001 IEEE International Conference on Robotics & Automation Seoul*, Korea, pp 3801-3806, 2001.

[13] Davor Jovanoski, The Gilbert – Johnson – Keerthi (GJK) Algorithm, Department of Computer Science, University of Salzburg, 2008

[14] Kaushik J, Vision Based Mobile Robot Navigation, Undergraduate Seminar Report, Department of Mechanical Engineering Indian Institute of Technology, Mumbai, 2007

[15] Troy Anthony Harden, Minimum Distance Influence Coefficients for Obstacle Avoidance in Manipulator Motion Planning, University of Texas, Ph.D Thesis, 2002

[16] Gino van den bergen, A Fast and Robust GJK Implementation for Collision Detection of Convex Objects, Department of Mathematics and Computing Science, Eindhoven University of Technology, Netherlands, 1999

[17] A. Zelinsky, R.A. Jarvis2, Byrne and S. Yuta, Planning Paths of Complete Coverage of an Unstructured Environment by a Mobile Robot, *Science Direct, Robotics and Autonomous Systems*, Vol,46, Issue 4, pp 195 – 204, 2004

[18] Jing-Sin Liu, Yuh-ren Chien, Shen-Po Shiang and Wan-Chi Lee ,Geometric Interpretation and Comparisons of Enhancements of GJK Algorithm for Computing Euclidean Distance Between Convex Polyhedra, Institute of Information Science, Academia Sinica, Taiwan, 2001

[19] Ray Jarvis, Distance Transform Based Visibility Measures for Covert Path Planning in known but Dynamic Environments, *International Conference on Autonomous Robots and Agents*, pp 396 – 400, 2004

[20] Sardjono Trihatmo, R.A. Jarvis, Short-Safe Compromise Path for Mobile Robot Navigation in a dynamic environment, *International Journal of Intelligent Systems*, Vol.20, pp 523-539, 2005

[21] Claudio Mirolo, Stefano Carpin, Enrico Pagello, Incremental Convex Minimization for Computing Collision Translations of Convex Polyhedra, *IEEE Transactions on Robotics*, Volume 23, Issue 3, pp 403 – 415, 2007

[22] Madhur Ambastha, Dídac Busquets, Ramon López de Màntaras,Carles Sierra, Evolving a Multiagent System for Landmark-Based Robot Navigation, *International Journal of Intelligent Systems*, Vol. 20, pp 523–539, 2005

[23] Stoytchev, A., Arkin, R., Incorporating Motivation in a Hybrid Robot Architecture, *Journal of Advanced Computational Intelligence and intelligent informatics* Vol.8,No.3, pp 100-105, 2004

[24] Jonas Buchli, Mobile Robots Moving Intelligence, *Advanced Robotic Systems* International and pro Literature Verlag, Germany, ISBN 3-86611-284-X, 2006

7

Navigation Among Humans

Mikael Svenstrup
Aalborg University
Denmark

1. Introduction

As robot are starting to emerge in human everyday environments, it becomes necessary to find ways, in which they can interact and engage seamlessly in the human environments. Open-ended human environments, such as pedestrian streets, shopping centres, hospital corridors, airports etc., are places where robots will start to emerge. Hence, being able to plan motion in these dynamic environments is an important skill for future generations of robots. To be accepted in our everyday human environments, the robots must be able to move naturally, and such that it is both safe, natural and comfortable for the humans in the environment.

Imagine a service robot driving around in an airport. The objective of the service robot is: to drive around among the people in the environment; identify people who need assistance; approach them in an appropriate way; interact with the person to help with the needs of the person. This could be showing the way to a gate, providing departure information, checking reservations, giving information about local transportation, etc. This chapter describes algorithms that handle the motion and navigation related problems of this scenario.

To enable robots with capabilities for safe and natural motion in human environments like in the above described scenario, there are a number of abilities that the robot must possess. First the robot must be able to sense and find the position of the people in the environment. Also, it is necessary to obtain information about orientation and velocity of each person. Then the robot must be able to find out if a person needs assistance, i.e. the robot needs to establish the intentions of the people. Knowing the motion state and the intention state of the person, this can be used to generate motion, which is adapted according to the person and the situation. But in a crowded human environment, it is not only necessary for the robot to be able to move safe and naturally around one person, but also able to navigate through the environment from one place to another. So in brief, the robot must be able to:

- estimate the pose and velocity of the people in the environment;
- estimate the intentions of the people;
- navigate and approach people appropriately according to the motion and intention state of the people;
- plan a safe and natural path through a densely populated human environment.

The overall system architecture is briefly presented in Section 3. Finding the position and orientation of people is done using a laser range finder based method, which is described in Section 4. For on-line estimation of human intentions a Case-Based Reasoning (CBR) approach is used to learn the intentions of people from previous experiences. The navigation around a person is done using an adaptive potential field, that adjusts according to the person's intentions. The CBR method for estimating human intentions and human-aware motion is described in Sections 5 and 6 respectively. In Section 7 the potential field is extended to include many people to enable motion in a crowded environment. Finally an adapted Rapidly-exploring Random Tree (RRT) algorithm is, in Section 8, used to plan a safe and comfortable trajectory. But first, relevant related work is described in the following section.

2. Related work

Detection and tracking of people, that is, estimation of the position and orientation (which combined is denoted pose) has been discussed in much research, for example in Jenkins et al. (2007); Sisbot et al. (2006). Several sensors have been used, including 2D and 3D vision (Dornaika & Raducanu, 2008; Munoz-Salinas et al., 2005), thermal tracking (Cielniak et al., 2005) or range scans (Fod et al., 2002; Kirby et al., 2007; Rodgers et al., 2006; Xavier et al., 2005). Laser scans are typically used for person detection, whereas the combination with cameras also produces pose estimates Feil-Seifer & Mataric (2005); Michalowski et al. (2006). Using face detection requires the person to always face the robot, and that person to be close enough to be able to obtain a sufficiently high resolution image of the face Kleinehagenbrock et al. (2002), limiting the use in environments where people are moving and turning frequently. The possibility of using 2D laser range scanners provides extra long range and lower computational complexity. The extra range enables the robot to detect the motion of people further away and thus have enough time to react to people moving at a higher speed.

Interpreting another person's interest in engaging in interaction is an important component of the human cognitive system and social intelligence, but it is such a complex sensory task that even humans sometimes have difficulties with it. CBR allows recalling and interpreting past experiences, as well as generating new cases to represent knowledge from new experiences. CBR has previously proven successful in solving spatio-temporal problems in robotics in Jurisica & Glasgow (1995); Likhachev & Arkin (2001); Ram et al. (1997), but not to estimate intentions of humans. Other methods, like Hidden Markov Models, have been used to learn to identify the behaviour of humans Kelley et al. (2008). Bayesian inference algorithms and Hidden Markov Models have also successfully been applied to modelling and for predicting spatial user information Govea (2007).

To approach a person in a way, that is perceived as natural and comfortable requires *human-aware navigation*. Human-aware navigation respects the person's social spaces as discussed in Althaus et al. (2004); Dautenhahn et al. (2006); Kirby et al. (2009); Sisbot et al. (2005); Takayama & Pantofaru (2009); Walters, Dautenhahn, te Boekhorst, Koay, Kaouri, Woods, Nehaniv, Lee & Werry (2005). Several authors have investigated the interest of people to interact with robots that exhibit different expressions or follow different spatial behaviour schemes Bruce et al. (2001); Christensen & Pacchierotti (2005); Dautenhahn et al. (2006); Hanajima et al. (2005). In Michalowski et al. (2006) models are reviewed that describe social engagement based on the spatial relationships between a robot and a person, with emphasis on the movement of the person. Although the robot is not perceived as a human when encountering people, the hypothesis is that robot behavioural reactions with respect to motion should resemble human-human scenarios. This is supported by Dautenhahn et al. (2006); Walters, Dautenhahn, Koay, Kaouri, te Boekhorst, Nehaniv, Werry & Lee (2005). Hall has investigated the spatial relationship between humans (proxemics) as outlined in Hall

(1966; 1963), which can be used for Human-Robot encounters. This was also studied by Walters, et al.Walters, Dautenhahn, Koay, Kaouri, te Boekhorst, Nehaniv, Werry & Lee (2005), whose research supports the use of Hall's proxemics in relation to robotics.

One way to view the problem of planning a trajectory through a crowded human environment, is to see humans as dynamic obstacles. The navigation problem can thus be addressed as a trajectory planning problem for dynamic environments. Given the fast dynamic nature of the problem, robotic kinodynamic and nonholonomic constraints must also be considered.

In the recent decade sampling based planning methods have proved successful for trajectory planning LaValle (2006). They do not guarantee an optimal solution, but are often good at finding solutions in complex and high dimensional problems. Specifically for kinodynamic systems Rapidly-exploring Random Trees (RRT's), where a tree with nodes correspond to connected configurations (vertices) of the robot trajectory, has received attention LaValle & Kuffner Jr (2001).

Various approaches improving the basic RRT algorithm have been investigated. In Brooks et al. (2009), a dynamic model of the robot and a cost function is used to expand and prune the nodes of the tree. Methods for incorporating dynamic environments, have also been investigated. Solutions include extending the configuration space with a time dimension ($\mathcal{C} - \mathcal{T}$ space), in which the obstacles are static van den Berg (2007), as well as pruning and rebuilding the tree when changes occur Ferguson et al. (2006); Zucker et al. (2007). To be able to run the algorithm on-line, the anytime concept Ferguson & Stentz (2006) can be used to quickly generate a possible trajectory. The RRT keeps being improved until a new trajectory is required by the robot, which can happen at any time.

These result only focus on avoiding collisions with obstacles. However, there have been no attempts to navigate through a human crowd taking into account the dynamics of the environment and at the same time generate comfortable and natural trajectories around the humans.

3. System architecture

The structure of the proposed system set-up is outlined in Fig. 1. The three main developed components are encaged by the dashed squares. First, the position of the people in the area are measured. The positions are then sent to the pose estimation algorithm, which estimates the person state using a Kalman filter and successively filters the state to obtain a pose estimate. This information about the peoples interest in interaction is sent to a person evaluation algorithm, which provides information to the navigation subsystem. The navigation subsystem first derives a potential field corresponding to the people's pose and interest in interaction. Then a robot motion subsystem finds out, how to move. This can either be by adapting the motion to interact with one specific person, or generating a trajectory through the environment. The loop is closed by the robot, which executes the path in the real world and thus has an effect on how humans move in the environment. The reactions of the people in the environment are then fed back to the person evaluation algorithm, to be able to learn from experience.

4. Person pose estimation

In this work we use a standard method to infer the position of the people in the environment from laser range finder measurements. This method however, only provides the position of

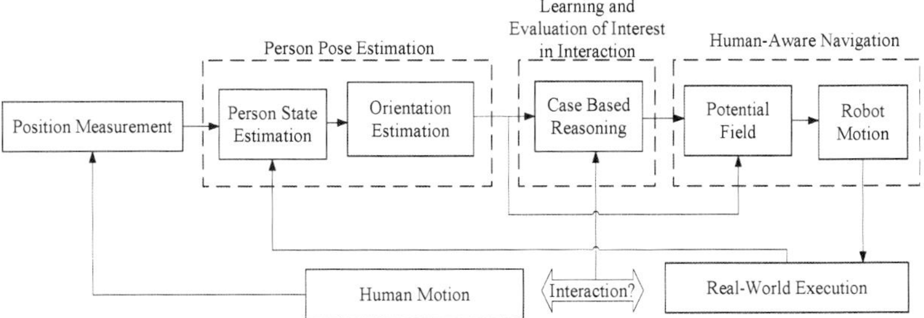

Fig. 1. An overview of how the different components are connected in the developed system. The three main parts encaged by the dashed squares.

a person. Thus, we develop a new Kalman filter based algorithm that takes into account the robot motion, to obtain velocity estimates for the people in the environment. This data is then post-filtered, using an autoregressive filter, which is able to obtain the orientation of the person as well. The method is briefly presented here, but is more thoroughly described in Svenstrup et al. (2009). The method is derived for only one person, but the same method can be utilised when several people are present.

We define the pose of a person as the position of the person given in the robot's coordinate system, and the angle towards the robot, as seen from the person (p_{pers} and θ in Fig. 2). The orientation θ is shown as approximately the angle between ϕ (the angle of the distance vector from the robot to the person) and v_{pers} (the angle of the person's velocity vector). The direction of v_{pers} is, however, only an approximation of θ, since the orientation of a person is not necessarily equal to the direction of the motion.

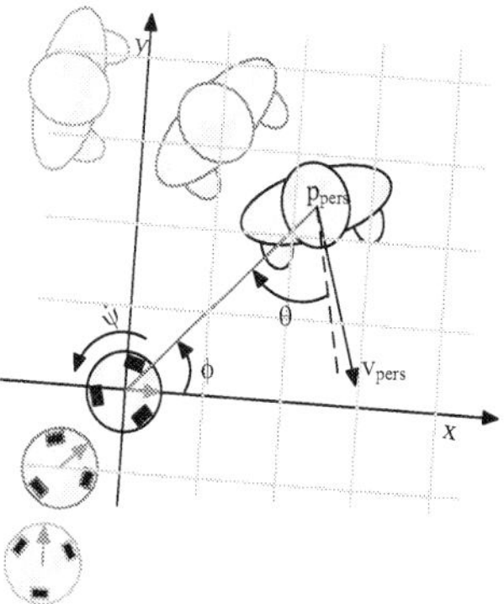

Fig. 2. The state variables p_{pers} and v_{pers} hold the position and velocity of the person in the robot's coordinate frame. θ is the orientation of the person and $\dot{\psi}$ is the rotational velocity of the robot.

The estimation of the person pose can be broken down into three steps:

1. Measure the position of the person using a laser range finder;

2. Use the continuous position measurements to find the state (position and velocity) of the person;

3. Use the velocity estimate to find the orientation (θ) of the person.

The position of the persons is estimated using a standard laser range finder based method, which is described in e.g. Feil-Seifer & Mataric (2005); Xavier et al. (2005). Our implementation is robust for tracking people at speeds of up to $2\frac{m}{s}$ in a real-world public space, which is described in Svenstrup et al. (2008).

The next step is to estimate velocity vector of the person in the robot's coordinate frame. This is done by fusing the person position measurements and the robot odometry in a Kalman filter, where a standard discrete state space model formulation for the system is used:

$$x(k+1) = \Phi x(k) + \Gamma u(k) \tag{1}$$

$$y(k) = Hx(k) \quad , \tag{2}$$

where x is the state, y is the measurements, u is the input and Φ, Γ, H are the system matrices, which are explained below.

The state is comprised of the person's position, person's velocity and the robot's velocity. The measurements are the estimate of the person's position and the robot odometry measurements.

$$x = \begin{bmatrix} p_{pers} \\ v_{pers} \\ v_{rob} \end{bmatrix} \quad , \quad y = \begin{bmatrix} \hat{p}_{pers} \\ v_{odom,rob} \end{bmatrix} \quad . \tag{3}$$

p denotes a position vector and v denotes velocities, all given in the robot's coordinate frame. The $\hat{p}$ is the estimate of the person's position from the person detection algorithm and $v_{odom,rob}$ the robot's odometry measurement vector. The rotation of the robot causes the measurement equation to be non-linear. To maintain a linear Kalman filter, the rotational odometry from the robot, can be added to the input, such that:

$$\Gamma(k)u(k) = \begin{bmatrix} p_{y,pers}(k) \\ -p_{x,pers}(k) \\ v_{y,pers}(k) \\ -v_{x,pers}(k) \\ 0 \\ 0 \end{bmatrix} T\hat{\psi}(k) \quad , \tag{4}$$

where p_x and p_y are the x and y coordinates of the vector p, T is the sampling time and $\hat{\psi}$ is the measured rotational velocity of the robot. The derived system matrices are then inserted into a standard Kalman filter to obtain a state estimate of the person.

The direction of the velocity vector in the state estimate of the person is not necessarily equal to the orientation of the person. To obtain a correct orientation estimate the velocity estimate is filtered through a first order autoregressive filter, with adaptive coefficients relative to the velocity. When the person is moving quickly, the direction of the velocity vector has a large weight, but if the person is moving slowly, the old orientation estimate is given a larger weight. The autoregressive filter is implemented as:

$$\theta(k+1) = \beta\theta(k) + (1-\beta)\arctan\left(\frac{v_{y,pers}}{v_{x,pers}}\right) \quad , \tag{5}$$

where β has been chosen experimentally relative to the absolute velocity v as:

$$\beta = \begin{cases} 0.9 & \text{if } v < 0.1m/s \\ 1.04 - 1.4v & \text{if } 0.1m/s \leq v \leq 0.6m/s \\ 0.2 & \text{else} \end{cases} . \qquad (6)$$

This equation means, that if the person is moving fast, the estimate relies mostly on the direction of the velocity, and if the person is moving slow, the estimate relies mostly on the previous estimate.

5. Estimate human intentions

To represent the person's interest in interaction, a continuous fuzzy variable, Person Indication (PI), is introduced, which serves as an indication of whether or not the person is interested in interaction. PI belongs to the interval $[0, 1]$, where $PI = 1$ represents the case where the robot believes that the person wishes to interact, and $PI = 0$ the case where the person is not interested in interaction.

Human intentions are difficult to decode, and thus difficult to hard code into an algorithm. So the robot needs to learn to find out if a person is interested in interaction. For this purpose, a Case-Based Reasoning (CBR) system, which enables the robot to learn to estimate the interest in interaction, has been developed in Hansen et al. (2009). The basic operation of the CBR system can be compared to how humans think. When we observe a situation, we use information from what we have previously experienced, to reason about the current situation. Using the CBR system, this is done in the following way. When a person is encountered, the specific motion patterns of the person is estimated as described above in Section 4. The estimates are compared to what is stored in a *Case Library*, which stores information about what happened in previous human encounters. The outcome, i.e. the associated *PI* values, of the previous similar encounters are used to update the *PI* in the current situation. When the interaction session with the person is over, the *Case Library* is revised with the new knowledge, which has just been obtained. This approach makes the robot able to learn from experience to become better at interpreting the person's interest in interaction.

5.1 Learning and evaluation of interest in interaction

The implementation of the CBR system is basically a database system which holds a number of cases describing each interaction session. There are two distinct stages of the CBR system operation. The first is the evaluation of the *PI*, where the robot estimates the *PI* during a session using the experience stored in the database. The second stage is the learning stage, where the information from a new experience is used to update the database. The two stages can be seen in Fig. 3, which shows a state diagram of the operation of the CBR system. Two different databases are used. The *Case Library* is the main database, which represents all the knowledge the robot has learned so far, and is used to evaluate *PI* during a session. All information obtained during a session is saved in the *Temporary Cases* database. After a session is over, the information from the Temporary Cases is used to update the knowledge in the Case Library.

Specifying a case is a question of determining a distinct and representative set of features connected to the event of a human-robot interaction session. The set of features could be anything identifying the specific situation, such as, the person's velocity and direction, position, relative position and velocity to other people, gestures, time of day, day of the week, location, height of the person, colour of their clothes, their facial expression, their apparent age

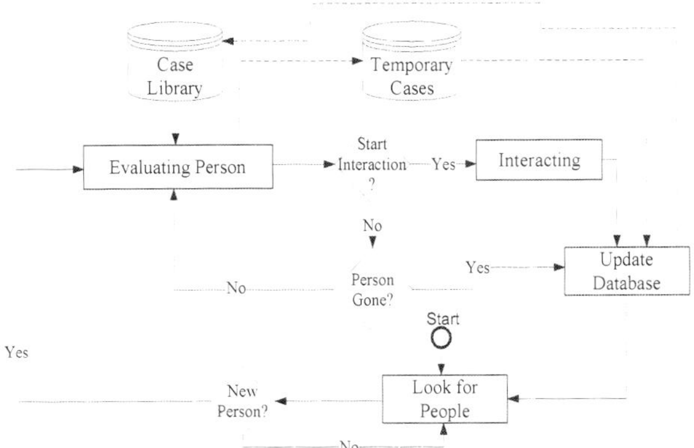

Fig. 3. Operation of the CBR system. First the robot starts to look for people. When a person is found, it evaluates whether the person wants to interact. After a potential interaction, the robot updates the knowledge library with information about the interaction session, and starts to look for other people.

and gender etc. The selected features depend on available sensors. For the system considered in this chapter, we consider only the human motion.

Initially, when the robot locates a new person in the area, nothing is known about this person, so PI is assigned to a default value $PI= 0.5$. After this, the PI of a person is continuously evaluated using the Case Library. First a new case is generated by collecting the relevant set of features above. The case is then compared to existing cases in the Case Library to find matching cases. If a match is found in the Case Library, the PI is updated towards the value found in the library according to the formula

$$PI_{new} = 0.2PI_{library} + 0.8PI_{old} \quad , \tag{7}$$

where PI_{new} is the new updated value of PI. This update is done to continuously adapt PI according to the observations, but still not trusting one single observation completely. If the robot continuously observes similar $PI_{library}$ values, the belief of the value of PI, will converge towards that value, e.g., if the robot is experiencing a behaviour, which earlier has resulted in interaction, lookups in the Case Library will result in $PI_{library}$ values close to 1. This means that the current PI will quickly approach 1 as well. After this, the case is copied to Temporary Cases, which holds information about the current session. If no match is found in the Case Library, the PI value is updated with $PI_{library} = 0.5$, which indicates that the robot is unsure about the intentions of the person. The case is still inserted into the Temporary Cases. When the session is over, the robot will know if it resulted in close interaction with the person, and thus if the person was interested in interaction. All the information in the Temporary Cases can thus be used to update the knowledge of the world, which is stored in the Case Library.

6. Adaptive human-aware navigation

The robot has two different tasks related to moving around in the environment, which it can perform. Either it can move around relative to one specific person that might want to interact, as described in the previous section. Otherwise it can have the objective to move from one point to another in the environment. This section describes the adaptive human-aware navigation around a specific person. The robot must move safe and naturally around the person, who might be interested in interaction. Furthermore, the motion of the robot must adaptively be adjusted according to the estimated PI value. One way to view this problem is to see humans as dynamic obstacles, that have social zones, which must be respected. The zones used here are developed by the anthropologist Hall (1963). Hall divides the area around a person into four zones according to the distance to the person:

- the public zone, where $d > 3.6m$

- the social zone, where $1.2m < d \leq 3.6m$

- the personal zone, where $0.45m < d \leq 1.2m$

- the intimate zone, where $d \leq 0.45m$

If it is most likely that the person does not wish to interact (i.e. $PI \approx 0$), the robot should not violate the person's personal space, but move towards the social or public zone. On the other hand, if it is most likely that the person is willing to interact or is interested in close interaction with the robot (i.e. $PI \approx 1$), the robot should try to enter the personal zone in front of the person. Another navigation issue is that the robot should be visible to the person, since it is uncomfortable for a person if the robot moves around, where it cannot be seen. Such social zones together with the desired interaction and visibility motion, can be represented by potential fields that govern the motion of the robot, see e.g. Sisbot et al. (2006); Svenstrup et al. (2009).

All navigation is done relative to the person, and hence no global positioning is needed in the proposed model. The potential field landscape is derived as a sum of several different potential functions with different purpose. The different functions are:

- **Attractor**. This is a negative potential used to attract the robot towards the person;

- **Rear**. This function ensures that the robot does not approach a person from behind;

- **Parallel**. This is an adaptive function, which is used to control the direction to the person and to keep a certain distance;

- **Perpendicular**. This function is also adaptive and works in cooperation with the parallel potential function.

All four potential functions are implemented as normalised bi-variate Gaussian distributions. A Gaussian distribution is chosen for several purposes. It is smooth and easy to differentiate to find the gradient, which becomes smaller and smaller (i.e. has less effect) further away from the person. Furthermore, it does not grow towards ∞ around 0 as, for example, a hyperbola (e.g. $\frac{1}{x}$), which makes both computational feasible and intuitively perceivable. The combined potential field around a person can be calculated as:

$$f(x) = \sum_{k=1}^{4} c_k \exp\left(-\frac{1}{2}[x - 0]^T \Sigma_k^{-1}[x - 0]\right) \quad, \tag{8}$$

where c_k are a normalizing constants, x is the position, 0 is the position of the person, in this case the origin, and Σ_k are the covariances of each of the Gaussian distributions.

The attractor and rear distribution are both kept constant for all instances of PI. The parallel and perpendicular distributions are continuously adapted, by adjusting Σ_k according to the PI value and Hall's proximity distances during an interaction session. Furthermore, the preferred robot-to-person encounter direction, reported in Dautenhahn et al. (2006); Woods et al. (2006), is taken into account by changing the width and the rotation of the distributions. The adaptation of the potential field distributions enables the robot to continuously adapt its behaviour to the current interest in interaction of the person in question.

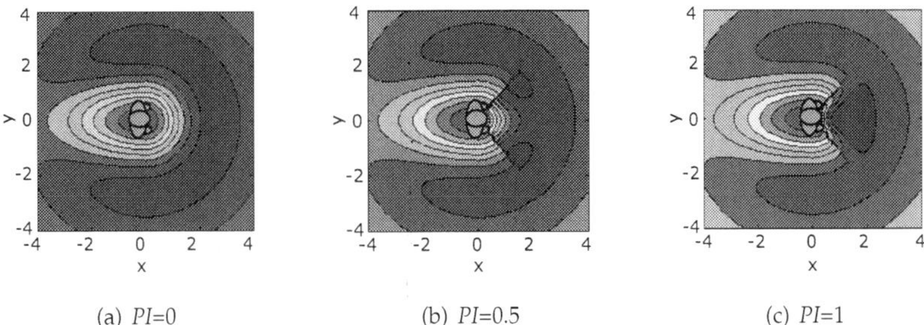

(a) *PI=0*   (b) *PI=0.5*   (c) *PI=1*

Fig. 4. Shape of the potential field around a person facing right for (a), a person not interested in interaction, (b) a person maybe interested in interaction, and (c) a person interested in interaction. The robot should try to get towards the lower points, i.e. the dark blue areas.

The resulting potential field contour around a person facing right can be seen in Fig. 4 for three specific values of *PI*. With $PI = 0$ the potential field will look like Fig. 4(a) where the robot will move to the dark blue area, i.e. the lowest potential approximately $3.6m$ in front of the person. The other end of the scale for $PI = 1$ is illustrated in Fig. 4(c), where the person is interested in interaction and, as a result, the potential function is adapted so the robot is allowed to enter the space right in front of the person. In between, Fig. 4(b), is the default configuration of $PI = 0.5$, in which the robot is forced to approach the person at approximately 45°, while keeping just outside the personal zone.
Instead of just moving towards the lowest point at a fixed speed, the gradient of the potential field $\nabla f(x)$, is used to set a reference velocity for the robot. This way of controlling the robot's velocity allows the robot to move quickly when the potential field is steep. On the other hand, the robot has slow comfortable movements when it is close to where it is supposed to be, i.e. near a minimum of the field.

7. Trajectory planning problem for crowded environments

The above described potential field governs the motion around one person. The navigation problem for moving through an environment with many people, can then be formulated by summing potential fields for all the people in the environment, plus a potential for the desired robot motion in environment. An example of this potential field landscape, together with three possible trajectories for a robot, is shown in Fig. 5. Notice, that even though a trajectory seems to pass through a person, it might not be a bad trajectory, since the person may have moved when the robot reaches the point of apparent collision. Conversely the robot may also run into a person, who was not originally on the path. Therefore it is important to take into account the dynamics of the obstacles (i.e. the humans), when planning trajectories. So the objective is to minimise the cost of traversing the potential field landscape that changes over time as the people move around.

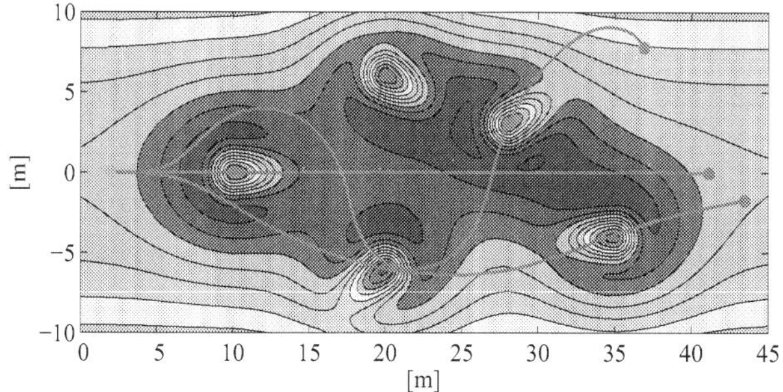

Fig. 5. Person landscape, which the robot has to move through. The robot starting point is the green dot at the point $(2,0)$. Three examples of potential robot trajectories are shown. Even though it looks like the trajectories goes through the persons, this is not necessarily the case, since the persons might have moved, when the robot comes to the point.

Given the dynamic nature of the problem, robotic kinodynamic and nonholonomic constraints must also be considered. Also the person motion, i.e. the change of the potential field over time must be taken into account.

7.1 Robot dynamics

The robot is modelled as a unicycle type robot, i.e. like a Pioneer, an iRobot Create or a Segway. A good motion model for the robot is necessary because it operates in dynamic environments, where even small deviations from the expected trajectory may result in collisions. So instead of using a purely kinematic robot model of the robot, it is modelled as a dynamical system, with accelerations as input. This describes the physics better, since acceleration and applied force are proportional. This dynamical model can be described by the five states:

$$
\boldsymbol{x}(t) = \begin{bmatrix} x_1(t) \\ x_2(t) \\ x_3(t) \\ x_4(t) \\ x_5(t) \end{bmatrix} = \begin{bmatrix} x(t) \\ y(t) \\ v(t) \\ \theta(t) \\ \dot{\theta}(t) \end{bmatrix} \begin{matrix} \rightarrow \text{x position} \\ \rightarrow \text{y position} \\ \rightarrow \text{linear velocity} \\ \rightarrow \text{rotation angle} \\ \rightarrow \text{rotational velocity} \end{matrix} \tag{9}
$$

The differential equation governing the robot behaviour is:

$$
\dot{\boldsymbol{x}}(t) = \boldsymbol{f}\left(\boldsymbol{x}(t),\boldsymbol{u}(t)\right) = \begin{bmatrix} \dot{x}(t) \\ \dot{y}(t) \\ \dot{v}(t) \\ \dot{\theta}(t) \\ \ddot{\theta}(t) \end{bmatrix} = \begin{bmatrix} v(t)\cos(\theta(t)) \\ v(t)\sin(\theta(t)) \\ u_v(t) \\ \dot{\theta}(t) \\ u_\theta(t) \end{bmatrix} = \begin{bmatrix} x_3(t)\cos(x_4(t)) \\ x_3(t)\sin(x_4(t)) \\ u_1(t) \\ x_5(t) \\ u_2(t) \end{bmatrix} , \tag{10}
$$

where $u_1 = u_v$ is the linear acceleration input and $u_2 = u_\theta$ is the rotational acceleration input.

7.2 Dynamic potential field

The value of the potential field, denoted G, at a point in the environment is calculated as a sum of the cost associated with three different aspects:

1. A cost related to the robot's desired position in the environment without obstacles. For example high costs might be assigned close to the edges of the environment.

2. A cost associated with the robot position relative to humans in the area.

3. A cost rewarding moving towards a goal.

The combined cost can be written as:

$$G(t) = g_1(\boldsymbol{x}(t))) + g_2(\boldsymbol{x}(t), \mathcal{P}(t)) + g_3(\boldsymbol{x}(t)) \quad . \tag{11}$$

$\mathcal{P}(t)$ is a matrix containing the position and orientation of persons in the environment at the given time. $g_1(\boldsymbol{x})$, $g_2(\boldsymbol{x})$ and $g_3(\boldsymbol{x})$ are the three cost functions. They are further described below.

7.2.1 Cost related to environment

This cost function is currently designed for motion in open spaces, such as a pedestrian street. It has the shape of a valley, such that it is more expensive to go towards the sides, but cheap to stay in the centre of the environment:

$$g_1(\boldsymbol{x}(t)) = c_y y^2(t) \tag{12}$$

where c_y is a constant determining how much the robot is drawn towards the centre, and y is the distance to the center line of the street.

7.2.2 Cost of proximity to humans

The cost of being near to humans is calculated by summing the potential fields for each person as described in Section 6. As described, the potential field for each person is a summation of four normalized bi-variate Gaussian distributions, which means that $g_2(\boldsymbol{x})$ for each individual person can be written as:

$$g_{2,person}(\boldsymbol{x}_{1:2}, \boldsymbol{\mu}) = \sum_{k=1}^{4} c_k \exp(-\frac{1}{2}[\boldsymbol{x}_{1:2} - \boldsymbol{\mu}]^T \Sigma_k^{-1} [\boldsymbol{x}_{1:2} - \boldsymbol{\mu}]) \quad , \tag{13}$$

where c_k are normalizing constants, $\boldsymbol{x}_{1:2}$ are the first two states of the robot state, i.e. the position where the cost function is evaluated. $\boldsymbol{\mu}$ is the position of the person and Σ_k are the covariances of each of the Gaussian distributions, which are related to the orientation and interest state of the person, as described in Section 6.

7.2.3 Cost of end point in trajectory

The cost at the end point penalizes if the robot does not move forwards, and if the robot orientation is not in a forward direction. An exponential function is used to penalize the position. It is set up, such that short distances are penalized much, while it is close to the same value for larger distances, i.e. it does not change much if the robot goes 19 or 20 meters from its starting position.

$$g_3(\boldsymbol{x}(t)) = c_{e1} \exp(c_{e2}(x(t) - \tilde{x}(0))) + c_\theta \theta^4(t) \quad , \tag{14}$$

where $c_{(.)}$ are scaling constants and $\tilde{x}(0)$ is the desired initial position. Note that c_{e2} must be negative to make the potential decrease as the robot gets further. The reason that θ is raised to the fourth, is to keep the term closer to zero in a larger neighbourhood of the origin. This means that the robot will almost not be penalized for small turns. On the other hand larger turns, like going the wrong way, will be penalized more.

7.3 Minimisation problem

Given the above cost functions the potential landscape may be formed as previously illustrated in Fig. 5 for a pedestrian street landscape with five persons. If the current time is $t = 0$, the planning problem can be posed as follows. Given an initial robot state x_0, and trajectory information for all persons until the given time $\tilde{P}_{start:0}$. Determine the control input $\tilde{u}_{0:T}$, which minimises the cost of traversing the potential field, subject to the dynamical robot model constraints and predicted human motions:

$$\begin{aligned}
minimise \quad & I(\tilde{u}_{0:T}) = \\
& \int_0^T [g_1(x(t)) + g_2(x(t), \mathcal{P}(t))]\, dt + g_3(x(T)) \\
s.t. \quad & \dot{x}(t) = f(x(t), \tilde{u}_t) \\
where \quad & g_1(x(t)) = c_y x_2(t)^2 \\
& g_2(x(t), \mathcal{P}(t)) = \\
& \sum_{j=1}^{p} \sum_{k=1}^{4} c_k \exp(-\frac{1}{2}[x_{1:2} - \mu_j]^T \Sigma_{j,k}^{-1}[x_{1:2} - \mu_j]) \\
& g_3(x(T)) = c_{e1} \exp(c_{e2}(x_1(T) - x_1(0))) + c_\theta x_4^4(T) \quad ,
\end{aligned}$$
(15)

were $x_{1:2} - [x_1(t), x_2(t)]$ is the position of the robot at time t, $\tilde{u}_{0:T}$ is the discrete input sequence to the robot. T is the ending time horizon of the trajectory, $g_x(\cdot)$ are cost functions and p is the number of persons in the area. The position and orientation of all persons at time t is predicted from the knowledge of the trajectories until the current moment ($\tilde{P}_{start:0}$), and given by $\mathcal{P}(t)$. μ_j is the center of the j-th person at a given time.

To be able to calculate the cost of a trajectory according to Eq. (15), only the prediction of the person trajectories, $\mathcal{P}(t)$, remains to be defined. A simple model is that the person will continue with the same speed and direction (Bruce & Gordon, 2004). More advanced human motion models could be used without changing the planning algorithm, but it is outside the scope of this chapter to derive a complex human motion model.

8. RRT Based trajectory planning

It has been chosen to solve the above described minimisation problem by using a Rapidly-exploring Random Tree algorithm (LaValle, 2006; LaValle & Kuffner Jr, 2001). The RRT algorithm is in Svenstrup et al. (2010) modified in several ways to obtain an algorithm that works for planning a trajectory for the given problem. The overall mission of the robot is, to move forward through the environment with a desired average speed and direction, which can be set by a top level planner. This chapter contributes by enhancing the basic RRT planning algorithm to accommodate for navigation in a potential field and take into account the kinodynamic constraints of the robot. The RRT is expanded using a control strategy, which ensures feasibility of the trajectory and a better coverage of the configuration space. The planning is done in $\mathcal{C} - \mathcal{T}$ space using an Model Predictive Control (MPC) scheme to incorporate the dynamics of the environment.

The structure of the proposed planning algorithm for planning a trajectory through a dynamic environment, as shown in Fig. 5, can be seen in Fig. 6. Comparing to Fig. 1, this figure corresponds to the *robot motion* block. The idea is that while a part of a calculated trajectory is executed, a new is calculated on-line. Input to the trajectory planner is the previous best trajectory, the person trajectory estimates, and the dynamic model of the robot.

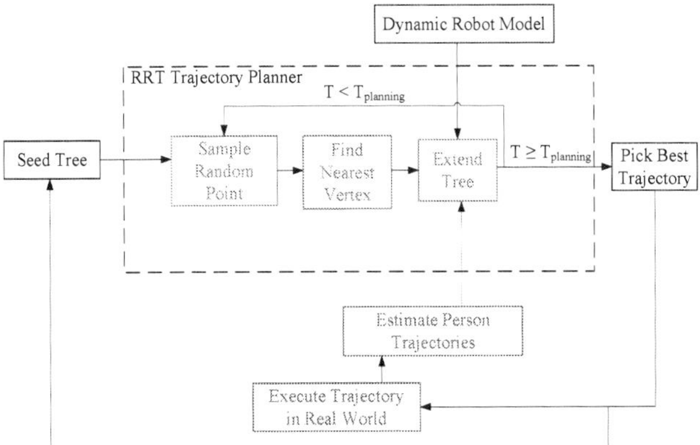

Fig. 6. The overall structure of the trajectory generator. The blue real world part and the red trajectory planning part are executed simultaneously.

The minimisation problem stated in Eq. (15) is addressed by a Rapidly-exploring Random Tree (RRT) algorithm. A standard RRT algorithm is shown in Algorithm 1, where the lines 4, 5, 6 correspond to the three blocks in the larger *RRT Trajectory Planner* box in Fig. 6.

Algorithm 1 Standard RRT (see Ferguson & Stentz (2006))

RRTmain()

1: Tree = q.start
2: q.new = q.start
3: **while** Dist(q.new , q.goal) < ErrTolerance **do**
4:    q.target = **SampleTarget()**
5:    q.nearest = **NearestVertex**(Tree , q.target)
6:    q.new = **ExtendTowards**(q.nearest,q.target)
7:    Tree.add(q.new)
8: **end while**
9: **return** Trajectory(Tree,q.new)

SampleTarget()

1: **if Rand()** < GoalSamplingProb **then**
2:    **return** q.goal
3: **else**
4:    **return RandomConfiguration()**
5: **end if**

The method presented here differs from the standard RRT in lines 1, 3, 6, 9, which are marked red. Furthermore, between line 6 and 7, node pruning is introduced. Since an MPC scheme is used, only a small portion of the planned trajectory is executed, while the planner is restarted to plan a new trajectory on-line. When the small portion has been executed, the planner has an updated trajectory ready. To facilitate this, the stopping condition in line 3 is changed. When a the robot needs a new trajectory, or when certain maximum number of vertices have been extended, the RRT is stopped. Even though the robot only executes a small part of the trajectory, the rest of the trajectory should still be valid. Therefore, in line 1, the tree is seeded with the remaining trajectory.

In line 9 the trajectory with the least cost according to Eq. (15) is returned, instead of returning the trajectory to the newest vertex. The tree extension function and the pruning method are described below.

8.1 RRT Control input sampling

When working with nonholonomic kinodynamic constrained systems, it is not straightforward to expand the tree towards a newly sampled point in the configuration space (line 6 in Algorithm 1). It is a whole motion planning problem in itself to find inputs, that drive the robot towards a given point Siciliano & Khatib (2008). The algorithm proposed here uses a controller to turn the robot towards the sampled point and to keep a desired speed. A velocity controller is set to control the speed towards an average speed around a reference velocity. The probabilistic completeness of RRT's in general, is ensured by the randomness of the input. So to maintain this randomness in the input signals, a random value sampled from a Gaussian distribution, is added to the controller input. The velocity controller is implemented as a standard proportional controller. The rotation angle is a second order system with θ and $\dot{\theta}$ as states, and therefore a state space controller is used for control of the orientation. The control input can be written as:

$$
u = \begin{bmatrix} u_1 \\ u_2 \end{bmatrix} = \begin{bmatrix} k_v(\mu_v - v(t)) \\ k_{\theta 1}(\phi_{point} - \theta(t)) - k_{\theta 2}\dot{\theta} \end{bmatrix} + \begin{bmatrix} \mathcal{N}(0, \sigma_v) \\ \mathcal{N}(0, \sigma_\theta) \end{bmatrix}.
\tag{16}
$$

μ_v is the desired average speed of the robot and ϕ_{point} is the angle towards the sampled point. $k_{(.)}$ are controller constants and σ_v, σ_θ are the standard deviations of the added Gaussian distributed input.

The new vertex to be added to the tree is now found by using the dynamic robot motion model and the controller to simulate the trajectory one time step. This ensures that the added vertex will be reachable.

8.2 Tree Pruning and trajectory selection

A simple pruning scheme, based on several different properties of a node, is used. If the vertex corresponding to the node ends up in a place where the potential field has a value above a specific threshold, then the node is not added to the tree. Furthermore a node is pruned if $|\theta(t)| > \frac{\pi}{2}$, which means that the robot is on the way back again, or if the simulated trajectory goes out of bounds of the environment. It is not desirable to let the tree grow too far in time, since the processing power is much better spend on the near future, because of the uncertainty of person positions further into the future. Therefore the node is also pruned if the time taken to reach the node is above a given threshold. Finally, instead of returning the trajectory to the vertex of the last added node, the trajectory with the lowest cost (calculated from Eq. (15)), is returned. But to avoid the risk of selecting a node, which is not very far in time, all nodes with a small time are thrown away before selecting the best node.

The final algorithm is shown in Algorithm 2.

9. Experiments and simulations

The pose and intention estimation algorithm together with the adaptive human-aware navigation is demonstrated to work in experiments with random test persons. Additionally

---

Algorithm 2 Modified RRT for human environments

RRTmain()

1: Tree = q.oldBestTrajectory
2: **while** (Nnodes < maxNodes) and (t < tMax) **do**
3:     q.target = **SampleTarget**()
4:     q.nearest = **NearestVertex**(Tree , q.target)
5:     q.new = **CalculateControlInput**(q.nearest,q.target)
6:     **if PruneNode**(q.new) == false **then**
7:        Tree.add(q.new)
8:     **end if**
9: **end while**
10: **return BestTrajectory**(Tree)

SampleTarget()

1: **if Rand** < GoalSamplingProb **then**
2:     **return** q.goal
3: **else**
4:     **return RandomConfiguration**()
5: **end if**

---

the trajectory planning through densely populated environments is demonstrated in a simulated pedestrian street environment.

9.1 Experimental set-up

The person state estimation and human-aware navigation subsystems are tested decoupled from the rest of the system in a laboratory setting in Svenstrup et al. (2009). Therefore, the experiments here focus on testing the function of the combined system including the intention estimation. The experiments are designed to illustrate the operation and the proof of concept of the combined methods. It took place in an open hall, with only one person at a time in the shared environment. This allowed for easily repeated tests with no interference from other objects than the test persons. The test persons were selected randomly from students on campus. None had prior knowledge about the implementation of the system.

9.1.1 Test equipment and implementation

The robot used during the experiments was a FESTO Robotino platform, which provides omnidirectional motion. A head, which is capable of showing simple facial expressions, is mounted on the robot (see Fig. 7). The robot is equipped with an URG-04LX line scan laser range finder for detection and tracking of people, and a button to press for emulating the transition to close interaction (see Fig. 7). If the test persons passed an object to the robot, they would activate the button, which was perceived as an interest in close interaction. If the test person did not pass an object (i.e. the button was not activated) within 15 seconds or disappeared from the robot's field of view, this was recognised as if no close interaction had occurred, and thus that the person was not interested in interaction.

9.2 Test specification

For evaluation of the proposed methods, two experiments were performed. During both experiments the full system, as seen in Fig 1, is used, i.e. the pose estimation and the human-aware navigation are running, as well as the interest learning and evaluation. All

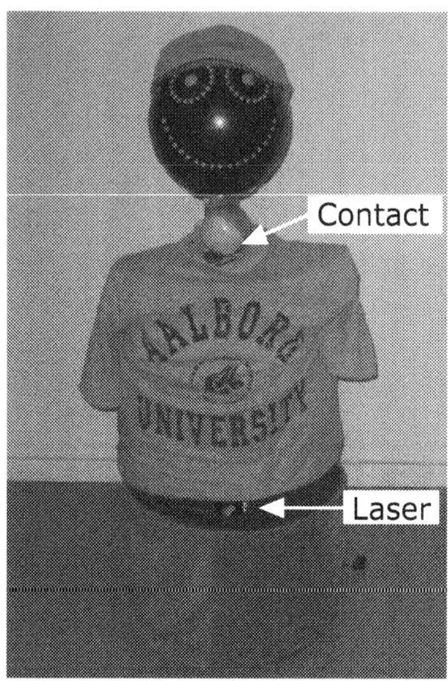

Fig. 7. The FESTO Robotino robot used for the experiments.

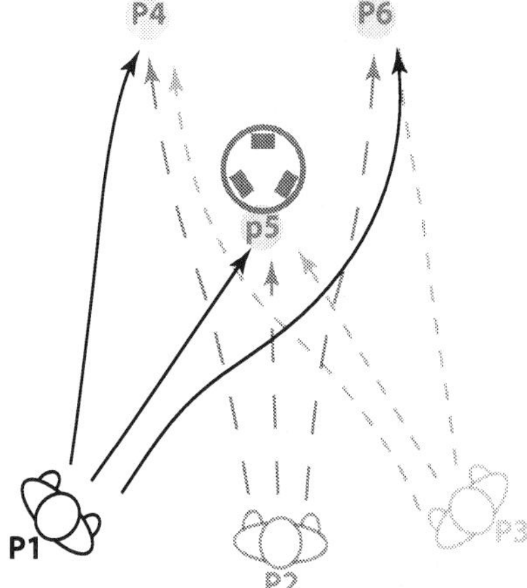

Fig. 8. Illustration of possible pathways around the robot during the experiment. A test person starts from points P1, P2 or P3 and passes through either P4, P5 or P6. If the trajectory goes through P5, a close interaction occurs by handing an object to the robot.

output values (*PI*), and input values (pose and velocity) were logged for later analysis during both experiments.

In Experiment 1, the objective was to see if the system was capable of learning to estimate *PI* based on interaction experience from several different people. As the number of cases increase, the system should be better able to estimate *PI* of a person and do it more quickly. Furthermore, the information in the CBR database should be generic, such that information obtained with some people can be used when other people occur. Starting from a CBR system with no knowledge, i.e. an empty database, a total of five test persons were asked to approach or pass the robot 12 times using different motion paths, which are illustrated in Fig. 8. The starting and end points of each session were selected randomly, while the specific route was chosen by the test person. The random selection was designed so the test persons would end up with close interaction in 50% of the sessions. In the other sessions, the test persons would pass the robot either to the left of the right without interacting.

In Experiment 2, the objective was to test the adaptiveness of the CBR system. The system should be able to change its estimation of *PI* over time if behaviour patterns change. A total of 36 test approaches were performed with one test person. The test person would start randomly at P1, P2 or P3 (see Fig. 8) and end the trajectory at P4, P5 or P6. In the first 18 sessions the test person would indicate interest in close interaction by handing an object to the robot from P5, while in the last 18 sessions the person did not indicate interest and the trajectory ended at P4 or P6.

9.3 Simulations in crowded environments

The algorithm for trajectory planning in crowded environments, described in Section 7, is implemented and demonstrated to work on a simulated pedestrian street, as shown in Fig. 5. The experiments consist of two parts. First, the algorithm is applied on the environment shown in Fig. 5. This will demonstrate that the algorithm is capable of planning a trajectory, which does not collide with any persons. It will also demonstrate how the tree expands. Next, a simulated navigation through several randomly generated worlds is performed. This will demonstrate the robustness of the algorithm over time. Specific parameters for the algorithm can be seen in Svenstrup et al. (2010).

9.3.1 Robustness test

The robustness test is performed in 50 different randomly generated environments, where the robot has to navigate forwards in during a one minute period. With an average speed of $1.5\frac{m}{s}$, this corresponds to the robot moving approximately $90m$ ahead along the street. In each simulation the robot's initial state is at position $(0, 0)$ and with zero velocity.

Initially a random number of persons (between 10 and 20) are placed randomly in the world. Their velocity is sampled randomly from a Gaussian distribution. The motion of each person is simulated as moving towards a goal $10m$ ahead of them. The goal position of the $y - axis$ of the street is sampled randomly, and will also change every few seconds. Additional Brownian motion is added to each person to include randomness of the motion. Over time new persons will enter at the end of the street according to a Poisson process. This means that at any given time, persons will appear and disappear at the ends of the street. Because of this randomness, the number of persons can differ from the initial number of persons, and ranges from 10 to around 40, which is different for each simulation.

At each time instant, the robot will only know the current position and velocity of each of the persons within a range of $45m$ in front of the robot, and it has no knowledge about where the persons will go in the future.

As it is a simulation, there are no real time performance issues, and nothing has been done to optimise the code for faster performance. So the tree is set to grow a fixed number of 2000 vertices at each iteration. The planning horizon is set to 20 seconds and at each iteration the robot executes 2 seconds of the trajectory, while a new trajectory is planned.

10. Results

10.1 Experiment 1

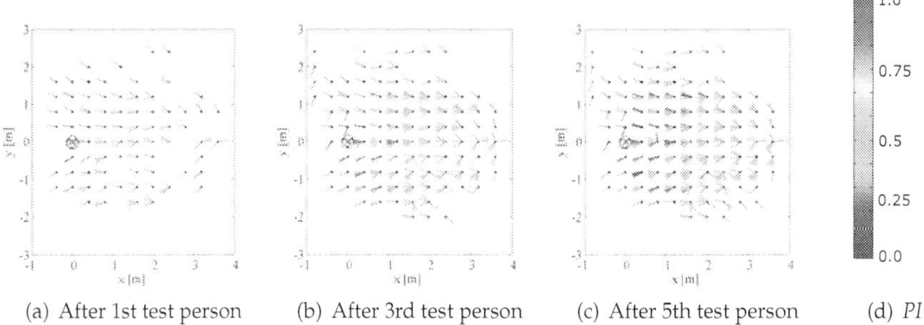

(a) After 1st test person   (b) After 3rd test person   (c) After 5th test person   (d) *PI*

Fig. 9. The figures show the values stored in the CBR system after completion of the 1st, 3rd and 5th test person. Note that the robot is located at the origin $(0,0)$, since the measurements are in the robot's coordinate frame, which follows the robot's motion. Each dot represents a position of the test person in the robot's coordinate frame. The direction of the movement of the test person is represented by a vector, while the level (*PI*) is indicated by the colour range.

As interaction sessions are registered by the robot, the database is gradually filled with cases. All entries in the database after different stages of training are illustrated by four-dimensional plots in Fig. 9. The (x, y) coordinates are the position coordinates (p_x, p_y) of the person in the robot's coordinate frame, as estimated by the pose estimation algorithm. The coordinates are the dots in the 40 x 40cm grid. At each position, the orientation of the person (θ) is illustrated by a vector. The colour of the vector denotes the value of *PI*. Blue indicates that the person does not wish close interaction, while red indicates that the person wishes to engage in close interaction, i.e. *PI* = 0 and *PI* = 1 respectively. A green vector indicates *PI* = 0.5.

Figs. 9((a)-(c)) show how information in the database evolves during the experiment. Fig. 9(a) shows the state of the database after the first person has completed the 12 sessions. Here, the database is seen to be rather sparsely populated with *PI* values mostly around 0.5, which means that the CBR system is not well trained yet. Fig. 9(b) shows the state after 3 test persons have completed the 12 sessions and, finally, Fig. 9(c) shows all cases (around 500) after all 5 test persons have completed the sessions. Here the database is more densely populated, and *PI* values are in the whole range from 0 to 1. As can be seen in Figs. 9((a)-(c)), the number of plotted database entries increases as more interaction sessions occur. This shows the development of the CBR system, and clearly illustrates how the CBR system gradually learns from each person interaction session.

In all three figures (Figs. 9((a)-(c))), the vectors in the red colour range (high *PI*) are dominant when the orientation of the person is towards the robot, while there is an excess of vectors not pointing directly towards the robot in the blue colour range (low *PI*). This complies with intuition and reflects that a person, who wishes to interact, has a trajectory moving towards the robot, which is as expected for a normal human-human interaction process.

In Fig. 10, the *PI* development for six individual sessions, are plotted as a function of time. This is done for test persons 1, 3 and 5. *PI* is plotted twice for each test person: once for a randomly selected session where the test person wishes interaction with the robot; and once for a randomly selected session where the test person passes the robot with no interest in interaction. For the first test person, *PI* increases to a maximum around 0.65 for a session ending with a close interaction. For the same test person, *PI* drops to a minimum of 0.48 for a session where no close interaction occurs. For the 3rd test person, *PI* ends with a value around 0.9 for a session where close interaction has occurred, while *PI* = 0.35 for a session where no close interaction has occurred. For the last test person, *PI* rapidly increases to a value around 1 for a session where close interaction occurs, and has *PI* around 0.18 when the person is not interested in interaction. Generally this illustrates that *PI* is estimated more quickly and with more certainty the more the system is trained. It also can be seen how maximum and

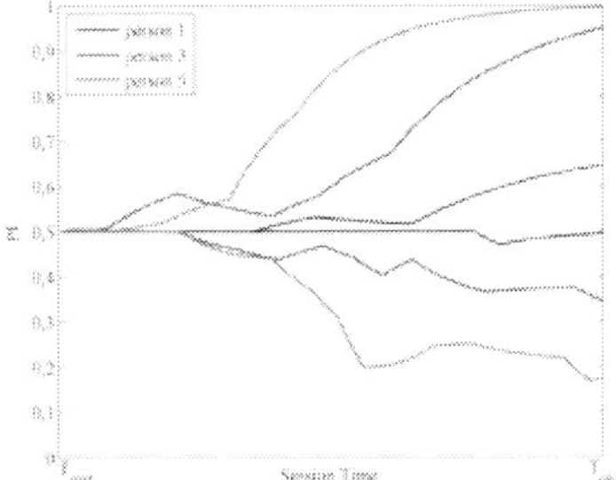

Fig. 10. *PI* as a function of the session time for three different test persons. For each test person, *PI* is plotted for a session where close interaction occurs and for a session where no close interaction occurs. The *x*-axis shows the session time. The axis is scaled such that the plots have equal length.

minimum values for *PI* increase as more test persons have been evaluated. After evaluating one test person, the robot has gathered very little interaction experience, and has difficulties in determining the correspondence between motion pattern and end result - hence *PI* stays close to 0.5. After the third test person, the robot has gathered more cases and, therefore, improves in estimating the outcome of the behaviour. For the last test person, the robot is clearly capable of estimating the intention state of the person, and thereby able to predict what will be the outcome of the interaction session.

10.2 Experiment 2

Experiment 2 tests the adaptiveness of the CBR system. In order to see the change in the system over time, the average *PI* value in the database after each session is calculated. The averages have been calculated as an average for three different areas (see Fig. 11(a)), to be able to compare how the database changes in different areas relative to the robot. The areas are:

- **Area 1:** The frontal area just in front of the the robot.

- **Area 2:** A small area around the robot, which includes some of the frontal area, and some to the sides as well.

- **Area 3:** All cases stored in the database.

Fig. 11(b) shows the development of the average values of *PI* for the 36 interaction sessions for one person.

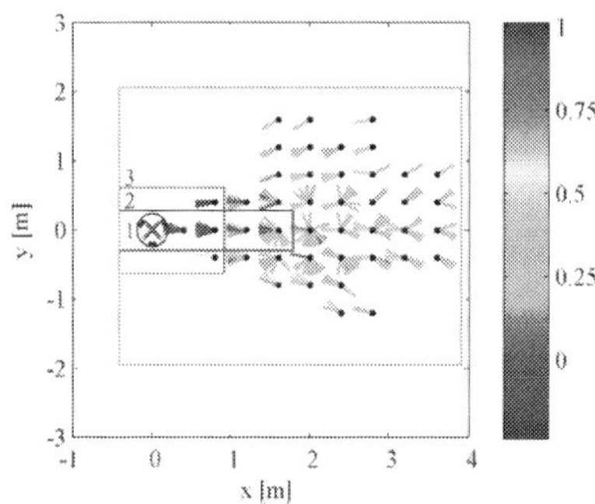

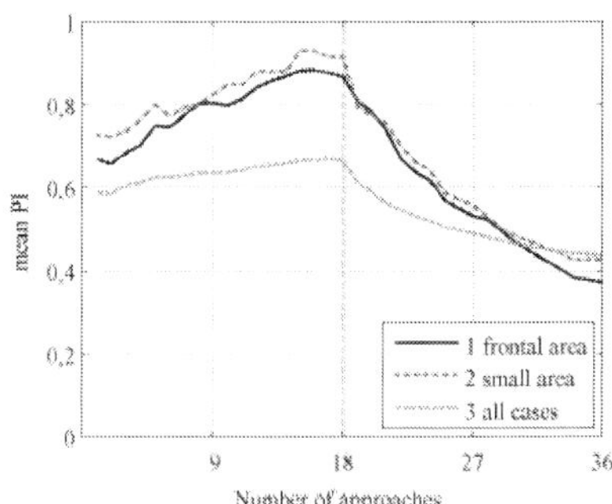

(a) A snapshot of the database after the second experiment was done. It shows how the mean value for *PI* is calculated for three areas: 1) the frontal area; 2) the small area and; 3) for all cases. The development of the mean values over time for all three areas are illustrated in Fig. 11(b)

(b) Graph of how the average of *PI* evolves for the three areas indicated in Fig. 11(a). 36 person interaction sessions for one test person is performed. The red vertical line illustrates where the behaviour of the person changes from seeking interaction to not seeking interaction.

Fig. 11. Plots of the database and how *PI* evolves from experiment 2

As can be seen from Fig. 11(b), the average value of *PI* increases for the first 18 sessions, where the person is interested in close interaction. This is especially the case for areas 1 and 2, which have a maximum value at 0.9 and 0.85 respectively, but less for area 3 (around 0.65). After 18 sessions, where the behaviour is changed, *PI* starts to drop for all areas. Most notably, area 1 drops to a minimum of 0.39 after 36 sessions. This is because in most sessions the person's trajectory goes through the frontal area, thereby having the highest number of updates of *PI*. To sum up, these experiments show that:

- Determination of *PI* improves as the number of CBR case entries increases, which means that the system is able to learn from experience.

- The CBR system is independent of the specific person, such that experience based on motion patterns of some people, can be used to determine the *PI* of other people.

- The algorithm is adaptive, when the general behaviour of the people changes.

Generally, the conducted experiments show that CBR can be applied advantageously to a robot, which needs to evaluate the behaviour of a person. The method for assessment of the person's interest in interaction with the robot is based on very limited sensor input. This is encouraging as the method may easily be extended with support from other sensors, such as computer vision, acoustics etc.

10.3 Trajectory generation results

An example of a grown RRT, with 2000 vertices, from the initial state can be seen in Fig. 12. The simulated trajectories of the robot are the red lines, and the red dots are vertices of the tree. It is seen how the RRT is spread out to explore the configuration space, although only every 10th vertex is plotted to avoid clutter on the graph. Note that the persons are static at their initial position on the figure, and some trajectories seem to pass through persons. But in reality, the persons have moved when the robot passes the point of the trajectory. The best of the all trajectories, which is calculated using Eq. (15), is the green trajectory.

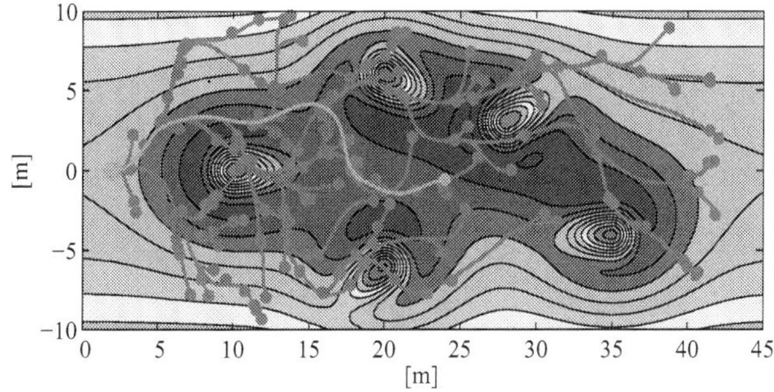

Fig. 12. An RRT for a robot starting at $(2, 0)$ and the task of moving forward through the human populated environment. Only every 10th vertex is shown to avoid clutter of the graph. The vertices are the red dots, and the lines are the simulated trajectories. The green trajectory is the least cost trajectory.

In Fig. 13 a typical scene from one of the 50 simulations can be seen. The blue dots are persons, and the arrows are velocity vectors, with a length proportional to the speed. The black star with the red arrow, is the robot position and velocity.

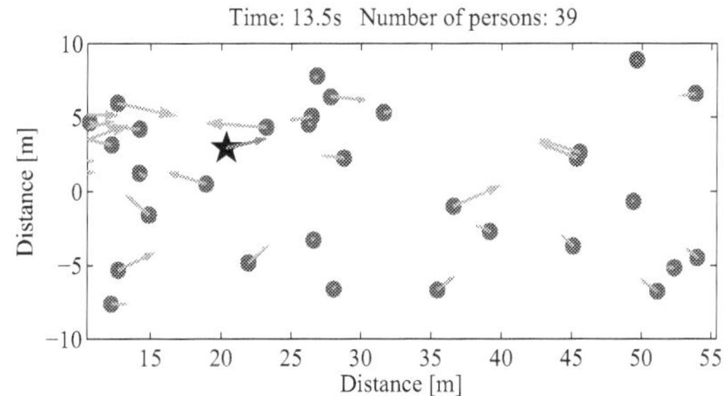

Fig. 13. A scene from one of the 50 simulations. The blue dots are persons, with their corresponding current velocity vectors. The black star is the robot.

The distance to the closest person over time, for a randomly selected simulation is shown on Fig. 14. Though it is only one sample, it is representative for all the simulations. It can be seen that very rarely the robot is closer to any person than $1.2m$, which is the distance of the personal zone of the humans.

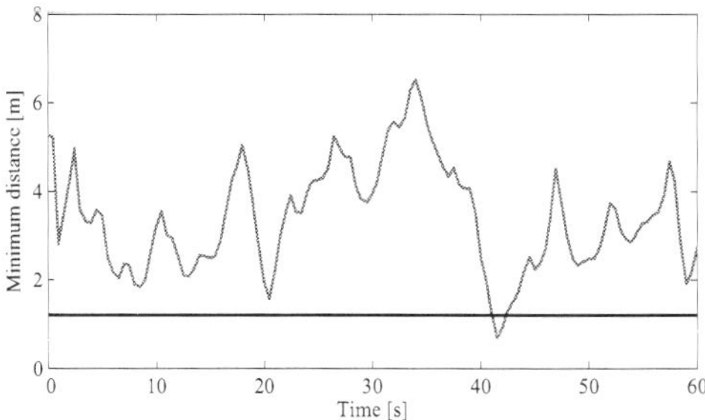

Fig. 14. The figure shows the closest distance of any person for one randomly chosen simulation. The horizontal black line, is at $1.2m$ distance, which corresponds to the transition between the social zone and the personal zone, which the robot should try to stay out of.

In none of the 50 one minute period simulations the robot ran into a person. This demonstrates that the algorithm is robust enough plan safe trajectories through an environment, where human motion is governed by changing goals and additional random motion, even though using a simple human motion model for prediction, when planning. A few close passes in the combined 50 minute run, down the pedestrian street, are seen. The time in each zone, in which the robot is located, for the person that is closest to the robot at any given time, is shown in Fig. 15. It is seen that the robot stays out of the personal zone of any of the persons in more than 97.5% of the time, and out of the intimate zone (a distance closer than $0.45m$) 99.7% of the time. This only occurs on 9 separate instances of the 50 minutes of driving.

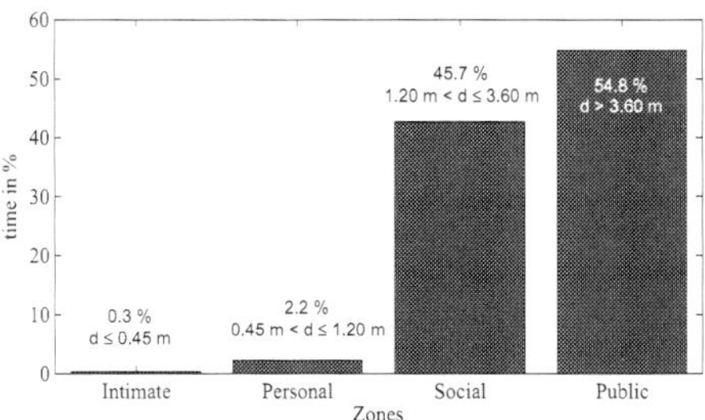

Fig. 15. The bar plot shows how large a part of the time the closest person to the robot has been in each zone. The robot should try to stay out of the personal and intimate zones. The distance interval for each zone, can also be seen in the plot.

Except in very densely populated environments, the model runs approximately one third of real time on a 2.0 GHz CPU running MATLAB. This is considered to be reasonable, since no optimisation for speed has been done. In very dense environments, the planning takes longer, since many new added vertices, are pruned again, and hence more points has to be sampled before 2000 vertices are expanded. Additionally the more persons in the area, the longer it takes to evaluate the cost of traversing the potential field. Generally, it is demonstrated, that the algorithm is able to plan and execute a trajectory through a human environment without colliding with the people walking in the environment.

11. Conclusions

In this work, we have described an adaptive system for safe and natural motion interaction between mobile robots and humans. The system forms a basis for human-aware navigation respecting a person's social spaces. The system consists of four independent components:

- A method for pose estimation of a human using laser rangefinder measurements.

- Learning to interpret human behaviour using motion patterns and Case-Based Reasoning (CBR).

- An adaptive human-aware navigation algorithm based on a potential field.

- A trajectory planning algorithm for planning a safe trajectory through a crowded human environment.

A Kalman filter based algorithm is used to derive pose estimates for the people in the environment. The pose estimates are used in a CBR system to estimate the person's interest in interaction. The spatial behaviour strategies of the robot are adapted according to the estimated interest by using adaptive potential field functions to govern the motion.

Furthermore a new algorithm for trajectory planning for a kinodynamic constrained robot in a human environment, has been described. The robot is navigating in a highly dynamic environment, which in this case is populated with humans. The algorithm, which is based on RRT's, enables the costs of traversing a potential field to be minimised, thereby supporting planning of comfortable and natural trajectories. A new control input sampling strategy, that together an MPC scheme is used to enable the planner to continuously plan a reachable trajectory on an on-line robotic system, has been presented.

The evaluation of the system has been conducted through two experiments in an open environment and simulation of robot navigation in a crowded environment. The first of the two experiments of the combined system shows that the CBR system is able to gradually learn from interaction experience. The experiment also shows how motion patterns from different people can be stored and generalised in order to predict the outcome of an interaction session with a new person. The second experiment shows how the estimated interest in interaction adapts to changes in behaviour of a test person. The trajectory generation algorithm proved in simulation that it is able to avoid collision with people in the environment. The algorithm is challenged, although still avoiding collisions, when the environments become very densely populated, but so are humans. Humans react by mutual adaptation and allowing violation of the social zones. This is not done here, where the robot takes on all the responsibility for finding a collision free trajectory.

The presented system is a step forward in creating socially intelligent robots, capable of navigating in everyday environments and interacting with human beings by understanding their interest and intention. In the long-term perspective, the results could be applied to service or assistive robot technology.

12. References

Althaus, P., Ishiguro, H., Kanda, T., Miyashita, T. & Christensen, H. (2004). Navigation for human-robot interaction tasks, *Proceedings of IEEE International Conference on Robotics and Automation, 2004. ICRA '04.*, Vol. 2, pp. 1894–1900.

Brooks, A., Kaupp, T. & Makarenko, A. (2009). Randomised mpc-based motion-planning for mobile robot obstacle avoidance, *Robotics and Automation, 2009. ICRA '09. IEEE International Conference on*, pp. 3962–3967.

Bruce, A. & Gordon, G. (2004). Better motion prediction for people-tracking, *Robotics and Automation, 2004. ICRA '04. IEEE International Conference on.*

Bruce, A., Nourbakhsh, I. & Simmons, R. (2001). The role of expressiveness and attention in human-robot interaction, *In Proceedings, AAAI Fall Symposium.*
URL: *citeseer.ist.psu.edu/article/bruce02role.html*

Christensen, H. I. & Pacchierotti, E. (2005). Embodied social interaction for robots, *in* K. Dautenhahn (ed.), *AISB-05*, Hertfordshire, pp. 40–45.

Cielniak, G., Treptow, A. & Duckett, T. (2005). Quantitative performance evaluation of a people tracking system on a mobile robot, *Proc. 2nd European Conference on Mobile Robots.*

Dautenhahn, K., Walters, M., Woods, S., Koay, K. L., Sisbot, E. A., Alami, R. & Simï£¡on, T. (2006). How may i serve you? a robot companion approaching a seated person in a helping context, *HRI Human Robot Interaction '06 (HRI06)*, Salt Lake City, Utah, USA.

Dornaika, F. & Raducanu, B. (2008). Detecting and tracking of 3d face pose for human-robot interaction, *Proceedings IEEE International Conference on Robotics and Automation*, pp. 1716–1721.

Feil-Seifer, D. & Mataric, M. (2005). A multi-modal approach to selective interaction in assistive domains, *Robot and Human Interactive Communication, 2005. ROMAN 2005. IEEE International Workshop on*, pp. 416–421.

Ferguson, D., Kalra, N. & Stentz, A. (2006). Replanning with rrts, *Proc. IEEE International Conference on Robotics and Automation ICRA 2006*, pp. 1243–1248.

Ferguson, D. & Stentz, A. (2006). Anytime rrts, *Proc. IEEE/RSJ International Conference on Intelligent Robots and Systems*, pp. 5369–5375.

Fod, A., Howard, A. & Mataric, M. J. (2002). Laser-based people tracking, *In Proc. of the IEEE International Conference on Robotics & Automation (ICRA*, pp. 3024–3029.

Govea, D. A. V. (2007). *Incremental Learning for Motion Prediction of Pedestrians and Vehicles*, PhD thesis, Institut National Polytechnique de Grenoble.

Hall, E. (1966). *The Hidden Dimension*, Doubleday.

Hall, E. T. (1963). A system for the notation of proxemic behavior, *American anthropologist* 65(5): 1003–1026.

Hanajima, N., Ohta, Y., Hikita, H. & Yamashita, M. (2005). Investigation of impressions for approach motion of a mobile robot based on psychophysiological analysis, *IEEE International Workshop on Robots and Human Interactive Communication ROMAN 2005*, pp. 79–84.

Hansen, S. T., Svenstrup, M., Andersen, H. J. & Bak, T. (2009). Adaptive human aware navigation based on motion pattern analysis, *Robot and Human Interactive Communication, 2009. RO-MAN 2009. The 18th IEEE International Symposium on*, Toyama, Japan, pp. –.

Jenkins, O. C., Serrano, G. G. & Loper, M. M. (2007). *Recognizing Human Pose and Actions for Interactive Robots*, I-Tech Education and Publishing, chapter 6, pp. 119–138.

Jurisica, I. & Glasgow, J. (1995). Applying case-based reasoning to control in robotics, *3rd Robotics and Knowledge-Based Systems Workshop, St. Hubert Quebec.*

Kelley, R., Tavakkoli, A., King, C., Nicolescu, M., Nicolescu, M. & Bebis, G. (2008). Understanding human intentions via hidden markov models in autonomous mobile robots, *HRI '08: Proceedings of the 3rd ACM/IEEE international conference on Human robot interaction*, ACM, New York, NY, USA, pp. 367–374.

Kirby, R., Forlizzi, J. & Simmons, R. (2007). Natural person-following behavior for social robots, *Proceedings of Human-Robot Interaction*, pp. 17–24.

Kirby, R., Simmons, R. & Forlizzi, J. (2009). Companion: A constraint-optimizing method for person-acceptable navigation, *Robot and Human Interactive Communication, 2009. RO-MAN 2009. The 18th IEEE International Symposium on*, pp. 607 –612.

Kleinehagenbrock, M., Lang, S., Fritsch, J., Lomker, F., Fink, G. & Sagerer, G. (2002). Person tracking with a mobile robot based on multi-modal anchoring, *Proceedings. 11th IEEE International Workshop on Robot and Human Interactive Communication (ROMAN), 2002.* 1: 423–429.

LaValle, S. (2006). *Planning algorithms*, Cambridge Univ Pr.

LaValle, S. & Kuffner Jr, J. (2001). Randomized kinodynamic planning, *The International Journal of Robotics Research* 20(5): 378.

Likhachev, M. & Arkin, R. (2001). Spatio-temporal case-based reasoning for behavioral selection, *Proc. IEEE International Conference on Robotics and Automation, ICRA*, Vol. 2, pp. 1627–1634.

Michalowski, M., Sabanovic, S. & Simmons, R. (2006). A spatial model of engagement for a social robot, *The 9th International Workshop on Advanced Motion Control, AMC06*, Istanbul.

Munoz-Salinas, R., Aguirre, E., Garcia-Silvente, M. & Gonzalez, A. (2005). People detection and tracking through stereo vision for human-robot interaction, *MICAI 2005: Advances in Artificial Intelligence* 3789/2005: 337–346.

Ram, A., Arkin, R. C., Moorman, K. & Clark, R. J. (1997). Case-based reactive navigation: A case-based method for on-line selection and adaptation of reactive control parameters in autonomous robotic systems, *IEEE Transactions on Systems, Man, and Cybernetics* 27: 376–394.

Rodgers, J., Anguelov, D., Pang, H.-C. & Koller, D. (2006). Object pose detection in range scan data, *Computer Vision and Pattern Recognition, 2006 IEEE Computer Society Conference on* 2: 2445–2452.

Siciliano, B. & Khatib, O. (2008). *Handbook of Robotics*, Springer-Verlag, Heidelberg.

Sisbot, E. A., Alami, R., Simï£¡on, T., Dautenhahn, K., Walters, M., Woods, S., Koay, K. L. & Nehaniv, C. (2005). Navigation in the presence of humans, *IEEE-RAS International Conference on Humanoid Robots (Humanoids 05)*, Tsukuba, Japan.

Sisbot, E. A., Clodic, A., Urias, L., Fontmarty, M., Brï£¡thes, L. & Alami, R. (2006). Implementing a human-aware robot system, *IEEE International Symposium on Robot and Human Interactive Communication 2006 (RO-MAN 06)*, Hatfield, United Kingdom, pp. 727–732.

Svenstrup, M., Bak, T. & Andersen, H. J. (2010). Trajectory planning for robots in dynamic human environments, *IROS 2010: The 2010 IEEE/RSJ International Conference on Intelligent Robots and Systems*, Taipei, Taiwan.

Svenstrup, M., Bak, T., Maler, O., Andersen, H. J. & Jensen, O. B. (2008). Pilot study of person robot interaction in a public transit space, *Proceedings of the International Conference on Research and Education in Robotics - EUROBOT 2008*, Springer-Verlag GmbH, Heidelberg, Germany, pp. 120–131.

Svenstrup, M., Hansen, S. T., Andersen, H. J. & Bak, T. (2009). Pose estimation and adaptive robot behaviour for human-robot interaction, *Proceedings of the 2009 IEEE International Conference on Robotics and Automation. ICRA 2009.*, Kobe, Japan, pp. 3571–3576.

Takayama, L. & Pantofaru, C. (2009). Influences on proxemic behaviors in human-robot interaction, *IROS'09: Proceedings of the 2009 IEEE/RSJ international conference on intelligent robots and systems*, IEEE Press, Piscataway, NJ, USA, pp. 5495–5502.

van den Berg, J. (2007). *Path planning in dynamic environments*, PhD thesis, Ph. D. dissertation, Universiteit Utrecht.

Walters, M. L., Dautenhahn, K., Koay, K. L., Kaouri, C., te Boekhorst, R., Nehaniv, C., Werry, I. & Lee, D. (2005). Close encounters: Spatial distances between people and a robot of mechanistic appearance, *Proceedings of 2005 5th IEEE-RAS International Conference on Humanoid Robots*, Tsukuba, Japan, pp. 450–455.

Walters, M. L., Dautenhahn, K., te Boekhorst, R., Koay, K. L., Kaouri, C., Woods, S., Nehaniv, C., Lee, D. & Werry, I. (2005). The influence of subjectsï£¡ personality traits on personal spatial zones in a human-robot interaction experiment, *Proc. IEEE Ro-man*, Hashville, pp. 347–352.

Woods, S., Walters, M. L., Koay, K. & Dautenhahn, K. (2006). Methodological issues in hri: A comparison of live and video-basedmethods in robot to human approach direction trials, *The 15th IEEE International Symposium on Robot and Human Interactive Communication (RO-MAN06)*, Hatfield, UK, pp. 51–58.

Xavier, J., Pacheco, M., Castro, D., Ruano, A. & Nunes, U. (2005). Fast line, arc/circle and leg detection from laser scan data in a player driver, *Robotics and Automation, 2005. ICRA 2005. Proceedings of the 2005 IEEE International Conference on*, pp. 3930–3935.

Zucker, M., Kuffner, J. & Branicky, M. (2007). Multipartite rrts for rapid replanning in dynamic environments, *Proc. IEEE International Conference on Robotics and Automation*, pp. 1603–1609.

Part 3

Robot Navigation Inspired by Nature

8

Brain-actuated Control of Robot Navigation

Francisco Sepulveda

BCI Group - School of Computer Science and Electronic Engineering, University of Essex
United Kingdom

1. Introduction

Brain-driven robot navigation control is a new field stemming from recent successes in brain interfaces. Broadly speaking, brain interfaces comprise any system that aims to enable user control of a device based on brain activity-related signals, be them conscious or unconscious, voluntary or evoked, invasive or non-invasive. Strictly speaking, the term should also include technology that directly affects brains states (e.g., transcranial magnetic stimulation), but these are not usually included in the terminology. Two main families of brain interfaces exist according to the usual terminology, although the terms are often used interchangeably as well: i) *Brain-computer interfaces* (or BCIs) usually refers to brain-to-computer interfaces that use non-invasive technology; ii) *Brain-machine interfaces* (or BMIs) often refers to implanted brain-interfaces. This chapter shall use these terms (BCI and BMI) as defined in this paragraph. Other sub-categories of BCIs are discussed below.

The idea of BCIs is credited to Jaques Vidal (1973) who first proposed the idea in concrete scientific and technological terms. Until the late 1990's the area progressed slowly as a result of work in but a handful of laboratories in Europe and North America, most notably the groups at the Wadsworth Centre (Albany, NY) and the Graz (Austria) group led by G. Pfurtscheller. Aside from the few researchers working on BCIs in the '70s and '80s, slow progress then was largely due to limitations in: i) our understanding of brain electrophysiology, ii) quality and cost of recording equipment, iii) computer memory and processing speed, and iv) the performance of pattern recognition algorithms. The state-of-the-art in these areas and the number of BCI researchers have dramatically increased in the last ten years or so. Yet, there is still an enormous amount of work do be done before BCIs can be used reliably outside controlled laboratory conditions.

In this chapter, an overview of BCIs will be given, followed by a discussion of specific approaches for BCI-based robot navigation control. The chapter then concludes with a summary of challenges for the future of this new and exciting technology.

1.1 Overview of BCIs

A typical – and simplified – BCI system is illustrated in Fig. 1. In principle, the easiest way for most users to control a device with their thoughts would be to have a computer read the words a user is thinking. E.g., if a user wants to steer a robot to the left, he/she would only need to think of the word 'left'. However, while attempts at doing this have been made, such approach currently leads to true positive recognition rates that are only slightly above chance – at best. At present BCIs work in two ways (see item A in Fig. 1): either i) brain signals are monitored while the user performs a specified cognitive task (e.g., imagination of hand movements), or ii) the computer makes decisions based on the user's brain's involuntary response to a particular stimulus (e.g., flashing of an object on a computer screen), although both approaches have been combined recently as well (Salvaris & Sepulveda, 2010).

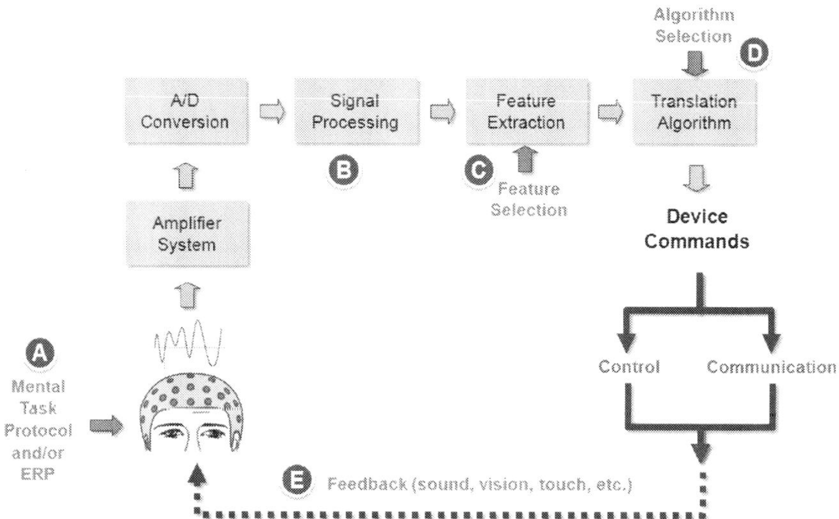

Fig. 1. Schematic of a brain-computer interface system

Once signals are recorded (which usually includes amplification, common mode rejection and antialising filtering) and digitized, they need to be further processed to increase the signal to noise ratio by applying frequency band filters, spatial filters, and various referencing methods (see step B in Fig. 1 and the Signal Processing section below). At this stage, we often have several hundred to several thousand data points per second, depending on the domain on which the data are analyzed. To reduce both the dimensionality of the pattern recognition task and the amount of irrelevant data (e.g., data that do not carry information related to the mental states of interest) feature selection algorithms (step C) are applied at least during offline testing, although they can also be applied on-line. Once features are extracted/selected, they are fed into a classifier (step D) that will attempt to infer the user's mental state. Finally, some BCI systems also provide specific feedback to the user (step E), such as a sample of the classifier's output or a parameter related to the user's level of concentration, amongst others. Some of the steps described here make use of methods that are common to other areas. Machine learning and feature selection algorithms (e.g., support vector machines, linear discriminant analysis, nerofuzzy inference, genetic algorithms, cluster overlap indices, etc.) used in BCIs are often the same as those applied in other fields such as computer vision, etc., or variations of them. These, as such, will not be discussed in this chapter (but see Lotte et al., 2007, for further information). On the other hand, a number of techniques are specific to the kind of data used in BCIs, i.e., usually suitable for encephalographic (EEG) data. These are discussed in some detail below.

1.2 Types of BCIs

Throughout the years, BCIs have been categorized in several different ways. Most accepted terminology falls under one of the following (Wolpaw et al., 2002):

- Invasive vs. non-invasive.
- Dependent vs. independent.
- Spontaneous vs. evoked vs. event-related.
- Synchronous vs. asynchronous.

So far, these have been studied mostly in a mutually exclusive manner (e.g., either synchronous or asynchronous). They are described in more detail below.

1.2.1 Invasive vs. non-invasive

In a narrow sense, there is an obvious difference between invasive interfaces (i.e., implanted) and those (non invasive) that go on the skin surface or farther from the body. In a strict sense, however, any technology that deposits external elements on the body, be it matter or even photons and magnetic fields, is invasive in that it directly affects the internal physical state of the body. As discussed under Recording Equipment, below, technologies such as near-infrared spectroscopy (NIRS, which deposits near-infrared light on tissue), magnetic resonance imaging (which applies magnetic fields) and positron emission tomography (which requires the administration of a radioactive substance) are all invasive as the very mechanisms by which they work requires that the observed tissue (and surrounding ones) be internally disturbed. For most of these technologies, the effects on the body are well known. For NIRS, however, the effects of the absorbed energy on the brain tissue have not been studied concerning long term and even short term but prolonged use (e.g., rare occasions, but with hours of use every time), and thus caution is recommended at this point in time.

Of the technologies described later in the chapter, only electroencephalography and magnetoencephalography can be considered non-invasive.

1.2.2 Dependent vs. Independent BCIs

BCIs have been classified as either dependent or independent (Wolpaw et al., 2000). A dependent BCI does not require the usual ways of brain output to express the internal mental state (e.g., speech, facial expression, limb movement, etc.), but it does require that some functionality (e.g., gaze control) remain beyond the brain. In practice what this means is that a dependent BCI is not entirely reliant on the brain signals alone. For example (see SSVEP BCIs below), in some cases the user must be able to fixate his/her gaze on a desired flashing object on a computer screen in order for the BCI to determine which object (or choice) the user wants amongst a finite set. This is a problem in principle as a 'pure' BCI should not require any body-based functionality beyond being conscious and being able to make decisions at the thought level. However, in practice very few users have no overt (i.e., observable via visual or auditory means) action abilities left. These, so called *totally* locked-individuals, would not be able to benefit from a dependent BCI, so independent BCIs are needed in this case. On the other hand, most disabled and otherwise functionally restricted people (including some locked in individuals), as well as able-bodied people, have at least some voluntary eye movement control, which motivates further research in dependent BCIs. Independent BCIs, in contrast, do not require any physical ability on the part of the user other than the ability to mentally focus and make decisions. In other words, even if the user has no voluntary control of any organ beyond the brain, an independent BCI would be able to infer the user's mental choices by looking at the brain signals. In this case, the signals are independent of whether or not the user has any control of any body parts. Examples of this are mental navigation, mental arithmetic, imagination of limb movements, etc.

1.2.3 Spontaneous vs. evoked vs. event-related

Evoked potentials (EPs) are observable brain responses to a given stimulus, e.g., a flashing letter, a sound, etc., whether the user is aware of or interested in the stimulus or not. EPs are time locked to the stimulus in that the observed brain signal will contain features that are consistently timed with respect to the stimulus. For example, if a user focuses his/her gaze on a flashing character on a computer screen, this flashing frequency (if it is between about 6Hz and 35Hz) will be observable in the visual cortex signals. Other brain signals can be *spontaneous*, i.e., they do not require a given stimulus to appear. Thoughts in general can be assumed to be spontaneous (although strictly speaking this is still debatable). An example of spontaneous potentials are those related to movement intentions in the sensory motor cortex and are thus not a result of specific input. Finally, a third class of signals is termed *'event-related potentials'* (ERP). They are related to evoked potentials but also include brain responses that are not directly elicited by the stimulus. I.e., they can include spontaneous or deliberate thoughts such as mental counting, etc. (Rugg and Coles, 1995), but they have a well controlled time window within which brain signals are monitored, whether spontaneous or as a result of a specific stimulus. The term *event related potential* is currently seen as more accurate for all but the most restricted stimulation protocols and it is preferred over the term *evoked potentials*.

1.2.4 Synchronous (cue based) vs. asynchronous (self-paced)

The three subcategories described in the previous paragraph are also referred to using two other terms, synchronous and asynchronous interfaces. BCIs based on EPs and ERPs are synchronous in that they restrict the interaction as the user is only allowed to convey an intention or command to the machine when the machine allows it. I.e., either the monitored signal is a response to a computer-timed stimulus, or it is a mental task executed only when the monitoring computer gives the 'go ahead' to the user, typically by means of a tone or an object on the screen. The user, thus, has control over **what** to convey to the machine, but not **when**. This is by far the most common approach in BCIs. For example, a common approach is to have the computer give a visual or auditory cue to let the user know that he/she is to perform a mental task (e.g., movement imagination) immediately afterwards. In this case, as in most BCIs, the user is told to stop the task after a few seconds. The computer then uses these few seconds of data to infer the mental state of the user. In another common synchronous approach, users choose from a set of flashing letters (see the P300 and SSVEP approaches later in the chapter). Obviously, in this case computer interpretation of the signals can only be done on data obtained while the object of interest in flashing, the timing for which is very precisely controlled in order to map specific data features to the correct flashing object. Synchronous BCIs are often called *'cue-based'* as well.

Asynchronous BCIs (e.g., Townsend et al., 2004), on the other hand, use brain signals that are produced any time by the user, with or without a specific computer-controlled stimulus. This makes classification of the user's intention difficult as the machine first needs to identify whether a deliberate intention-related signal has been produced (the so called 'onset detection' problem, e.g., see Tsui et al., 2006) to then be able to identify what intention took place. An alternative is to use continuous classification of the signals with 'idle' or 'no specific state' as one of the classes, but this may reduce classification performance overall as it adds a class to the number of possible outputs from the translation algorithm. An example of an asynchronous BCI is the use of movement imagination (e.g., left hand movement vs. right hand movement) to steer a robot left or right when the user decides this must be done and not when the robot/computer demands a command. Asynchronous BCIs are often called 'self-paced' as well.

The main problem with asynchronous BCIs is the difficulty in determining training and validation labels for the classifier. In essence, if the computer is not able to determine when an onset took place with a precision in the order of a few hundred milliseconds, it is unlikely that the data will be correctly labelled for (re)training purposes. To circumvent this problem, often the user is asked to perform the spontaneous mental task for relatively long periods, e.g., near 10s, so that onset timing errors become irrelevant (see e.g., Sepulveda et al., 2007). However, this approach puts serious limitations on the rate of information transfer between the user and the machine.

Due to the timing and labelling problems with asynchronous (self-paced) BCIs, most work to date has used synchronous (cue-based) interfaces. However, self-paced BCIs are much more natural to the user as they do not require that the subject be paying full attention to a given stimulus or cue. Thus, not only does the user have timing freedom with self-paced BCIs, but he/she is also free to multi-task and interact with the environment beyond the BCI. This is the ultimate aim of BCIs.

1.3 Recording equipment

A number of devices have potential for use in BCIs. Some candidates are briefly discussed below. As we will see, only one class of equipment is currently suitable for widespread use, but, depending on the circumstances, the other devices may be useful as well.

- *Functional magnetic resonance imaging (fMRI)* (Belliveau et al., 1991): This is a powerful technology used for functional brain mapping based on hemodynamics (i.e. , blood flow and oxygenation changes).
  - Pros: It provides excellent spatial resolution.
  - Cons: The equipment is very large, heavy and expensive. Thus, portability is not a possibility for at least a few decades, if ever. The temporal response is slow compared to, e.g., electroencephalography (EEG, discussed on the next page). As fMRI monitors hemodynamics, a few seconds of changed and sustained neural activity go by before significant changes are seen (Raichle et al., 2006). This poses a major problem for real-time BCIs, in which case a particular mental state of interest may have come and gone without being detected. This is because much of BCI-relevant brain activity is of a transient nature (but see SSVEP later in the chapter for an exception to this). On the other hand, if a mental task is maintained for several seconds, in semi or actual steady-state, fMRI will allow detection of this process. An additional problem is the use of strong magnetic fields, which poses safety issues, especially if metals (e.g., electrodes) are in the proximity.
- *Positron emission tomography (PET)* (Ter-Pogossian et al., 1975): In principle this technology can be used for brain mapping, usually through radioactive oxygen or glucose given to the user.
  - Pros: spatial resolution is better than with EEG.
  - Cons: First and foremost, then use of radioactive substances precludes use of this technology in BCIs, although in extreme cases (e.g., in totally locked in individuals)

it can be useful for validating other methods as it is a well established technology, having been available for several decades. Like fMRI, the approach also suffers from poor time resolution, aside from the fact that long delays (up to hours) are required between radioisotope ingestion and the brain imaging procedure. The recording equipment is very large and expensive as well.

- *Near infrared sprectroscopy (NIRS)* (Wolf et al., 2007): This method too is based on hemodynamics. In this case blood oxygenation changes are linked to the amount of reflected near-infrared light applied on the brain through transmitters on the scalp, the receiver being placed nearby on the scalp as well. The approach is similar to that used in existing sensors using mid-range infrared, but near infra-red has much deeper penetration in tissue (up to a few centimetres), lending itself to brain monitoring.
  - Pros: This is currently the cheapest hemodynamics-based technology available, although the equipment is still more expensive than for EEG. Compared to other hemodynamics devices, NIRS equipment is also fairly portable, and wireless systems have been recently developed as well (Muehlemann et al., 2008).
  - Cons: As in other hemodynamics-based systems, time resolution is poor. On the other hand, different from PET and fMRI, spatial resolution is poor due to significant scattering of the near-infrared light in tissue. NIRS systems are also very sensitive to transmitter and sensor motion and environmental NIR sources.
- *Magnetoencephalography (MEG)* (Cohen, 1972): MEG records the magnetic fields orthogonal to the electric fields generated by ensemble neural activity, although there is evidence suggesting that the source of detectable magnetic fields in the brain is physiologically different from those generating EEG (Hamalainen et al., 1993).
  - Pros: It has much better time resolution than hemodynamics-based systems. Electrical and magnetic field changes reflect the underlying neural activity within a few milliseconds. Also, in contrast with fMRI, PET and NIRS, MEG only monitors brain signals and does not deposit any matter or energy on the brain. It is thus a truly non-invasive technology in that it does not disturb the object of study.
  - Cons: MEG equipment is still very large, comparable in size with fMRI equipment. It is also very costly.
- *Electroencephalography (EEG)* (Niedermeyer et al., 2004): This is by far the oldest of all the devices discussed here, having been available at least since the 1920's (Swartz and Goldensohn, 1998). In EEG, the electrodes are usually placed on the scalp and record the electrical activity taking place in the brain tissue underneath, which reaches the electrode region by volume conductor processes. In order for neural activity to be detectable using EEG, it must be both fairly near the cortical surface and include many millions of cells in synchrony so that the total sum of the activity is large enough to be detected from the scalp. Still, the largest EEG potentials seen under most conditions have amplitudes in the order of a few tens of microvolts.
  - Pros: EEG is the least expensive technology for brain monitoring. EEG systems are also very portable and provide excellent time resolution. Due to their passive nature (from the brain's point of view), they are very safe as well.
  - Cons: There are two main limitations in EEG systems. One (poor spatial resolution) is inherent while the other (poor usability) can still be tackled. Poor spatial resolution is inherent due to the volume conductor effects through which signals from nearby (even up to a few cm apart) areas are irreversibly mixed together. While various approaches exist to minimize this problem, sub-centimeter

EEG features have little meaning. Poor usability stems from the need to use electrode gel to reduce the impedance between the electrodes and the scalp, but there are commercial systems currently available that employ user-friendly wet electrodes or dry (usually capacitive) electrodes, at the expense of signal quality.

- *Implanted Brain Interfaces, or Brain-Machine Interfaces (BMIs)* (Lebedev & Nicolelis, 2006): Various approaches have been developed that require the implantation of electrodes and arrays thereof to record brain electrical signals much closer to their source than with MEG and EEG. These record local potentials and in some cases signals from as few as tens of cells can be recorded. These brain interfaces have been implanted at various depth levels under the skull, from the surface of the protective tissue surrounding the brain to near a centimetre into the cortex.
  - Pros: The main advantage of implanted devices is that they have the potential to simultaneously provide the best spatial and time resolution.
  - Cons: Very high cost, risky surgery and post-surgery damage risks (including possible irreversible loss of neural tissue) are the main issues. These are currently of such high level, however, that (implanted) BMIs are still experimental, although there is currently at least one user with a working BMI in place (Hochberg et al., 2006).

Of all the devices described above, EEG is so far the best candidate for routine BCI use as it is portable, safe, relatively inexpensive, and has good temporal resolution. For these reasons it is the device of choice in the vast majority of BCI research and development. Hence, hereafter in this chapter all methods under discussion refer to EEG unless otherwise specified.

A typical EEG set up is illustrated in Fig. 2. In the picture electrodes have been placed on the scalp on locations anterior and posterior to the areas of the brain that control limb movements (see Motor Imagery below). In this case differential (bipolar) recordings are obtained for each anterior/posterior electrode pair, providing relevant information on movement-related intentions.

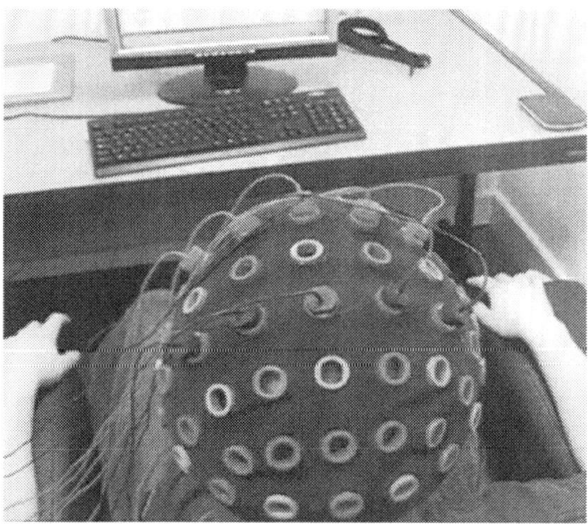

Fig. 2. Typical EEG cap for use in BCIs. In the picture, only electrode locations used for monitoring hand and foot movement imagination are included in the set-up

1.4 Signal processing

The signal-to-noise ratio in EEG signals is significantly <1. This is largely due to the small amplitude of the recorded signals (in the order of microvolts), but also due to a number of other factors, such as: irreversible summation of sources due to volume conduction in tissue, brain multitasking, less than suitable skin-electrode impedances, evoked potentials resulting from unwanted or unaccounted for stimuli, motion artifacts (electrode and cable movement, etc.), environmental noise, strong interference from muscle signals, eye motion artifacts, etc. On the whole this produces a very noisy signal, which, at first glance, has little if any information about the underlying brain function. For the simplest cases, basic features can be extracted (e.g., closing of one's eyes or relaxing produces a visible amplitude increase in the alpha band – 8Hz to 10Hz), but in most cases sophisticated feature extraction and machine learning algorithms need to be employed to obtain even partially reliable information. A typical EEG signal set is shown on the left panel in Fig. 3. The figure illustrates the recorded signals at various locations on the scalp after they have been submitted to digital filtering and ear-referencing (discussed in the next subsections).

Three characteristics can be easily identified in the EEG plot in Fig. 3: i) the strong correlation between signals from nearby electrodes, thus illustrating the poor spatial resolution mentioned above; ii) the lack of obvious events during movement imagination, starting at the green arrows and lasting 3s; and iii) the strong artifact caused by rolling of the eyes, shown in the red box. Notice that while the eye-movement artifact is more prominent in the more frontal areas, it does spread as far as the back of the head.

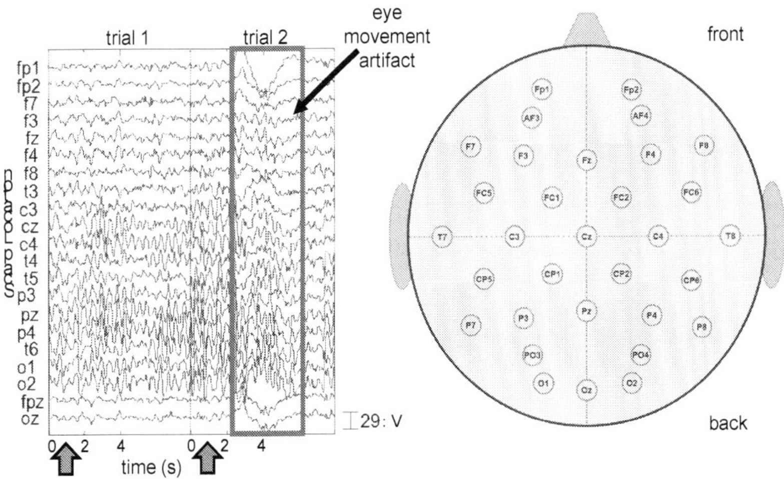

Fig. 3. EEG time-domain signal sample and standard electrode locations. *Left panel*: multichannel recordings during two trials (i.e., attempts) of hand movement imagination. *Right panel*: standard scalp location of electrodes for a 32-channel setup using the 10-20 system (Cooper et al., 1969). Fp: frontal pole, AF: antero-frontal, F: frontal, FC: fronto-central, C: central, T: temporal, CP: centro-parietal, P: parietal, PO: parieto-occipital, O: occipital, z: mid-sagittal line. The (red) box on the left panel shows the effect of eye movement on the signals. The green arrows show when a visual cue was given to the user to begin mental imagination of right hand movement, which lasted 3s

The figure above illustrates how challenging information extraction is even after digital filtering and ear-referencing EEG signals. Without these pre-processing steps, however, the signals are even less usable. We thus proceed to discuss the minimum pre-processing stages.

1.4.1 Frequency band filtering

EEG signal energy is optimal in the 0Hz-80Hz range, although historically most studies have ignored frequencies above about 45Hz (as most processes of interest to the medical community take place below 45Hz). In this range, there are three main sources of noise which must be removed or minimized: i) motion artifacts caused by electrode and cable movements (including slow electrode drift), which are mostly below 0.5Hz; ii) mains interference (50Hz in the UK, 60Hz in the USA); and iii) muscle signals, i.e., electromyography (EMG, e.g., from jaws, facial muscle twitches, swallowing, etc.), some of which actually overlaps with EEG as EMG produces relevant information between near 0Hz and about 500Hz (up to 1kHz if implanted EMG is recorded). EMG cannot be fully removed due to the EEG/EMG overlap, but it can be minimized by avoiding muscle contractions in areas near the brain and by applying a lowpass digital filter to the EEG signal (if EMG is simultaneously recorded, it can be used with methods such as independent component analysis to reduce the EMG interference on the EEG signal). Most motion artifacts can be removed with a highpass filter at ~0.5Hz (some researchers will apply a cutoff as high as 5Hz if they wish to ignore the EEG delta band). Mains interference can be eliminated by referencing (see next subsection). But, if no referencing will be applied, a notch or stopband filter must be used to remove mains interference. Overall, both analogue and digital filters are needed as a first step in EEG processing. Typical filters suitable for BCIs are illustrated in Fig. 4, which are shown only as basic guidelines as researchers might use different filter types, orders and cutoff frequencies.

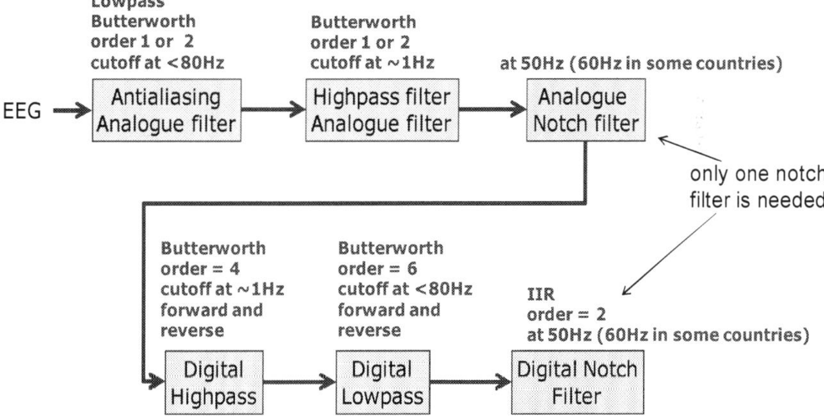

Fig. 4. Typical frequency band filtering of EEG signals

1.4.2 Referencing

EEG signal referencing is the subtraction of the potential recorded at a scalp location (usually already subtracted from a scalp-based common mode rejection point at the hardware stages) from a nearby overall reference location. This is done to remove common environmental noise from the recorded EEG. To this end, the reference point must be near enough to a scalp electrode so that it has a similar noise content, but it should not have any signal sources itself. There are two typical referencing methods:

- Outside the scalp (ear or mastoid referencing): one of the ear lobes or mastoid locations (or the average between the left and right ones) is used as the reference. This is the standard approach for overall removal of environmental noise for most experimental scenarios.
- Scalp average: this is used when the goal is to investigate the difference between one channel and the rest of the scalp. It is useful also for rough localization of function (e.g., movement imagination vs. other tasks) or to study waves that are over several, but not all, channels (e.g., the P300 wave discussed later in the chapter).

Although referencing is very effective in removing common environmental noise, it does nothing to improve spatial resolution, i.e., the difference between signals from adjacent electrodes. To this end, spatial filtering is often used, the most common approaches being bipolar and Laplacean processing, as follows:

- Bipolar: This is a simple subtraction between signals from two adjacent electrodes. It will give a good estimate of activity in the area between the two electrodes. For example, subtraction of channel CP1 from channel FC1 (see Fig. 3 above) gives good information about activity related to right arm movement, whose control is the area between these two electrodes.
- Laplacean: the subtraction of one channel from the ones surrounding it. This is very useful for maximizing spatial resolution, e.g., to distinguish between imagination of movement for different limbs as their control areas are near each other in the cortex. For example, to monitor signals related to foot movement, the Cz signal (Fig. 3) can be subtracted from the average of the signal from the {FC1, FC2, CP1, CP2} electrode set. In this way, the Cz signal would yield less information about irrelevant areas nearby and more about what is directly underneath the Cz electrode.

The bipolar and Laplacean methods are also called *referenceless* as any previous signal referencing done will drop out during the subtraction process.

Referencing and referenceless methods can also reduce eye-movement artifacts, but often these persist and must be reduced by more sophisticated methods such as independent component analysis (Vigario, 1997), at the expense of processing speed and risking losing relevant information. However, many BCIs ignore eye-movement artifact removal altogether as the pattern recognition algorithms can learn to ignore the artifact and the increase in computer memory use and processing time is often not worth the effort.

2. Approaches for BCI control of robot navigation

As mentioned above, there are many approaches currently under development in BCIs. Some will more easily lend themselves to applications in robot navigation, but almost every approach can be used for this purpose with minor modifications. Due to space and topic relevance restrictions, it is not possible to cover all approaches within this chapter. Instead, in the next subsections the three main candidates for brain-actuated robot navigation using (non-invasive) BCIs are discussed. The subsection will conclude with a discussion of how to employ a particular approach towards BCI control of robot navigation.

2.1 Motor Imagery (MI)

Imagination or mental rehearsal of limb movements is a relatively easy cognitive task for BCI users, especially able-bodied ones. Some individuals will not find this task as straight forward, but most become better at motor imagery (MI) with practice. Another advantage of this approach is that it allows the user to multitask, e.g., he/she does not need to focus on the BCI computer and can thus interact with the environment more freely than with methods such as P300 and SSVEP discussed below.

In addition, MI benefits from the fact that movement-related brain activity is well localized. Several areas of the brain handle movement-related intentions before these are executed, but, at the execution stage, the primary motor cortex (PMC) is the main control center (right panel in Fig. 5). The area immediately posterior to the PMC, the somatosensory cortex, receives sensory information from the equivalent body parts controlled by the PMC. Within the PMC, subregions of the body are distributed in a well localized functional map as well. For example, a cross section of the left primary motor cortex area is illustrated on the right panel in Fig. 5, where the labels indicate which part of the (right side of) the body is controlled. We can clearly see how one might use signals from different channels to be able to distinguish between movements of different body parts, e.g., hand vs. foot. However, the functional map shown below can only be fully explored by means of implanted devices, intra-cortical ones in particular. Due to the volume conductor effects mentioned above, EEG electrodes will also pick up signals from areas near the region underneath the electrode. For example, an EEG electrode on the scalp right above the hand area will likely contain signals related to other areas as well, from arm to neck, at least. This problem, however, can be lessened by applying multichannel recordings and bipolar or Laplacean processing, as discussed above.

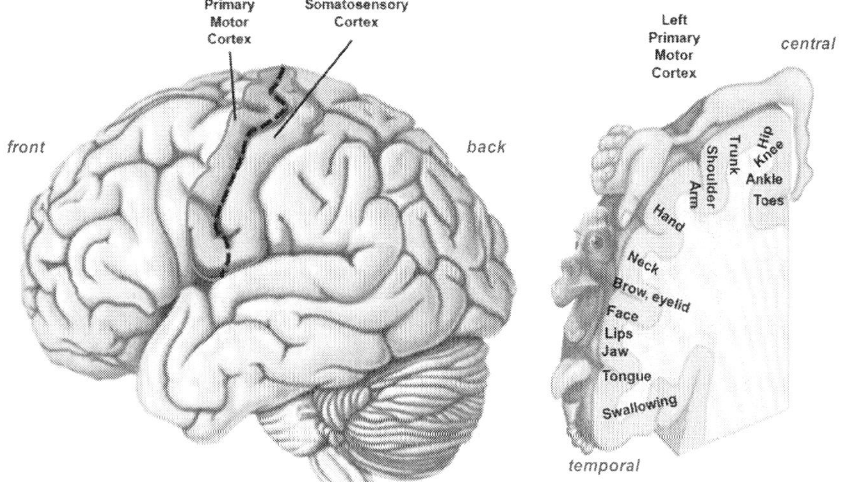

Fig. 5. Brain localization of primary movement control

2.1.1 Motor Imagery (MI) towards robot navigation

As mentioned above, motor imagery is an intuitive cognitive task for most, although it may require practice. Control of robot navigation with this method can thus be easily mapped to limb movements. For example (Fig. 6), to steer a robot to the right, the user can imagine or mentally feel (also known as kinaesthetic motor imagery) a movement of the right hand (e.g., hand closing, wrist extension, etc.).   The example below shows only three movements. Other motor imagery tasks can be added to increase the number of robot movement classes (i.e., choices). For example, imagination of tongue movement is often used as an additional class.

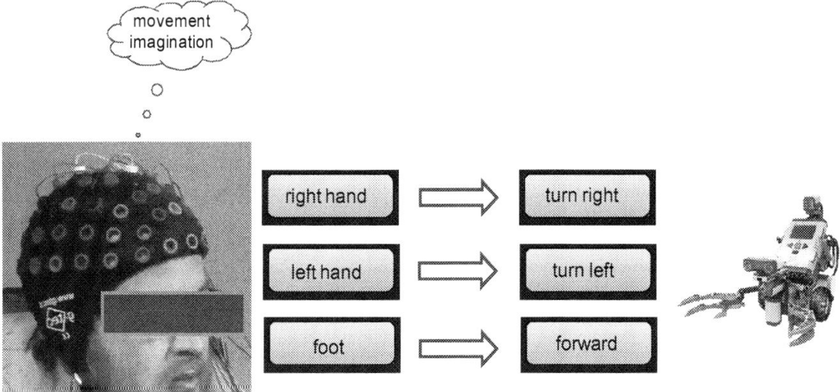

Fig. 6. Possible use of motor imagery for robot navigation control

Notice from Fig. 5 above that using separate movements of the right and left feet should not be expected to yield two separate classes with EEG as the brain areas that control both feet are next to each other and deep in the brain, which means the same electrode (i.e., Cz in Fig. 3) will pick up signals from both feet.

Motor imagery will produce features that can be used for classification. A common feature used with MI is band power, in which case the power of the (previously pre-processed) signal in specific frequency bands (notably alpha: 8-12Hz and beta: 13-30Hz) yields good classification of right vs. left movements. A similar feature commonly used with MI is event-related desynchronization and synchronization (ERD/ERS) which compares the energy of the signal in specific bands with respect to an idle state (i.e., a mentally relaxed period). In either case the most appropriate electrodes are usually the ones over or near the relevant primary motor cortex areas.

Motor imagery can be used with any timing protocol. It can be used by itself in a cue based approach, in a self-paced system, or used in combination with the P300 approach discussed below (as in Salvaris & Sepulveda, 2010), although the latter has not been applied to robot navigation.

One of the limitations of MI-based BCIs for robot control is that usually a few seconds of EEG data are needed for each control decision and for the motor cortex to fully return to a neutral state. Typically this will give an information transfer rate (from user to robot) of <10 bits/min. MI approaches similar to the one discussed above have been applied to robot navigation (e.g., Millan et al., 2004).

2.2 P300

This approach falls under the event-related potential category.   In this method, the user is presented with a visual array of choices (left panel, Fig. 7, based on Farwell & Donchin,

1988), although sound and touch can be used as the stimulus as well. Typically each row and column will flash for a short period (about 100ms) in a random sequence on a computer screen. When the row or column containing the desired choice flashes, the user adds 1 to a mental counter to signal that a target has flashed. For example, if the user wants to type the letter P using a BCI, she/he will count every time a row/column containing it flashes. On average, when a target row/column flashes, a strong signal is seen (especially in the centro-parietal electrodes, Fig. 3) which will peak at about 300ms after the desired object flashed, hence the P300 name. Until recently it was assumed that eye gaze did not significantly affect P300 responses, but there is now evidence suggesting that this is not the case (Brunner et al., 2010).

The right panel in Fig. 7 illustrates signal differences between target, non-target and near-target events). In most cases, the target P300 peak is only easily distinguishable from non-target events if an average of several trials is performed, and often up to ten target trial responses are needed to have a true positive rate of about 90%.

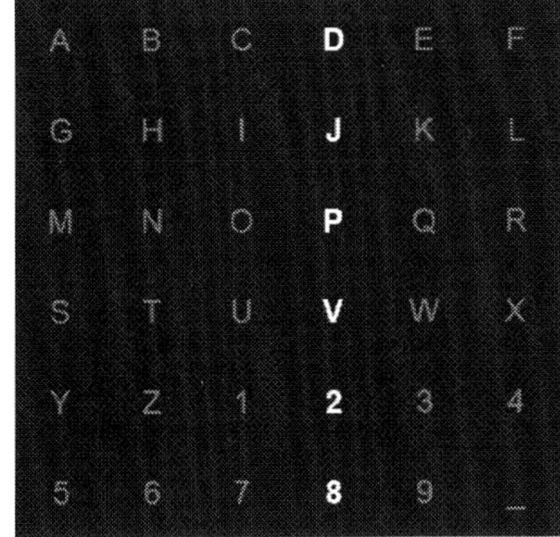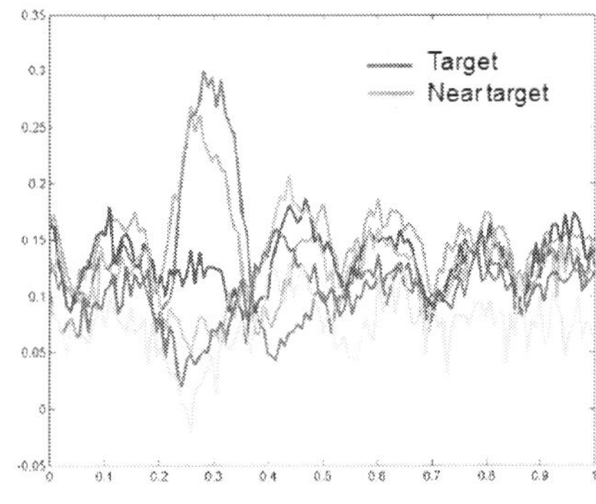

Fig. 7. Typical P300-based stimulus array and EEG responses (modified from Citi et al., 2004)

2.2.1 P300 towards robot navigation

The array in Fig. 7 is used for communication BCIs (e.g., as a speller) and does not directly lend itself to use in robot navigation control. However, if each object on the array represents a command to a robot, the user can employ the BCI to give the robot a sequence of commands which may include variables such as direction, timing schedule, proportional control parameters (e.g. , for angular displacement, speed), etc. But, one of the problems with this interface is that the user must wait for all rows and columns to flash before a new flashing cycle begins. With current standard timing parameters, this would take several seconds per trial, per chosen letter. If, as mentioned above, several trials are used to increase true positive recognition rates, choosing one letter can take more than 10s, which is not suitable in many robot navigation cases. To minimize this problem, an array with less elements can be used, although this will reduce the difference between target and non-target events as this difference increases when target events are much less probable than non-target ones.

An alternative to the P300 standard array and one that is suitable for robot navigation (at least in a 4-direction 2D scenario) is shown in Fig. 8. The figure is based on a system designed for mouse control (Citi et al., 2004), but it can be easily employed for robot navigation. For example, the four flashing objects can represent left/right/back/forward. One limitation that would still exist, however, is that the user must have full attention on the screen showing the 4-object array. In this case, the user would count every time the desired direction flashes, as a result of which the robot would turn in the desired direction.

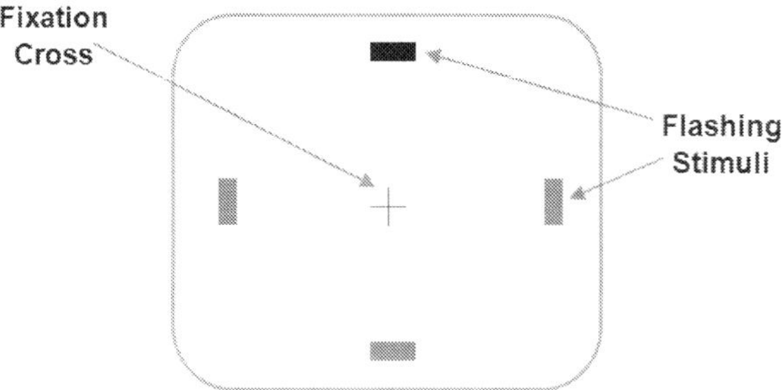

Fig. 8. P300-based interface for basic robot steering

P300 approaches similar to the one shown in Fig. 8 have been applied to robot navigation recently. Also, Rebsamen et al. (2007) produced a P300 system in which the objects on the monitor are pictures of the landmarks to which the robot (a wheelchair in this case) must go. In that system, the user chooses the end point and the robot uses autonomous navigation to get to it.

The information transfer rate of a P300-based BCI with four classes will yield a higher information transfer rate than with motor imagery, possibly >20bits/minute, but, as mentioned above, it has the disadvantage that it demands the user's full attention on the visual interface.

2.3 Steady-State Visual Evoked Potentials (SSVEP)

The P300 method above is similar to the SSVEP approach in that the user is presented with an array containing flashing objects from which the user chooses one. However, in the SSVEP method each object flashes at a different frequency, usually between 6Hz and about 35Hz (Gao et al., 2003). When the user fixates his/her gaze on a flashing object, that object's flashing frequency will be seen as a strong frequency-domain element in the EEG recorded from areas above the visual cortex (occipital areas, Fig. 3). For example (Fig. 9), if the user is interested in number 7 on a number array, fixating his/her gaze on that object (which is this example is flashing at 8Hz) will produce the power spectrum shown on the right panel in Fig. 9, which is an average of five trials (i.e., target flashing cycles).

Notice that the user must have eye gaze control for this approach to work, but, as mentioned above, this ability is retained by the vast majority of potential BCI users, both disabled and able-bodied.

2.3.1 SSVEP towards robot navigation

Using an SSVEP-based BCI for robot navigation control is similar to the case with the P300 method, i.e., a suitable array of flashing objects can be designed specifically for robot navigation.

SSVEP-based BCIs have been used for robot navigation control (e.g., Ortner et al., 2010). The information transfer rate will yield a higher information transfer rate than with motor imagery, >40bits/minute, but, as is the case with the P300 approach described above, it has the disadvantage that it demands the user's full attention on the visual interface.

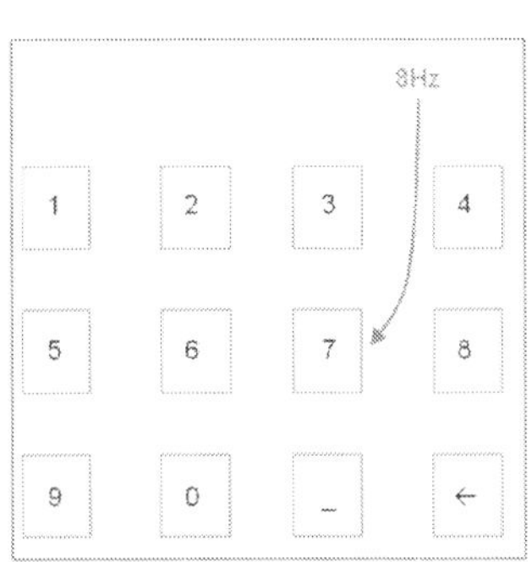

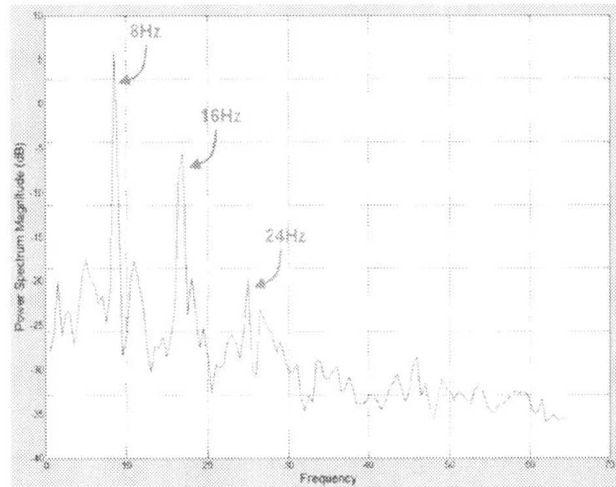

Fig. 9. SSVEP BCI. Left: example of a multi-object array in which the object of interest (number 7) flashes at 8Hz. Right: power spectrum of the recorded EEG when the user fixates his/her gaze on number 7 in the interface (notice the strong harmonic components)

2.4 Choosing the most suitable BCI type

The best BCI type will depend on the scenario to be tackled. For example, for robot navigation in an environment for which landmarks are stored in its memory, either the P300 or the SSVEP approaches can be used only when necessary by allowing the user to choose the desired landmark and letting the robot use its autonomous system to get to the landmark. If, on the other hand, the environment is novel or the robot encounters unexpected obstacles, motor imagery can be used for direct control of robot steering. All approaches can be used in combination as well, e.g., using motor imagery for initial navigation while the robot saves information about the environment and then later using P300 or SSVEP to perform landmark-based navigation (as in Bell et al. 2010). Recently, wheelchair navigation control was done using a BCI that relied on the so called error potentials (an involuntary brain response to undesired events; not discussed here) to allow the robot to determine which of the routes it found was suitable to the user (Perrin et al., 2010).

3. Future challenges

In order for BCIs to be routinely used in robot navigation control, a number of factors will need to be improved. Amongst other, the following will need to receive high priority:

- *Recording equipment*: while systems based on dry electrodes exist, they do not yet give as reliable a signal as standard wet EEG electrodes. The latter require the use of electrode gel or water. Systems that require the use of electrode gel are the most reliable ones, but they require about 1min per electrode to set up, and the gel needs to be changed after a few hours. Water-based systems are quicker to set up, but at present they provide less reliable signals. As dry sensor technology improves, it is likely that such devices will be preferred, especially by users outside the research community.

- *Degrees of freedom*: The number of classes available in a BCI depends on which type of BCI is used. P300 BCIs can provide a large number of classes (>40 in principle, although clutter will decrease true positive recognition performance), but this will come at the expense of longer processing times for each individual choice. The same applies to SSVEP-based interfaces. MI-based BCIs can provide only a small number of classes at the moment, usually 4 or less if more than 90% true positive rate is desired (although up to 20 classes have been successfully classified in a small but well controlled study, Lakany & Conway, 2005).
- *Proportional control*: BCI control of proportional variables such as robot angular displacement and speed has received little attention so far. This is an important area of research for future use of BCI-based robot navigation.
- *Intuitiveness and user freedom*: The most intuitive approach is motor imagery, but more classes would be needed to make this approach more useful in robot navigation control. P300 and SSVEP approaches require full attention on the visual interface and thus give no freedom to the user. Other cognitive tasks have been used in off-line BCI studies (e.g., Sepulveda et al., 2007), but these should be investigated further before they are used for robot navigation.
- *Speed issues*: If information transfer rate alone is the main concern, SSVEP would be the best choice, followed by P300, but the required focus on the interface will remain a major problem for the future. It will thus be crucial to find fast approaches that rely on motor imagery or other cognitive tasks that are intuitive and give the user freedom from the interface.

4. Conclusions

BCIs have come of age in many ways and are now being used outside controlled laboratory settings. However, a number of limitations in the current state-of-the-art will need to be addressed in order to make this technology more reliable, low cost, user friendly and robust enough to be used for routine robot navigation control. Until then, BCIs will remain largely an experimental tool in robot navigation, or as an additional tool within a multi-modality approach. Nonetheless, brain-actuated or brain-assisted robot navigation control will bring benefits to the field, especially in difficult scenarios in which the robot cannot successfully perform all functions without human assistance, such as in dangerous areas where sensors or algorithms may fail. In such cases BCI intervention will be crucial until a time when robots are intelligent and robust enough to navigate in any environment. But, even then, human control of the robot will probably still be desirable for overriding robot decisions, or merely for the benefit of the human operator. In another case, when the robot is a wheelchair, frequent user interaction will take place, in which case BCIs are essential for at least some form of brain-actuated navigation control.

5. References

Bell, C.; Sdhenoy, P.; Chalodhorn, R. & Rao, R.P.N. (2008). Control of a humanoid robot by a noninvasive brain–computer interface in humans. *J. Neural Eng.*, Vol. 5, 2008, pp. 214-220. doi:10.1088/1741-2560/5/2/012

Belliveau, J.W. ; Kennedy, D.N.; McKinstry, R.C.; Buchbinder, B.R.; Weisskoff, R.M.; Cohen, M.S. ; Vevea, J.M.; Brady, T.J. & Rosen, B.R. (1991). Functional mapping of the human visual cortex by magnetic resonance imaging. *Science*, Vol. 254, pp. 716–719.

Brunner, P.; Joshi, S.; Briskin, S.; Wolpaw, J.R.; Bischol, H. & Schalk, G. (2010). Does the 'P300' speller depend on eye gaze? *J. Neural Eng.*, 7 056013 doi: 10.1088/1741-2560/7/5/056013.

Citi, L.; Poli, R.; Cinel, C. & Sepulveda, F. (2008). P300-based BCI Mouse with Genetically-Optimised Analogue Control. IEEE Trans. Neur. Systems and Rehab. Eng., Vol. 16, No. 1, pp. 51 - 61.

Citi, L.; Poli, R.; Cinel, C. & Sepulveda, F. (2004). Feature Selection and Classification in Brain Computer Interfaces by a Genetic Algorithm. *Proceedings of the Genetic and Evolutionary Computation Conference* - GECCO 2004, Seatle, 10pp.

Cohen, D. (1972). Magnetoencephalography: detection of the brain's electrical activity with a superconducting magnetometer. *Science,* Vol. 175, pp. 664-66.

Cooper, R.; Osselton, J.W. & Shaw, J.C. (1969). *EEG Technology*, 2nd ed. Butterworths, London.

Farwell, L. & Donchin, E. (1988). Talking off the top of your head: toward a mental prothesis utilizing event-related brain potentials. *Electroenceph Clin Neurophysiol*, Vol. 70, pp. 510–523.

Gao, X.; Xu, D.; Cheng, M. & and Gao, S. (2003). A BCI-based environmental controller for the motion-disabled. *IEEE Trans.Neural Syst. Rehabil. Eng.*, Vol. 11, pp. 137–40.

Hamalainen, M.; Hari, R. ; Ilmoniemi, R.J.; Knuutila, J. & Lounasmaa, O.V. (1993). Magnetoencphalography- Theory, instrumentation, and applications to noninvasive studies of the working human brain. *Reviews of Modern Physics*, Vol. 65, pp. 413–497.

Hochberg, L.; Serruya, M.D.; Friehs, G.M.; Mukand, J.A.; Saleh, M.; Caplan, A.H.; Branner, A.; Chen, D.; Penn, R.D. & Donoghue, J.P. (2006). Neuronal ensemble control of prosthetic devices by a human with tetraplegia. *Nature*, Vol. 442, pp. 164–171.

Lakany, H. & Conway, B. (2005). Classification of Wrist Movements using EEG-based Wavelets Features. 27th Annual International Conference of the IEEE Engineering in Medicine and Biology Society, Shanghai, 17-18 Jan. 2006, pp. 5404 – 5407.

Lebedev, M.A. & Nicolelis, M.A. (2006). Brain-machine interfaces: past, present and future. *Trends in neurosciences*, Vol. 29, No. 9, pp. 536–46.

Lotte, F.; Congedo, M.; L'ecuyer, A.; Lamarche, F. & Arnaldi, B. (2007). A review of classification algorithms for EEG-based brain–computer interfaces. *J. Neural Eng.*, Vol. 4 (2007) doi:10.1088/1741-2560/4/2/R01.

Millan, J. del R.; Renkens, F.; Mouriño, J. & Gerstner, W. (2004). Non-Invasive Brain-Actuated Control of a Mobile Robot by Human EEG. *IEEE Trans. on Biomedical Engineering*, Vol. 51, pp. 1026–1033.

Muehlemann, T.; Haensse, D. & Wolf, M. (2008). Wireless miniaturized in-vivo near infrared imaging. *Optics Express*, Vol. 16, No. 14, pp. 10323-30.

Niedermeyer, E. & da Silva, F.L. (Eds.) (2004). *Electroencephalography: Basic Principles, Clinical Applications, and Related Fields* (5th Ed.). Lippincot Williams & Wilkins, ISBN 9780781751261.

Ortner, R.; Guger, C.; Prueckl, R.; Grunbacher, E. & Edlinger, G. (2010). SSVEP Based Brain-Computer Interface for Robot Control. *Lecture Notes in Computer Science*, Volume 6180/2010, 85-90, DOI: 10.1007/978-3-642-14100-3_14.

Perrin, X.; Chavarriaga, R.; Colas, F.; Siegwart, R. & Millan, J. del R. (2010). Brain-coupled interaction for semi-autonomous navigation of an assistive robot.

Raichle, M.E. & Mintun, M.A. (2006). Brain Work and Brain Imaging. *Annual Review of Neuroscience*, Vol. 29, pp. 449–76.

Rebsamen, B.; Burdet, E.; Cuntai Guan; Chee Leong Teo; Qiang Zeng; Ang, M. & Laugier, C. (2007). Controlling a wheelchair using a BCI with low information transfer rate. IEEE 10th International Conference on Rehabilitation Robotics, ICORR 2007, Noordwijk, Netherlands, 13-15 June 2007, pp. 1003 – 1008.

Rugg, M.D, & Coles, M.H. (1995). *Electrophysiology of mind: event-related brain potentials and cognition.* Oxford University Press – Oxford.

Salvaris, M. & Sepulveda, F. (2010). Classification effects of real and imaginary movement selective attention tasks on a P300-based brain--computer interface. *Journal of Neural Engineering*, 7 056004, doi: 10.1088/1741-2560/7/5/056004.

Sepulveda, F.; Dyson, M.; Gan, J.Q. &; Tsui, C.S.L. (2007). A Comparison of Mental Task Combinations for Asynchronous EEG-Based BCIs. *Proceedings of the 29th Annual International Conference of the IEEE Engineering in Medicine and Biology Society EMBC07*, Lyon, August 22-26, pp. 5055 – 5058.

Swartz, B.E. & Goldensohn, E.S. (1998). Timeline of the history of EEG and associated fields. *Electroencephalography and clinical Neurophysiology*, Vol. 106, No. 2, pp. 173-176.

Ter-Pogossian, M.M.; Phelps, M.E.; Hoffman, E.J. & Mullani, N.A. (1975). A positron-emission transaxial tomograph for nuclear imaging (PET). *Radiology*, Vol. 114, No. 1, pp. 89–98.

Townsend, G.; Graimann, B. & Pfurtscheller, G. (2004). Continuous EEG classification during motor imagery — simulation of an asynchronous BCI. *IEEE Trans. Neural Syst. Rehabil. Eng.*, Vol. 12, No. 2, pp. 258– 265.

Tsui, C.S.L.; Vuckovic, A.; Palaniappan, R.; Sepulveda, F. & Gan, J.Q. (2006). Narrow band spectral analysis for movement onset detection in asynchronous BCI. *3rd International Workshop on Brain-Computer Interfaces*, Graz, Austria, 2006, pp. 30-31.

Vidal, J.J. (1973). Toward direct brain-computer communication. *Annual Review of Biophysics and Bioengineering*, Vol. 2, pp. 157–80.

Vigario, R.N. (1997). Extraction of ocular artefacts from EEG using independent component analysis. *Electroencephalography and Clinical Neurophysiology*, Vol. 103, No. 3, pp. 395-404.

Wolf, M.; Ferrari, M. & Quaresima, V. (2007). Progress of near-infrared spectroscopy and topography for brain and muscle clinical applications. *Journal of Biomedical Optics*, Vol. 12, No. 6, 062104 doi:10.1117/1.2804899.

Wolpaw, J.R.; Birbaumer, N.; McFarland, D.J.; Pfurtscheller, G. & Vaughan, T.M. (2002). Brain-computer interfaces for communication and control. *Clin Neurophysiol*, Vol. 113, No. 6, pp 767–791.

9

A Distributed Mobile Robot Navigation by Snake Coordinated Vision Sensors

Yongqiang Cheng, Ping Jiang and Yim Fun Hu
University of Bradford
UK

1. Introduction

To date research in intelligent mobile agent have mainly focused on the development of a large and smart "brain" to enable robot autonomy (Arkin 2000; Murphy 2000). They are, however, facing a bottleneck of complexity due to the dynamics of the unstructured environments. Steering away from this smart brain approach, this chapter investigates the use of low level intelligence, such as insect eyes, and combines them to produce highly intelligent functions for autonomous robotic control by exploiting the creativity and diversity of insect eyes with small nervous systems (Land & Nilsson 2002) that mimics a mosaic eye.

A mosaic eye transmits information through the retina to the insect's brain where they are integrated to form a usable picture of the insect's environment in order to co-ordinate their activities in response to any changes in the environment. Applying this concept to robotic control, the mosaic eye is used to assist a robot to find the shortest and safest path to reach its final destination. This is achieved through path planning in a dynamic environment and trajectory generation and control under robot non-holonomic constraints with control input saturations, subject to pre-defined criteria or constraints such as time and energy. By utilising pervasive intelligence (Snoonian 2003) distributed in the environment, robots can still maintain a high degree of mobility while utilising little computational functions and power. However, navigation techniques assisted by an environment with distributed information intelligence are different from conventional ones that rely on centralised intelligence implemented in the robot itself. These distributed navigation techniques need to be reconsidered and developed.

The contour snake model (Kass et al. 1988) is broadly used and plays an important role in computer vision for image segmentation and contour tracking. Similar concepts have been applied to path planning with centralised robot navigation control using onboard sensors, such as elastic bands and bubbles (Quinlan & Khatib 1993; Quinlan 1994), connected splines (Mclean 1996) and redundant manipulators (Mclean & Cameron 1993; Cameron 1998). They all require a global planner to gather and process information. On the other hand, most of the existing work for robot navigation in an environment with small scale sensor networks considers only the high level path or discrete event planning(Sinopoli et al. 2003; Li & Rus 2005), ignoring issues related to low level trajectory planning and motion control due to sensor communication delay, timing skew, and discrete decision making. Low level functions are usually given to robots to conduct local control relying on on-board sensors. Due to the limited information provided by local sensors, tracking speed and accuracy have to be compromised.

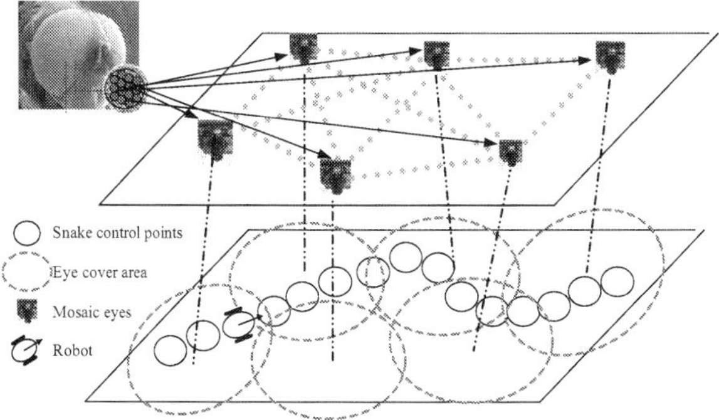

Fig. 1. Mosaic eye inspired intelligent environment

Building upon the WIreless Mosaic Eyes towards autonomous ambient assistant living for the ageing society (WiME) system(Website 2006; Cheng et al. 2008), this chapter aims at creating an intelligent environment with distributed visions for the navigation of unintelligence mobile robots in an indoor environment. The mosaic eye intelligent environment is illustrated in Fig. 1. It resembles that of insect eyes connected by neurons. The structure is formed using a set of distributed wireless vision sensors (mini-cameras, mosaic eye) mounted on a physical structure. Each vision sensor represents an eye in the mosaic eye structure. Neighbouring eyes are connected by wireless eye communications. Each eye covers a certain area of the workspace and holds a segment of the whole path. Thus, by considering a distributed sensor network, robots can be guided by a larger set of information concerning its surrounding environment to enable better predictive capability to be achieved. Predefined projection relations are calibrated in advance after mounting the mosaic eye in the structural environment. Once the start positions and target positions of a path are specified by an operator and written into the system profile files of all eyes, each eye will search its profile file and exchanges information with its neighbours for its role in the routing table, and generates a segment of the global distributed reference snake path as required. A mobile robot controlled by the mosaic eye only equips with wireless receiver and actuator without intelligent processing capability on-board. If an eye detects an abnormal situation within its coverage area, it will send a signal to inform its neighbouring eyes of this situation for their considerations in the path planning process. If an area is only covered by one eye, a robot is controlled only by this node. When a robot enters into an overlapping area covered by two neighbouring eyes, one of them will be elected to be the dominant eye to control the robot through negotiation between the two eyes based on some pre-defined criteria, for example, whether the robot is observed in the central or edge area of the eye coverage.

The rest of the chapter is organised as follows. Section two states the problem and gives a general idea of mosaic eye controlled snake based robot navigation; Section three summarises the generation of the Reference snake (R-snake) with curvature constraints; The

Accompany snake (A-snake) spatial position planning algorithm and time series trajectory based on R-snake are discussed in Section four and five respectively; Section six focuses on the control dedicated protocol that connects all distributed vision sensors; Experiment results and conclusions are given in section seven and section eight respectively.

2. Problem statement and overview of a snake based robot navigation by mosaic eye

In general, a snake is defined as a series of control points connected one by one to represent a collision free path. At initialisation, the start and target (or the end) control points of the snake will be input by an operator manually. Other control points between the start and target points are generated by a global search algorithm, such as Dijkstra's search algorithm (Cormen et al. 2001). The snake shape is dynamically deformed by two kinds of forces exerted on all the control points (Kass, Witkin et al. 1988). Internal forces are forces exerted by other control points within the snake body, such as the attraction force used to reduce the distance between two control points or the bending force used to reduce the sharpness of the snake body. External forces are actions generated from the environment rather than the control points. For example, the repulsive force from obstacles is an external force. The operation for deforming a snake body only requires interactions between adjacent joints (hereafter referred to as control points in this chapter) and reactions to surrounding obstacles in a certain range, e.g. one segment will move according to the locally observed obstacles approaching to it and this movement will affect its neighbouring segments, as a result, the whole snake will deform into a new optimised shape to avoid the obstacles. Therefore, it is suitable to apply the snake algorithm in distributed environment, such as distributed wireless sensor network, to plan a navigation path using only local information exchange between adjacent control points to alert a navigation robot in advance of any obstacles ahead of its navigation path with global effect.

The snake algorithm proposed in this chapter is designed for path planning as well as trajectory generating and robot motion control in an architectural environment installed with distributed vision sensors compliant to the non-holonomic constraints and control saturations. Each distributed vision sensor will maintain one part of the global path dynamically. Local environment information will be exchanged by communications between adjacent vision sensors. By negotiation, one of the vision sensors will plan the local trajectory and control the robot. This is rather different from previous applications where the generation of the snake path relies on centralised processing and global information. The snake will evolve and adapt dynamically to the local environment in an elastic manner, forming a collision free and constraint compliant reference global path, i.e. the R-snake path, for a navigation robot.

While the R-snake provides a reference path for a robot to travel, controlling the robot to follow the path is another difficult task. It involves trajectory generation and motion control subject to non-holonomic constraints and saturated torques, slippage speed etc. A proposed approach to take into account such constraints in this chapter is to develop a distributed control scheme, providing the environment with the ability to perceive information from a large area using distributed sensors to maintain the robot navigation performance up to its maximum driving speed limit. Therefore, an A-snake based on the R-snake is introduced to cope with all these constraints as well as to plan the shortest travel time trajectory. The A-snake is further divided into two phases: 1) A-snake spatial position planning; and 2) A-snake time series trajectory generation and motion control. Phase one only deals with path geometry features without considering the time factor. The primary goal is to generate an associated path that converges to the R-snake path and at the same time complies with the dynamic and non-holonomic constraints, and control saturation. Phase two selects predictive control (Maciejowski 2001) to optimise the forthcoming tracking. The model based prediction also alleviates effects due to the slow feedback from vision sensors. A rolling window optimisation (Xi & Zhang 2002) is carried out to generate the optimum velocity profile of the mobile robot up to a certain distance from its current position.

3. Planning a R-snake under curvature constraints

Let p_i be a Euclidian coordinate representing the Cartesian configuration (x_i^{cp}, y_i^{cp}) in space R^2, where $i \in Z$ and Z is the set of integers. For a positive integer n, $\{p_0, p_1, ..., p_n\}$ denotes a sequence of configurations in space R^2. A snake is created by connecting adjacent coordinates sequentially. Each coordinate, p_i, represents a control point, which can be moved by exerted internal and external forces from obstacles and adjacent control points. An obstacle q_i is defined as a circle with a radius d_o, centred at (x_i^o, y_i^o). The total number of obstacles in a physical space covered by a vision sensor node is m. Then the objective of the snake algorithm is to adjust the n control points $\{p_0, p_1, ..., p_n\}$ dynamically for keeping the robot within a safe distance away from m obstacles $q_1, ..., q_m$, satisfying the given curvature constraint and maintaining the shortest path length from its start point to the goal point via intermediate control points.

As discussed above, the safe path for a robot is the R-snake path maintained by the distributed mosaic eye. Define the internal and external energy functions in space R^2 as the energy caused by attractive actions from adjacent control points and repulsive actions from obstacles respectively, then the total energy, E^{snake}, of the snake can be expressed as(Quinlan & Khatib 1993),

$$E^{snake} = E^{int\,ernal} + E^{external} \tag{1}$$

where the internal energy, $E^{int\,ernal}$, is only concerned with the intrinsic actions of the snake, such as its shape and length while the external energy, $E^{external}$, is concerned with the effect from the environment, such as obstacles.

To minimize the energy exerted on a snake, p_i should move along the negative energy gradient direction so that the total energy of the snake decreases. The total force, F^{snake}, exerted on the snake, in terms of $E^{int\,ernal}$ and $E^{external}$ can be expressed as:

$$F^{snake} = F^{int\,ernal} + F^{external}$$
$$= (-\nabla \eta_{int} E^{int\,ernal}) + (-\nabla \eta_{ext} E^{external}) \tag{2}$$

where, η_{int} and η_{ext} are positive coefficients representing the force strength, ∇ is the gradient operator.

In Eq. (1), different forces serve different purposes. The aim of path planning is to find an obstacle free and the shortest length path that satisfies the curvature constraints. Thus, the elastic contraction energy and the curvature bending energy are considered as internal energy and the obstacles repulsive energy is considered as external energy. Let f^o be the obstacle force, f^e be the elastic force and $f^{curvature}$ be the curvature constraints force. By adding all internal and external forces, one gets the resultant force f_i^r on a control point i where $f_i^r = \sqrt{f_{i,x}^r + f_{i,y}^r}$ and

$$f_{i,x}^r = f_{i,x}^o + f_{i,x}^e + f_{i,x}^{curvature}$$
$$f_{i,y}^r = f_{i,y}^o + f_{i,y}^e + f_{i,y}^{curvature}$$

$$(3)$$

Readers can refer to (Cheng, Hu et al. 2008) for more detailed descriptions on obstacle, elastic and curvature forces. A three-state R-snake for guaranteed curvature constraints can also be found in (Cheng, Hu et al. 2008).

4. A-snake spatial position planning

Feedback control of distributed vision sensors is adopted for the dynamic generation of an A-snake spatial position. The A-snake extends from the robot's current position and orientation to approach the R-snake path by taking into account the limited steering torque under the non-holonomic constraints. This will correct the deviation of the robot's position from the reference path. A key issue in this phase is whether the A-snake can converge to the R-snake path without violating the steering torque and driving force limitations.

Fig. 2 denotes a coordinate system with the doted circles representing the R-snake control points and the square box indicating the robot. θ_d is the desired direction which the robot should follow at each iterative step; θ is the robot's current direction; $\vec{i}$ and $\vec{j}$ are the unit tangential vector and normal vector of the robot's local coordinates along its direction of movement respectively; $\vec{i}_0$ is the tangential vector on the nearest reference control point; $\vec{r}$ is the robot's location vector, $\vec{r}_0$ is the vector of the nearest reference control point of the snake; θ_e is the direction error between the desired direction and the robot's current direction; ξ is a positive coefficient. The A-snake will always start from the robot current position.

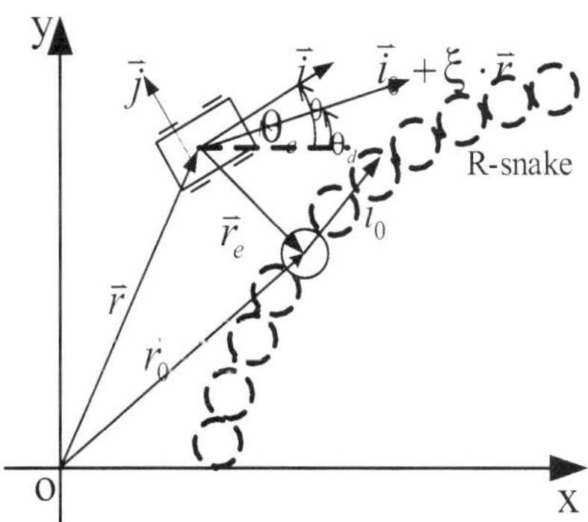

Fig. 2. Coordinates definitions

From (Cheng et al. 2010), a proper desired direction θ_d which can lead the A-snake to converge to the R-snake is,

$$\theta_d = \theta_0 + \arctan\left(\frac{\Delta r_{\tilde{j}}}{\Delta r_{\tilde{i}}}\right) \tag{4}$$

where,

$$\begin{cases} \Delta r_{\tilde{i}} = 1 \\ \Delta r_{\tilde{j}} = \xi_1 \cdot r_e \end{cases} \tag{5}$$

ξ_1 is the positive gain along the vector $\vec{r}_e$ and,

$$r_e = sign(\vec{r}_e) \cdot \left\| \vec{r}_0 - \vec{r} \right\|, \tag{6}$$

$$sign(\vec{r}_e) = \begin{cases} -1, & \text{robot is on the left side of the R - snake} \\ 1, & \text{robot is on the right side of the R - snake} \end{cases}$$

Eq. (4) gives the desired direction for the A-snake to follow so as to converge to the R-snake. In practice, the robot's moving direction cannot always reach the desired value due to the non-holonomic constraints (maximum steering torque) and dynamic constraints (maximum driving force and frictions). The maximum robot velocity v_{max} should be obtained as,

$$v_{max} = \min\left(v_{\tau max}, v_{f max}\right) \tag{7}$$

where,

$$v^2_{\tau max} = \frac{\tau_{max}}{J \left| \partial k / \partial s \right|} \tag{8}$$

$$v^2_{f max} = \frac{(\mu N)_{max}}{M \left| k \right|} = \frac{g \mu_{max}}{\left| k \right|}$$

M and J are the mass and the inertia of the robot respectively; g is the Gravity factor; μ is the friction coefficient; N is the normal force with the ground; k is the trajectory curvature; s is the arc length along the snake and the saturated torque of a robot τ_{max}.
Thus, the control points of A-snake can grow iteratively according to Eq. (9) ,

$$\begin{pmatrix} x' \\ y' \end{pmatrix} = \begin{bmatrix} \cos(\theta) & -\sin(\theta) \\ \sin(\theta) & \cos(\theta) \end{bmatrix} \cdot \int \begin{pmatrix} \frac{\partial x}{\partial s} \\ \frac{\partial y}{\partial s} \end{pmatrix} ds + \begin{pmatrix} x \\ y \end{pmatrix} \tag{9}$$

where, $\begin{pmatrix} x \\ y \end{pmatrix}$ and $\begin{pmatrix} x' \\ y' \end{pmatrix}$ are the current and newly calculated control point positions respectively, and ,

$$\begin{pmatrix} \frac{\partial x}{\partial s} \\ \frac{\partial y}{\partial s} \end{pmatrix} = \begin{pmatrix} \cos(\int \frac{\partial \theta}{\partial s} ds) \\ \sin(\int \frac{\partial \theta}{\partial s} ds) \end{pmatrix} \tag{10}$$

5. A-snake time series trajectory generation and motion control

Although the A-snake spatial position provides a reference path for a robot to travel, due to the limited field of view of the onboard sensors, the tracking speed has to compromise with safety. In fact, the far sight provided by a large scale distributed sensor network is developing the foundation and potential for the optimal control of vehicles. A vehicle is envisaged to be able to respond to changes on its way ahead and be driven with optimal time or energy in a dynamic environment. Distributed control to achieve high performance tracking up to the driving limit becomes a promising technique.

In (Cheng, Jiang et al. 2010), a predictive control scheme combining trajectory planning and dynamic control is developed to achieve optimal time tracking, taking into account the future path that needs to be tracked, subject to non-holonomic constraints, robot kinematic and dynamic constraints, the maximum velocity without slippage, driving force and steering torque saturation.

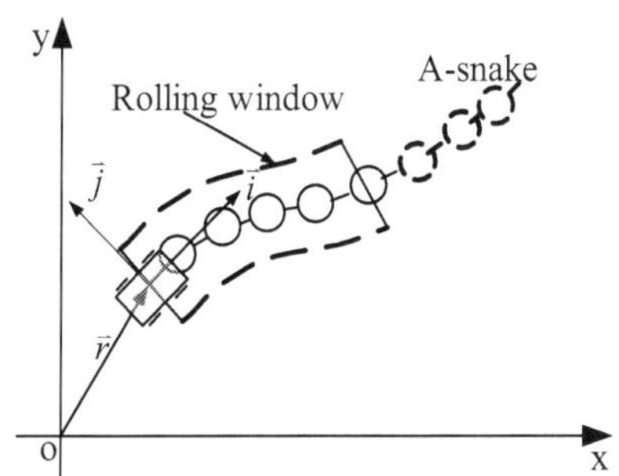

Fig. 3. Robot, A-snake and rolling window

Define a rolling window with length l along a snake as shown in Fig. 3, which could be distributed in several wireless sensors and evolved by individual vision sensors asynchronously. The optimal control for a robot can be achieved by optimizing,

$$\min_{F^d,\tau}(\Gamma) = \min_{F^d,\tau}(\int_0^l 1 / v(s)ds \big|_{s \in A}) \tag{11}$$

with boundary conditions: $v(0) = v_{r0}, v(l) = 0$; subject to

$$\begin{cases} \left| f^{friction} \right| < (\mu N)_{max}, & for\, non-slippage \\ \left| F^d \right| < F^d_{max}, & for\, limited\, driving\, force \\ \left| \tau \right| < \tau_{max}, & for\, limited\, steering\, torque \end{cases} \tag{12}$$

where A is the A-snake; $v(s)$ is the velocity profile of the robot; v_{r0} is the sampled velocity of the robot at any instant; f is the friction of tires with coefficient μ and the normal force N ; F^d and τ are the driving force and steering torque of the robot with upper bounds of F^d_{max} and τ_{max} respectively. The objective equation Eq.(11) for predictive control is to minimise the robot's travelling time Γ which is also called a servo period along the snake from its current location until the end of the l-window. However the robot should be able to stop at the end such that $v(l) = 0$ in order to respond to the worst possible circumstances which are not covered by the current rolling window.

In order to optimise Eq.(11), the area under the velocity profile $v(s)$ will be maximised so that the area of its reciprocal can be minimised according to the maximum uniform velocity obtained in Eq.(7), which is the maximum allowable velocity for the robot to travel along the A-snake without any effort for acceleration or deceleration, this section will obtain the optimal force and torque approaching this maximum allowable velocity as much as possible, considering the dynamic constraints and satisfying the boundary conditions.

In order to satisfy the two boundary conditions in Eq. (11), one needs to design optimal control inputs such that the robot can safely travel a path and is able to stop at the end of the rolling window, considering the dynamic constraints. A sharp bend on the way requires the robot to decelerate in advance due to the limited driving force and steering torque. The optimisation of Eq. (11) can be solved by maximising the area of $v(s)$, which can be achieved by squeezing the velocity profile from the two ends towards the middle using the maximum force and torque.

The maximum allowable positive acceleration can be obtained as

$$a_{F\,max+} = F^d_{max} / M$$

$$a_{\tau\,max+} = \frac{\tau_{max}}{J\,|\,k\,|} - \frac{v^2}{k}\frac{\partial k}{\partial s} \tag{13}$$

$$a_{max+} = \min(a_{F\,max+}, a_{\tau\,max+})$$

If $v \leq v_{max}$, then $a_{max+} \geq 0$, this implies that a positive acceleration exists. Therefore, the acceleration process has to be bounded by v_{max}.

Similarly, the maximum allowed negative acceleration can be obtained as

$$a_{F\,max-} = -F^d_{max} / M$$

$$a_{\tau\,max-} = -\frac{\tau_{max}}{J\,|\,k\,|} - \frac{v^2}{k}\frac{\partial k}{\partial s} \tag{14}$$

$$a_{max-} = \max(a_{F\,max-}, a_{\tau\,max-})$$

A negative acceleration exists if the velocity is bounded by v_{max}.

The squeezing process is approximated by segments of uniform acceleration/deceleration movements from two boundary velocities with an incremental step δ :

For acceleration at s_+ , forward planning is carried out

$$v^2_+(s_+) = v^2_+(s_+ - \delta) + 2\alpha_{max+}\delta \tag{15}$$

For deceleration at s_- , backward planning is carried out

$$v_-^2(s_-) = v_-^2(s_- + \delta) + 2\alpha_{\max-}\delta \tag{16}$$

During the squeezing process, it is needed to ensure that the values of $v_+^2(s_+)$ and $v_-^2(s_-)$ in Eq. (15) and Eq. (16) do not exceed $v_{\max}$ for the segment in between s_+ and s_- . If this happens at any point $s_\#$, the velocity profile can be squeezed for the segment from $v_+(s_-)$ to $v_-(s_\#) = v_{\max}(s_\#)$. The process continues until the acceleration segment and the deceleration segment encounter each other. The velocity profile will be obtained by repeating this squeezing process for the remaining segments. Working in this way, the area of $v(s)$ is maximised and therefore the travelling time is minimised. The generated velocity profile informs the robot when to accelerate or decelerate in advance in order to safely track the dynamic snake in a predictive l-window. The algorithm is summarised as below and is shown in Fig. 4:

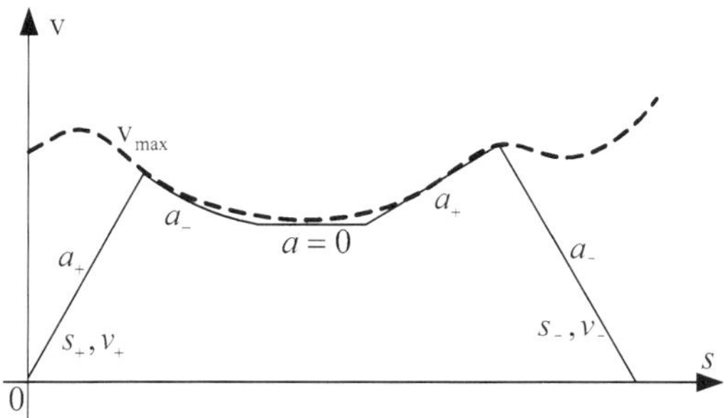

Fig. 4. Rolling window optimisation for trajectory generation (assume $v_{r0} = 0$)

1. According to the snake, obtain the maximum allowable velocities $v_{\max}$ from Eq.(7) in rolling window l ;
2. Initialise the squeezing process with the following boundary conditions: initial state $s_+ = 0, v_+(0) = v_{r0}$ and terminate state $s_- = l, v_-(l) = 0$;
3. Plan/increase v_+ and v_- in parallel: if $v_+ \leq v_-$, increase v_+ by Eq. (15) and $s_+ = s_+ + \delta$; If $v_+ > v_-$, increase v_- by Eq. (16) and $s_- = s_- - \delta$;
4. If $s_+ = s_-$ and there is any unplanned segment, set s_+ and s_- to be the unplanned segment and go to 3); if the maximum allowable velocity is found at $s_\#$ between $s_+ \sim s_-$, create two new segments, $s_+ \sim s_\#$ and $s_\# \sim s_-$ then go to 3), otherwise go to 5);
5. Calculate the driving force and steering torque for $s = 0$ as control signals for time t :

$$F^d(t) = Ma_{\max}(0)$$

$$\tau(t) = Ja_{\max}(0)k(0) + Jv^2(0)\frac{\partial k}{\partial s}\Big|_{s=0} \tag{17}$$

where $a_{\max} = a_{\max+}$ or $a_{\max-}$ obtained in step 3);

6. Send $F^d(t)$ and $\tau(t)$ to the robot for control and shift the rolling window one step forward;

7. For every servo period Γ, $F(t+n\Gamma)$ and $\tau(t+n\Gamma)$ will be continuously generated from the obtained velocity profile to control the vehicle until a new profile is received from a vision sensor;

8. For every image sampling period, the mosaic eye updates the A-snake and then repeats (1).

6. Communication empowered distributed mobile robot navigation

The purpose of this section is to design a control dedicated communication protocol connecting all vision sensors and mobile robot thus enabling the mobile robot navigation functionality in the intelligent environment. Meanwhile the protocol will establish a reliable and precise data exchange among the intelligent environment in order to support the path planning and motion control.

6.1 Overview

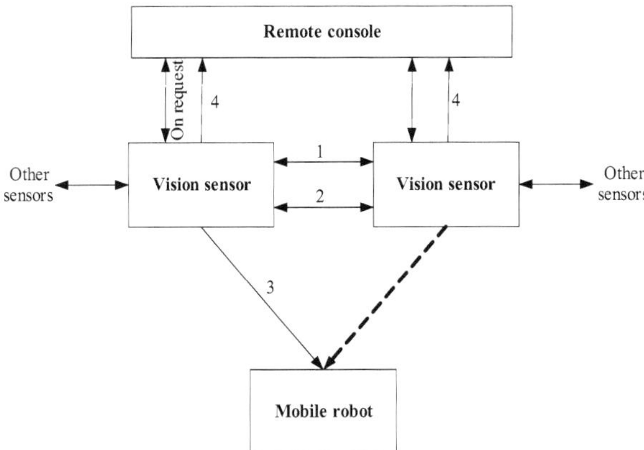

Fig. 5. Communication protocols overview

Fig. 5 is an outline of all the communication parties and the links between them. As the key intelligent component, vision sensors are involved in all communications, either as a sender or as a receiver. Except the *'on request'* commands originated by an operator in the remote console and the subsequent responses to these requests, commands are invoked periodically in the following sequence:

1. **Exchanging of control points and/or obstacles**: Control points coordinates are used to calculate internal forces to deform a snake. Snake segments in two neighbouring vision sensors can interact with each other by adjusting their positions according to the forces generated by the received control points coordinates from other vision sensors. Obstacles observed by one vision sensor will be sent to its neighbouring sensors if localisation fusion is required. After snake deformation, the vision sensor will send the planned control points to its neighbouring sensors;

2.   **Control token negotiation**: At a specific time, one robot should be controlled by only one vision sensor. All vision sensors which have the robot in view will compete for the token. The vision sensor with a control token will become the dominant vision sensor and broadcast its ownership of the token periodically or initiate a token handover procedure if required;

3.   **Mobile robot control**: The dominant vision sensor sends control to the robot; the one without a control token will skip this step;

4.   **Monitoring purpose reporting**: If a vision sensor is marked by an operator to send monitoring related information, such as control points, it will send out the corresponding information to the remote console.

6.2 Protocol stack structure

The proposed control protocol is built on top of the IEEE 802.15.4 protocol which has the following data structure (Zhang 2008),

```
typedef struct __TOS_Msg
{
        __u8 length;      // data length of payload
        __u8 fcfhi;           // Frame control field higher byte
        __u8 fcflo;           // Frame control field lower byte
        __u8 dsn;             // sequence number
        __u16 destpan; // destination PAN
        __u16 addr;      // destination Address
        __u8 type;            // type id for Active Message Model handler
        __u8 group;      // group id
        __s8 data[TOSH_DATA_LENGTH]; // payload
    __u8 strength;//signal strength
    __u8 lqi;
    __u8 crc;
    __u8 ack;
    __u16 time;
    } TOS_Msg;
```

As seen in the TOS_Msg structure, 16 bytes are used as headers, the maximum payload length, TOSH_DATA_LENGTH, should be 112 bytes. The control protocol packets are encapsulated and carried in the payload. The protocol stacks at different interfaces are discussed in the following subsections.

6.2.1 Protocol stack between vision sensors

As shown in Fig. 6, the control protocol layer is built on top of the physical lay and MAC layer of the 802.15.4 protocol stack to enable vision sensors to communicate with each other. The information processing and robot navigation control algorithms are resided within the control protocol layer.

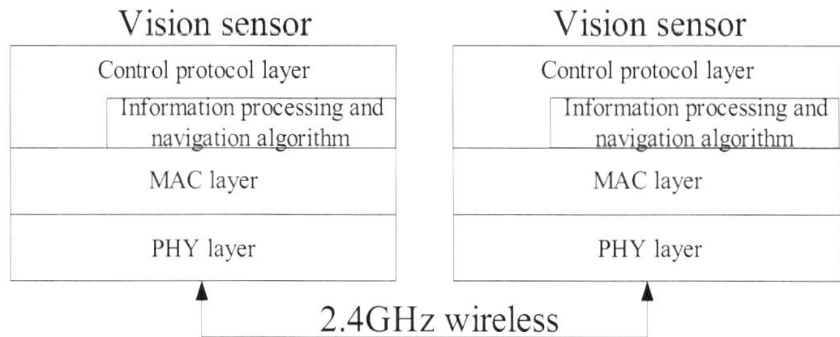

Fig. 6. Protocol stack between vision sensors

6.2.2 Protocol stack between vision sensor and mobile robot

Similar to the protocol stack between visions, the control protocol stack between vision sensor and mobile robot is shown in Fig. 7.

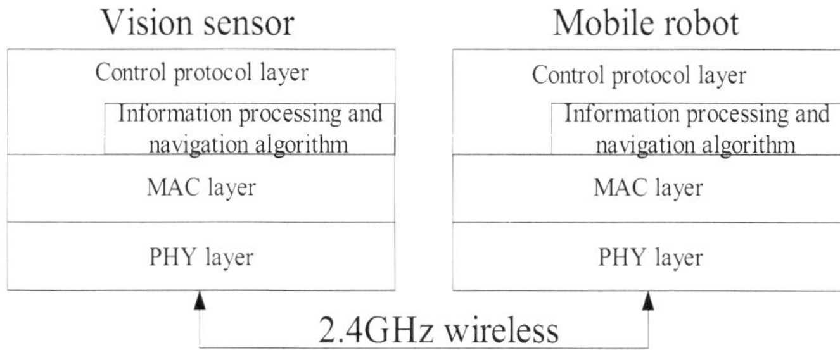

Fig. 7. Protocol stack between vision sensor and mobile robot

6.2.3 Protocol stack between vision sensor and remote console

To enable the communication between a normal PC and the vision sensor, a wireless adaptor is used to make conversion between 2.4GHz wireless signal and USB wire connection. The GUI application in the remote console PC will act as a TCP server which listens to the connection request from the wireless adaptor. The protocol stack is shown in Fig. 8.

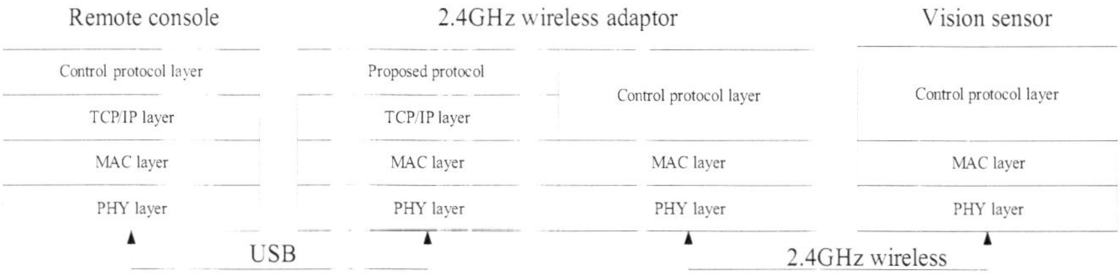

Fig. 8. Protocol stack between vision sensor and remote console

6.3 Generic packet structure

As mentioned above, the control protocol will be based on the TOS_Msg data structure. All packets are carried within the *data* area of the TOS_Msg structure. The generic packet format is defined as below Table 1.

Byte 0 0 1 2 3 4 5 6 7	Byte 1 0 1 2 3 4 5 6 7	Byte 2 0 1 2 3 4 5 6 7	Byte 3 0 1 2 3 4 5 6 7
CHK	CMD	SrcAddr	
SN		TotalNum	
User payload......			

Table 1. Generic packet structure

The fields are,
- CHK: check sum which is the remainder of the addition of all fields except the CHK itself being divided by 256;
- CMD: type of commands which identifies different control protocol payloads;
- SrcAddr: Sender short address from 1 to 65535 (0 is broadcast address);
- SN: Packet sequence number;
- TotalNum: Total number of packets to be transmitted;
- User payload: the length varies from 0 to 104 bytes depending on the CMD value; the structures of different payloads will be discussed in the next subsection.

6.4 Detailed design of the proposed control protocol

There are basically 5 commands designed to meet the data exchange and control requirements. Their descriptions are listed in Table 2.

CMD	Description	Message direction
1	Control points	Vision sensor ←→ vision sensor
2	Obstacles	Vision sensor ←→ vision sensor
3	Token negotiation	Vision sensor ←→ vision sensor
4	Mobile robot control commands	Vision sensor ←→ mobile robot
5	Monitoring purpose	Vision sensor ←→ remote console

Table 2. Command lists

The following subsections will discuss the detailed usage and packet structure of each command. It is organized according to the command sequence.

6.4.1 Control points

This is a vision sensor to vision sensor command. The purpose of this command is to transmit the planned control points from one vision sensor to another. To reduce the communication burden and save frequency resource, only the preceding vision sensors send border control points to the succeeding ones, as shown in Fig. 9.

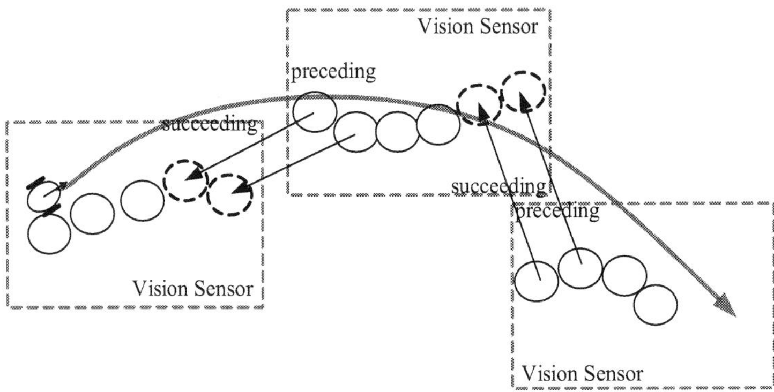

Fig. 9. Sending border control points from preceding vision sensor to succeeding ones

The signal flow is shown in Fig. 10. Border control point coordinates are transmitted periodically by all the vision sensors to their succeeding vision sensors if they exist. Destination address is specified in the TOS_Msg header.

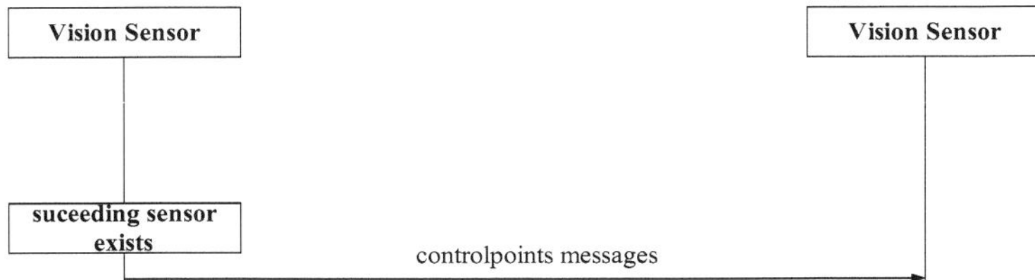

Fig. 10. Exchange border control points signal flow

The corresponding packet format is shown in Table 3,

Byte 0 0 1 2 3 4 5 6 7	Byte 1 0 1 2 3 4 5 6 7	Byte 2 0 1 2 3 4 5 6 7	Byte 3 0 1 2 3 4 5 6 7
CHK	CMD	SrcAddr	
SN		TotalNum	
NCP			
Series of control point coordinates ……			

Table 3. Control point packet format

where,
- CHK, SrcAddr, SN and TotalNum are referred to section 6.3
- CMD = 1
- NCP: Total number of control points to be sent, maximum 25 (103/4) control points can be sent within one packet
- Control point coordinates (x, y) are followed by format below,

Byte 0	Byte 1	Byte 2	Byte 3
0 1 2 3 4 5 6 7	0 1 2 3 4 5 6 7	0 1 2 3 4 5 6 7	0 1 2 3 4 5 6 7
x		y	

6.4.2 Obstacles

This is a vision sensor to vision sensor command. It is created to provide information for multiple geometry obstacle localisation. If obstacles are observed by one vision sensor, and this vision sensor has overlapping areas with the dominant one, it will transmit the observed obstacles to the dominant sensor. This function can be disabled to reduce the communication burden in the program.

The data format is shown in Table 4.

Byte 0	Byte 1	Byte 2	Byte 3
0 1 2 3 4 5 6 7	0 1 2 3 4 5 6 7	0 1 2 3 4 5 6 7	0 1 2 3 4 5 6 7
CHK	CMD	SrcAddr	
SN		TotalNum	
NOB			
Series of obstacle coordinates			

Table 4. Obstacle packet format

where,
- CHK, SrcAddr, SN and TotalNum are referred to section 6.3
- CMD = 2
- NOB: Total number of obstacles to be sent
- The obstacles coordinates are as the same format as control points in section 6.4.1

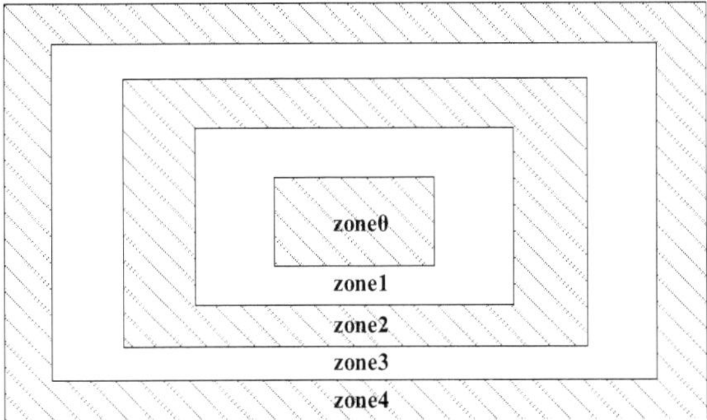

Fig. 11. Division of the observation area into zones in one vision sensor

6.4.3 Token negotiation

At a specific time, only the dominant vision sensor can send control command to the mobile robot. In the proposed distributed environment, there is no control centre to assign the control token among vision sensors. Therefore all vision sensors have to compete for the control token. By default, vision sensors with the mobile robot in view will check whether other visions broadcast the token ownership messages. If there is no broadcast messages received within a certain period of time, it will try to compete for the control token based on two criteria: 1) the quality of the mobile robot being observed by the vision sensors and 2) a random number generated by taking into account the vision sensor short address as the seed. The quality of the mobile robot being observed is identified by different zones shown in Fig. 11. Zone0 is in the inner area which denotes the best view and zone4 is in the outer area which represents the worst view. Different zones are not overlapped and divided evenly based on the length and width of the view area.

The control token negotiation procedures are interpreted as following four cases.

Case 1: One vision sensor sends request to compete for the token and there is no other request found at the same time. A timer is set up once the command is broadcasted. If there is no other token request messages received after timeout, the vision sensor takes the token and broadcast its ownership of the token immediately. Fig. 12 shows the signal flow.

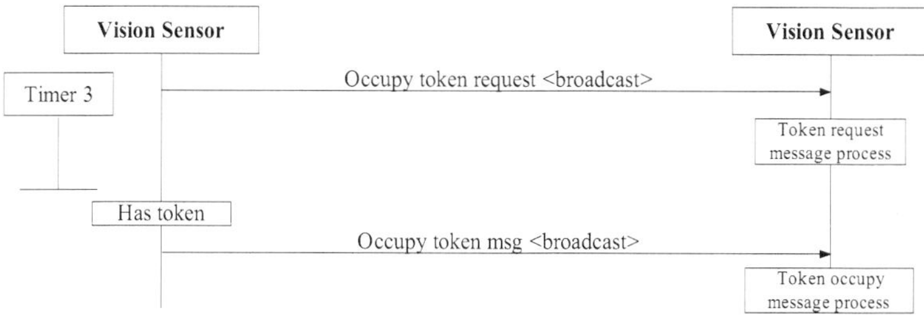

Fig. 12. Control token init signal flow, case 1

Case 2: If a control token request message is received before timeout, the vision sensors will compare its observation quality with the one carried in the broadcast message. The one with the less zone number will have the token. It might be a possibility that the zone numbers are the same, then the values of their short addresses are used to determine the token ownership, i.e. smaller value of the address will be the winner. Fig. 13 depicts the signal flow.

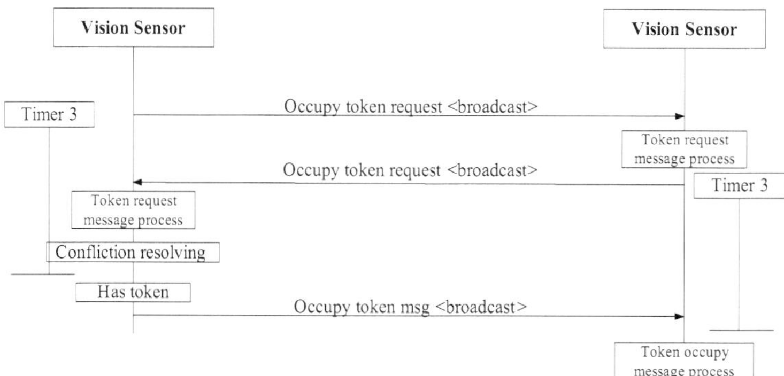

Fig. 13. Control token init signal flow, case 2

Case 3: Once a vision sensor has the control token, it will broadcast its ownership periodically. Upon receipt of this message, other vision sensors will set up a timer which should be greater than the time for a complete processing loop (image processing, path planning and trajectory generation). During the lifetime of this timer, it assumes that the ownership is still occupied by others and will not send request message during this time. If the dominant vision sensor receives a token request message, it will reply with an token already being occupied message immediately to stop other vision sensor from competing for the token. Fig. 14 shows the signal flow.

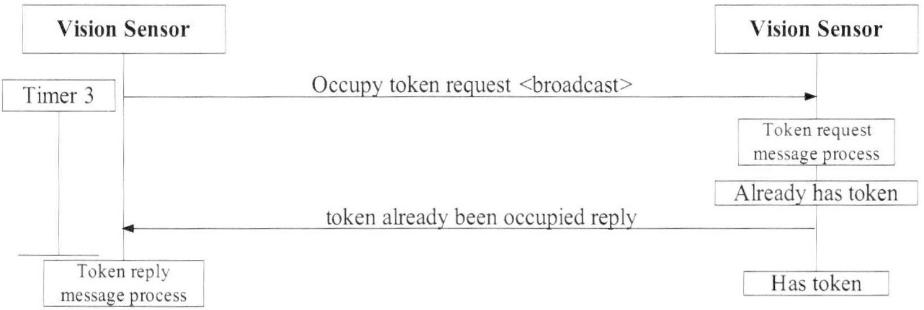

Fig. 14. Control token init signal flow, case 3

Case 4: When the mobile robot moves from an inner area to an outer area in the vision, the dominant vision sensor will try to initiate a procedure to handover the token to other vision sensors. First it broadcasts a token handover request with its view zone value and setup a timer (Timer 1). Upon receipt of the handover message, other vision sensors will check whether they have a better view on the robot. Vision sensors with better views will send token handover reply messages back to the dominant vision sensor and setup a timer (Timer 2). If the dominant vision sensor receives the response messages before the Timer 1 expires, it will choose the vision sensor as the target and send token handover confirmation message to that target vision sensor to hand over its ownership. If there is more than one vision sensors reply the handover request message, the dominant one will compare their view zone values and preferably send the handover confirmation message to the vision sensor with less zone value. If they have the same view quality, vision sensor short address will be used to decide the right one. If token handover confirmation message is received, the target vision sensor will have the token, as shown in Fig. 15. However if no handover confirmation messages received before the Timer 2 expires, i.e. the handover confirmation message does not reach the recipient, a token init procedure will be invoked as no other sensors apart from the dominant vision sensor has the token to broadcast the occupy token message which is shown in Fig. 16.

The packet format is listed in Table 5.

Byte 0 0 1 2 3 4 5 6 7	Byte 1 0 1 2 3 4 5 6 7	Byte 2 0 1 2 3 4 5 6 7	Byte 3 0 1 2 3 4 5 6 7
CHK	CMD	SrcAddr	
SN		TotalNum	
type	zone		

Table 5. Token packet format

where,

- CMD = 3
- CHK, SrcAddr, SN and TotalNum are referred to section 6.3
- type: Token message types.

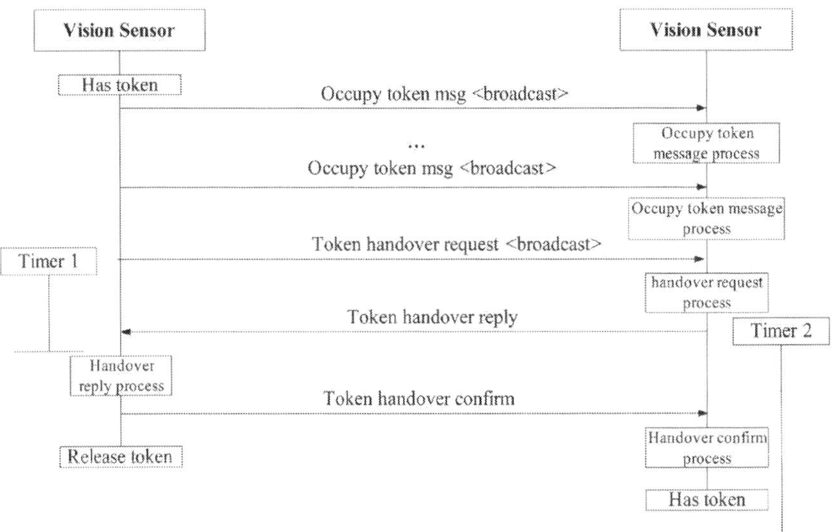

Fig. 15. Control token handover signal flow - successful

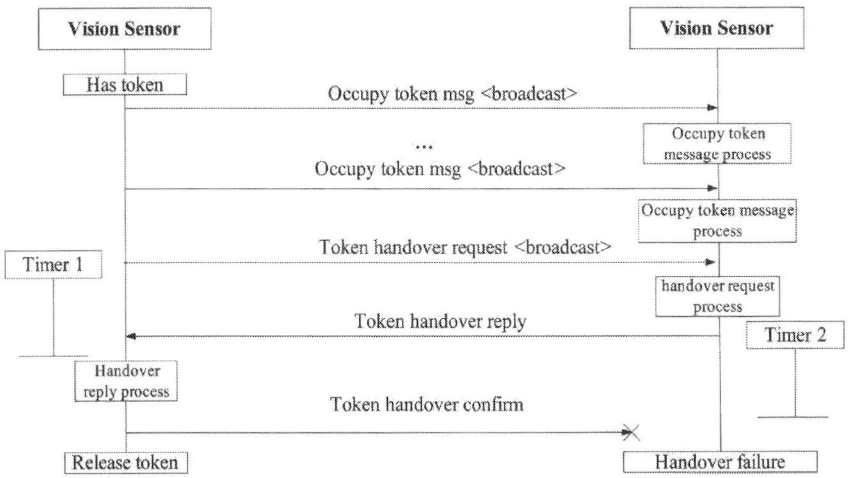

Fig. 16. Control token handover signal flow - failure

The descriptions and possible values for type is listed in Table 6,

type value	Description
0	Init token request
1	Occupy token msg
2	token already occupied reply
3	Token handover request
4	Token handover reply
5	Token handover confirmation

Table 6. Token messages

- zone: view zones. It is used to indicate the quality of mobile robot being observed in one vision sensor. The zone0, zone1, zone2, zone3 and zone4 are represented by 0, 1, 2, 3 and 4 respectively.

6.4.4 Mobile robot control

This is a vision sensor to mobile robot command. After planning, the dominant vision sensor will send a series of commands to the robot with time tags. The signal flow is shown in Fig. 17.

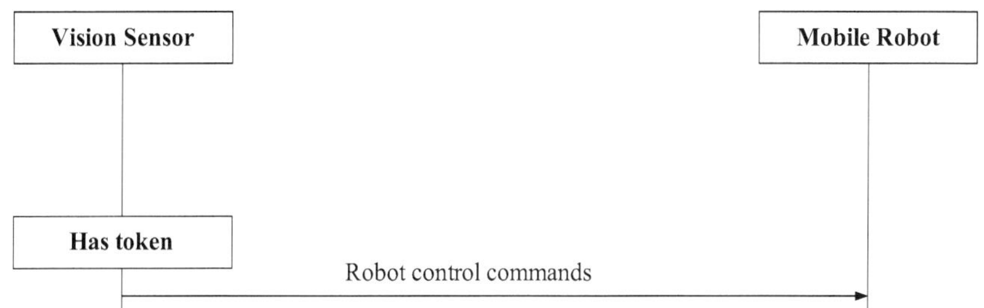

Fig. 17. Robot control signal flow

The packet format is shown in Table 7,

Byte 0 0 1 2 3 4 5 6 7	Byte 1 0 1 2 3 4 5 6 7	Byte 2 0 1 2 3 4 5 6 7	Byte 3 0 1 2 3 4 5 6 7
CHK	CMD	SrcAddr	
SN		TotalNum	
Num of steps	Control parameters		

Table 7. Robot control commands packet format

where,
- CMD = 4

- CHK, SrcAddr, SN and TotalNum are referred to section 6.3
- Num of steps: Number of control commands in one packet. It could be one set of command or multiple set of commands for the mobile robot to execute
- Control parameters: one set of control parameter includes five values as below,

Byte 0 0 1 2 3 4 5 6 7	Byte 1 0 1 2 3 4 5 6 7	Byte 2 0 1 2 3 4 5 6 7	Byte 3 0 1 2 3 4 5 6 7
timet	Vvalue	Vsign	Dvalue
Dsign			

Timet is an offset value from the previous one with the unit millisecond. The velocity *Vvalue* is the absolute value of the speed with the unit ms^{-1}. The *Dvalue* is the angle from the current direction. The *Timet* and *Vvalue* are multiplied by 100 before they are put in the packet to convert float numbers into integers. The value ranges are listed in Table 8,

Field	Value
Dsign	0: left or centre, 2: right
Dvalue	0~45 degree
Vsign	0: forward or stop, 2: backward
Vvalue	0~255 cm/s

Table 8. Robot control parameter values

6.4.5 Remote console

This is a vision sensor to remote console PC command. The remote console is responsible for system parameters setting, status monitoring, vision sensor node controlling and etc.. The communication protocol between vision sensors and console is designed to provide the foundations of these functions. After configuration of all the parameters, the system should be able to run without the remote console.

As a transparent wireless adaptor for the remote console, the wireless peripheral will always try to initiate and maintain a TCP connection with the remote console PC to establish a data exchange tunnel when it starts.

6.4.5.1 Unreliable signal flow

On the one hand, the operator can initiate requests from the remote console PC to vision sensors, e.g. restart the sensor application, set the flags in the vision sensor to send real time image and/or control points information, instruct vision sensor to sample background frame and etc.. The wireless module attached with the remote console will be responsible for unpacking IP and sending them wirelessly to vision sensors; On the other hand, vision sensors will periodically send control points, real time images, path information, robot location etc. to the remote console according to the flags set by the operator. The loss of messages is allowed. It is illustrated as Fig. 18.

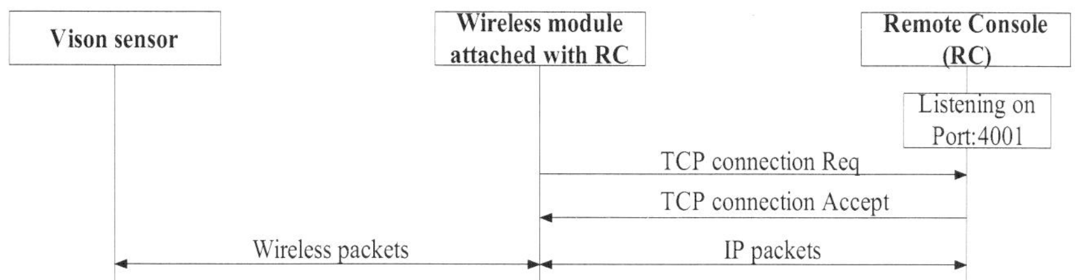

Fig. 18. Unreliable signal flow between remote console and vision sensor

6.4.5.2 Reliable signals

Reliable transmission is also provided in case packet loss is not tolerant, e.g. downloading vision sensor system drivers, updating user programs, transferring setting profile files and etc.. All data packets are required to be acknowledged by the recipient. Retransmission will be invoked if no confirmation messages received within a given time. The signal flow is illustrated in Fig. 19. The wireless module will buffer the packets and make sure all the packets sent to the vision sensor are acknowledged to ensure a reliable transmission.

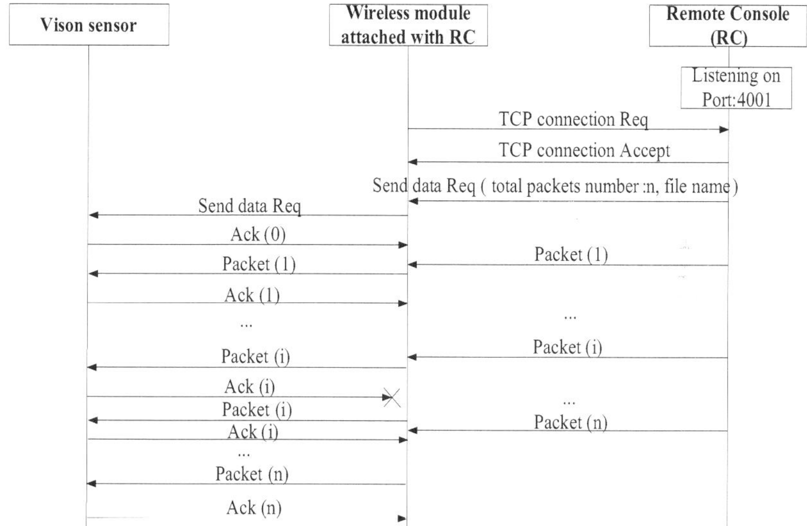

Fig. 19. Signal flow between remote console and vision sensor

7. Simulation and experiment results

Trajectory tracking of a car like robot using the mosaic eye is experimented. Four eyes are mounted on a room ceiling forming a closed continuously running room such that each eye will have a neighbouring eye at each side, one on the left and another on the right. An independent remote monitor terminal is setup to capture the mosaic eye working status on demand and to maintain mosaic eye when needed. The main processor of the car like robot is a Motorola MC9S12DT128B CPU which is used to execute the received commands from mosaic eye. The mosaic eye, the remote monitor terminal and the robot are all 802.15.4 communication enabled. The car like robot is marked by a rectangle with red and blue blobs on top of it which is used to locate the robot's position and to distinguish the robot from its obstacles, as shown in Fig. 20.

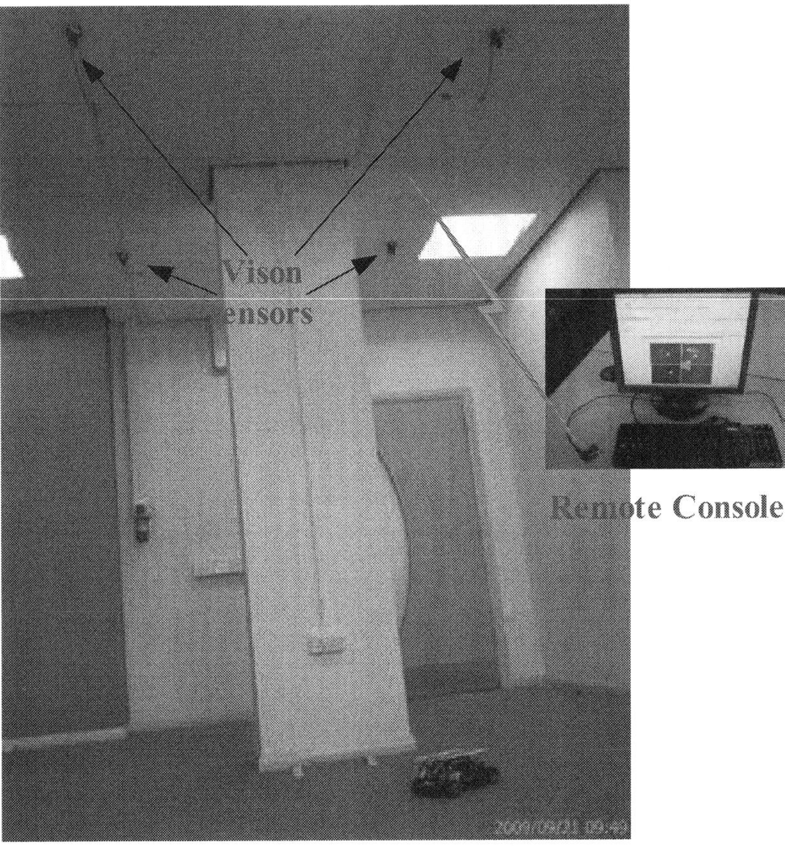

Fig. 20. Car like robot marked by a rectangle with red and blue blobs on it

The predictive control has a rolling window with $l = 20$ (control points). The maximum travelling speed is 0.8 m/s, the maximum driving force is $F_{max}^{d} = 4.4(N)$ with a 0.56(kg) robot mass and the friction factor $\mu_{max} = 0.6$ and $\tau_{max} = 2.0(N \cdot m)$.

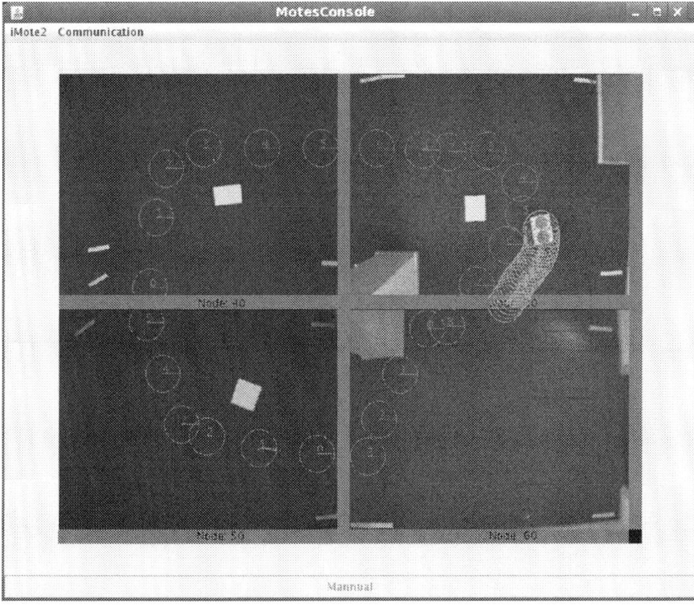

Fig. 21. Robot moving from eye-30 to obstacles free eye-60

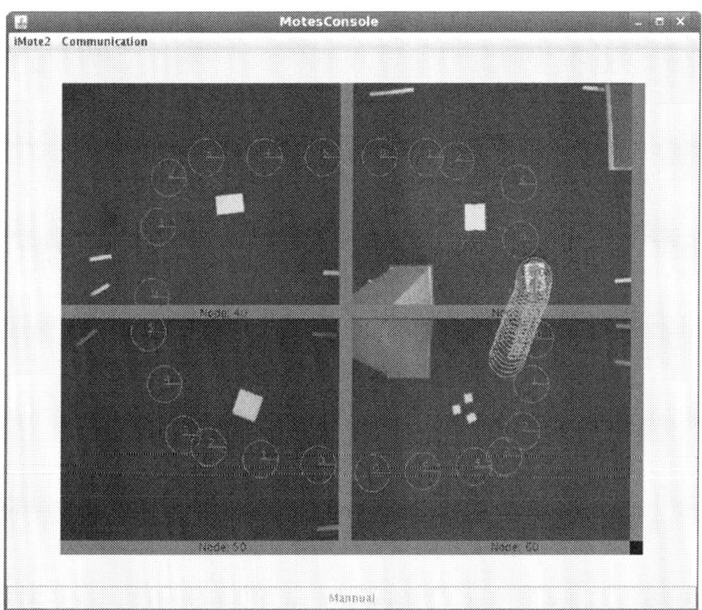

Fig. 22. Obstacles appear in eye-60

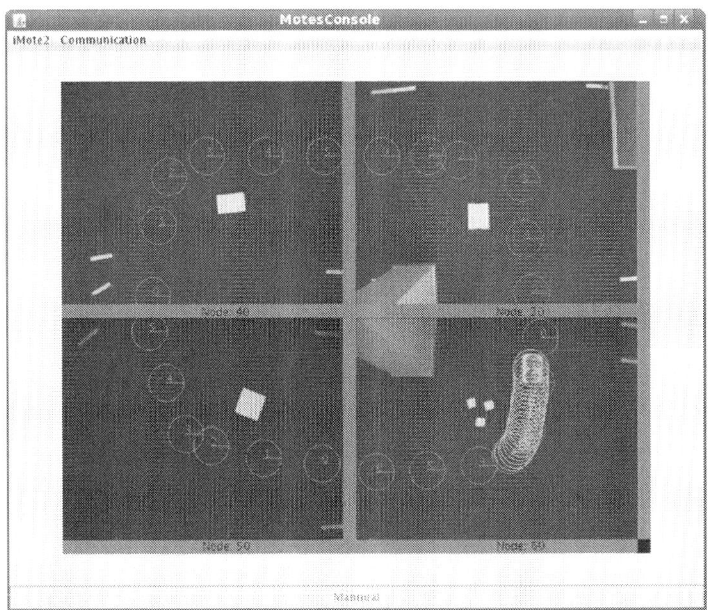

Fig. 23. Robot passing obstacle area in eye-60

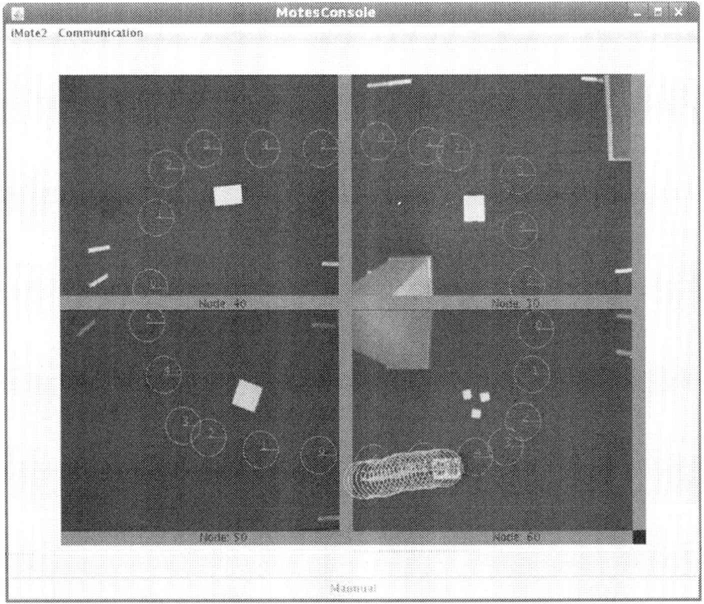

Fig. 24. Robot passed obstacles area in eye-60 and move to eye-50

Fig. 21, Fig. 22, Fig. 23 and Fig. 24 show the real time experiments of robot control by the mosaic eye. Each figure displays four views from each of the four eyes. Let eye-30, eye-40, eye-50 and eye-60 be the names of the mosaic eye starting from top-right one and counting anti-clockwise. In Fig. 21, the robot is controlled by eye-30 heading to the control area of eye-60. The sparse white circles with numbers in the centre represent the desired path that the robot should follow. The white rectangle blobs represent dynamic obstacles. As one can see in Fig. 21, the dynamic obstacles are within the views of eye-30, eye-40 and eye-50 but out of sight of eye-60. In Fig. 22, an obstacle appears within the sight of eye-60. At this point, the robot is under the control of eye-30 and eye-30 does not know the existence of the new obstacle. With the information sent from eye-60 notifying eye-30 of the obstacle, the predictive path is updated to avoid the obstacle. In Fig. , the robot control is handed over from eye-30 to eye-60. The figure shows that with the predictive path updated by eye-30 and with the control of eye-60, the robot has successfully avoided the obstacle and continued to move along the updated predictive path.

8. Conclusion

As an attempt to steer away from developing an autonomous robot with complex centralised intelligence, this chapter proposes a scheme offering a complete solution for integrating communication with path planning, trajectory generation and motion control of mobile robots in an intelligent environment infrastructure where intelligence are distributed in the environment through collaborative vision sensors mounted in a physical architecture, forming a wireless vision sensor network, to enable the navigation of unintelligent robots within that physical architecture through distributed intelligence. A bio-mimetic snake algorithm is proposed to coordinate the distributed vision sensors for the generation of a collision free R-snake path during the path planning process. Segments of a path distributed in individual sensors from a start position to a goal position are described as an elastic band emulating a snake. By following the R-snake path, an A-snake method that complies with the robot's nonholonomic constraints for trajectory generation and motion control is introduced to generate real time robot motion commands to navigate the robot from its current position to the target position. A rolling window optimisation mechanism subject to control input saturation constraints is carried out for time-optimal control along the A-snake.

The scheme has been verified by the development of a complete test bed with vision sensors mounted on a building ceiling. Results obtained from the experiments have demonstrated the efficiency of the distributed intelligent environment infrastructure for robot navigation.

9. References

Arkin (2000). Behavior-based Robotics. Cambridge, MIT Press.
Cameron (1998). Dealing with Geometric Complexity in Motion Planning. New York, Wiley.
Cheng, Hu, et al. (2008). A distributed snake algorithm for mobile robots path planning with curvature constraints. *IEEE Int. Conf. on SMC*, Singapore.
Cheng, Jiang, et al. (2010). A-Snake: Integration of Path Planning with Control for Mobile Robots with Dynamic Constraints. ICCAE.
Cormen, Leiserson, et al. (2001). Introduction to Algorithms, MIT Press and McGraw-Hill.

Kass, Witkin, et al. (1988). Snake: Active contour models. *International Journal of Computer Vision* 1(4): 321-331.

Land and Nilsson (2002). Animal Eyes, Oxford University Press.

Li and Rus (2005). Navigation protocols in sensor networks. *ACM Trans. on Sensor Networks* 1(1): 3-35.

Maciejowski (2001). Predictive control with constraints.

Mclean (1996). Dealing with geometric complexity in motion planning. *Int. Conf., IEEE in Robotics and Automation.*

Mclean and Cameron (1993). Snake-based path planning for redundant manipulators. *Robotics and Automation, IEEE International Conference on*, Atlanta, USA.

Murphy (2000). Introduction to AI robotics. Cambridge, MIT Press.

Quinlan (1994). Real-time modification of collision-free paths. Department of Computer Science, Stanford. PhD.

Quinlan and Khatib (1993). Elastic bands: connecting path planning and control. *IEEE Int. Conf. Robotics and Automation*, Atlanta, USA.

Sinopoli, Sharp, et al. (2003). Distributed control applications within sensor networks. *Proceedings of IEEE.*

Snoonian (2003). Smart buildings. *IEEE Spectrum* 40(8).

Website (2006). http://www.inf.brad.ac.uk/~pjiang/wime/.

Xi and Zhang (2002). Rolling path planning of mobile robot in a kind of dynamic uncertain environment. *Acta Automatica Sinica* 28(2): 161-175.

Zhang (2008). TOS_MAC Driver based on CC2420 radio chip.

Part 4

Social Robotics

10

Knowledge Modelling in Two-Level Decision Making for Robot Navigation

Rafael Guirado, Ramón González, Fernando Bienvenido and
Francisco Rodríguez
Dept. of Languages and Computer Science, University of Almería
Spain

1. Introduction

In recent years, social robotics has become a popular research field. It aims to develop robots capable of communicating and interacting with humans in a personal and natural way. Social robots have the objective to provide assistance as a human would do it. Social robotics is a multidisciplinary field that brings together different areas of science and engineering, such as robotics, artificial intelligence, psychology and mechanics, among others (Breazeal, 2004). In this sense, an interdisciplinary group of the University of Almería is developing a social robot based on the *Peoplebot* platform (ActivMedia Robotics, 2003). It has been specifically designed and equipped for human-robot interaction. For that purpose, it includes all the basic components of sensorization and navigation for real environments. The ultimate goal is that this robot acts as a guide for visitors at our university (Chella et al., 2007). Since the robot can move on indoor/outdoor environments, we have designed and implemented a two-level decision making framework to decide the most appropriate localization strategy.

Knowledge modelling is a process of creating a model of knowledge or standard specifications about a kind of process or product. The resulting knowledge model must be interpretable by the computer; therefore, it must be expressed in some knowledge representation language or data structure that enables the knowledge to be interpreted by software and to be stored in a database or data exchange file. CommonKADS is a comprehensive methodology that covers the complete route from corporate knowledge management to knowledge analysis and engineering, all the way to knowledge-intensive systems design and implementation, in an integrated fashion (Schreiber et al., 1999).

There are several studies on the knowledge representation and modelling for robotic systems. In some cases, semantic maps are used to add knowledge to the physical maps. These semantic maps integrate hierarchical spatial information and semantic knowledge that is used for robot task planning. Task planning is improved in two ways: extending the capabilities of the planner by reasoning about semantic information, and improving the planning efficiency in large domains (Galindo et al., 2008). Other studies use the CommonKADS methodology, or any of its extensions, to model the knowledge; some of the CommonKADS extensions that have been used in robotics are CommonKADS-RT, for real time systems, and CoMoMAS (Conceptual Modelling of Multi-Agent Systems), for multi-agent systems. The first one is based on CommonKADS with the addition of necessary elements to model real time restrictions and it is applied to the control of autonomous mobile robots (Henao et al., 2001). The second one extends CommonKADS towards Multi-Agent Systems development. A Nomad200 mobile robot is used to analyse two agent architectures, AIbot and CoNomad, by reverse engineering and to derive conceptual descriptions in terms of agent models (Glaser, 2002). Nowadays the knowledge engineering focuses mainly on domain knowledge, using reusable representations in the form of ontologies (Schreiber, 2008).

One fundamental task to achieve our goal is robot navigation, which includes the subtasks of path planning, motion control, and localization. Generally, in the process of developing robots, robotics engineers select, at design time, a single method (algorithm) to solve each of these tasks. However, in the particular case of social robots (usually designed with a generic purpose, since its ultimate goal is to act as a human) it would be more interesting to provide several alternatives to solve a specific task and the criteria for selecting the best solution according to the current environment conditions. For instance, for the specific task of localization, the robot could decide to use a GPS-like solution, if it is moving on an open space, or dead-reckoning if it is in an indoor environment.

The main contribution of this work is the development of an operational knowledge model for robot navigation. This model leads to a generic and flexible architecture, which can be used for any robot and any application, with a two-level decision mechanism. In the first level, the robotics engineer selects the methods to be implemented in the social robot. In the second level, robot applies dynamic selection to decide the proper method according to the environment conditions, taking into account a suitability criteria table. Dynamic selection of methods (DSM) lets to choose the best alternative to perform a task. It uses several suitability criteria, criterium weights, selection data and knowledge, and an aggregation function to make the decision (Bienvenido et al., 2001).

The chapter is organized as follows. The second section presents the description of the robot system used in this work. In the third section, the methodology for the knowledge representation based on DSM is shown. Next, the fourth section shows the knowledge modelling for the localization subsystem needed to develop the generic multi-agent system for the social robot *Peoplebot*. The next section discusses the results of a physical experiment carried out to analyze the proposed methodology. The last section is devoted to conclusions and further works.

2. System description

In this work, the mobile robot called *Peoplebot* of *ActivMedia Robotics Company* has been used to test through physical experiments the proposed decision making approach. It is a mobile robot designed and equipped specifically for human-robot interaction research and applications. It includes all the basic components of sensorization and navigation in real environments, which are necessary for this interaction (see Fig. 1). It has two-wheel differential with a balancing caster and it feeds on three batteries that give an operational range of about ten hours. It also has installed a touch screen which displays a map of the University of Almería. Furthermore, for speech communication, it has two microphones to capture voice and two speakers. In this way, a user can interact with the robot either by manually selecting a target in the touch screen showing the environment map or by speaking directly to the robot.

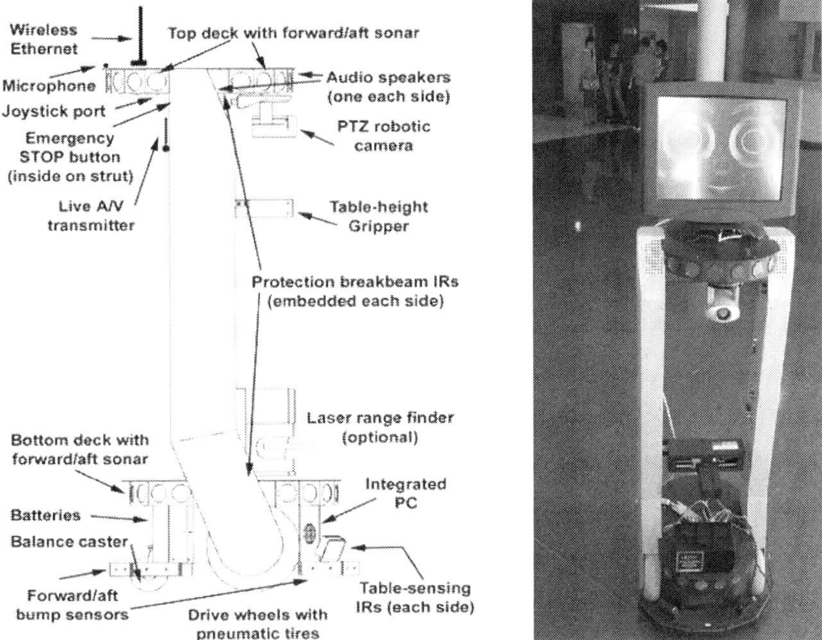

Fig. 1. Peoplebot robot: components (ActivMedia Robotics, 2003) and picture in action

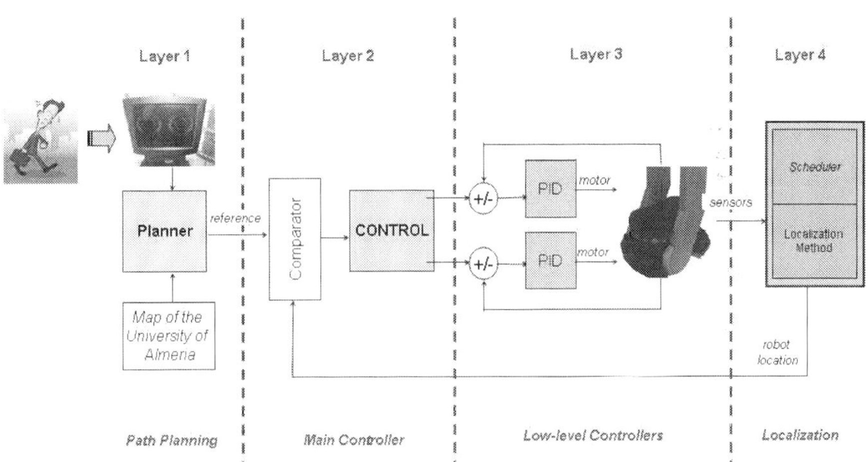

Fig. 2. Navigation architecture

For navigation purposes, a typical four-layer navigation architecture has been implemented (see Fig. 2). The top layer is devoted to path planning, that is, the generation of the reference trajectory between the current robot position and the target commanded by the user (touch screen or speech recognition modules). Then, a motion controller based on pure-pursuit (Coulter, 1992) is used to generate the actual wheel velocities. In order to ensure that the wheels move at the desired setpoints two low-level PID controllers were tuned. Finally, a layer devoted to localization is implemented. This localization layer is detailed subsequently.

3. Methodology

The knowledge model, about the localization for social robots described in this work, is based on some extensions of knowledge representation methodologies (like CommonKADS) and the DSM. Here, we introduce those approaches and a short summary of the localization algorithms implemented in the system.

3.1 Knowledge representation: the CommonKADS methodology

The CommonKADS methodology was consolidated as a knowledge engineering technique to develop knowledge-based systems (KBS) in the early 90's (Schreiber et al., 1994). This method provides two types of support for the production of KBS in an industrial approach: firstly, a lifecycle enabling a response to be made to technical and economic constraints (control of the production process, quality assurance of the system, ...), and secondly a set of models which structures the development of the system, especially the tasks of analysis and the transformation of expert knowledge into a form exploitable by the machine (Schreiber et al., 1999). Our proposal supposes to work in the expertise or knowledge model, one of the six models in CommonKADS. The rest are organizational (it supports the analysis of an organization, in order to discover problems and opportunities for knowledge systems), task (it analyzes the global task layout, its inputs and outputs, preconditions and performance criteria, as well as needed resources and competences), agent (it describes the characteristics of agents, in particular their competences, authority to act, and constraints in this respect), communication (it models the communicative transactions between the agents involved in the same task, in a conceptual and implementation-independent way) and design models (it gives the technical system specification in terms of architecture, implementation platform, software modules, representational constructs, and computational mechanisms needed to implement the functions laid down in the knowledge and communication models). Fig. 3 presents the kernel set of models used in the CommonKADS methodology (Schreiber et al., 1994).

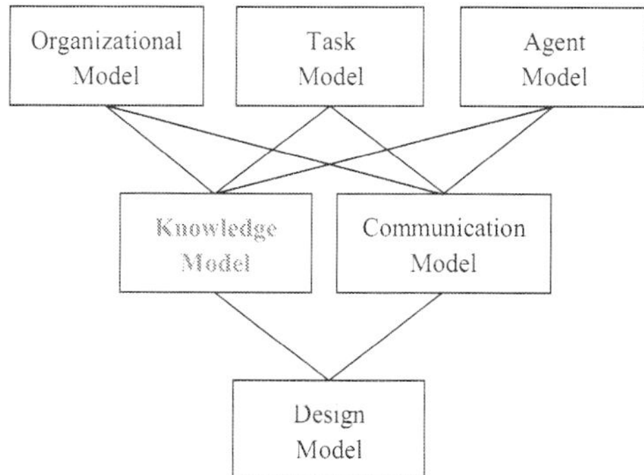

Fig. 3. CommonKADS kernel set of models

The purpose of the knowledge model is to detail the types and structures of the knowledge used in performing a task. It provides an implementation-independent description of the role that different knowledge components play in problem solving, in a way that is understandable for humans. This makes the knowledge model an important vehicle for communication with experts and users about the problem solving aspects of a knowledge system, during both development and system execution (Schreiber et al., 1999). So, its final goal is to analyze the tasks (objectives), methods (possible solution mechanisms), inferences (algorithms or agents) and domain knowledge elements (context and working data) for the KBS to be developed. These four elements permit to represent the knowledge involved in our mobile robot system. So, we have decided to use this knowledge engineering methodology.

The Task-Method Diagrams (TMD) (Schreiber et al., 1999) to model the solution mechanism of the general problem represented by the highest-level task (main objective) are used. TMD presents the relation between one task to be performed and the methods that are suitable to perform that task, followed by the decomposition of these methods in subtasks, transfer functions and inferences (final implemented algorithms). Fig. 4 shows an example of TMD tree, where the root node represents the main task (*Problem*). It can be solved using two alternative methods (*Met 1* and *Met 2*). First of them is implemented by the inference *Inf 1*, a routine executed by an agent. Second method requires the achievement of three tasks (really are two transfer functions *Tran. Fun. 1* and *Tran. Fun. 2* –special type of task, so it is represented by the same symbol- and one task *Task 1*). Transfer functions are tasks whose resolution is responsible for an external agent (for instance, it could be used for manual tasks). There are two methods to solve *Task 1*; they are *Met 3* and *Met 4*. Second one is implemented by the inference *Inf 2*, while *Met 3* requires the performance of four tasks: *Task 3*, *Task 4*, *Task 5* and *Task 6*; each one is solved by a correspondent method (*Met 5*, *Met 6*, *Met 7* and *Met 8*, respectively). These four methods are implemented by the inferences *Inf 3*, *Inf 4*, *Inf 5* and *Inf 6*.

CommonKADS proposes that the different elements (tasks, methods and inferences) of the TMD are modelled using schemas like CML or CML2 (Guirado et al., 2009). These schemas formalize all the knowledge associated to each one of these elements.

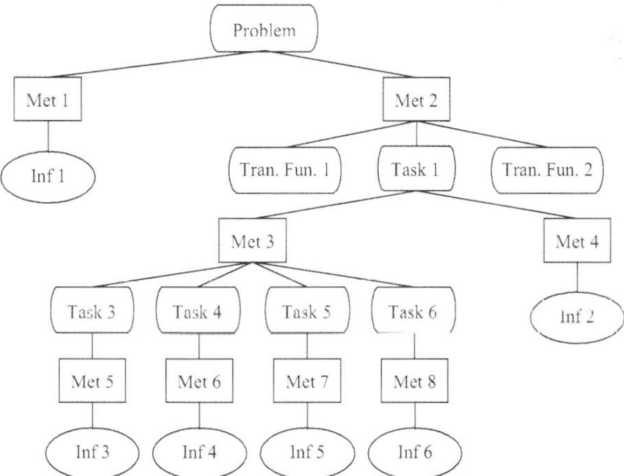

Fig. 4. Simple TMD

3.2 Dynamic selection of methods

A given task, at any level, can be performed by several alternative methods, and these can be only applied at specific conditions. DSM is based on a general decision module that, taking into account the suitability criteria defined for each alternative method and actual data, would activate the most appropriate method. These suitability criteria have assigned weights whose values are calculated through functions that depend on the current knowledge of the problem and modify the suitability criteria values of the alternative methods to solve a given task (Bienvenido et al., 2001). For example, Table 1 shows the structure of the suitability criteria for a set of alternative methods. There are criteria that must be completely fulfilled, and others are conveniently weighted to offer a condition that increase or not the suitability of a given method. This technique was previously used in greenhouses design (Bienvenido et al., 2001), and robot navigation (Guirado et al., 2009).

Method	Criterion 1	Criterion 2	Criterion 3	Criterion 4	Criterion 5
Method 1	4	3	$f_1(\ )$	1	$g_1(\ )$
Method 2	1	1	$f_2(\ )$	3	$g_2(\ )$
Method 3	2	2	$f_3(\ )$	2	$g_3(\ )$
Method 4	5	5	$f_4(\ )$	1	$g_4(\ )$
Method 5	2	2	$f_5(\ )$	2	$g_5(\ )$

Table 1. Example of structure of the suitability criteria table

In this example, criteria 3 and 5 are hard constraints or critical (C). Notice that corresponding functions $f_M()$ and $g_M()$ can only take the values 0 or 1 (depending on environment conditions), where a value of 0 means that the method is not applicable if this criterion is not met, and a value of 1 means that it can be used. The other criteria (C1, C2 and C4) can take values between 1 and 5 according to the suitability of the method. These criteria are called soft constraints or non-critical (N).

In this case, the global suitability value S for the method M (M = {1, 2, 3, 4, 5}) is given by the following equation:

$$S_M = f_M() * g_M() * (1 + W1 * C1_M + W2 * C2_M + W4 * C4_M) \qquad (1)$$

Where Ci_M is the value of the criterion i for the method M, and Wi is the weight for the criterion i. These weights depend on the environment conditions and their sum must be equal to 1. For instance, assuming that W1 = 0.5, W2 = W4 = 0.25 and that the suitability criteria table is as shown in the table above (with $f_1() = f_5() = 0$, $f_2() = f_3() = f_4() = 1$, $g_1() = g_2() = g_3() = 1$, and $g_4() = g_5() = 0$), then the selected method would be the number 3 ($S_1 = 0$, $S_2 = 2.5$, $S_3 = 3$, $S_4 = 0$, and $S_5 = 0$). Notice that if there are two or more methods with the highest suitability value, the current method remains as selected, and if not, the method is selected randomly.

3.3 Localization algorithms

Robot localization is defined as the process in which a mobile robot determines its current position and orientation relative to an inertial reference frame. Localization techniques have to deal with the particular features of environment conditions, such as a noisy environment (vibrations when the robot moves, disturbance sources, etc.), changing lighting conditions, high degrees of slip, and other inconveniences and disturbances.

Method	Indoor/ Outdoor	Computing Time	Light Conditions	Precision	Cost	Sensors	Fault-tolerant
Odometry	Both, not advisable for slip conditions	Fast	There is no inconve-nience	Error grows with distance	Cheap	Encoders	It only depends on encoders readings
Dead-reckoning	Both	Fast	There is no inconve-nience	Error grows with distance, although it is reduced taking IMU data	More expensive than odometry	Encoders and IMU	It depends on encoders and IMU
Beacons	Mainly indoor	Middle	Beacons must be observable from robot	Absolute position (no error growth)	Expensive (installation of markers)	Beacons, landmarks, etc.	It uses many beacons
GPS-based	Only outdoor	Middle	There is no inconve-nience	Absolute position (no error growth)	High cost of accurate GPS	GPS, DGPS, RTK-GPS	It depends on the number of available satellites
Visual odometry	Both, advisable for slip conditions	Usually high	It depends on light conditions	Error grows with distance, although it is reduced taking visual data	Cheap	Camera(s)	It depends on camera(s)
Kalman-filter-based	Both	Usually high	There is no inconve-nience	Small error (redundant sources)	Expensive (redundant sensors)	It depends on fused sensors	Yes, since it generally uses several redundant sourccs

Table 2. Main characteristics of the localization techniques

In this work, we have analyzed different localization methods, in order to evaluate the most appropriate ones according to the activity of the robot. In order to achieve this objective, we have firstly studied the typical localization methods for the mobile robotics community and we discuss the advantages and disadvantages of these methods to our specific case.

The most popular solutions are wheel-based odometry and dead-reckoning (Borenstein & Feng, 1996). These techniques can be considered as relative or local localization. They are based on determining incrementally the position and orientation of a robot from an initial point. In order to provide this information, it uses various on-board sensors, such as encoders, gyroscopes, accelerometers, etc. The main advantage of wheel-based odometry is that it is a really straightforward method. The main drawback is, above all, an unbounded growth of the error along time and distance, particularly in off-road slip conditions (González, 2011).

We have also analyzed global or absolute localization techniques, which determine the position of the robot with respect to a global reference frame (Durrant-Whyte & Leonard, 1991), for instance using beacons or landmarks. The most popular technique is GPS-like solutions such as Differential GPS (DGPS) and Real-Time Kinematics GPS (RTK-GPS). In this case, the error growth is mitigated and the robot position does not depend on time and initial position. The main problems in relation to GPS are a small accuracy of data (improved using DGPS and RTK-GPS) and the signal is lost in closed spaces (Lenain et al., 2004). Other solutions such as artificial landmarks or beacons require a costly installation of the markers on the area where the robot operates.

On the other hand, there are some localization techniques based on visual information (images). One of the most extended approaches is visual odometry or Ego-motion estimation, which is defined as the incremental on-line estimation of robot motion from an image sequence (Nistér et al., 2006). It constitutes a straightforward-cheap method where a single camera can replace a typical expensive sensor suite, and it is especially useful for off-road applications, since visual information estimates the actual velocity of the robot, minimizing slip phenomena (Angelova et al., 2007).

Finally, probabilistic techniques based on estimating the localization of the mobile robot combining measurements from different data sources are becoming popular. The most extended technique is the Kalman filter (Thrun et al., 2005). The main advantage of these techniques is that each data source is weighted taken into account statistical information about reliability of the measuring devices and prior knowledge about the system. In this way, the deviation or error is statistically minimized.

Summing up, in Table 2 the considered localization methods for our social robot are presented. We also detail some key parameters to decide the most appropriate solution, depending on the task to be performed.

4. Modelling the localization system

In order to model the knowledge that the social robot needs to take decisions, we have analyzed the characteristics of the localization methods to decide the necessary parameters for the best selection in different environment conditions. Firstly, all available alternatives have been evaluated. Since it would be inefficient to implement all the methods in the robot, it is applied a first decision level in which the human experts select the methods that the social robot may need taking into account the scenarios to be found at the University. In this sense, we are considering a social mobile robot working at indoor and outdoor scenarios. The main purpose of this mobile robot is to guide to the people at our University, that means, the robot could guide a person inside a building (for instance, the library) or it could work outdoors between buildings.

We propose a two-level multi-agent architecture for knowledge modelling of the localization strategy. Fig. 5 shows a schema for this architecture. Firstly, the expert selected the most proper methods for the kind of activities that the robot has to make (move at the campus of the University of Almería). These localization methods were: wheel-based odometry since it is a straightforward method to estimate the robot position. This approach is especially used for indoor environments (like inside the library). On the other hand, for outdoor motions, the visual odometry approach and a DGPS-like solution are used. Finally, it is also considered to use a Kalman filter fusing data from visual odometry and DGPS.

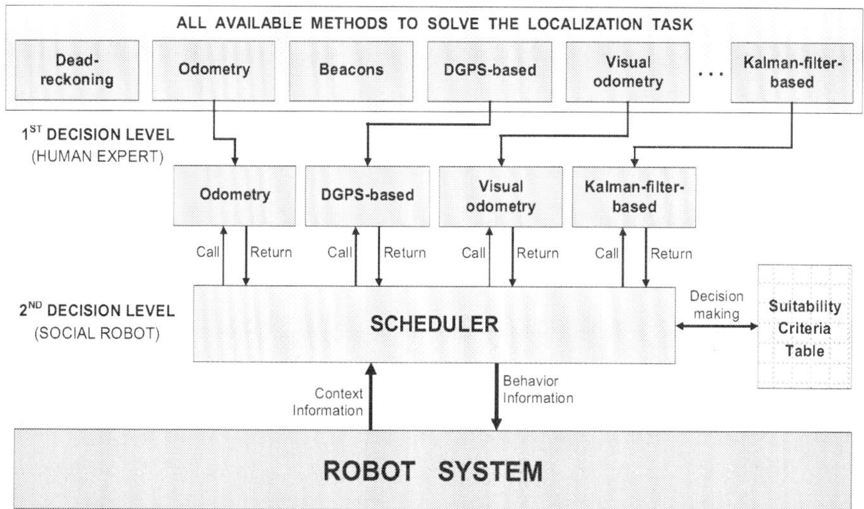

Fig. 5. Schema for the proposed two-level multi-agent architecture

The first selection process (filter applied by the engineer) lets that the robot chooses only between useful and independent methods, according to the kind of activities to be accomplished by the mobile robot. In this way, redundant and useless localization methods will be avoided.

The second decision level of this architecture considers a general scheduler module implemented in the social robot. This planner is permanently running. When the robot has to take a decision (selecting an alternative among several options to accomplish a particular task) it calls to the scheduler agent. This agent uses the context information, the suitability criteria table and a dynamic cost function (depending on the scenario) to select the most appropriate localization method.

Some of the main advantages of this architecture are that the robot can choose the most appropriate localization method according to the surrounding environment and new decisions can be incorporated simply including its suitability criteria table.

Fig. 6 shows the lower-level TMD elements, simplified to four testing alternatives of localization. This is a branch of the most general navigation subsystem TMD (Guirado et al., 2009).

DSM is applied to choose the most efficient method using an aggregation function that integrates the suitability criteria and the weights to generate a suitability value for each method. In our particular case, the criteria for decision-making are Computing Time (CT), GPS-Signal Necessity (GN), Luminosity (L), Fault-Tolerance (FT) and Precision (P). These criteria are related to the method characterization done in the previous section. CT, L, FT and P are directly considered in the Table 2, while GN is related to the Indoor/Outdoor and Sensors method parameters. The economic Cost of implementation is used by the expert in the first decision level in order to choose the methods to be implemented in the robot, but it does not make sense to use it as a suitability criterion for selecting the best alternative method among those that are implemented in the robot.

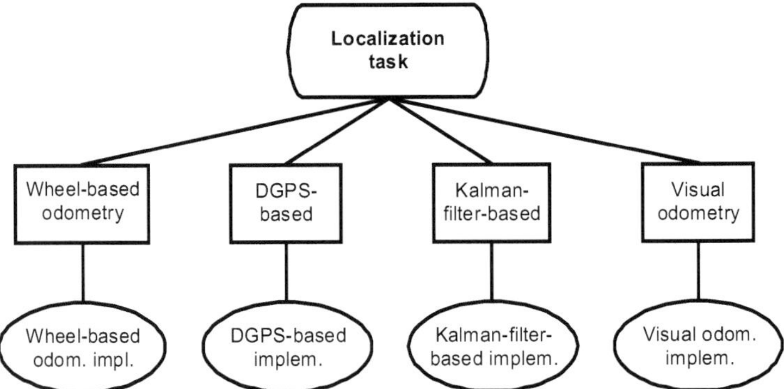

Fig. 6. Representation of a TMD for a pre-filtered localization system

CT is inversely proportional to the execution time of each method, favouring the faster method to calculate the exact position of the robot. We have considered this criterion because some instances need a fast response and it is necessary to use the fastest algorithm. CT is considered a non-critical (N) and static (S) criterion that means it is not used to discard any alternative method and its value is considered fixed for each method because the variations in testing are minimal.

GN indicates if a method needs a good GPS signal to be considered in the selection process. This criterion is critical (C) only for the DGPS-based method because the robot cannot apply it if the received signal to get the position is low (less than 4 satellite signals). The other methods do not use the GN criterion because they do not use the GPS data; so, it is convenient or non-critical (N) for those methods. The criterion is dynamic (D) for all the methods, taking values 0 or 1 for DGPS-based method, and values between 1 and 5 for the rest.

L represents the intensity of the light in the place where the robot is. If the luminosity is low, algorithms that require the use of conventional cameras for vision cannot be used. This is a dynamic (D) criterion since the robot must operate in places more or less illuminated with natural or artificial light. So, the value of this criterion is changing and its value is discretized between 1 and 5. As this criterion does not exclude any method in the selection process, it is considered non-critical (N). Notice that, in our case, luminosity is obtained analyzing the histogram of an image.

FT is a parameter that indicates if the robot system is able to continue operating, possibly at a reduced level, rather than failing completely, when the applied method fails. This criterion is static (S) for each method. Its values have been obtained from our experiences. As in the previous criterion, this is also considered non-critical (N).

P is related to the accuracy of the sensor data that each method uses. It has a dynamic (D) value because the environment conditions are changing. For instance, GPS signal quality is fine in an open area; therefore, the precision of DGPS-based method is high. This is another non-critical (N) criterion because it does not discard any method by itself.

As previously explained, the human expert has chosen four localization methods in the first decision level. These alternatives are wheel-based odometry (O), DGPS-based (G), Kalman-filter-based (K) and visual odometry (V); each of them has assigned a set of suitability criteria.

The cost function considers the criteria with their associated weights,

$$S_M = GN_M() * (1 + W_{CT} * CT_M + W_L * L_M + W_{FT} * FT_M + W_P * P_M) \tag{2}$$

The weights (W_i) are dynamic functions, so they can change depending on environment and performance requirements.

The function for the critical criterion GN is defined as follow.

$$GN() = \begin{cases} 1 & \text{if the method does not work with GPS} \\ GPS - signal() = \begin{cases} 1 & \text{if GPS signal is available} \\ 0 & \text{if GPS signal is not available} \end{cases} \end{cases} \tag{3}$$

So, it can only be equal to 0 for the DGPS-based method, and the GPS signal must also be insufficient.

The description of the elements (tasks, methods and inferences) has been represented using the CML notation, as CommonKADS methodology proposes (Schreiber et al., 1999). Here is an example for the localization task:

```
TASK Localization;
   GOAL:     "Obtain the exact position and orientation of the robot at any
             given time";
   INPUT:
     sensor-data:
       "Readings from sensors (GPS, cameras, encoders, ...)";
   OUTPUT:
     robot-position-and-orientation:
        "x, y and θ coordinates of the robot position and rotation angle on
        the reference system";
   SELECTION-CRITERIA:
     NS Computing-time =    "Speed factor for calculating the exact
                            position of the robot";
     CD GPS-necessity =     "Necessity to use the GPS signal";
     ND Luminosity =        "Light conditions near the robot";
     NS Fault-tolerance =   "Resilience to failure";
     ND Precision =         "Accuracy in calculating the robot position";
   CRITERION-WEIGHTS:
     Computing-time-weight =   "if a quick answer is needed, this criterion
                               is very important";
     Luminosity-weight =       "methods using camera (eg. visual odometry)
                               need good lighting conditions";
     Fault-tolerance-weight =  "if there is a high fault probability, this
                               criterion will have a high weight";
     Precision-weight =        "it the robot is moving on a narrow space,
                               this criterion will have a high weight";
   AGREGATION-METHOD:         Multi-criteria function S_M;
 END-TASK Localization;
```

Each selection criterion has two letters in front of his name. The first one is the severity of the criterion, where N indicates non-critical and C indicates critical, and the second one is if the criteria can change or not, using D for dynamic and S for static.

5. Results

The proposed methodology was tested through several physical experiments showing how the robot applies the knowledge model-based architecture using the suitability criteria values (depending on the environmental conditions) to select the appropriate method in every moment.

In this section, we analyze the proposed methodology in a real scenario. Our real case has been that the mobile robot has guided a person at our University (see Fig. 7) from the bus stop (start) to the library (goal). Firstly, the visitor tells the robot to guide him to the library. In this case, the user used the touch screen. Then, the mobile robot calculated the optimal route according to several parameters (we are not detailing it here). The solution of this stage was the line marked in Fig. 7 (left). The mobile robot is moving at 0.5 m/s with a sampling time of 0.2 s. In order to avoid sudden transitions from one method to another, due to sensor noises and disturbances, we have tuned a filter, where a decision will not be taken until a method is not selected 10 consecutive times.

In this case, the robot moves through four areas along the trajectory. The path labelled with "a" is a wide-open space. The path labelled with "b" is a narrow way with some trees. Finally, the path labelled with "c" is open space but close to buildings. Notice that the robot moved on a pavement terrain, which leads to slip phenomena, is not expected. The real trajectory followed by the robot is shown in Fig. 7 (right); note that the x-axis has a different scale from y-axis in the plot.

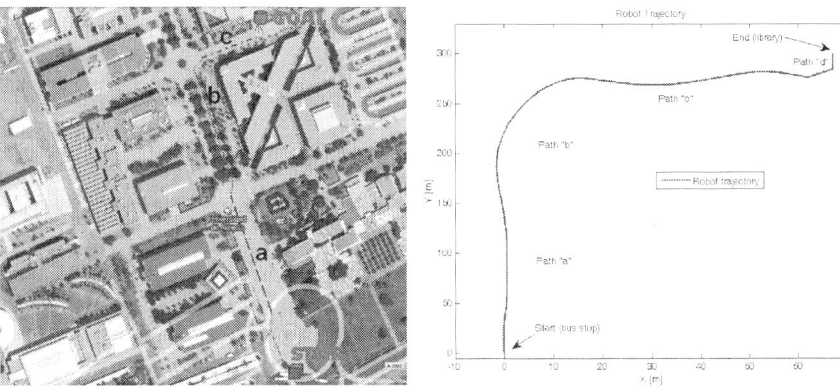

Fig. 7. Real scenario (University map) and followed trajectory. The mobile robot has guided a person from bus stop (start) to the library (goal)

As previously explained, the GN criterion is critical for the DGPS-based method. This means that method is not selectable if GPS signal is insufficient (less than 4 satellites available). So, we represent in Fig. 8 the number of satellites detected by the GPS justifying the necessity to use other alternatives localization methods in some trajectory paths.

CT and FT are static criteria and so they have the same values in all situations, since they are related to independent characteristics of the environment (CT_O=5, CT_G=2, CT_K=1, CT_V=4, FT_O=2, FT_G=4, FT_K=5 and FT_V=3). Other criteria (GN, L and P) are dynamic, that means they can change depending on the environment conditions.

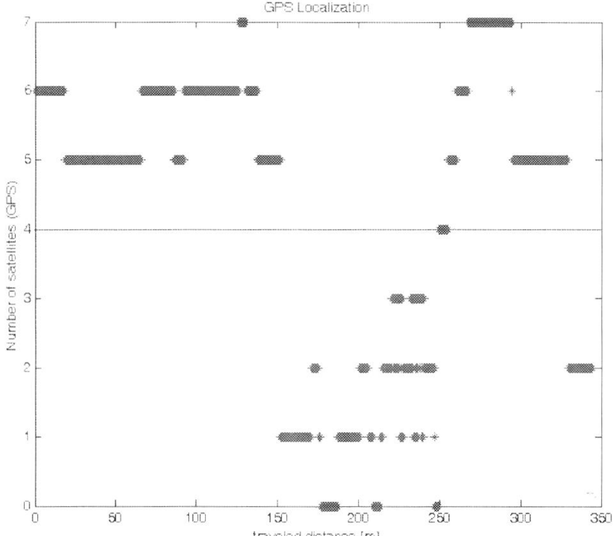

Fig. 8. GPS signal during the robot travel

In the first area ("a"), the GN and L criteria was equal for all methods, since all of them could be used without problems in current conditions. In addition, the robot initially considered the same weights for all criteria ($W_{CT} = W_L = W_{FT} = W_P = 0.25$). Applying the cost function, robot obtained the following suitability values for each method:

$$S_O = 1 * (1 + 0.25 * 5 + 0.25 * 5 + 0.25 * 2 + 0.25 * 2) = 4.5$$

$$\mathbf{S_G = 1 * (1 + 0.25 * 2 + 0.25 * 5 + 0.25 * 4 + 0.25 * 5) = 5}$$

$$S_K = 1 * (1 + 0.25 * 1 + 0.25 * 5 + 0.25 * 5 + 0.25 * 3) = 4.5$$

$$S_V = 1 * (1 + 0.25 * 4 + 0.25 * 5 + 0.25 * 3 + 0.25 * 3) = 4.75$$

As expected, robot used the DGPS-based localization method, since it obtains the larger suitability value. Notice in Fig. 8 that there are more than three satellites available during this path.

In the second area ("b"), the GN and L criteria remained the same for all methods. Factors for P criterion changed for some methods with respect to the previous area. The GPS signal was frequently lost due to the trees and the error increased considerably (see Fig. 8). In addition, the user increased the velocity of the robot, which led to give a higher weight to TC criterion, keeping a constant value for the other ($W_{CT} = 0.4$; $W_L = W_{FT} = W_P = 0.2$). These were the obtained suitability values for each method:

$$S_O = 1 * (1 + 0.4 * 5 + 0.2 * 5 + 0.2 * 2 + 0.2 * 2) = 4.8$$

$$S_G = 0 * (1 + 0.4 * 2 + 0.2 * 5 + 0.2 * 4 + 0.2 * 2) = 0$$

$$S_K = 1 * (1 + 0.4 * 1 + 0.2 * 5 + 0.2 * 5 + 0.2 * 3) = 4$$

$$\mathbf{S_V = 1 * (1 + 0.4 * 4 + 0.2 * 5 + 0.2 * 3 + 0.2 * 4) = 5}$$

The selected method was visual odometry. DGPS method got a low suitability value due to "b" was a cover area (trees) and the GPS signal was temporary lost (see Fig. 8).

In the third area ("c"), the GN and L criteria remained the same for all methods. Factors for the P criterion slightly changed from the previous area (GPS signal was slightly better since there were not trees, although still affected by the proximity to the buildings). The user reduced the velocity of the robot, and it led to reduce the weight of the TC criterion, keeping a constant value for the other (W_{CT} = 0.1; W_L = W_{FT} = W_P = 0.3). The obtained suitability values were:

$$S_O = 1 * (1 + 0.1 * 5 + 0.3 * 5 + 0.3 * 2 + 0.3 * 2) = 4.2$$

$$S_G = 1 * (1 + 0.1 * 2 + 0.3 * 5 + 0.3 * 4 + 0.3 * 3) = 4.8$$

$$\mathbf{S_K = 1 * (1 + 0.1 * 1 + 0.3 * 5 + 0.3 * 5 + 0.3 * 3) = 5}$$

$$S_V = 1 * (1 + 0.1 * 4 + 0.3 * 5 + 0.3 * 3 + 0.3 * 3) = 4.7$$

The Kalman-filter-based obtained the larger suitability value since "c" was an open area where DGPS and visual odometry work fine.

In the last area (inside the library), the GN criterion was zero for the DGPS-based method, since the signal was completely lost; moreover, the L criterion decreased slightly for visual odometry method due to changing light conditions. When the robot goes inside the library, it considers the same weights for all criteria again (W_{CT} = W_L = W_{FT} = W_P = 0.25). The obtained suitability values were:

$$\mathbf{S_O = 1 * (1 + 0.25 * 5 + 0.25 * 5 + 0.25 * 2 + 0.25 * 3) = 4.75}$$

$$S_G = 0 * (1 + 0.25 * 2 + 0.25 * 5 + 0.25 * 4 + 0.25 * 1) = 0$$

$$S_K = 1 * (1 + 0.25 * 1 + 0.25 * 5 + 0.25 * 5 + 0.25 * 3) = 4.5$$

$$S_V = 1 * (1 + 0.25 * 4 + 0.25 * 4 + 0.25 * 3 + 0.25 * 3) = 4.5$$

Finally, as expected, when the mobile robot guided to the person inside the library, wheel-based odometry method obtained the larger suitability value.

Fig. 9 shows the average values during the experiment for the localization methods. This information has been used in the test of the proposed methodology.

6. Conclusions and future works

The main objective of this work is to take a further step in developing a generic and flexible decision mechanism to select the most proper localization algorithm for a social robot. We present the preliminary results for a single decision between four alternatives (selected by the human expert in the first decision level). More tests will be performed within the same operating environment in the future.

The main advantages of the proposed architecture are to facilitate further addition of new algorithms that could be developed in the future and the capacity of deciding in real-time the most appropriate technique to be used in the current conditions.

From a practical point of view, and according to our physical experiments, the proposed methodology permits to successfully guide users at our university by choosing the best localization method taking into account the surrounding environment.

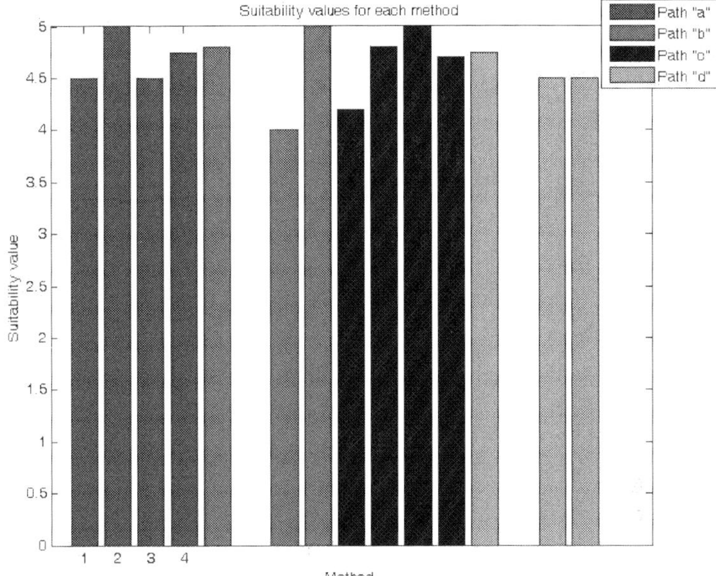

Fig. 9. Average suitability values for the localization methods in every path ("a", "b", "c", "d")

Here we have applied a direct DSM that means the best method is the one with the highest suitability value (or one of them if there is more than one), but we are considering to incorporate fuzzy logic to the cost function and to apply other types of membership functions to the DSM.

In order to follow evaluating the proposed mechanisms of DSM in robotics, we are extending the use of these techniques to other social robot tasks. The final goal is to build an ontology in the domain of social robotic.

7. References

ActivMedia Robotics. (August 2003). Performance PeopleBot Plus Operations Manual, (version 4), In: *Mobile Robots*, 29.03.2011, Available from
http://www.ing.unibs.it/~arl/docs/documentation/Aria%20documentation/Old %20and%20useless/Misc.%20Mob.%20Robots%20doc./PeopleBotMan4.pdf

Angelova, A.; Matthies, L.; Helmick, D. & Perona, P. (2007). Learning and Prediction of Slip from Visual Information. *Journal of Field Robotics*, Vol.24, No.3 (Special Issue on Space Robotics, Part I), (March 2007), pp. 205-231, ISSN 1556-4967

Bienvenido, J.F.; Flores-Parra, I.M.; Guirado, R. & Marín, R. (2001). Knowledge Based Modeling of the Design Processes as a Base of Design Tools. Application to the Development of Agricultural Structures, In: *Lecture Notes in Computer Science 2178*, R. Moreno-Diaz et al. (Eds.), pp. 209-222, Springer-Verlag, ISBN 3-540-45654-6, Berlin Heidelberg

Borenstein, J. & Feng, L. (1996). Measurement and Correction of Systematic Odometry Errors in Mobile Robots, *IEEE Transactions on Robotics and Automation*, Vol.12, No.6, (December 1996), pp. 869-880, ISSN 1042-296X

Breazeal, C.L. (2004). *Designing Sociable Robots* (new edition), The MIT Press, ISBN 0-262-52431-7, Cambridge, Massachusetts, London, England

Chella, A.; Liotta, M. & Macaluso, I. (2007). CiceRobot: A Cognitive Robot for Interactive Museum Tours, *Industrial Robot: An International Journal*, Vol.34, No.6, (October 2007), pp. 503-511, ISSN 0143-991X

Coulter, R.C. (1992). *Implementation of the Pure Pursuit Path Tracking Algorithm*, Technical Report CMU-RI-TR-92-01, The Robotics Institute, Carnegie Mellon University, Pittsburgh

Durrant-Whyte, H. & Leonard, J. (1991). Mobile Robot Localization by Tracking Geometric Beacons, *IEEE Transactions on Robotics and Automation*, Vol.7, No.3, (June 1991), pp. 376-382, ISSN 1042-296X

Galindo, C.; Fernández-Madrigal, J.A.; González, J. & Saffiotti, A. (2008). Robot Task Planning using Semantic Maps, *Robotics and Autonomous Systems*, Vol.56, No.11, (November 2008), pp. 955-966, ISSN 0921-8890

Glaser, N. (2002). *Conceptual Modelling of Multi-Agent Systems: The CoMoMAS Engineering Environment*, Kluwer Academic Publishers, ISBN 1-4020-7061-6, Boston/Dordrecht /London

González, R. (2011). *Contributions to Modelling and Control of Mobile Robots in Off-Road Conditions*, Doctoral Dissertation, University of Almería, Almería, Spain

Guirado, R.; Miranda, C.M. & Bienvenido, J.F. (2009). Path Planning Knowledge Modeling for a Generic Autonomous Robot: A Case Study, In: *Lecture Notes in Artificial Intelligence 5712*, J.D. Velásquez et al. (Eds.), pp. 74-81, Springer-Verlag, ISBN 978-3-642-04592-9, Berlin Heidelberg

Henao, M.; Soler, J. & Botti, V. (2001). Developing a Mobile Robot Control Application with CommonKADS-RT, *Lecture Notes in Artificial Intelligence 2070*, L. Monostori, J. Váncza and M. Ali (Eds.), pp. 651-660, Springer-Verlag, ISBN 3-540-45517-5, Berlin Heidelberg

Lenain, R.; Thuilot, B.; Cariou, C. & Martiner, P. (2004). A New Nonlinear Control for Vehicle in Sliding Conditions: Application to Automatic Guidance of Farm Vehicles using RTK GPS, *IEEE International Conference on Robotics and Automation*, Vol.5, (May 2004), pp. 4381-4386, ISSN 1050-4729

Nistér, D.; Naroditsky, O. & Bergen, J.R. (2006). Visual Odometry for Ground Vehicle Applications, *Journal of Field Robotics*, Vol.23, No.1, (January 2006), pp. 3-20, ISSN 1556-4967

Schreiber, G.; Wielinga, B.; de Hoog, R.; Akkermans, H. & Van de Velde, W. (1994). CommonKADS: A comprehensive methodology for KBS development, *IEEE Expert*, Vol.9, No.6, (December 1994), pp. 28–37, ISSN 0885-9000

Schreiber, G.; Akkermans, H.; Anjewierden, A.; de Hoog, R.; Shadbolt, N.; Van de Velde, W. & Wielinga, B. (1999). *Knowledge Engineering and Management: The CommonKADS Methodology*, The MIT Press, ISBN 0-262-19300-0, Cambridge, Massachusetts, London, England

Schreiber, G. (2008). Knowledge Engineering, In: *Handbook of Knowledge Representation*, van Harmelen, F.; Lifschitz, V. & Porter, B. (Eds.), pp. 929-946, Elsevier Science, ISBN 978-0-444-52211-5, Oxford, UK

Thrun, S.; Burgard, W. & Fox, D. (2005). *Probabilistic Robotics*, The MIT Press, ISBN 0-262-20162-3, Cambridge, Massachusetts, London, England

11

Gait Training using Pneumatically Actuated Robot System

Natasa Koceska[1], Saso Koceski[1], Pierluigi Beomonte Zobel[2]
and Francesco Durante[2]
[1]Faculty of Computer Science, University "Goce Delce" – Stip, Stip,
[2]Applied Mechanics Laboratory, DIMEG, University of L'Aquila, L'Aquila
[1]Macedonia
[2]Italy

1. Introduction

Locomotor disability is the most commonly reported type of disability. It is defined as a person's inability to execute distinctive activities associated with moving both himself and objects, from place to place and such inability resulting from affliction of musculoskeletal and/or nervous system. In this category entered the people with paraplegia, quadriplegia, multiple sclerosis, muscular dystrophy, spinal cord injury, persons affected by stroke, with Parkinson disease etc.

The number of people with locomotor disabilities is growing permanently as a result of several factors, such as: population growth, ageing and medical advances that preserve and prolong life. Worldwide statistics about locomotor disability show that:

- in Australia: 6.8% of the Australian population had a disability related to diseases of the musculoskeletal system, which is 34% of the persons with any kind of disability;
- in USA: there are more than 700.000 Americans who suffer a stroke each year, making it the third most frequent cause of death and the leading cause of permanent disability in the country. 10.000 suffer from traumatic spinal cord injury, and over 250.000 are disabled by multiple sclerosis per year;
- in Italy: 1.200.000 people have declared the locomotor disabilities.

Rehabilitation is very important part of the therapy plan for patients with locomotor dysfunctions in the lower extremities. The goal of rehabilitation is to help the patient return to the highest level of function and independence possible, while improving the overall quality of life - physically, emotionally, and socially.

Locomotor training in particular, following neurological injury has been shown to have many therapeutic benefits. Intensive training and exercise may enhance motor recovery or even restore motor function in people suffering from neurological injuries, such as spinal cord injury (SCI) and stroke. Repetitive practice strengthens neural connections involved in a motor task through reinforcement learning, and therefore enables the patients a faster and better re-learning of the locomotion (walking). Practice is most effective when it is task-specific. Thus, rehabilitation after neurological injury should emphasize repetitive, task-specific practice that promotes active neuromuscular recruitment in order to maximize motor recovery.

Conventional manual therapy includes specific exercises for strengthening and practicing of one single movement at time. The more sophisticated therapy which over the years has established itself as an effective intervention for improving over-ground walking function, involves practice of stepping on a motorized treadmill with manual assistance and partial bodyweight support (BWS). This kind of therapy makes use of a suspension system to provide proper upright posture as well as balance and safety during treadmill walking. This is accomplished through a harness that removes a controllable portion of the weight from the legs, redistributing it to the trunk and groin, and in the same time allowing free movement of the patients' arms and legs. The movement is provided by a slow moving treadmill. The treadmill constant rate of movement provides rhythmic input which reinforces a coordinated reciprocal pattern of movement. Proper coordination is further assisted by the manual placement of the feet by the therapist. The   BWS   reduces   the demands on muscles, which may enable the patient to work on improving the coordination of the movement while gradually increasing the strength of muscles (Miller et al., 2002). The controlled environment may also increase patient confidence by providing a safe way to practice walking (Miller et al., 2002). As patients progress, the BWS can be gradually decreased, challenging the patient to assert more postural control and balance (Miller et al., 2002).

This rehabilitation strategy was derived from research showing the effect of suspending spinalized cats in harnesses over treadmills (Visintin & Barbeau, 1989) From this work with spinalized cats, it was determined that not only a reciprocal locomotor program can be generated at a spinal cord level by central pattern generators, but also, this pattern can be controlled through sensory input. By pulling the stance leg back with the pelvis stabilized in a harness, the treadmill causes extension to the hip of the weight bearing leg, which triggers alternation in the reciprocal pattern controlled by the central pattern generator (Grillner, 1979). Since it was demonstrated by (Barbeau & Rossignol, 1987) that the quality of locomotion in spinalized cats improved if they were provided a locomotor training program, it seems reasonable to expect that humans with locomotor disabilities might benefit from this type of training.

Clinical studies have confirmed that individuals who receive BWS treadmill training following stroke (Hesse et al., 1994) and spinal cord injury (Wernig et al., 1999) demonstrate improved electromyographic (EMG) activity during locomotion (Visintin et al., 1998), walk more symmetrically (Hassid et al., 1997), are able to bear more weight on their legs.

However, manual assistance, during the BWS treadmill training, relies on physiotherapy procedures which are extremely labour intensive. It is carried out by 2 or 3 physiotherapists, sitting next to the treadmill, and manually guiding patient's legs in coordination with a treadmill. For therapists this training is exhaustive, therefore, training sessions tend to be short and may limit the full potential of the treatment. Manual assistance also lacks repeatability and precision. During the manual therapy it is very difficult for even the most proficient and skilled therapist to provide a proper gait pattern and in that way to maintain high-quality therapy across a full training session of patients, who require this type of attention. Also, manually assisted treadmill training lacks objective measures of patient performance and progress.

A promising solution for assisting patients during rehabilitation process is to design robotic devices. They may enhance traditional treatment techniques by enabling rehabilitation of all the joints together, which is more effective that training only one joint at time; they will provide more precise and repetitive gait trajectory, which was the main problem with the manual therapy; they could accurately measure and track the patient's impairments over the rehabilitation course; they could potentially augment recovery of ambulation in people following neurological injury by increasing the total duration of training and reducing the labor-intensive assistance provided by physical therapists. In the general setting of these robotic systems, a therapist is still responsible for the nonphysical interaction and observation of the patient by maintaining a supervisory role of the training, while the robot carries out the actual physical interaction with the patient.

2. Robot devices for gait training - state of the art

Several research groups are working on development of robot devices for "gait training".
One example of automated electromechanical gait training device is 'Lokomat' (Colombo et al., 2000). It is a motor driven exoskeleton device that employs a body weight support suspension system and treadmill. Locomat has four rotary joints that drive hip and knee flexion/extension for each leg. The joints are driven in a gait-like pattern by precision ball screws connected to DC motors. The patient's legs, strapped into an adjustable aluminum frame, are moved with repeatable predefined hip- and knee-joint trajectories on the basis of a position-control strategy. Lokomat systems enables longer and individually adapted training sessions, offering better chances for rehabilitation, in less time and at lower cost compared to existing manual methods.

Another commercially available gait training device is Gait Trainer. It is a single degree-of-freedom powered machine that drives the feet trough a gait-driven trajectory. Gait Trainer applies the principle of movable footplates, where each of the patients' feet is positioned on a separate footplate whose movements are controlled by a planetary gear system, simulating foot motion walking. Gait Trainer use a servo-controlled motor that sense the patients' effort, and keeps the rotation speed constant (Hesse et al., 2000). A potential limitation with the Gait Trainer is that the system does not directly control the knee or hip joints, so a manual assistance of one physiotherapist is needed to assist their proper movements. Gait Trainer might not be suitable for non-ambulatory people with weak muscles but only for those that have some degree of control of the knee/hip joints.

HapticWalker is programmable footplate machine, with permanent foot machine contact (Schmidt et al., 2005). The system comprises two 3 DOF robot modules, moving each foot in the sagittal plane. Foot movement along the two base axes in this plane (horizontal, vertical) is performed by linear direct drive motors, which move independently on a common rail, but are connected via a slider-crank system. A limitation of the HapticWalker is that the interaction only takes place at the foot sole so that typical poor joint stability of stroke patients cannot be controlled, for example to prevent hyperextension of the knee (similar to the GaitTrainer). Furthermore the cutaneous input at the foot sole with such a system is unnatural, which might disturb training effectivity.

LOPES (Lower Extremity Powered Exoskeleton) robot is a combination of an exoskeleton robot for the legs and an externally supporting end-effector robot for the pelvis (Veneman et al., 2005). The joints of the robot (hip, knee) are actuated with Bowden-cable driven series elastic actuators. Impedance control is used as a basic interaction control outline for the exoskeleton.

PAM is a device that can assist the pelvic motion during stepping using BWST, and it's used in combination with POGO- the pneumatically operated gait orthosis (Aoyagi et al., 2007). Most of these devices are using electric motors as actuators. The use of electric motors, together with the specifically designed mechanism for converting their motion, is increasing the production costs of these devices.

This research is focused on design of pneumatically driven exoskeletal device for gait rehabilitation (developed in the Laboratory of Applied Mechanics at University of L'Aquila, Italy). The use of the pneumatic actuators is reasonable due to their large power output at a relatively low cost. They are also clean, easy to work with, and lightweight. Moreover, the choice of adopting the pneumatic actuators to actuate the prototype joints is biologically inspired. Indeed, the pneumatic pistons are more similar to the biological muscles with respect to the electric motors. They provide linear movements, and are actuated in both directions, so the articulation structures do not require the typical antagonistic scheme proper of the biological joints.

In summary, the pneumatic actuators represent the best tradeoff between biological inspiration, ease of employment and safe functioning due to the compliance of air, on one hand, and production costs, on the other.

3. Mechanical design of the rehabilitation system

Designing an exoskeleton device for functional training of lower limbs is a very challenging task. From an engineering perspective, the designs must be flexible to allow both upper and lower body motions, once a subject is in the exoskeleton, since walking involves synergy between upper and lower body motions. It must be also a light weight, easy wearable and must guarantee comfort and safety. From a neuro-motor perspective, an exoskeleton must be adjustable to anatomical parameters of a subject.

Considering these characteristics an exoskeleton structure with 10 rotational DOF was studied and realized. An optimal set of DOF was chosen after studying the literature on gait, and in order to allow the subject to walk normally and safely in the device.

The degrees of freedom are all rotational, two of them are on the pelvis level, two for the hips, two for the knees, and four for the ankles (Fig.1).

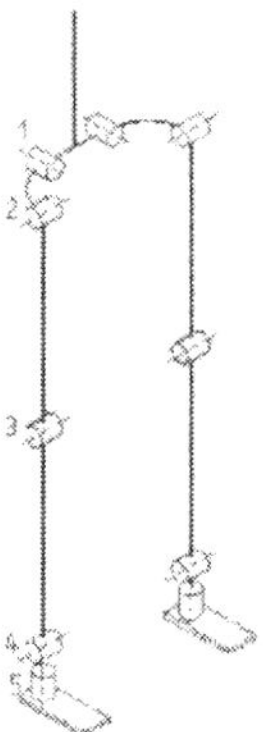

Fig. 1. DOF of the developed exoskeleton

The robot moves in parallel to the skeleton of the patient, so that no additional DOF or motion ranges are needed to follow patient motions.

The mechanical structure of the shapes and the dimensions of the parts composing the exoskeleton are human inspired and have an ergonomic design.

The inferior limbs of the exoskeleton are made up of three links corresponding to the thighbone, the shinbone and the foot. The thighbone link is 463 mm long and has a mass of 0.5 kg and the shinbone link is 449 mm long and has a mass of 0.44 kg. For better wearability of the exoskeleton an adjustable connection between the corset of polyethylene (worn by the patient) and the horizontal rod placed at the pelvis level is provided. Moving the exoskeleton structure up for only 25 mm, the distance between the centre of the knee joint and the vertical axes of the hip articulation, is reduced to 148 mm, while the corset remains in the same position. This way the system is adaptable to different patient dimensions.

In order to realize a prototype with anthropomorphic structure that will follow the natural shape of the human's lower limbs, the orientation and position of the human leg segments were analyzed. In the case of maximum inclination, the angle formed by the vertical axis and a leg rod is 2.6°, observed in frontal plane (Fig. 2).

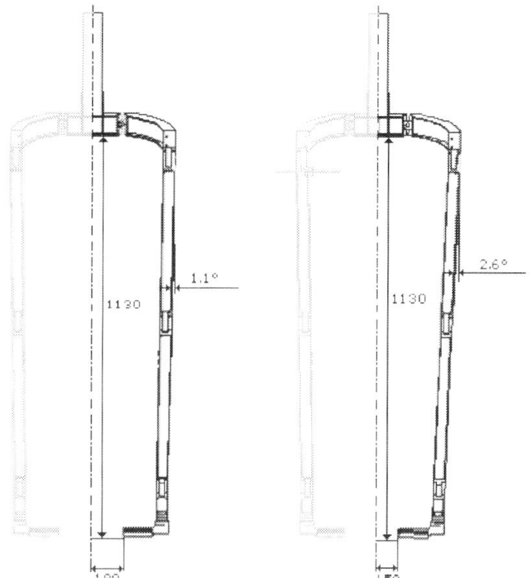

Fig. 2. Positioning of the exoskeleton shinbone and thighbone link, realized following the human leg position

The inclination of 1.1° was chosen for the stand position, while other 1.5° are given by a lateral displacement of 30 mm, when the banking movement occurs. In this way the ankle joint is a little bit moved towards the interior side with respect to the hip joint, following the natural profile of the inferior limbs in which the femur is slightly oblique and form an angle of 9° with the vertical while for the total leg this angle is reduced to 3° (Fig. 3).

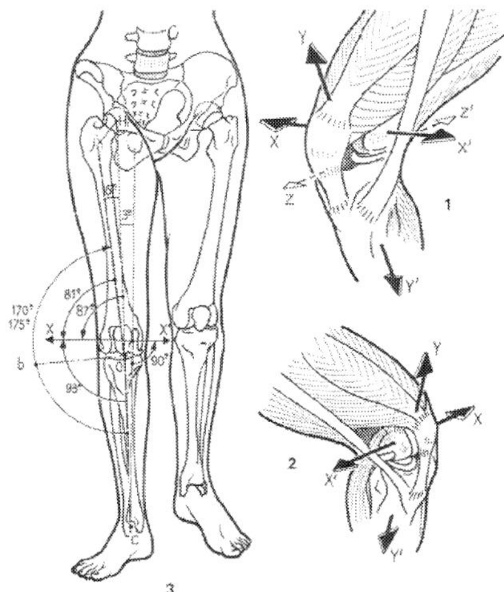

Fig. 3. Orientation and position of the human leg segments

The structure of the exoskeleton is realized in aluminum which ensures a light weight and a good resistance.

Rehabilitation system is actuated by 4 pneumatic actuators, two for each inferior limb of the exoskeleton (Fig. 4). The motion of each cylinder's piston (i.e. supply and discharge of both cylinder chambers) is controlled by two pressure proportional valves (SMC-ITV 1051-312CS3-Q), connected to both cylinder chambers.

Hip and knee angles, of our rehabilitation system, are acquired by rotational potentiometers.

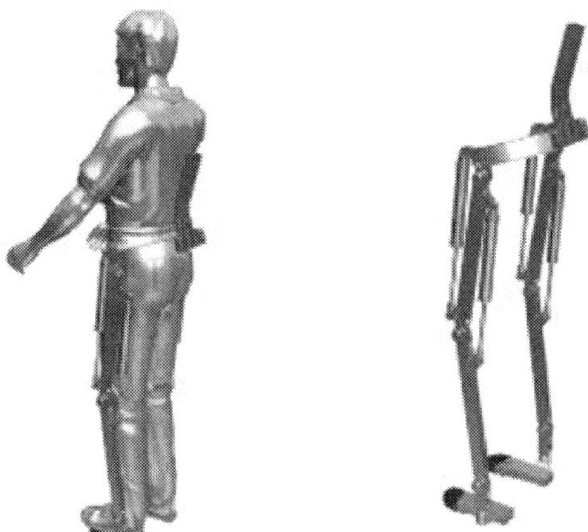

Fig. 4. Mechanical ergonomic structure of the exoskeleton with pneumatic actuators

In order to guarantee the safety of the patient, mechanical safety limits (physical stops), are placed on extreme ends of the allowed range of motion of each DOF.

The overall exoskeleton structure is positioned on a treadmill and supported, at the pelvis level, with a space guide mechanism that allows vertical and horizontal movements. The space guide mechanism also prevents a backward movement caused by the moving treadmill belt. Space guide mechanism is connected with the chassis equipped with a weight balance system (Fig.5), which ensure balance during walking. The developed system is capable to support person heavy less than 85kg.

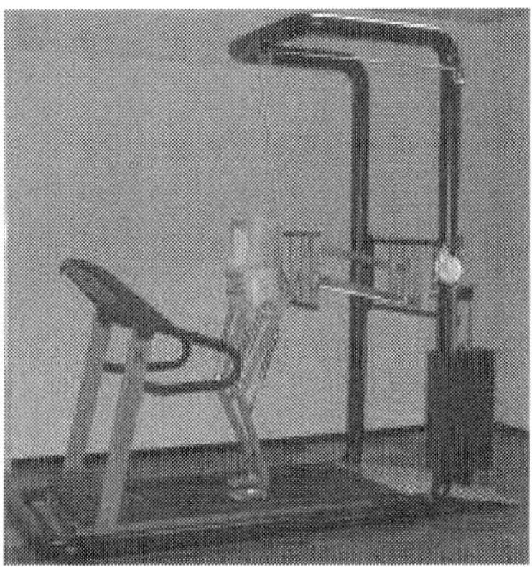

Fig. 5. Realized prototype of the overall rehabilitation system

4. Kinematical behaviour and joint forces

In order to develop the control system, it is useful to analyze the actuator forces necessary to move the mechanical system with reference to the shinbone and thighbone angular positions. Since the system is a rehabilitation one, with slow velocities, dynamic loads will be neglected in the following. The articulations have only one DOF or they are actuated by only one pneumatic actuator, Fig.4. The kinematic scheme of the leg is shown on the Fig.6a.

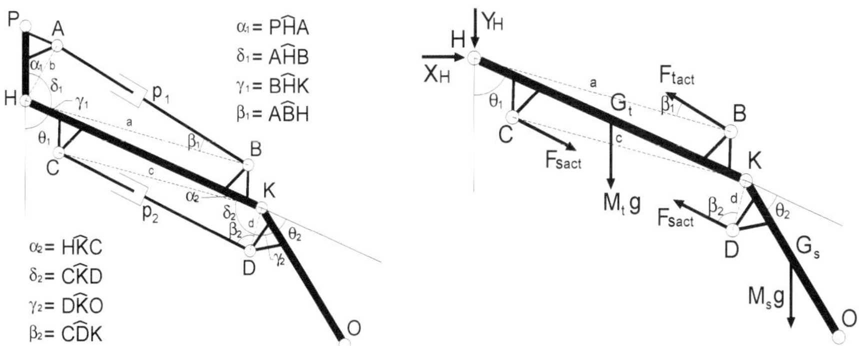

Fig. 6. a) Kinematic articulation scheme and b) free body diagram of the leg

The p_1 segment represents the pneumatic actuator of the thighbone, the p_2 segment represents the pneumatic actuator of the shinbone whereas the hip angle position is indicated by the θ_1 angle with reference to the vertical direction and the knee angle position is indicated by the θ_2 angle with reference to the thighbone direction.

By means of simple geometric relations the process that calculates the length of the actuator of the shinbone once known the rotation angle θ_2 is described with (1). The equations (1) show this process for the shinbone, considering the geometrical structure and the connections between different components.

$$\begin{cases} \delta_2 = \pi - \theta_2 - \gamma_2 - \alpha_2 \\ \\ p_2 = \sqrt{c^2 + d^2 - 2cd\cos\delta_2} \end{cases} \tag{1}$$

After the calculation of the actuators length p_2, the angle β_2 can be easily deduced as in (2):

$$\beta_2 = \sin^{-1}(\frac{c\sin\delta_2}{p_2}) \tag{2}$$

F_{Sact} represents the force supplied by the shinbone pneumatic actuator, whereas the arrow indicated by $M_S g$ shows the opponent force caused by the gravity as for the shinbone. M_S is the approximate sum of the mass of the shinbone and the foot applied in the centre of mass of the shinbone.

From a simple torque balance with respect to the point K, Fig. 6b, the relation between F_{Sact} and the angular positions θ_1 and θ_2 is derived as in (3).

$$F_{Sact} = \frac{M_S g L_{KGs} \sin(\theta_1 - \theta_2)}{d\sin(\beta_2)} \tag{3}$$

From (1), (2) and (3) it can be seen that the force supplied by the shinbone pneumatic actuator can be expressed as a function of the θ_1 and θ_2 angle, obtained by the rotational potentiometers.

As the knee articulation also the hip articulation of the prototype has only one DOF and thus is actuated by only one pneumatic actuator as it can be seen on Fig.4. The hip articulation scheme is again shown on the Fig.6a as a part of the overall scheme of the leg.

By simple geometric relations, the process that calculates the actuator length knowing the rotation angle θ_1, is described with (4).

$$\begin{cases} \delta_1 = \pi - \theta_1 - \gamma_1 - \alpha_1 \\ \\ p_1 = \sqrt{a^2 + b^2 - 2ab\cos\delta_1} \end{cases} \tag{4}$$

For a certain actuator length p_1, the angle β_1 can be easily deduced as in (5).

$$\beta_1 = \sin^{-1}(\frac{b\sin\delta_1}{p_1}) \tag{5}$$

F_{Tact} indicates the force supplied by the thighbone pneumatic actuator, whereas the arrow indicated by $M_T g$ shows the opponent force caused by the gravity as for the thighbone. M_T is the approximate sum of the weights of the thighbone applied in the centre of mass of the thighbone.

From a simple torque balance with respect to the point H, Fig. 5b, the F_{Tact} value depending on the angular positions of hip and knee is derived. Equation (6) shows the relation found for the hip articulation.

$$F_{Tact} = \frac{M_T g L_{HG_T} \sin\theta_1 + M_S g[L_{HK}\sin\theta_1 + L_{KG_S}\sin(\theta_1 - \theta_2)]}{a\sin\beta_1} \tag{6}$$

From equations (4), (5) and (6) it can be seen that the force supplied by the thighbone pneumatic actuator also can be expressed as a function of the θ_1 and θ_2 angles obtained by the rotational potentiometers.

So, analytic relations between the forces provided by the pneumatic actuators and the torques needed to move the hip and knee articulations have been found. In particular, in our case it is useful to analyze the forces necessary to counteract the gravitational load acting on the thighbone and shinbone centre of mass, varying the joints angular position, because it offers the possibility of inserting a further compensation step in the control architecture in order to compensate the influence of errors, due to modelling and/or external disturbances, during the movements.

5. Numerical solution of the inverse kinematic problem

Walking is a complicated repetitious sequence of movement. The human walking gait cycle in its simplest form is comprised of stance and swing phases.

The stance phase which typically represents 60% of gait cycle is the period of support, while the swing phase for the same limb, which is the remaining 40% of the gait cycle, is the non-support phase [13]. Slight variations occur in the percentage of stance and swing related to gait velocity.

Fig. 7. Position of the markers

To analyze the human walking, a camera based motion captured system was used in our laboratory. Motion capturing of a one healthy subject walking on the treadmill, was done with one video camera placed with optical axis perpendicular in respect of the sagittal plane of the gait motion. The subject had a marker mounted on a hip, knee and ankle.

An object with known dimensions (grid) was placed inside the filming zone, and it was used like reference to transform the measurement from pixel to distance measurement unit (Fig. 7). The video was taken with the resolution of 25 frame/s.

The recorded video was post-processed and kinematics movement parameters of limbs' characteristic points (hip, knee and ankle) were extracted. After that, the obtained trajectory was used to resolve the problem of inverse kinematics of our lower limb rehabilitation system. The inverse kinematic problem was resolved in numerical way, with the help of Working Model 2D software (Fig. 8). By the means of this software the target trajectory that should be performed by each of the actuators was determined.

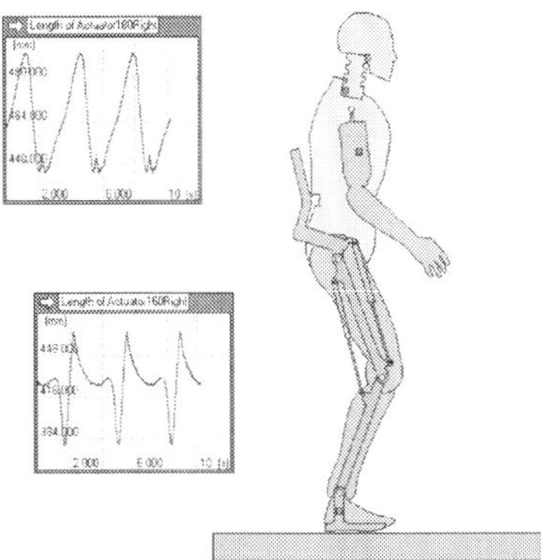

Fig. 8. Working Model 2D was used to obtain the actuators length, velocity and forces applied

6. Control architecture

The overall control architecture is presented with the diagram on the Fig. 9. In particular, it is based on fuzzy logic controllers which aim to regulate the lengths of thighbone and shinbone pneumatic actuators. The force compensators are calculating the forces necessary to counteract the gravitational load acting on the thighbone and shinbone center of mass, varying the joints angular position.

The state variables of the pneumatic fuzzy control system are: the actuator length error E, which is the input signal and two output control signals $Urear$ and $Ufront$ which are control voltages of the valves connected to the rear chamber and front chamber respectively.

Actuator length error in the system is given by:

$$E(kT) = R(kT) - L(kT) \tag{7}$$

where, $R(kT)$ is the target displacement, $L(kT)$ is the actual measured displacement, and T is the sampling time.

Based on this error the output voltage, that controls the pressure in both chambers of the cylinders, is adjusted. Seven linguistic values non-uniformly distributed along their universe of discourse have been defined for input/output variables (negative large-NL, negative medium-NM, negative small-NS, zero-Z, positive small-PS, positive medium-PM, and positive large-PL). For this study trapezoidal and triangular-shaped fuzzy sets are chosen for input variable and singleton fuzzy sets for output variables.

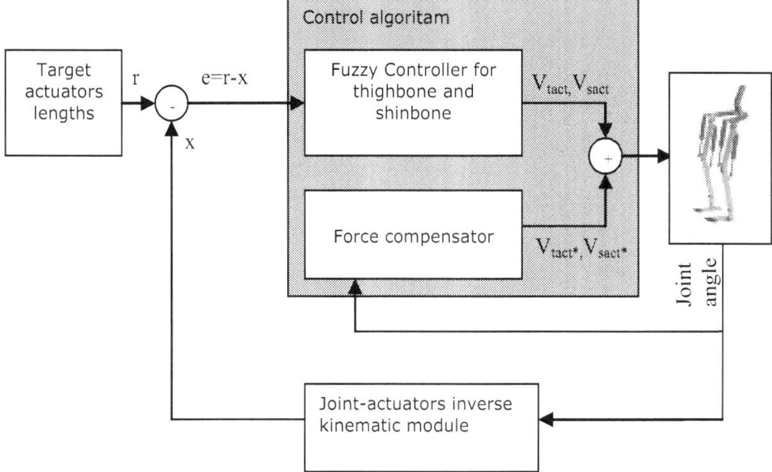

Fig. 9. Control architecture diagram

The membership functions were optimized starting from a first, perfectly symmetrical set. Optimization was performed experimentally by trial and test with different membership function sets. The membership functions that give optimum results are illustrated in Figs. 10, 11 and 12.

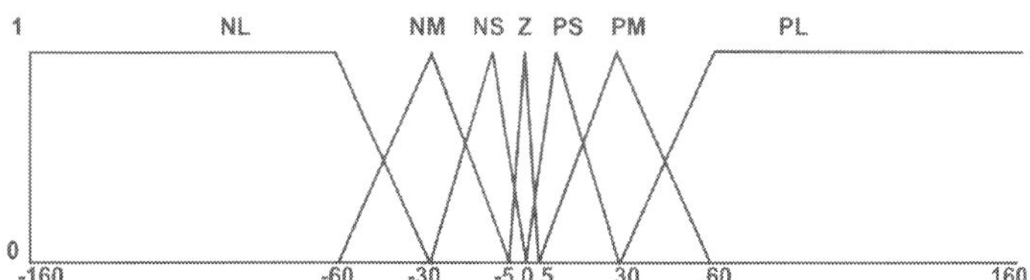

Fig. 10. Membership functions of input variable E

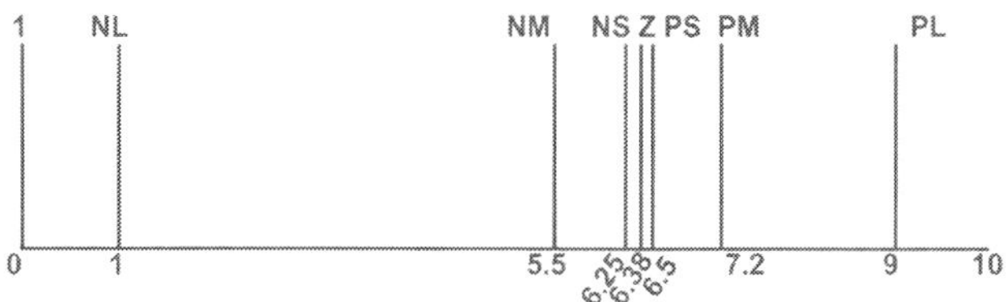

Fig. 11. Membership functions of output variable U_{front}

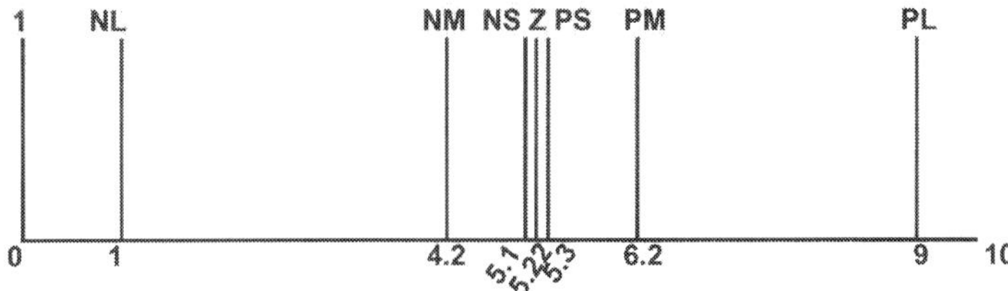

Fig. 12. Membership functions of output variable U_{rear}

The rules of the fuzzy algorithm are shown in Table 1 in a matrix format.
The max-min algorithm is applied and centre of gravity (CoG) method is used for deffuzzify and to obtain an accurate control signal. Since the working area of cylinders is overlapping, the same fuzzy controller is used for both of them. The force compensators are calculating the forces necessary to counteract the gravitational load acting on the thighbone and shinbone centre of mass, varying the joints angular position.

Rule n °	E	ANT	POS
1	PL	PL	NL
2	PM	PM	NM
3	PS	PS	NS
4	Z	Z	Z
5	NS	NS	PS
6	NM	NM	PM
7	NL	NL	PL

Table 1. Rule matrix of the fuzzy controller

Target pneumatic actuators lengths obtained by off-line procedure were placed in the input data module. In this way there is no necessity of real-time calculation of the inverse kinematics and the complexity of the overall control algorithm is very low. The feedback information is represented by the hip and knee joint working angles and the cylinder lengths.
The global control algorithm runs inside an embedded PC104, which represents the system supervisor. The PC104 is based on Athena board from Diamond Systems, with real time Windows CE.Net operating system, which uses the RAM based file system. The Athena board combines the low-power Pentium-III class VIA Eden processor (running at 400 MHz) with on-board 128 MB RAM memory, 4 USB ports, 4 serial ports, and a 16-bit low-noise data acquisition circuit, into a new compact form factor measuring only 4.2" x 4.5". The data acquisition circuit provides high-accuracy; stable 16-bit A/D performance with 100 KHz sample rate, wide input voltage capability up to +/- 10V, and programmable input ranges. It includes 4 12-bit D/A channels, 24 programmable digital I/O lines, and two

programmable counter/timers. A/D operation is enhanced by on-board FIFO with interrupt-based transfers, internal/external A/D triggering, and on-board A/D sample rate clock.

The PC 104 is directly connected to each rotational potentiometer and valves placed onboard the robot.

In order to decrease the computational load and to increase the real-time performances of the control algorithm the whole fuzzy controller was substituted with a hash table with interpolated values and loaded in the operating memory of the PC104.

7. Experimental results

To test the effectiveness of the proposed control architecture on our lower limbs rehabilitation robot system, experimental tests without patients were performed, with a sampling frequency of 100 Hz, and a pressure of 0.6 MPa.

The larger movements during the normal walking occur in the sagittal plane. Because of this, the hip and the knee rotational angles in sagittal plane were analyzed. During normal walking, the hip swings forward from its fully extended position, roughly −20 deg, to the fully flexed position, roughly +10 deg. The knee starts out somewhat flexed at toe-off, roughly 40 deg, continues to flex to about +70 deg and then straightens out close to 10 deg at touch-down. Schematic representation of the anatomical joint angle convention is shown in Figure 13.

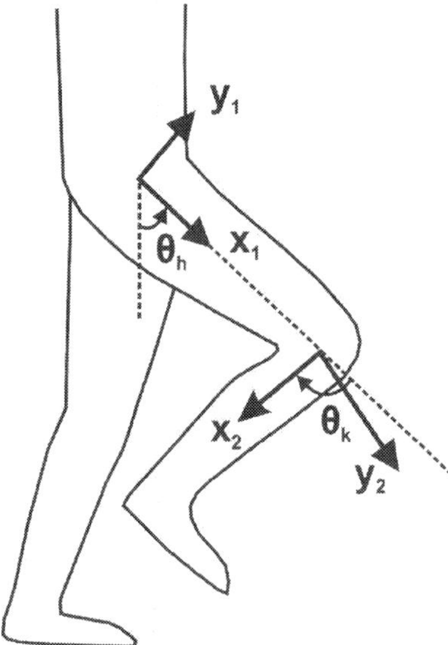

Fig. 13. Schematic representation of the anatomical joint angle convention

Figure 14 and Figure 15 show the sagittal hip and knee angle as function of time, of both human (position tracking measurement with leg-markers) and robot (joint angle measurements).

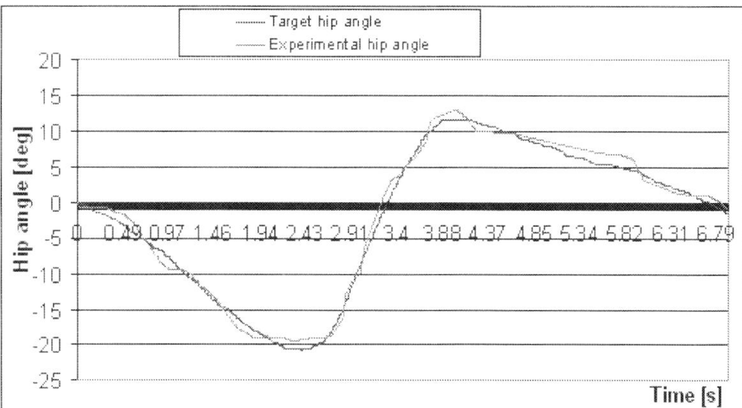

Fig. 14. Comparison of target and experimentally obtained hip angle as function of time

The results from the experiments show that the curves have reached the desired ones approximately. However, error (which is max. 5 degrees) exists, but doesn't affect much on final gait trajectory.

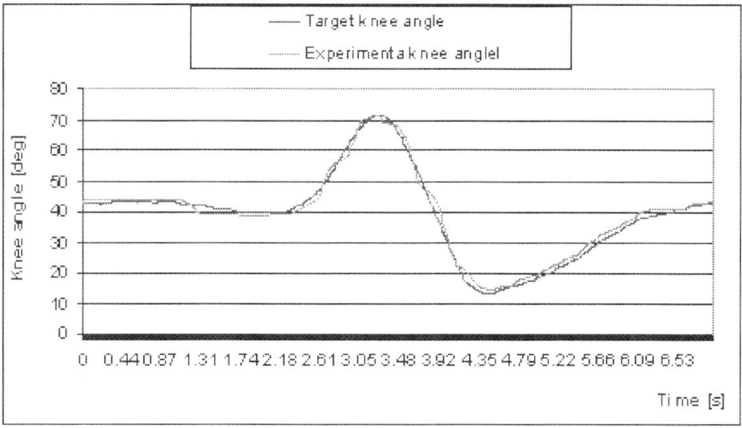

Fig. 15. Comparison of target and experimentally obtained knee angle as function of time

8. Conclusion

Powered exoskeleton device for gait rehabilitation has been designed and realized, together with proper control architecture. Its DOFs allow free leg motion, while the patient walks on a treadmill with its weight, completely or partially supported by the suspension system.
The use of pneumatic actuators for actuation of this rehabilitation system is reasonable, because they offer high force output, good backdrivability, and good position and force control, at a relatively low cost.

The effectiveness of the developed rehabilitation system and proposed control architecture was experimentally tested. During the experiments, the movement was natural and smooth while the limb moves along the target trajectory.

In order to increase the performance of this rehabilitation system a force control loop should be implemented as a future development. The future work also foresees two more steps of evaluation of the system: experiments with voluntary healthy persons and experiments with disable patients.

9. References

Aoyagi, D.A., Ichinose, W. E. I., Harkema, S. J. H, Reinkensmeyer, D J. R, & Bobrow, J. E. B. (Sep. 2007) A Robot and Control Algorithm That Can Synchronously Assist in Naturalistic Motion During Body-Weight-Supported Gait Training Following Neurologic Injury, *IEEE Transactions on neural systems and rehabilitation engineering*, vol.15, no. 3.

Barbeau H, Rossignol S. Recovery of locomotion after chronic spinalization in the adult cat. *Brain Res.* 1987; 412(1):84–95.

Colombo G., Joerg M., Schreier R., Dietz V., Treadmill training of paraplegic patients using a robotic orthosis, *J. Rehabil. Res. Dev.* 17 (2000) 35–42.

Grillner S. Interaction between central and peripheral mechanisms in the control of locomotion. *Prog Brain Res.* 1979;50:227–235.

Hassid, E.H., Rose, D.R., Commisarow, J.C., Guttry, M.G. & Dobkin, B.D. (1997), Improved gait symmetry in hemiparetic stroke patients induced during body weight supported treadmill stepping, *J. Neurol. Rehabil.* 11, 21–26.

Hesse, S.H., Bertelt, C.B., Schaffrin, A.S., Malezic, M. M., & Mauritz, K.M. (October 1994), Restoration of gait in non-ambulatory hemiparetic patients by treadmill training with partial body weight support, *Arch. Phys. Med. Rehabil.* 75, 1087–1093.

Hesse, S.H. & Uhlenbrock, D.U. (2000), A mechanized gait trainer for restoration of gait, *J. Rehabil. Res. Development*, vol. 37, no. 6, pp. 701–708.

Hornby, T.H., Zemon, D.Z. & Campbell, D.C. (Jan. 2005), Robotic-assisted, body-weightsupported treadmill training in individuals following motor incomplete spinal cord injuri, *Physical Therapy*, vol. 85, no. 1, 52-66.

Jezernik, S.J., Colombo, G.C., Keller, T.K., Frueh, H.F. & Morari, M. M. (Apr. 2003), Robotic orthosis lokomat: A rehabilitation and research tool, *Neuromodulation*, vol. 6, no. 2, pp. 108–115.

Miller EW, Quinn ME, Seddon PG. Body weight support treadmill and overground ambulation training for two patients with chronic disability secondary to stroke. *Phys Ther.* 2002;82:53–61.

Schmidt H., Hesse S., Bernhardt R., Kruger J., Hapticwalker — A novel haptic foot device, *ACM Trans. Appl. Perception* (TAP), vol. 2, no. 2, pp. 166–180, Apr. 2005.

Veneman J, Kruidhof R, van der Helm FCT, van der Kooy H. Design of a Series Elastic- and Bowdencable-based actuation system for use as torque-actuator in exoskeleton-type training robots. *Proceedings of the ICOOR 2005*. 2005.

Visintin M, Barbeau H. The effects of body weight support on the locomotor pattern of spastic paretic patients. *Can J Neurol Sci.* 1989;16:315–325.

Visintin, M.V., Barbeau, H.B, Bitensky, N.B, & Mayo, N.M. (1998), Using a new approach to retrain gait in stroke patients through body weight support and treadmill training, *Stroke* 29,1122–1128.

Wernig, A.W., Nanassy, A.N. & Muller, A.M. (1999), Laufband (treadmill) therapy in incomplete paraplegia and tetraplegia, *J. Neurotrauma* 16, 719–726.